The Story of All Things

W9-BJL-507

Post-Contemporary Interventions

Series Editors: Stanley Fish and Fredric Jameson

The Story of All Things

Writing the Self in English Renaissance Narrative Poetry

Marshall Grossman

Duke University Press *Durham & London* 1998

© 1998 Duke University Press

All rights reserved

Printed in the United States of America on acid-free paper ∞

Typeset in Minion by Tseng Information Systems, Inc.

Library of Congress Cataloging-in-Publication Data appear

on the last printed page of this book.

for Joel

Contents

Acknowledgments

Material from the following previously published articles have been revised and incorporated in the present study.

"Augustine, Spenser, Milton and the Christian Ego," *New Orleans Review* 11 (1984): 9–17.

"Authoring the Boundary: Irony, Allegory and the Rebus in 'Upon Appleton House,' " in *The Muses' Commonweal: Poetry and Politics in the Seventeenth Century,* ed. Claude Summers and Ted-Larry Pebworth (Columbia: University of Missouri Press, 1988), pp. 191–206.

"Housing the Remains of Culture: From Absolute Knowledge to Absolute Monumentality," *Surfaces* 2 (1993), electronic publication, 18 pp.

"The Hyphen in the Mouth of Modernity," in *Postmodernism Across the Ages,* ed. Bennett Schaber and William Readings (Syracuse: Syracuse University Press, 1994), pp. 75–87.

"Literary Form and Historical Consciousness in Late Renaissance Poetry," *Exemplaria* 1 (1989): 247–64.

"Servile/Sterile/Style: Milton and the Question of Woman," in *Milton and the Idea of Woman,* ed. Julia Walker (Champaign: University of Illinois Press, 1988), pp. 148–68.

"The Subject of Narrative and the Rhetoric of the Self," *Papers on Language and Literature* 18 (1982): 398–415.

Permission to publish this material is gratefully acknowledged.

Preface

The most general goal of my work is to understand better the interaction of historical change and literary form. Such interaction includes both personally exigent and climatically historical determinants: the accidents of the everyday life of individuals and the shared experiences of the changing conditions of material social life. Thus, I am interested in the coming together of large movements—the progress of agricultural technology, the experiences of civil war and regicide, the emergence of republican state institutions—and local occurrences—Augustine's stressed relationship with his mother, the marital disharmony of Milton and Mary Powell, the (apparently) coincidental sharing of the name Elizabeth by Spenser's mother, wife, and queen. In this study of the representation of character in English narrative poetry from Spenser to Milton, I try to understand how exigent events, both determined and adventitious, are accommodated by and in literary developments that on occasion become themselves world historical events.

My method is to identify and categorize the interactions among the specific figures of speech that poets use to represent their characters' choices and actions in relation to the worlds of and beyond their poems. By noting trends and innovations in this rhetoric of the self, while also attending to the exigent material out of which significance is formed, I try to construct a picture of how representative narratives respond to the major changes in the way that people perceive and represent themselves in relation to technological innovation, economic instability, and civil war and revolution in the sixteenth and seventeenth centuries. Since literary representations of the self-in-action form as well as reflect the historical subject, I take the narratives under study to be, themselves, mediators of cultural change through which poets join the social project of rendering meaningful the inchoate turbulence of everyday life, and I explore the cognitive efficacy of rhetoric in assimilating social change as individual experience.

I argue that the rhetoric through which subjectivity is represented in Renaissance poetic narrative can be seen as part of the response of language to historical trends, like the technological mastery of nature and the integration of a worldwide market economy, and to the far more local needs of individual writers in peculiar situations. An environmental confluence of the two integrates some works as social mediations, making them part of language, while discarding others.

During the great midwestern floods of the summer of 1993 the provisional confluence of the Mississippi and Missouri Rivers suggested a metaphor for this collaboration of historical contingency and literary innovation. Technological intervention had all but effaced the floodplains of these rivers, until an excess of river material (water) discovered again (some of) the archaic traces of what human intervention had negated. The result was a great deal of standing water, much of it in awkward places. Eventually most of this water returned to its culturally appointed path; some simply vanished or dried up, but here and there, according to an unforeseen and unintended collaboration of nature (or what we might now properly call, natural history) and the U.S. Army Corps of Engineers (whose dams and levies had altered the rivers in the interests of an anticipated human history), new channels appeared; new confluences and an altered structure emerged.

My point is that the surge of events now and in the Renaissance tends at times to resemble the high waters of the Missouri and the Mississippi and that these events — in order that they may become and remain events — flow through and around the austerely limited yet endlessly supple system of an underlying rhetoric of the self. Like the watercourses and floodplains of the Midwest, the rhetoric of the self may be manipulated and all but effaced, yet it remains a latent and virtual presence. I propose, therefore, a literary history that records the interaction of exigent high water and formal geography — the points when an excess of material, in the form of human experience, overflows the narratives into which it is generically channeled, and a significantly changed symbolic landscape is left behind. If this metaphor of confluent rivers constructed from the daily news of 1993 seems adventitious, perhaps baroque, it gains a certain poignancy when we recall that it could have been drawn as well from Spenser's narration of the marriage of the Medway and the Thames in the fourth book of *The Faerie Queene.*

My hypothesis is that figures of speech such as metaphor, metonymy, synecdoche, and irony define underlying patterns—riverbeds and floodplains. Each relates narrative characters to their fictional worlds in ways that project distinctly different experiences of time and action. This is neither a psychological nor a historical assertion. It is rather an attempt to make explicit the logical structure of rhetoric at its highest level of generalization.

As the most casual reader of George Puttenham's *Arte of English Poesy* knows, rhetorical nomenclature in the sixteenth-century was already a vexed issue. It is important, therefore, at the outset to stress the fact that my use of rhetorical terms does not imply any particular historical argument about their reference or provenance. Although one could find a good beginning to such a historical argument in the organization of seventeenth-century Ramistic rhetorics such as those of Omar Talon and his English follower Abraham Fraunce, I am concerned here only to assert now (and argue more elaborately in chapter 2) that the four tropes I invoke *logically* form coherent and dialectically interrelated categories.

Briefly, I will argue that metaphor identifies similarities and continuities between self and world, while metonymy emphasizes differences and discontinuities; synecdoche allows an individual to relate his or her experiences to an inclusive whole or providential design, and irony underlines the discontinuity between what is said and what is meant, what is planned and what occurs. Specific narratives shift from one figure to another in ways that characterize distinctive conceptions of the self in relation to historical action. Once we understand the underlying logic of the tropes, we can construct a literary history that attends to the way that poets represent and sometimes mediate tensions between shifting ideologies by shifting from one rhetorical register to another.

For example, in sixteenth-century narratives, plot complications are sometimes resolved when characters discover that they are long-lost relatives, or when shepherd girls, beloved of princes, turn out in the end to be of royal blood. These typical narratives develop by shifting from figures of difference to ones of similarity. By doing so, they represent a self that is essential and unchanging; in them, a character's "true nature" determines his or her actions in various circumstances, and the divagations of the self from its original character—for example, the princess's humble circumstances and pastoral attire—

turn out to be accidental or apparent. Thus, for instance, in *The Winter's Tale* on the level of plot, the conflict represented by the social distance between Florizel and Perdita, the shepherd girl, disappears as soon as Perdita is found to be a princess; while, on the ideological level, the contradiction between Perdita's evident and manifest nobility and her humble station is shown to be no contradiction at all, but rather an affirmation of the primacy of breeding: noble blood shows its quality regardless of circumstances. Only apparently a shepherdess, "*in reality*" Perdita was always her royal self.

Alternatively, in *The Faerie Queene* the inclusive magnificence of Arthur is decomposed into the component virtues of various knights, thus effecting a shift in the reverse direction: from the unity of virtue in the synecdochic Arthur to the more conflicted and complicating discourse of difference governing the narratives of the metonymic knights. In both cases, difference generates plot complications that may or may not be resolved through identity. Broadly speaking, narration achieves closure when metonymy becomes metaphor; closure fails, as it does in *The Faerie Queene,* when characters differ from themselves (over time) in ways that cannot be recuperated as self-identity.

By the second half of the seventeenth-century an alternative to this clash of essences appears in the form of narratives that represent the self as developing in response to experience. In them, historical action becomes a medium through which the self is constructed as well as expressed. Individuals become, in Milton's phrase, "authors to themselves." Shifting episodically from figures of difference to figures of identity, presenting various versions of a character and unifying them only through the total action of the story, these narratives of the historical self relate an individual's choices and actions not to the person he or she always essentially was but to the person he or she will become by the story's end. Identity is no longer a question of disguise or misprision but of narrative characters who manage to change, to differ from their previous selves, and to accommodate the differences in a temporally determined affirmation of self-identity. In effect, the cumulative assimilation of experience in the formation of a developing self-identity is the plot of this sort of narrative. In its deferral of self-identification to the end of a sequence of temporally unfolding events, this plot expresses a conception of the self that answers to an experience of history as the medium in which progress is achieved through a growing technological mastery of "second causes." It poses and attempts to resolve a question fundamental to any conception of historical progress: How do we change, yet remain the same?

To ask this as a literary historical question: How do we get from one plot configuration to another? In offering a literary history of the writing of the self in Renaissance narrative poetry, it will be my very specific contention, with respect to the rhetorical shifts evidenced in sixteenth- and seventeenth-century poetic narratives, that ideological tensions arising from the reorganization and "modernization" of social life in revolutionary England were experienced as an inward division of the self, and that the major poets of the time represented this division with writings that are suspended between iconic and verbal representation and lyric and narrative genres.

For example, when, in *Eikonoklastes*, Milton argues that the king is subordinate to parliamentary law, he reverses James I's assertion that the king speaks the law. The positions taken by James on the one side and Milton on the other closely parallel the alternative conceptions of the self that I have been studying in the poetry of the period. James's king is king a priori; Milton's king fits himself, as best he can, to the role that the law creates for him. In fact, Milton portrays James's son and successor, Charles I, as unable to mature and become an effective king because of his refusal to submit to the law. The argument of *Eikonoklastes* separates the king's person from his historical role and provides an explicit rationale for a model of the self that is fully developed in Milton's later poetry and, in fragmentary and contradictory form, in the earlier poets I have studied. Milton's polemic thus reproduces in an explicitly political context the shift from image to text, from presence to word, that characterizes the changing representation of the self in this period.

I have compared the processes of literary history to those that form and reform a great river system. To some extent this comparison applies to the presentation of my argument as well. Again, as with the Mississippi and Missouri Rivers, a number of tributaries, in this case critical, theoretical, and methodological lines of argument, converge to form the mainstream and force. The course of the argument has proved complicated. I have tried to attend as carefully as possible to the interrelations and interactions among the river system's many contributing streams so that it would, in the end, be coherent and traceable from its source to its mouth.

In attempting to relate narrative form to historical consciousness, I follow

Paul Ricoeur and Charles Taylor in arguing that the model of the narrative text is paradigmatic for human action. Also relevant is some discussion of historical cognition among analytic philosophers of history. Louis Mink, for example, shows how a specifically historical understanding of human action necessarily resembles the construal of a narrative plot. In arguing that various narrative configurations can be generated from a systematically related quartet of rhetorical tropes, I draw largely on the work of Kenneth Burke and Hayden White, especially the theory of narrational genres given in White's *Metahistory.*

Among the more widely influential studies of Renaissance literature that provide a context for the present work are Barbara Lewalski's *Protestant Poetics and the Seventeenth-Century Religious Lyric* and Stephen Greenblatt's *Renaissance Self-Fashioning.* Lewalski documents the impact on lyric poetry of the Reformation tendency to interpret Old Testament stories as foreshadowing the Christian revelation. My work suggests that typological interpretation is especially congenial to a view of the self as developing toward completion, and it argues that the doctrinal emphasis on the type is part of a larger historical development in the understanding of the individual's relation to history. Greenblatt has shown that the Renaissance is a period in which the conscious crafting of a "self" that is suited to differing public and private situations is a crucial project. While I share Greenblatt's interest in "self-fashioning," my emphasis is on the interaction of literary forms and historical developments immediately subsequent to those that he has studied, and I focus more directly on the ways in which rhetoric generates logical categories that represent and create opportunities for individual agency. The complex and conflictual agents so formed elude the new historical polarities of containment and subversion.

I argue in chapter 1 that this focus on an implicit logic of rhetorical tropes yields a more thoroughly formalized understanding of the relation of history to literature than does the anecdotal method typical of the New Historicism. In chapter 4 I undertake to show in some detail the ways in which New Historicist assumptions actually thwart a historical understanding of *The Faerie Queene.*

I try in this book to address a considerable range of literary and critical issues by keeping a tight focus on the vicissitudes of the literary subject. In this and, to some extent, in the thematic emphasis I place on the relationship between literary and critical languages, I owe my greatest debt to Joel Fineman. The object of my study lies adjacent to the canonical subject delineated in *Shakespeare's Perjured Eye* and the compact body of essays that represent Fineman's short but intense career. Locating the invention of poetic subjectivity in Shakespeare's sonnets, Fineman delineates the formal characteristics of a new poetic "I," and he accounts for the effect of psychological depth that it projects. This poetic subject encounters itself as the subject of an open-ended desire. Fineman's study of the subject of Shakespearean desire sets a certain agenda for my own. While pursuing my own method, I attempt to continue his practice of using the close study of Renaissance texts as a way to address issues of contemporary critical theory. However, as will be apparent in the chapters that follow, I have wanted to address the issue of history—both literary and material—in a way that is less rigorously oblique than his. I am particularly interested in the ways in which the subject of narrative poetry develops alongside Shakespeare's lyric and dramatic subject, and I will argue that in *Paradise Lost* narrative poetry finds a decisive way to stabilize and make thematic the rhetorical duplicity of the Shakespearean subject that Fineman described.

Suffice it to say that Fineman's project is in an essential and a historical way the occasion of my own, and that while I accept and parallel his understanding of psychoanalysis as the *theoretical* expression of Renaissance poetic subjectivity, my choice of nontheatrical proof-texts published between 1590 and 1681 is also intended to offer him, as it were, a posthumous provocation by making more complicated the contingent role of Shakespeare in a development of poetic subjectivity that may have had a somewhat longer and less entirely formal duration than Fineman recognized. In making my turn from Shakespeare to other Renaissance poets, I mean to ask: what happens when we extend the *literary* history of poetic subjectivity to the moments before and after the canonization of the Shakespearean "subjectivity effect"—that is, before and after the coming to be of a literary character assumed to know more than he or she can say, assumed to have, as Hamlet puts it, "that within which passes show"? Thus, in my account of literary subjectivity I trace an early and, I believe historically important, confrontation of structure and duration—the assimilation of difference within a narrated self-identification.

The first three chapters of this book comprise a theoretical discussion of rhetoric and the articulation of literary and material history. By way of situating my notion of literary history with respect to the New Historicism, chapter 1 advances a definition of the literary historical event and tracks its appearance in Marvell's "The Garden." Chapter 2 considers the relationship of narrative to subjectivity and elaborates a structural theory of narrative configurations for use in subsequent chapters. Chapter 3 seeks, through a close reading of Augustine's *Confessions,* to delineate the constitutive elements of a canonical literary subject that is part of the cultural patrimony of early modern England and to explore its passage through and transformation in *La Vita Nuova,* the *Rime sparse,* and the ironic pastoral of Marvell's mower poems.

The remaining chapters present an episodic literary history of sixteenth- and seventeenth-century poetic narrative: Spenser and the metonymies of virtue; Donne's refiguring of the remains of the world in the *Anniversaries;* irony, allegory, and ideological contradiction in Marvell; and historical time and the narration of concepts in Milton. Finally, in a brief epilogue, I try to suggest something of the afterlife of the subject of historical cause as it emerged from seventeenth-century literary narrative and continued into the present.

It remains to say something—at the beginning—about my reasons for choosing the particular poets represented in this study as the bases on which to establish a literary history of the representation of subjectivity in Renaissance narrative poetry. To do so, I want to advance a very restricted notion of canonicity. I will argue, in chapter 1, that the literary historical event per se occurs in the moment that a figure comes to stand not so much for as in the place of "reality." Insofar as the theme of my study is the linguistic projection of subjectivity and the processes and conditions that allow it to change over time, I have selected texts that exemplify, both historically and formally, a comprehensive vision and revision of the self in relation to time and action. By way of asserting a certain unity or coherence to this selection, I will argue that in some significant sense the texts of Augustine, Spenser, Donne, Marvell, and Milton that preoccupy the body of this study, though they vary greatly in their overt ambitions, all tell—in a structurally significant way—the story of all things.

The major poetic texts of Spenser and Milton may be taken as the respective beginning and conclusion of a historic revision of the Augustinian ego as it is established and canonized in the *Confessions.* Both Spenser and Milton engage, in an astonishingly self-conscious way, the making of a poet and the making of a man. The title page of Spenser's 1596 volume reads: "*The Faerie Qveene. Disposed into twelve bookes, fashioning XII. Morall vertues.*" This project of fashioning extends itself in time. Spenser's poem fashions the moral virtues by embodying them in individual knights whose stories, that is, whose actions, are somehow read in the superimposed mirrors of ancient and secret books and a contemporary court from which Spenser was excluded. The stories, fashioned in mirrors, are, subsequently, to become the mirrors in which perfect English gentleman will see themselves so that they may become what they see.

Milton's intention to "soar/Above th' *Aonian Mount*," pursuing "Things unattempted yet in Prose or Rhyme" (*Paradise Lost* 1.15–16) is elaborated by his early ambitions to produce a poem "doctrinall to the nation" (*Reason of Church Government*) and "to see and tell/Of things invisible to mortal sight" (*Paradise Lost* 3.53–54). As he chronicles the stages of his own career as a prophetic poet in the poems collected in 1645, Milton also narrates the coming into power of human agents in their dynamically differing relations to eternity under the law and under the spirit.

Donne and Marvell are included because their generically innovative responses to the perceived decay of the power of the epideictic lyric are meticulous in their detailing of a crisis befalling the lyric "I" and prescient in their move toward what I will later want to describe as narrative montage. Both Donne and Marvell engage an ironic wit that draws one of its principal themes from the systematic transgression of the lyric frame and that directly treats the contradictions between providential time and historical progress.

All four of these poets perceive a need for a relationship of time to eternity that is more *timely* and more dynamic than that which can be comfortably contained within the Augustinian opposition between a transitory world and an eternal spirit. Thus, I have chosen four distinct and, I think, crucial moments in the history of the revision of the more or less stable notion of the self presented by Augustine to illustrate a process of change that is neither wholly literary nor wholly historical, but properly both. Still, it should be acknowledged that many other moments — for example, that of the dialectically poised counterpoint of lyric and narrative in George Herbert's *The Temple* — could have been made to serve an equally exemplary function and that the choices represented retain a significant element of the frankly arbitrary, which is to say, I suppose, that they represent my taste and, of course, the exigencies of a teaching schedule.

Finally, in seeking to articulate a literary history within contemporary critical discourse, I have found it necessary to reflect in some detail on the discursive relations that exist between poetic practice and critical theory. A result of this reflection is what may seem a digressive preoccupation with the hermeneutic systems that, explicitly or implicitly, inform contemporary critical discourse—most notably psychoanalysis. The presence of these theoretical meditations in what purports to be a work of literary history may perhaps be approached through a brief explanation of the rather presumptuous title of this study.

The title is drawn from the commendatory poem *"In Paradisum Amissam,"* contributed by S.B. for the second edition of *Paradise Lost:*

> *Qui legis Amissam Paradisum, grandia magni*
> *Carmina Miltoni, quid nisi cuncta legis?*
> *Res cunctas, & cunctarum primordia rerum,*
> *Et fata, & fines continet iste liber.*

> You who read *Paradise Lost,* Milton's great song, what do you read, if not all things? This book contains [keeps in, surrounds] all things, their beginnings, their ends and their fates. (my translation)

What does it mean to say that *Paradise Lost* is the story of all things? My title is meant to draw attention to an ambition common in lesser and greater degree to the poems that I have chosen to study: the ambition to join in orderly fashion the disparate and chaotic universe of things within narrative form, to reach the reality of things through story. It may be useful to think of the configuring power of narrative in terms of Saussure's distinction between a group of sounds and an acoustic image. When we hear a language with which we are unfamiliar, it is often difficult to pick out individual words. We do not know how the sounds of the language fit together to form larger units. When we hear a language that we know, however, we recognize even unfamiliar words as words because we already have an expectation of how the sounds will fit together. When we hear a word, rather than noise, we are actually matching the sounds we hear to an already conceptualized *sound image* that serves to mediate for us the transition from sound to sign.[1] Similarly, stories mediate to us the noise of experience as images of human life.

The works in this study approach their ambition through the process that S.B. acutely perceives; to join things to story and in story is to contain their beginnings and their ends in a way that recognizes the journey from the one to the other as fate. It is integral to my argument that certain versions of history and theory are formally related to specific ways of narrating the self-in-action. To make this point, I try to attend to the historical development of theory on the one hand and the theoretical development of history on the other. Because I am trying to establish a definition of the object of literary history that invites us to seriously rethink the relationship of history to literature, I want to respond — with the substance of my study — to current criticism that is in my view overly casual both in its theory and its history. The theory in my book is there to situate history within literature and thus to argue for a renewed emphasis on literary history as opposed to the historicist study of literature. Substantively, I argue that discourses like Marxism and psychoanalysis, which seem mutually preemptive: (1) appear to be complementary when they are viewed as alternative theorizations of similar narrative practices, rather than as disclosures of some underlying truth (e.g., class struggle or the Oedipus complex); and (2) that the formulation of these approaches forms part of the *literary* history of the narrative construction of the self. The dialectical interaction of the four tropes, presented in chapter 2, allows me to characterize both the narrative poems and the theoretical discourses that I discuss in terms of their underlying rhetoric.

What is literary history for? The history I mean to recount aspires to take its place as a part of the story of the story of all things; in general, it is a tale of how nonsignifying material things are named and experienced through the mediation of historically specific symbolic systems. These symbolic systems, into which *things* effectively disappear, have, in themselves, formal characteristics whose logic can be understood and whose development over time can be tracked. Thus, I hope to point to a narrative practice, exemplified specifically by the tale of the Renaissance canonization of a symbolic system marked by narrative temporality and closure, for which the great hermeneutic systems of modernity are properly the theory. In bringing the discourse of psychoanalysis into the thematics of my literary history, I mean to offer a nonhermeneutic (or as I prefer to put it, a nondiagnostic) model of its use, one that situates it alongside rather than above the literary narratives that I consider. In this telling, psychoanalysis is not *applied* to Renaissance literature, but rather it is put in conversation with it. By recording this conversation, I hope to extend the province of literary history into a consideration of contemporary discourse, and it is for this reason that I conclude, perhaps rather curiously, with a brief consideration of postmodernism as seen from the prospect of Renaissance literary history.

This book has taken rather a long time to write, and the debts have accumulated along with the years. Of these, the institutional ones are the easiest to identify and acknowledge. I thank the National Endowment for the Humanities for a fellowship that, combined with a grant from the Faculty Research Council of Fordham University, provided a year of uninterrupted study in 1988–89, and the General Research Board of the University of Maryland for a summer grant in 1990 and a semester research award in the fall of 1993.

I also have had the great benefit of extended proximity to and use of two very special environments: The Allen Room of the New York Public Library, the home base where this work began, and the Folger Shakespeare Library, where it was completed. In very different ways, both of these places combine the service of knowing staff, immediate access to unparalleled collections, and the unique camaraderie of parallel study in a room quietly full of diverse readers. Special thanks go also to the staffs of the Bobst Memorial Library of New York University, the McKeldin Library of the University of Maryland, and the Library of Congress, especially the preservation department, where my wife, Annlinn Grossman, and her colleagues work without end to maintain the material remnants of culture against the ravages of time and the follies of humankind.

The list of individuals to whom I am indebted is long: Joel Fineman, over fifteen years, and Hayden White, in six intense weeks (at the School of Criticism and Theory) and several years of generous follow-up, made decisive contributions to my thinking, such as it is, and the modes of my being in the world, such as they are. Special thanks go to David Lee Miller, whose monumental patience and generosity allowed him to argue about, listen to, read, and suggest improvements on at least three complete drafts of the manuscript, and to the anonymous reader for Duke University Press whose detailed and sympathetic comments and bibliographical suggestions were invaluable.

I am grateful, too, for the moral, intellectual, and practical support I have received from Charles Altieri, Ann Baynes Coiro, Stanley Fish, Noam Flinker, Ernest Gilman, Richard Harrier, Richard Helgerson, Barbara Lewalski, Perry Meisel, Mary Ann Radzinowicz, Jason Rosenblatt, John Shawcross,

David Harris Sacks, Julie Solomon, Reynolds Smith, Patricia Stablein, Edward Tayler, and Gordon Teskey. Louis Marin and Bill Readings also have their place in this list; I wish they were here to read this book and tell me what they think.

John Maynard and Anthony Low of the English Department at New York University provided office space, library privileges, and collegial hospitality during my fellowship year, and I am grateful for the sympathetic attention of my colleagues at the University of Maryland, especially Neil Fraistat, Gary Hamilton, Ted Leinwand, Tom Moser, Bill Sherman, Mark Turner, and Orrin Wang. I also want to thank my graduate students, especially Catherine Calloway Dauterman, J. Andrew Hubbell, and Karen Nelson, for teaching me Spenser, and Amy Stackhouse for keeping my Milton up to date and for her generous and invaluable help checking the manuscript.

Finally, in a paragraph by himself: Like every other Miltonist I know, I owe innumerable special debts of gratitude to Joseph Wittreich, whose ability to survive his instinct to take responsibility for the well-being of everyone and everything, everywhere, and at all times, is a beacon to us all.

And finally, on another level, I wish to thank my sternest interlocutors, Jacob Linn Grossman and Annlinn Grossman, whose presence in the household performs the feats necessary to a perpetual reengagement with the Real.

Part One ❧

Lasso, che son? che fui?

Chapter 1

Literary Forms and Historical Consciousness in Renaissance Poetry

1

This book is conceived as a work of literary history. In it I am concerned to account for the differences among various representations of the self-in-action in sixteenth- and seventeenth-century narrative poetry, to explore the historical question of the ways in which literary forms change over time, and to suggest ways in which such changes relate at once to changes in the material conditions of social life in the period and to exigent events in the lives of individual writers. It has, therefore, a literary and a historical face. The first three chapters explore the relations that inhere between these two primary objects of investigation: literature and history. It will be my contention that because it articulates a sequence of identity and difference mediated by time, the narration of a subject over time, effecting and experiencing change yet maintaining a recognizable self-identity, provides the paradigmatic case for any self-consciously historical understanding.

The articulation I am trying to describe may be illustrated by a simple thought experiment. Imagine a group of adults around a table on which are spread some photographs of infants. After some brief study, one of the adults indicates one or more pictures and says, "That's me." The others, in turn, each identify *their* baby pictures. Although it will probably seem precious to make the point that the infant in the photograph is manifestly not the adult who identifies the picture, doing so calls attention to the complexity of reference concealed in the simple sentence, "That's me." Two aspects of that complexity indicate the interdependency of narrative and history: (1) The utterance exemplifies, in a concrete and commonplace way, the Lacanian observation that the subject is acknowledged and recognized in and through its representation.[1] This moment in which the speaker identifies herself or himself with the temporally distant representation of his or her own past is both complex and poignant, for it forges a sense of continuity in time that at once grasps the past and acknowledges its loss.[2] (2) Recognition of our identity with past versions of ourselves joins two moments of time: that in which the photograph was taken and that in which it is acknowledged. It thus constitutes a temporal space separating, yet also connecting, these moments, so that despite the present-tense verb, the relation "That's me" can only be established *historically;* it is both formally retrospective and substantively determined by the contingent experiences it encompasses. Lacan's universalizing presentation notwithstanding, the *subject* referred to in this study is, therefore, always the subject of an actually existing literary history.

It is not enough, however, simply to assert the historicity of the subject and go on. To refer to "*the* subject," even of a particular literary history, is to tread dangerous ground, for it demands that we find ways to avoid reifying the ideological force that is always carried by one (as opposed to another) particular identification of *the* subject. In its social functioning such a subject of representation stands in for and obscures a multiplicity of subjects, differentiated by the experiences of class, race, gender, and the contingencies of material circumstance. If we are to appreciate the historicity of the subject as it appears in a particular early modern literature, we need to understand its appearance as contingent on a set of circumstances that allowed it to emerge at the expense of other possible configurations. In short, if we are to be historical, we must consider the fact that the universalizing subject we discover in our literary history is maintained at the expense of other, historically excluded possibilities. The obvious example in the case of early modern English poetry is the exclusion of the feminine and maternal subject effected by the positing of a masculine and paternal literary historical subject.

One of the anomalies brought out by the experiment of the baby pictures is that the gender of the baby will generally be far less defined than it is in the adult who accepts the picture as his or hers. Apart from the appearance of the genitals (which, concealed by a diaper or a pose, often will not appear in the photo), we distinguish the infant girls from the infant boys by accidents of cultural ascription — a pink ribbon, blue booties — purposefully added to impose or enforce anatomically determined expectations. We rely on symbolic identifications of an anticipated gender that will, in fact, precondition the meaning of secondary sexual characteristics when they do appear. For the adult identifying (and identifying with) the photo a complex history of desires, experiences, and expectations is at once recalled and concealed by the juxtaposition of past and present versions of the self. Consider from the historically situated point of view of the adult, for example, the possible resonances of such photo album sentences as "That's me when I was a boy"; "There I am as a girl."

The story that I wish to tell concerns the relations between subjective cognition and some very broad rhetorical configurations; it is crucial that these configurations also be understood to include the smudges and erasures that necessarily occur when the particular is called upon to identify itself with the general. I therefore want to say something at the outset about the erasure of women in the dialectical construction of what I have been calling *the* subject of early modern literary history. The works I will be discussing (and later ones) generally identify both the specifically male and the generically human subject as masculine.[3] How do we describe this ideological subject, yet avoid complicity with it? In dialectic, what is negated is not destroyed.

This canonically male subject construes itself as the subject of desire, and it is, of course, no coincidence that in each of the texts which I study, this constitutive desire is encountered in dialectical relation to figures of elusive femininity. Gender per se is a structure of difference. An agent can be masculine only in relation to something that is not, and the story of the patriarchal subject must include some account of the formal as well as the historically contingent construction of the dialectical other in opposition to which it is gendered. Thus, in chapter 3 we will have occasion to consider Augustine's displacement of desire from his mother, Saint Monica, to his mistress, the mother of Adeodatus, and finally to the "Mother Church" of Christ, and we will trace the transformations of Augustinian desire as it reappears in Dante's and Petrarch's figurations of the ideal in Beatrice and Laura and in Marvell's pastoral femme fatale, Juliana, in the mower poems. Chapter 4 charts the construction of the Spenserian subject in relation to the complex superpositions of Britomart, Elizabeth, and Gloriana in *The Faerie Queene,* on the one hand, and the curious onomastic superposition of three Elizabeths—Spenser's mother, his wife, and his queen—on the other. In chapter 5 we will find in Donne's *Anniversaries* a self-conscious reflection on the crucial rhetorical role of idealized feminine perfection in the organization of the patriarchal ego. Returning to Marvell in chapter 6, we will see how the poet and his patron, Thomas Fairfax, understood the exigencies of an immediate political decision in relation to the figure of young Mary Fairfax in "Upon Appleton House." Finally, in chapter 7 the figure of Eve in *Paradise Lost* will provide the opportunity for a formal articulation of the constitutive role of feminine desire in the dialectical construction of the patriarchal subject.

The experience of gender, as it emerges from the combination of experience, expectation, and representation is one of a number of cognitive adventures in the vicissitudes of the subject. The medium in which the ideological, representational, cultural, and historically exigent are experienced as the continuity of an identity is, I shall argue, narrative time. Our sense, when we look at our baby pictures, that the infant and the adult are in fact "me," that we persist meaningfully over time and through change is an effect that we support by filling the intervening time — as best we can — with story. What connects us to the temporally remote versions of ourselves that we might see in a scrapbook is — what we take to be — the story of our lives, and our encounter with the image of our infant selves demands of us that we supply its episodes.

A similar demand may arise — in the third person, as it were — with regard to the reception of literary character. Take, for example, the coordination in *I Henry IV* of Hal's soliloquy at the end of act 1 scene 2 and the encounter with Hal in Vernon's report to Hotspur before the battle of Shrewsbury. After initiating with Poins the plot to rob the robbers at Gadshill, Hal concludes his first scene in the play with a comparison of himself to the sun and his unsavory associates to clouds, suggesting that his madcap persona is, at least in part, a stratagem:

> Yet herein will I imitate the sun,
> Who doth permit the base contagious clouds
> To smother up his beauty from the world,
> That when he please again to be himself,
> Being wanted, he may be more wond'red at
> By breaking through the foul and ugly mists
> Of vapors that did seem to strangle him.
> . . . . .
> So when this loose behavior I throw off
> And pay the debt I never promised,
> By how much better than my word I am,
> By so much shall I falsify men's hopes,

And like bright metal on a sullen ground,
My reformation, glitt'ring o'er my fault,
Shall show more goodly and attract more eyes
Than that which hath no foil to set it off. (1.2.197–203, 208–15)⁴

In the fourth act, Vernon, returning from an embassy to the King's camp, reports on Hal's appearance in terms that resume the sun and clouds metaphor to suggest the fulfillment of Hal's act 1 promise. "The nimble-footed madcap Prince of Wales,/And his comrades, that daff'd the world aside/And bid it pass" (4.1.95–97) are now:

All furnish'd, all in arms;
All plum'd like estridges, that with the wind
Bated like eagles having lately bath'd,
Glittering in golden coats like images,
As full of spirit as the month of May,
And gorgeous as the sun at midsummer;
Wanton as youthful goats, wild as young bulls.
I saw young Harry with his beaver on,
His cushes on his thighs, gallantly arm'd,
Rise from the ground like feathered Mercury,
And vaulted with such ease into his seat
As if an angel dropp'd down from the clouds
To turn and wind a fiery Pegasus,
And witch the world with noble horsemanship. (4.1.98–110)

The audience's sense that Vernon reports precisely the sunrise promised in the first act soliloquy is quickly validated by Hotspur's dry response: "No more, no more! worse than the sun in March,/This praise doth nourish agues" (4.1.111–12). Yet one could also imagine alternative scenarios in which we are victims of a deception, in which the Hal of the fourth act is simply a different person who happens to have the same name as the character who spoke the first act soliloquy. From within the play, the King almost invites us to suspect as much when he remarks on the tenuous relations of name and person:

O that it could be prov'd
That some night-tripping fairy had exchang'd
In cradle-clothes our children where they lay,

And call'd mine Percy, his Plantagenet!
Then would I have his Harry and he mine. (1.1.86–90)

Just as the possibility of constructing a story supports our experience of self-identity over time, so the experience of difference within identity, in ourselves and others, supports our ability to read a story. The construction of identity within each of these registers may be more or less successful. Thus, in the case of *I Henry IV* the intervening episodes prepare us for Hal's success at Shrewsbury, and our relative comfort in assuming the continuity of his character is reflected in our interest in searching those intervening episodes for clues to its presumed unity. On the other hand, we may be much less comfortable with, say, the sudden reformation of Oliver in *As You Like It* or of Alonzo, Sebastion, and Antonio in *The Tempest,* preferring in these cases to evade the issue of character continuity on the assumption that the author's interest lies elsewhere. Without pausing to cite examples, I will trust the readers' experience to confirm that identities in the world (as opposed to literature) vary similarly in their ability to attain the "authenticity effect," and I will recall here Freud's trenchant clinical observation that hysterics suffer from memories that they cannot remember, that is, from an inability to situate themselves as the subjects of a coherent history.[5]

The distinction between the literary and the lived is tenuous with respect to the construction of the self. From a formal or narratological point of view there can be neither success nor interest in categorizing the narration of selves-in-action as either fiction or nonfiction, biography or autobiography. First because each is the support of the other, and second because insofar as the continuity of the self is mediated to us as a life-story, the literary form of history appropriates to itself our extraliterary experience. As Lacan puts it: "every truth has the structure of fiction."[6] Thus, I will be arguing that "history" is a specifically literary formalization of experience, whose development can be traced in a representative group of narrative poems, and my exploration of the relations of literature and history will include a synoptic view of the ways in which selected poems represent the self-in-action. This practical literary history is presented in part 2 of this book, which examines exemplary works of Spenser, Donne, Marvell, and Milton in terms of their participation in a brief history of history.

Attention to history has figured largely in literary studies of late. But the history of history I have in mind is distinct from historicism. The renewed interest in history and its subsequent development in the direction of "cultural studies" make more urgent the need to think clearly about the relationship of history to literary history and about the impact of historicism on how and why poetry is read (when it is read at all). Insofar as the goal of this study is the literary history of a certain sense of the self as historical, I want to begin by distinguishing the literary historical interest from the historicist.

2

In recent years the New Historicism has made fashionable the recognition that literary history errs when it constitutes the history of literature as an autonomous, self-enclosed system. We are reminded that literature responds to the material circumstances in which it is produced as well as to intertextual processes like imitation or the anxieties that may accompany the exhaustion, real or perceived, of established styles and genres.

This salutary return to history puts in question — explicitly or implicitly — the universalizing and transcendental ideology underlying the various formalisms of recent critical practice. At the same time, it distinguishes itself from the old historicism's effort to re-create — as it were, on the level of reception — the contexts that engaged a work's first readers. New Historical studies have helped to show how formalists and old historicists, each in their own way, bind the social energy of the literary artifact to its own uniqueness: either as a transcendental expression of "the human condition" or as a wholly determined response to a specifiable and nonrepeatable set of material circumstances.

Some years ago, in a survey introducing an issue of the journal *English Literary Renaissance* dedicated to New Historical studies, Louis Montrose summarized the New Historical response to both of these positions. In the survey, situating the New Historicism as a reaction against the perceived formalism of then recent critical theory, he distinguishes both the methods and the ideology of the new from the old historicism, cautiously suggesting that the New Historicism negotiates a via media between the new (poststructuralist) formalism and the old (naively ideological) historicism by appropriating the methods of each. Acknowledging that the New Historicism "sometimes reproduc[es] the shortcomings of older modes of historical criticism" while "also often appropriating their scholarly labors," Montrose argues that "the newer historical criticism is *new* in its refusal of unproblematized distinctions between 'literature' and 'history,' between 'text' and 'context,' " and in its resistance to "a prevalent tendency to posit and privilege a unified and autonomous individual—whether an Author or a Work—to be set against a social background." Having thus identified what is "new" in the New Historicism, Montrose went on to characterize its "collective project" as being: "to resituate canonical literary texts among the multiple forms of writing, and in relation to the non-discursive practices and institutions, of the social formation in which those texts have been produced—while, at the same time, recognizing that this project of historical resituation is necessarily the textual construction of critics who are themselves historical subjects."[7]

I quote this exemplary passage at length so as to situate, here at the outset, my project for a new and properly historical literary history with respect to what has become—at least in Renaissance studies—a thriving academic industry. The point at which I shall enter—or, better, slide behind—this discursive corporation may be located along the demarcation between literature and history that Montrose both makes and denies. If the New Historicist project is to bring together literature and history, my point of hesitation is the inevitable assumption of a *history* that remains, despite various and assertive efforts to deny the fact, prior to literature. While, in a characteristic move, Montrose proclaims the New Historicism's awareness of the textual construction of history by critics who are themselves historically situated, the precise content of that awareness remains untheorized and elusive.

Situated as they are between the two alternatives of formalism and a semiotically naive historicism, attempting to appropriate what remains useful in each, the challenge of the New Historical studies is, I take it, to render the literary work *exemplary,* that is, resuscitating to a degree the Renaissance topos of the macrocosm inscribed in the microcosm, to locate within it the fissures and patterns of the cultural discourse in which it participates. Before advancing an argument for a somewhat different new *literary history,* I want to focus briefly on the necessarily formal structure of a historicism that both produces and assumes the exemplarity of the literary text.

The notion of a cultural discourse that is itself the medium through which social power circulates is an ideal or virtual construction. It produces the image of a reified and reifying *culture* that unifies its disparate discursive codes, each of which we otherwise might assume to be developing diachronically in accord with its *own* material exigencies, on the level of a cultural *langue* that allows us to know its documents—for example, the literary *parole*—through which and in which cultural discourse is itself disclosed.

The New Historicist assumption that a culture may be defined at the level at which the unity of its discourse becomes evident is manifest in the anecdotal method that has become the self-parodic marker of its practice. The juxtaposition—in paired formal analyses—of a snippet of discourse that is taken to be the textual representative of *something that happened* and its *exemplary* literary image is supported by the virtual formal unity of the text of the event, on the one hand, and the eventual (literary) text, on the other, at an undefined and undefinable level of sociosemiotic generalization. However, we may question whether texts and events, properly understood, do exemplify each other by exemplifying a "poetics of culture," and we may further question how the assumption that they do might inform the practice of literary history.[8]

The very project of constructing such a cultural poetics presupposes a specifically narrative disposition of history; in fact, it joins history to narrative in a way that subsequently becomes the model for exactly the relation of reciprocal exemplarity it finds to inhere among the various voices of the "poetics of culture." The synchronic shuttling between anecdotal example and the presumed structure of a cultural poetics—no doubt inspired, at least initially, by the early Foucault—parallels the narrative of historical causation in and through its shared faith in a revelatory but always virtual underlying design or set of structuring principles of which the anecdotal narrative will prove exemplary.[9]

Joel Fineman provides a careful analysis of the paradoxical interdependence of the anecdote that is ahistorical because it resists causal determination only until it is absorbed by the narrative of determined causes which it is used to exemplify. Thus, in an essay entitled (with specific reference to Greenblatt) "The History of the Anecdote: Fiction as Fiction," by way of a prolegomena to a response to the New Historicism, Fineman uses a literary history of the anecdote to historically reach the formalist position:

> that the anecdote is the literary form that uniquely *lets history happen* by virtue of the way it introduces an opening into the teleological, and therefore timeless, narration of beginning, middle, and end. The anecdote produces the effect of the real, the occurrence of contingency, by establishing an event as an event within and yet without the framing context of historical successivity.[10]

Thus, by interrupting the formal structure of historical narration, the anecdote opens a space for the contingent, but, paradoxically, so long as that space remains open, the contingent, as contingent, remains eccentric to and in excess of the historical narration it interrupts; once brought into the larger series of causes it ceases to be an anecdote and becomes an episode within a narrative frame that replaces the anecdote's apparently accidental openness and indeterminacy — its character as something that could have, if not for wholly contingent circumstances, not happened — with a retrospective narrative necessity:

> the opening of history that is . . . traced out by the anecdote within the totalizing whole of history is something that is characteristically and ahistorically plugged up by a teleological narration that, though larger than the anecdote itself, is still constitutively inspired by the seductive opening of anecdotal form — thereby once again opening up the possibility, but, again, *only* the possibility, that this new narration, now complete within itself, and thereby rendered formally small — capable, therefore, of being anecdotalized — will itself be opened up by a further anecdotal operation, thereby calling forth some yet larger circumcising circumscription, and so, so on and so forth. (ibid.)

Thus, Fineman argues:

> the aporetic operation of anecdotal form . . . allows us to understand the characteristic writing practice of the New Historicism — those essays that begin with an introductory anecdote that introduces history, followed by an amplification, followed by a moralizing conclusion that serves to put an end to history, this then sometimes followed by another anecdote that strives to keep things open." (p. 75)

I will suggest later that these mutually exemplary examples — the realization of action through an anticipatory narrative and the contextualization of discourse through the assumption of a virtual but incompletely known structure — are, in some important ways, twinned products of the Renaissance.

The presupposition that a culture has or is a coherent synchronic structure that may be known — retrospectively — through the progressive disclosure of its particular manifestations parallels the unfolding of meaning in narrative. Narrative enjoins a double reading in which events represented as unfolding in time are themselves structured by a presupposed closure. The ending of a narrative allows its readers retroactively not only to assign meaning to its episodes but to grasp them as episodes — that is, as *causally* connected components of a single action.[11] In this way, narrative establishes — formally and intrinsically — a dialectical relation of time and structure. Any narrative is itself a synchronic structure which — in an act of reading that has necessarily a temporal duration — represents temporal successivity.

According to the logic of narrative, the causes of events are understood through their effects or, to put it a bit more strongly, revealed over the course of time to have been their effects. This reversal of temporal sequence, in which the origin of the object is located in its representation, provides the literary form of the historical event as such. Thus, the literary form of the historical event takes its shape within a rhetoric for the integration of novel occurrences into a formal narrative of what precedes and what follows.

The formal structure of the narrative of historical causation articulates events and meanings by referring the temporal unfolding of episodes forward to the consequences they will reveal at some future point of closure. *Narrative thus operates a shift of meaning from origin to end point in a constructed sequence of events.* The point of closure of a narrative, the point at which it is presented that *something has happened,* is also the point at which diachrony is retrospectively subsumed into synchrony, sequence is construed as consequence, and — however provisionally — time is absorbed by structure.[12]

The *virtual* unity of event and discourse, within the doubled registers of narrative design and cultural poetics, governs a necessary hierarchy of mutual implication, through which discrete discourses — for example, literary and historical discourses — take their determined places within an ahistorical and putatively totalizing structural synchrony. In practice, this implicit and irresistible pressure of hierarchy creates the temptation either to treat literature as epiphenomenal to some extratextual and prior "reality" (the naive historicist's sin) or to reduce the material world to a textual system (the formalist's heresy). In either case, the virtual presence of an endlessly recuperating structure retrospectively forecloses the element of chance necessary to the emergence of anything that might qualify as a historical contingency.

When an overly generalized and insufficiently articulated notion of textuality allows the literary text to be assimilated, as it were, empirically, to another discourse — medical, political, judicial, or what have you — *literary* history becomes a subfield of just that sort of positive history that historians, under the

pressure of literary theory, have put in question.[13] To treat literature as the reflection or handmaiden of some earlier material "reality" that is understood
to be the true object of history is to forget that our understanding of the "real"
as a set of related events or circumstances is itself a literary effect.[14]

But to simply replace the diverse exigencies of material life by a syncretic
semiotics would allow the unfolding of experience to slip away beneath the
protective cover of an a priori formal structure. To seek, as the best of the
New Historicists do, the socially productive patterns of representation that
join literature to a generalized discursive economy (however heuristic) produces interesting results, but we ought not leave unexamined the distinct roles
that different discourses play in the genesis of the cultural categories — such as
history and character — on which we depend, and we ought to specify as rigorously as possible the mechanisms through which discourse assimilates for,
and mediates to, its subjects their own experience.

The Foucauldian, New Historicist view of the subject as the precipitate of
a discursive formation that always preexists and determines either obscures
or denies any approach to the historical agency of individual human subjects.
The notably historical questions of origin, cause, and change are thus folded
back onto a description of structure that cannot account for its own beginning or end, emergence or disappearance: thus the radical discontinuities
that mark the (temporal) space between *épistèmes* in Foucault's *The Order of
Things* and the displacement in New Historicist readings of subjective agency
onto a "poetics of culture" that contains and recuperates the discourse of its
inmates.[15]

Greenblatt's masterful *Renaissance Self-Fashioning* is wholly exemplary in
that it presents not self-fashioning, but the poignant story of the failure of
self-fashioning as a defense against the penetrating incursions of a discourse
that is irreducibly exterior to the individual, who is doomed, despite talent
and heroic effort, to be fashioned by social forces of which he or she does not
partake and in which he or she is necessarily contained: "We may say that self-
fashioning occurs at the point of encounter between an authority and an alien,
that what is produced in this encounter partakes of both the authority and
the alien that is marked for attack, and hence that *any achieved identity* always
contains within itself the signs of its own subversion or loss" (p. 9; emphasis mine).[16] I have italicized the universalizing phrase "any achieved identity"
in the above passage because Greenblatt's divagations regarding the loss of

"self" in "self-fashioning" are illustrative. When, in its memorable epilogue, the writing of the book is recounted as a narrative of discovery over time, we learn that the author came to see this loss of self as constitutive of the "modern subject" only in the course of losing his first, more optimistic, intention:

> When I first conceived this book several years ago, I intended to explore the ways in which major English writers of the sixteenth century created their own performances, to analyze the choices they made in representing themselves and in fashioning characters, to understand the role of human autonomy in the construction of identity. It seemed to me the very hallmark of the Renaissance that middle-class and aristocratic males began to feel that they possessed such shaping power over their lives, and I saw this power and the freedom it implied as an important element in my own sense of myself. But as my work progressed, I perceived that fashioning oneself and being fashioned by cultural institutions — family, religion, state — were inseparably intertwined. In all my texts and documents, there were, so far as I could tell, no moments of *pure, unfettered subjectivity;* indeed, the human subject itself began to seem remarkably unfree, the ideological product of the relations of power in a particular society. Whenever I focused sharply upon a moment of apparently autonomous self-fashioning, I found not an epiphany of identity freely chosen but a cultural artifact. If there remained traces of free choice, the choice was among possibilities whose range was strictly delineated by the social and ideological system in force. (p. 256; my emphasis)

A curious absolutism seems to take hold in this passage as it relinquishes the hope of understanding "the role of human autonomy in the construction of identity" in the face of a failure to find "moments of pure, unfettered subjectivity." Must the question of autonomy take the form of "either/or"? Autonomy either expresses pure subjectivity or is subsumed by an ideological system that *precedes* it? Self-fashioning either results from "an epiphany of identity freely chosen" or is merely a "cultural artifact"? Is the deck not stacked against autonomy, if the card we must find corresponds to "pure, unfettered subjectivity"? Insofar as the notion of subjectivity implies a relationship to objects (some of which themselves may also be subjects), this phrase is surely an oxymoron. If the world disappears, so does the self that, as a subject, resides perforce within it. I readily accept Greenblatt's conclusion that human autonomy is compromised by the belatedness of the subject with respect to the symbolic systems within which subjectivity is necessarily precipitated, but the reduction of autonomy to "an epiphany of identity freely chosen" is not compelling.

As we shall see in chapter 2, the new literary history I propose places the determinative force of discourse not in a "poetics of culture," the elements of which can never be specified, but rather in the cognitive implications of a linguistically conditioned rhetorical usage. In this model, the structures of language and rhetoric, determined as they are by a negotiation of mutual comprehensibility — that is, by how widely innovative usages are understood and repeated and for how long — are viewed as configuring cognitive paradigms that integrate the individual into social discourse. At once occupying the individual subject formed within them, yet also perceptibly external to it, these purely formal structures configure a structural unconscious, opening up a space from which historical agents can selectively employ and manipulate a determined range of rhetorical possibilities to achieve authentically indeterminate results. *Over time* these cognitive adjustments transform the contents of a culture and its normative discourse in ways that allow both a discursive culture and the individuals comprising and comprised by it to change.[17] Because such change emerges from a confrontation of exigent circumstance and a definite number of formalizing configurations, *as acted upon* by subjects who may find themselves situated within variously conflicting configurations, it may be characterized as determinately indeterminate. I will argue that within this determined indeterminacy, the constitutive belatedness of the subject is precisely what allows it the ethical privilege of self-fashioning. The subject recognizing itself as the unique locus of multiple and exigent determinations constitutes itself as a succession of retrospections, anticipations, and choices. As the world we confront changes, it provides numerous moments in which the rhetoric of the self in relation to its world and its actions in that world is multiple, fluid, subject to adjustment — moments in which two or more possibilities hold out a choice, and it is in such moments that the subject of history also becomes its agent. My project is to identify and follow such moments of change as they constitute literary historical events.

3

How do we know when a literary historical event has occurred and in what domains might such an event matter? In attempting to define the literary historical event, I want to pay proper attention to the literary form in which history always already comes to us, and thus to posit, as the first task of *literary* history, the recovery of the historicity of history itself. Accordingly, I shall be arguing that history receives the paradigmatic form through which we moderns (a term that pointedly includes the Renaissance and excludes the medieval) achieve our specifically mediated access to the exigencies of the material world in and through the representation of character in Renaissance narrative.

What, then, would constitute a properly *literary* history? Literature is informed by its own linguistic and rhetorical constraints and by the historical conditions in which it is produced. Both the material of contingent experience and the conventions of rhetoric and language in force in a given time and place condition not only the content but the structures—generic and architectural—of literature. At the same time, the literary product in circulation at a given time is a historical fact with demonstrably historical results. When Hamlet tells the actors that the end of playing is "to hold as 'twere, the mirror up to nature" (3.2.21–22), he states a generalized expectation of long standing. At the same time, he asserts for Shakespeare a functionalist position within the contemporary theater that situates his play with respect to a passé declamatory acting style, on the one hand, and the nouveau popularity of the children's companies, on the other.

Literary characters also may serve as cultural templates within whose patterns living characters are formed. Between the writings and the actions of Sir Philip Sidney, to take another Renaissance example, there exists a determined reciprocity. A certain ideal of knightly behavior is taken to be exemplified in the writing and by the life. In the course of time, this reciprocal exemplarity of life and text shifts genres, combines with other exemplary texts, and enters *The Faerie Queene,* where, becoming an image in yet another literary mirror, it serves to fashion—to some undetermined and no doubt limited degree—the lives of younger gentleman who seek to cast themselves in Spenser's mold.

My interest, then, is the procedures according to which human subjects write themselves into stories and read themselves out of stories. I want to be able to specify how it comes about that, as Oscar Wilde remarks with respect to the interdetermination of impressionist painting and the appearance of the London fog, life imitates art.[18]

The goal of a properly *literary* history should be to specify the relationship of text to exigent experience and explain as far as possible how change in one affects (and effects) change in the other. To do this it is necessary to recognize and articulate the distinctness of the literary tradition as an active participant in the formation of material experience.

Thus, a properly *literary* history would study how in a given historical moment a particular accommodation of experience and textuality is consolidated, in such a way that the text produced is *subsequently* thought of as referring to — even opening a transparent window on — an earlier extratextual "reality." Although it is the characteristic mark of such reference to imply the existence of a "reality" before signification, it is only through the mediation of the signifier that this putatively prior reality can be *discursively* encountered.[19]

A history that takes as its object the moment in which specifically literary processes mediate our access to "the Real" will be at once literary and historical, because a literary text matters historically precisely when it gives form to exigent experience and thus takes part in the self-constitution of subjects whose choices and actions affect the substance of material history. Because it seeks "history" in literature and, specifically, in the historical nature of literary forms, this literary history may seem excessively formalist to readers whose initial interest is literature *and* history, where history is construed to be a set of material facts to be placed in a determinate relation to contemporary literary productions.

This apparent inflation of the formal until it surrounds and encompasses the historical is neither casual nor expedient. The reciprocal imitation of life and art cannot be confined to the consideration of themes. History is a question not simply of content, of textual references and material events, but of the *forms* in and through which the particularities of art and life become manifest. That the formal structures through which a literary character is situated within the world of his or her actions are more powerful than the discursive comments that may be made about them is apparent in our unfailing trust of form over content whenever the two are brought into contradiction, as in, for example, the famously vexed case of the narrator's thematic denigration of Satan over against the existential sweep of his actions and rhetoric in *Paradise Lost*, or the suspicious dissatisfaction we may feel with the too quick reformation of Oliver in *As You Like It*. Tropes and schemes and generic expectations define a rhetorical logic out of which the themes and action of a literary work are built. They are also the generative ground of the categories into which the thematic material is disposed. By determining how character and action may be joined, a text's figurative modalities determine also the emergence of its themes and resolutions. The mechanism through which this disposition takes place will be elaborated in chapter 2.

To grasp the literary event as a historical event and to show why it is that historical events are always already literary, it remains necessary, however, to separate for one more moment what cannot really be separated, that is, literary and material history. As a gesture toward this impossible project, I propose a *nearly* dialectical approach to literary historiography. I say nearly dialectical, because a truly dialectical approach would claim to mediate moments that are in fact contradictory and determinately different. But dialectic itself, insofar as it imparts a naturalizing narrative form to a series of exigent events, may be viewed as a formal event that takes place wholly within literary history. To posit a dialectical literary history, therefore, would engage the most common of epistemological tropes, metalepsis, or the metonymy of effect for cause, to predicate the literary historical event on a process that can only be constructed as its posterior effect.

Therefore, I offer a dialectical approach to the literary history of the Renaissance, with the provision that the advent of dialectic itself ultimately falls within that history. While it may appear that with this formulation I resort to the sort of preemptive confession that I earlier cited as the mark in the New Historicism of its strategic undertheorization, I would argue that a specific and *theoretically determined and elaborated* dependence on dialectical argument has the advantage over an untheorized assertion of the critic's embeddedness in the textuality that he or she explores, on the one hand, or the (implicit) assertion that dialectic simply gives the structure of the world, on the other.[20]

In an interview with Jean-Louis Houdebine and Guy Scarpetta, Jacques Derrida situates the project of deconstruction as an informed resistance to dialectic: "If there were a definition of *différance*, it would be precisely the limit, the interruption, the destruction of the Hegelian *relève* [*Aufhebung*] *wherever* it operates."[21] Referring to the "interminable" labor of "elucidating the relationship [of deconstruction] to Hegel," Derrida goes on to say:

I have attempted to distinguish *différance* (whose *a* marks, among other things, its productive and conflictual characteristics) from Hegelian difference, and have done so precisely at the point at which Hegel, in the greater *Logic,* determines difference as contradiction only in order to resolve it, to interiorize it, to lift it up (according to the syllogistic process of speculative dialectics) into the self-presence of an onto-theological or onto-teleological synthesis. (p. 44; pp. 59–60 in the French text)

If, however, we offer, as I intend to do, not a general economy of the Spirit, but rather a carefully restricted dialectic of self-representation, we may consider that *différance* names also a series of sites at which the experience of difference between the self and its speculations evokes a desire that manifests itself in the dynamic action of individual agents. The fact that absolute knowledge will not be achieved, that each *Aufhebung* will be followed by a reinscription of the *différance* it had sought to overcome, does not invalidate the potential dynamism of the self, even in and through its self-division. Insofar as *différance,* "at a point of absolute proximity to Hegel" (p. 44), may be thought of as producing a "master narrative" in suspense, a restless dialectic in which what is left over is thematized in and as narrative rather than sublated as concept, the method I am proposing, may, I suppose, peacefully coexist with deconstruction, if not, indeed, go under its name (though with the rather specific reservation of a refusal to privilege metonymy over metaphor).[22]

The *nearly* dialectical articulation of experience and literature needs to be distinguished, however, from the *truly* dialectical interaction of tropes developed in chapter 2. Because this interplay of *rhetorical forms* takes place wholly within the representation, it forms a homogenous discourse, which may be formalized according to its inherent logic. The moment of incoherence that I attempt to take into account by the adverb "nearly" occurs when the representation of events belatedly organizes the disparate and multifaceted manifestations of "reality" according to just such a rhetorical paradigm. It is in such moments that the self in its dynamism encounters the irreducible lack around which it is constituted, encounters itself precisely as the excess of the real over signification.

This awkward process, by which my methodology seeks to erase itself in advance of the arguments it generates, will reappear at several key moments in the studies that follow, with particular and insistent reference to the two great dialectical hermeneutics that explicitly or implicitly, consciously or unconsciously, inform our modern retrospections of the literary past: Marxism and psychoanalysis, the one for its articulation of the material and the literary within the hierarchy of base and superstructure, the other for its theory of the subject as specifically the subject of a structure (complex) of the remembered traces of its own history. It is my historical contention that something occurred in the Renaissance that specifically enabled both these systems by creating and formally representing the human agent that is their subject and the temporal medium in which its agency has its play.

Thus, the moment of literary historical innovation that I wish to construct out of the literary moments here considered is that in which the self is confirmed as the experience of a mutable yet self-consistent inwardness passing through time. It is this historically determined "self" that is the subject and object of Marxist (Hegelian) and psychoanalytic interpretation. Insofar as the constitution of historical agents in and through this discursive subjectivity is the theme of my own narrative, I indulge a certain confidence that my occasional but persistent juxtaposition of Marxist and psychoanalytic categories will eventually clarify and justify both itself and the provisionality I now, at the beginning, invoke.

4

Having stressed the discontinuities of material and literary history, I will, in constituting my *near* dialectic, use *time* as a mediating term between them, because in its textual and experiential aspects time is an intimate player in the interchange of experience and signification.[23] Time, as Thomas Aquinas notes, is implicit in the verb: "To signify with time is to signify time principally, as a thing, which is appropriate to the name; however, it is another thing to signify time, which is not proper to the name but to the verb."[24]

Literary texts necessarily articulate a time of reading and a sense of duration interior to the discourse. Because we understand history to be the content of a duration, this coming together of the duration of the signifier and the signification of duration takes part in any formal conception of history. Thus, our expectations of history, understood as the course of events written on the passage of time, condition our experience of time itself.

In the poetic production of the Renaissance one sees clearly the presence of two contradictory conceptions of time. One view places little value on the arena of historical events. The other looks forward, with, for example, Francis Bacon, to a time when the mastery of second causes will restore, "even in this life," the dominion over nature lost through Adam's sin. The older of these views looks back to a long tradition of Christian thought that sees Adam's fall and Christ's passion as punctuation marks in a homogeneous human history that is winding down to the appointed moment of a messianic apocalypse. The contrary view, exemplified by Bacon's new scientific faith, looks forward to a time when time will be experienced not as the repetition of a homogeneous cycle of labors prolonging exile from the light of heaven, but as the medium of progress, the preparation "by tract of Time" — to borrow Milton's phrase — of regeneration.[25] These two experiences of time coincide through much of the Renaissance, and both persist in our own time; however, I think it fair to say that, at least in the West, the identification of history with progress becomes ascendant during the seventeenth century and remains so at least until, let us say, in remembrance of the cold war, 1945.[26]

We also ought to notice that this change in the experience of time coincides with the beginnings of technological control over "second causes." Such projects as fen drainage, enclosure, and especially, wintering-over of livestock and establishing international circulation of agricultural produce and manufactured commodities, superimposed over the yearly cycles of the agricultural calendar an expectation that wealth would accumulate over an extended time. The ancient cycle of sowing and reaping is eclipsed in the Renaissance by the vision of increased productivity, geometrically enlarging herds, and accumulating stocks of gold.[27] I have argued elsewhere that the experience of time as a medium of accumulation (of experiences, of goods, of revelations) correlates with a general revision of the way in which people ascribe meaning to the events of their daily lives.[28] Put briefly, meaning is displaced from an originary essence (as in, for example, humor psychology, or tropological hermeneutics) to an always deferred ending (as in, for example, Freudian psychoanalysis, or typological hermeneutics).[29] There is thus the ground of an apparent alliance between the emergence of narrative as the paradigmatic form for the understanding of events in relation to the self as historical agent and the rhetoric of accumulation associated with contemporary technological and economic development. In each, meaning accretes toward some anticipated repletion: the self is realized as the dialectical synthesis of its encounters over time, and the world it occupies is realized as the result—again, over time—of a collaboration of natural law and human agency.

What has all this to do with the history of literary forms? Let us imagine for the moment a Renaissance person. During this person's life, changes in the organization of agriculture and the development of a world market economy, the shift away from the land as the dominant medium of wealth, the opening of a "new" world—all these occasions—work, in various ways, to sever the experience of time from its former close association with the agricultural calendar. What had been experienced as homogeneous and cyclical becomes differentiated and linear. Can we think of this person apart from his or her contradictory experience of time? If we imagine, perhaps anachronistically—but the Renaissance revival of Neoplatonism invites us to do so—that this Renaissance person is constituted, as we are, by the memories that he or she possesses, we can see that he or she experiences a passing of present days which is different from the passing that he or she remembers. In what form does this individual encounter the disparity? His or her language and cultural history are still dominated by forms that answer to the older, fading experience of time, and these forms, this language, reproduce the discontinuity of time in its own changing relationship to the literary tradition it embodies.

The literary *event* I am seeking is, then, the formal assimilation of this experience of division and its representation as constitutive of a human subject unified by the writing out of this division in time—that is, the production of literary forms through which the individuals who lived through these changes were able to imagine themselves in new ways, accommodating their experience of internal discontinuity by envisaging themselves as works-in-progress. Through this recognition—and only after a time—a new "reality" is established.

One place in which this literary historical event can be seen is the production in the Renaissance of a body of poetry that more or less self-consciously engages a formal tension between lyric and narrative. In this context, we can identify narrative with the tendency to defer meaning until the end of the work. Only from the perspective of a temporal closure can the episodes of a narrative be assigned stable meanings.

As we have seen, narratives always have two lives, one the temporal unfolding of a plot, the other the semantic design of a completed set of events, reread from the perspective of their conclusion. Narrative indulges time as the medium in which the exigent contents of experience must be encountered, only to negate this medium in a moment of closure that converts the apparently contingent episodes to elements in an atemporal structure. Narrative is thus a formal rhetoric by which a sequence of diachronically unfolding events is joined to a synchronic design through an act of metaleptic anticipation.

The literary historical moment at issue occurs when this epistemological rhetoric is granted ontological force, as, for example, when typological hermeneutics contain the historical episodes of the Hebrew Scriptures as prophetic signifiers by at once preserving these episodes as literal history and converting them to signifiers whose ultimate significance derives from their participation in an apocalyptic anagogy. Narrative, then, is a literary form through which exigent events are contained within a more or less universal history.

Lyric, on the other hand, resists this displacement forward by dwelling on the presence of a speaker in the time of the poem's enunciation. If the lyric voice generalizes from within its setting, the appeal to design, to law, to stable and timeless structure is more immediate, less likely to be deferred through a temporal sequence of discovery. The discontinuity between an agrarian ideology that organizes time as homogeneous and cyclical and an only partially formed ideology of accumulation can be seen in the tension that sometimes surfaces between lyric and narrative inscriptions of time in Renaissance poetry. By presenting itself as the repetition of a lived moment, lyric also represents the momentary escape of history from its narrative containment.

We can see the creative tension between lyric and narrative in the hybrid forms that appear as early as *La Vita Nuova* and the *Rime sparse* and become more common in the Renaissance: in the extraordinarily popular sonnet sequences, in the not quite serious dynastic plots of the epic romances of Ariosto, Tasso, and Spenser, in a typologically narrativized collocation of lyrics like Herbert's *The Temple,* in the generic anomaly of Donne's *Anniversaries,* which, as I shall argue in chapter 5, perform a funeral oration over their own lyric procedures, and in the ironic and self-conscious narratives incorporated in Marvell's lyrics.

Finally, I will point to *Paradise Lost* as the moment when the experience of time as a medium of accumulation is fully expressed and recognized as if it were the manifestation of a natural law. In this last English epic, Milton decisively revises the Renaissance hybrid of dynastic romance and classical epic into a fully imbricated plot in which the narrative deferral of meaning explicitly dismantles the immediate semantic values of the old inherited orders of classical and Christian iconography and genre.

5

In this chapter, in very general terms, I have sketched something of my own narrative history of Renaissance literature. This narrative, embedded in a preliminary discussion of its means and purposes, includes a number of large claims, which, in turn, depend on a series of subsidiary arguments. Before entering the detailed account of the method of this study, presented in chapter 2, I think some recapitulation and illustration is in order. The purpose of the history outlined here and elaborated in the ensuing chapters is to achieve an understanding of a certain inscription of subjective agency—of the self in relation to its acts. I understand this inscription to be, precisely, a *literary historical event. Literary* because the subject is inscribed *in* a set of linguistically determined rhetorical configurations developed and represented in the narrative poetry of the Renaissance. *Historical* because the configuration and reconfiguration of the mimesis presented in these poems responds to and effects the integration of exigent experience—both social and personal—into the understanding of self and world from which the historical subject emerges. An *event* because the emergence and revision of the subject can be identified with dialectical moments in which one rhetorical configuration of experience becomes opaque and difficult and another, after a period of time, becomes associated with a "transparent" representation of "reality." In the case at issue, the writing of the self as historical subject in Renaissance English narrative poetry, the event comprises a number of episodes in which the pressure of specifiable social, technological, and economic developments may be traced in a tense transition from lyric to narrative representations of the self. These representations use narrative to articulate the self as an agent and subject of history, mutable yet able to construct its identity over time. Time is thus rendered as the medium within which an individual's self-consistency is both challenged and maintained.

To give some idea of how in its details the literary history I am proposing might lead us first to discern in a lyric the pressure of narrative beneath the generic surface and then to engage the larger issues that I have just summarized, I will conclude this introduction with a brief discussion of the way in which time and action are articulated in one of the most anthologized lyrics of the late Renaissance.

Marvell's "The Garden" presents a speaker who generalizes about social activity while withdrawn from it—in a pleasant place and a specific time. But the time and place of "The Garden" are impossible to sort out, and the critical history of the poem testifies to its many indeterminacies. What is the relationship of Eden to the Garden from which the poet speaks (ll. 57–64)? What happens to the poet's mind and thoughts after Mind "Annhilat[es] all that's made / To a green Thought in a green Shade" (ll. 47–48)?[30] What joins the industrious bee, the poet, and the sundial in the final stanza? To whom and for what purpose does the poet speak from within "this delicious Solitude" (l. 16)?

Taking these indeterminacies as themselves thematic, I would argue that the poem records the impossibility of the poet's dwelling either in Eden or in the fallen world. Caught between two distinct matrices of experience, he can organize his thoughts and actions neither in the homogeneous time of the past nor the cumulative time of the future. He can only write his poem in the historical world by constantly referring it to the "natural" world of the garden. In other words, the first phase of narrative, the temporal unfolding of exigent events, can be unified and made meaningful only by preemptively assimilating it to the second, the retrospective configuration of those events as parts of the same story. Thus, the poet alternatively, even noncommittally, looks to "nature" or "Mind" to reduce sequence to consequence, to assimilate contingency to design. Like God, the poet creates a world in which to incarnate his own sign, but, unlike God, he can only dwell within the time of his own writing; the voice that he incarnates in discourse is necessarily alienated from the body from which it issues. What, in my view, marks this poem as participating in a literary historical event is the self-conscious way in which the poet, neither wholly within nor without the realms of his "fancy," encounters himself as the supplement of his own signifier, suspended between alternative modes of representation.[31]

"The Garden" begins in a timeless present in which "vainly men themselves amaze / To win the Palm, the Oke, or Bayes" (ll. 1–2). Along with the verbal aspect of the universal present, the invocation of the classical signs of success in distinct areas of endeavor suggests a timeless ambition timelessly expressing itself as an aspect of human nature. The second stanza shifts to the more definite past tense to place the poet's discovery of "Fair quiet" against this universal ambition:

> Fair quiet, have I found thee here,
> And Innocence thy Sister dear!
> Mistaken long, I sought you then
> In busie Companies of Men.
> Your sacred Plants, if here below,
> Only among the Plants will grow.
> Society is all but rude,
> To this delicious Solitude. (ll. 9–16)

The normative social ambition of the first stanza is now seen as a period of personal error, delaying rather than achieving the speaker's contentment. The third stanza continues an assertive description of the Garden as a substitutive or superseding norm, quite as universal as the ambition of the first stanza.

The signs of social attainment, sacrificed in the first stanza for the "Fair Quiet" of the second, are now joined by a parallel purging of the *signs* of passionate desire in favor of a self-affirming sylvan solitude:

> No white nor red was ever seen
> So am'rous as this lovely green.
> Fond Lovers, cruel as their Flame,
> Cut in these Trees their Mistress name.
> Little, Alas, they know, or heed,
> How far these Beauties Hers exceed!
> Fair Trees! where s'eer your barkes I wound,
> No Name shall but your own be found. (ll. 17–24) [32]

The narrative containment of experience may be preserved through either of two alternatives, which we now recognize as the active and the contemplative lives. The critical point at which these apparent alternatives cross or coincide comes in the central fifth stanza:

> What wond'rous Life is this I lead!
> Ripe Apples drop about my head;
> The Luscious Clusters of the Vine
> Upon my Mouth do crush their Wine;

The Nectaren, and curious Peach,
Into my hands themselves do reach;
Stumbling on Melons, as I pass,
Insnar'd with Flow'rs, I fall on Grass. (ll. 33–40)

The alternative universal history of the contemplative life is brought from the quasi-historical past of stanzas one to four into the iterative present of lyric time — but only until the final couplet intersects the highly determinate historical narrative evoked by the climactic "I fall." The fact that, after this couplet, the poem shifts immediately to a meditation on the conflictual relations of mind and body — of universal being and temporal becoming — argues that Empson was right to hear in the phrase "I fall on Grass" an echo of Isaiah 40:6, "All flesh is grass" and to read the line as an allusion to the Fall of man, an allusion confirmed by the reference in the eighth stanza to Adam's life in Eden before the creation of Eve.[33] The lyric present is fractured by an allusion that speaks to the poem from elsewhere. The words of Isaiah, which are not quite repeated by the poet, mark the eruption into the present of a historical and prophetic text that takes possession of the lyric moment. This splitting of the word becomes *thematically* significant when we recall that the passage in Isaiah goes on to contrast the mutability of the flesh-grass to the permanence of the divine word, reproducing — as it were a type — the tension between the universal and the temporal that underlies Marvell's evocation of pastoral contemplation as an escape from social engagement.[34]

The allusion to the flesh and the Fall ironically reanimates the poem's human subject after several lines in which all the active verbs are assigned to the fruit and the poet is portrayed as the passive victim of an excessive nature. It is precisely when the poet falls on grass, when flesh becomes grass, that history begins. The poet's "I" emerges — as the active subject of a verb — from the background of a nature that is defined by a common mortality. Human action occurs only within the historical time of the fallen world. The fallen poet, subject to death, is joined to the grass, as is Marvell's mower character when he complains: "For *Juliana* comes, and She / What I do to the Grass, does to my Thoughts and Me," ("The Mower's Song," ll. 29–30). But in choosing his actions, he has recourse to a Platonic memory of a timeless garden world in which the will of man was not distinct from the design of God, in which time was not the medium of one's self-differing.

The evocation of Eden without Eve in the eighth stanza makes it clear that both intercourse and discourse, what Milton refers to in Book 8 of *Paradise Lost* as the "conversation" of Adam and Eve, are called forth to repair the defect of our mortality, "But twas beyond a Mortal's share / To wander solitary there: / Two Paradises 'twere in one / To live in Paradise alone" (ll. 61–64).

But what would be the status of language and poetry in solitude? The praise of solitude is the logical conclusion of the opening stanza's rejection of cultural symbols — palm, oak, bayes — in favor of a language of endlessly repeated denomination, "where s'eer your barkes I wound, / No Name shall but your own be found" (ll. 23–24).[35] The poet, in such a condition, could be grass, but he could not "fall on grass." To be one with the voice is to stand mutely outside time and discourse.

As Fineman has shown in another context, the epideictic poet traditionally aspires to be that which he contemplates, so that the very distinctness of his voice evokes his failure, drawing attention to his poetic activity as the rhetorical supplement of a purely deictic mimesis; the Johannine gesture of pointing is always necessarily corrupted by an accompanying self-indication: "behold the Lady (as *I* have deftly drawn her according to the figure in *my* heart)."[36] In "The Garden" the poet who seeks "Fair quiet" "among the Plants" stumbles over the rhetorical excess of his own evocation, becoming one with nature only through the historical exigency of a fatal fall, after which "All flesh is grass."[37]

Thus, we see illustrated in "The Garden" a decisive tension between the traditional epideictics of the lyric, in which, through the mediation of his representation, the poet becomes one with that which he represents, and the beginnings of an ex-pressive subjectivity; that is, a subjectivity that manifests itself as witness to its own incessant failure to express "that within which passes show" (*Hamlet* 1.2.85). The poet in "The Garden" is at one with neither the object of his poem nor his representation of it. Instead, he records the irreducible exteriority of his own voice, tracing man's expulsion from timeless nature into self-consciously mortal historicality. From within history, this subject reflects upon its own finitude and attempts to negotiate an existential relationship to time; it encounters itself through what Heidegger calls "the being toward death."[38] In this moment, the poet becomes the supplement of his own discourse, the effaced origin of his own voice.[39] But also in this moment, and perhaps only for a moment, he opens in that space between the voice and its origin, a space for history, a space in which something just might happen. As Fineman points out, we may find a structurally similar opening theorized (as opposed to narrated) in contemporary psychoanalytic theory, in Lacan's category of the Real: "different both from the Imaginary and the Symbolic—a Real that can be neither specularized nor represented" (TSE, p. 71).[40] History is a trace suspended over and only partly occluding this void.

In the course of the Renaissance the constitution of the self around this constitutively empty space comes to be represented as the identification of the self with the story of its accumulations, including the memory of its accumulated experiences. Here again, we may find an uncanny resonance in contemporary critical discourse, when, in the (apparently) ahistorical Oedipal narrative of Lacanian psychoanalysis, the subject enters, through its acquisition of language, into the Symbolic register and encounters itself as the unseen point from which it sees.

In the course of developing his argument for dialectic in opposition to contemporary historicist and deconstructive criticism, Altieri argues that the spatialized rhetoric prevailing in contemporary theory cannot account for time: "It is temporality, not specularity, that makes it impossible to gather the self into an image. . . . Instead, the impossibility of so staging the self indicates the need to turn entirely from the ideal of representation as a measure of identity."[41] In the chapters that follow, I will suggest some specific reasons for what amounts to a contemporary repetition in a theoretical register of the literary history of Renaissance self-representation. For the moment, I wish to make the point that this literary historical metalepsis, because it records a moment in which, under the pressure of temporal change, the lyric image gives way to an inherently dialectical narrative of historical causation, offers in a peculiar way the possibility of historicizing Altieri's return to dialectic.

The rhetoric of this narrative installs the expectation that the lost origin, the lost unity of an integral subject, will be recuperated not by the restoration of its past but by the realization of its future, not by a return to Eden but by a transfiguring second coming that ends history and thereby seals its meaning with the finitude of completion. Marvell, writing on the cusp of this literary and historical moment, is able to thematize this interpretive strategy in a way that playfully discloses the metalepsis through which it operates:

> When we have run our Passions heat,
> Love hither makes his best retreat.

> The *Gods*, that mortal beauty chase,
> Still in a tree did end their race.
> *Apollo* hunted *Daphne* so,
> Only that She might Laurel grow.
> And *Pan* did after *Syrinx* speed,
> Not as a Nymph, but for a Reed. (ll. 25–32)

An alternative to the "annihilation" of solitude is found in the fourth stanza's typological parody of Ovidian metamorphosis—which is, of course, equally, an Ovidian parody of typology. Through the metaleptic redefinition of contingent ends as intended, explanatory meaning is recast as that which is promised at the end of history, in contrast to that from which history falls.

What is most interesting to me about this stanza is that it so ostentatiously employs metalepsis as the *historical* explanation of subjective intention. The narrative containment of the exigent event—what we call history—suppresses the *unspeakable* passions of Apollo and Pan and constructs *in their place* a *hortitory* intention. This metalepsis is at once literary in formal and material registers; the examples are literary, taken from Ovid's *Metamorphoses*. Moreover, they are *about* literature, for they tell how two desired females were transformed by another's desire into instruments of mimesis: the reed that forms a shepherd's breath into a Doric strain and the laurel with which his privileged station is culturally marked and recognized.

In the ninth stanza the sun dial alludes at once to the natural time of the seasons and the intervention of a "skilful Gardner," who cannot be securely placed within or beyond nature, drawing the cycle of blooms into a dial. He is the product and the producer of time's map. His mimetic representation of what the sun has already written imposes on, or discovers in, its motion the atemporal design of the zodiac. Through the gardener's skill, the movement of the sun is captured within and interpreted by its participation in a totalizing structure. Situated neither here nor there, but shuttling between a lyric presence and a narrative design, the poem's speaker reproduces the position of a subjectivity that exists on the borderline between the mundane present and eternity, and acts from the place where retrospection and anticipation cross. By a similar doubling—in fact, a metaleptic doubling back—the poem's self-conscious, self-representing depiction of its rhetorical process leaves for us the trace of meaning's trajectory from origin to terminus, from specular lyric to narrative dialectic, from a medieval to a modern experience of time, from an originary subject to a (pre)destined one.

6

I began this chapter with a discussion of the New Historicism. Having now offered a summary expedition into literary historical practice, I think it may be useful to round on that discussion and make note of what I have not done. I have not sought to join Marvell's discourse to the anecdotal narration of any contemporary event, nor have I, in this instance, made any consistent attempt to contextualize his poem with respect to specific events unfolding in the 1650s in England or elsewhere. Still, I make my claim to a properly literary historical approach, one that seeks to understand the language of poetry not as a *parole* governed by a virtual but present *langue,* but rather as a place where language participates in the long, slow, and properly dialectical process of mediating to its users the determinate contradictions through which they live.

In choosing this approach I do not simply neglect the details of life in Marvell's time, as they may be discovered in various archives, but rather I consciously ally myself with the *histoire de mentalités.* For social contradictions find their way into discourse, become visible within discourse, slowly, fitfully. And these slow changes — like the reassimilation of time to which I have alluded — respond to exigent social life in an inherently conservative way, struggling to project continuity where we will later perceive rupture.

This is not to say that detailed information about a text's immediate context is necessarily irrelevant or pernicious. Such information can help us understand a text in a local way and, more importantly, understand how the local and the contingent enter history by entering a text. But an unexamined preoccupation with the narratable event also can distract and mislead someone interested in the linguistic and literary mediation of significant change. The history of a literary text is not the same as literary history.

In the chapters that follow, I will further elaborate a narrative literary history of the Renaissance by studying the rhetoric of the self in a selection of works, chosen because each work marks a significant and distinctive moment in the quasi-dialectical accommodation of rhetoric to experience. Taken together in a retrospective glance, these moments can be made to represent significant steps in a major rearticulation of the self, understood as a historical agent, that occurs in England over the course of time from the mid-sixteenth to the late seventeenth century.

From within this perspective it will be possible to see in the work of Spenser the breakdown of an epideictic subject more or less in place since the *Confessions* of Saint Augustine. In Donne, we will find a turn from the implicit narrative romances of the sonnet sequences to a thematic exploration of the condition of an epideictic epistemology confronted by scientific disenchantment. Donne marks precisely the passing of a visionary knowledge, supported by a symbolic order that presumes the material world has been given to the senses as immediately significant, as divine *meaning*. Donne sees the historical distress of the subject of *The Faerie Queene* as a failure to confine the contingent within an always deferred and deferring typological frame. Marvell's lyric narrativizations—the mower poems, the "Garden," and especially the long and generically anomalous "Upon Appleton House"—just as explicitly violate and exceed this frame. In them, the immediate historical exigencies of life in the 1650s are brought to question, and finally to overwhelm, the conventions that would allow him to preserve and encode in (and as) isolated moments an Augustinian subjectivity.

In Milton's works we can trace both the final decomposition of Augustinian epideixis and the initial completion of a recuperative movement that yields the subject of modernism, a represented human agent, whose theorization has been and will continue to be the preoccupation of our own time. Thus, I conclude with Milton because in an important sense his historical ontology recapitulates the phylogeny it succeeds.[42]

Before proceeding to the elaboration of this history, however, it will be necessary to consider, in some detail, the formal properties that allow narrative to structure subjectivity along the boundary between figurality and experience— that is, between literature and what we may modestly conceive to be history.

Chapter 2

The Subject of Narrative and the Rhetoric of the Self

1

The construction of narrative is an essential activity of the human mind.[1] Because the articulation of experience into story is the primary process through which individual and collective subjects disclose themselves, the study of the individual resolves in the psychoanalytic process into the study of personal narrative, and the study of culture resolves into the writing of history or collective narrative.

To make intelligible the large claims that I am making for narrative, I want to begin by recalling some of the more general claims of language on subjectivity. In a number of provocative and influential essays, Émile Benveniste has argued that "linguistic form is not only the condition for transmissibility, but first of all the condition for the realization of thought." This now widely accepted belatedness of thought with respect to language opens the way for the study of narrative form to become an investigation of the subject's way of coming to be, not only socially, but for itself.[2]

Before discussing the coming to be of the subject in the special conditions of narrative, however, it will be useful to consider the relations obtaining between subjectivity and discourse in general. Benveniste again provides an initial formulation, by linking subjectivity to grammatical person:

> The capacity of the speaker to posit himself as a "subject" . . . is defined
> not by the feeling which everyone experiences of being himself (this
> feeling, to the degree that it can be taken note of, is only a reflection) but
> as the psychic unity that transcends the totality of actual experiences it
> assembles and that makes the permanence of the consciousness. Now
> we hold that "subjectivity," whether it is placed in phenomenology or

psychology, as one may wish, is only the emergence in the being of a fundamental property of language. "Ego" is he who *says* "ego." That is where we see the foundation of "subjectivity," which is determined by the linguistic status of "person." [3]

Thus, Benveniste argues, the realization of thought presupposes language, and "Language is possible only because each speaker sets himself up as a *subject* by referring to himself as *I* in his discourse." This *I* must posit another person to whom its discourse is addressed. Thus, *I* and *You* are necessarily produced as the poles of any and every communication. Although the poles indicated by the pronoun shifters are neither equal nor symmetrical: " 'ego' always has a position of transcendence with regard to *you*. Nevertheless, neither of the terms can be conceived without the other; they are complementary, although according to an 'interior/exterior' opposition, and at the same time, they are reversible." [4]

Benveniste's "linguistic turn" on ego-formation is, of course, a classically structuralist argument, situating the subject as that which appears as an effect of language and occupies a spatial position determined by it. In a 1989 study, however, Charles Taylor reaches strikingly similar conclusions on more broadly philosophical grounds. Taylor concludes that "to study persons is to study beings who only exist in, or are partly constituted by, a certain language." [5] Since "a language only exists and is maintained within a language community. . . one is a self only among other selves. A self can never be without reference to those who surround it" (p. 35):

> I am a self only in relation to certain interlocutors: in one way in relation to those conversation partners who were essential to my achieving self-definition; in another in relation to those who are now crucial to my continuing grasp of languages of self understanding — and, of course, these classes may overlap. A self exists only within what I call "webs of interlocution." (p. 36)

When considering narrative, I shall be occupied with the emergence of the subject — in its relations with its partners in conversation — as it occurs within a specific form of discourse. [6] Some years before the publication of Benveniste's "Subjectivity in Language," Lacan argued (in a seminar attended by Benveniste) that, even before language acquisition, the subjective polarity of

I and *You* structures an internal dialectic in which the ego will be formed. The subject escapes the diadic oscillation between *I* and *You* by subsuming a specular version of self-awareness (that is, a self constructed according to an image) within what I will argue is a narrative construction of the self, that is, a self identified with the stories that may be told about it.

Thus, Lacan situates the ego at the juncture of an *Imaginary* oscillation between *I* and *You* and a *Symbolic* identification with the name, that is, with third-person nomination:

> Every imaginary relation comes about via a kind of *you or me* between the subject and the object. That is to say — *If it's you, I'm not. If it's me, it's you who isn't*. That's where the symbolic element comes into play. On the imaginary level, the objects only ever appear to man within relations which fade. He recognises his unity in them, but uniquely from without. And in as much as he recognises his unity in an object, he feels himself to be in disarray in relation to the latter. . . . That is where the symbolic relation comes in. The power of naming objects structures the perception itself.[7]

"The power of naming," however, is exterior to the poles of *I* and *You*. It occurs when a third person (the father in Lacan's psychoanalytic story) appropriates the subject position for *him*self by naming another as the (grammatical) *third person*. The ego emerges in the Symbolic (in and as the third person) when the subject accepts this name (the "Name of the Father") as its own. Thus, one could say in the context of the present argument that narrative functions symbolically to overcome the ephemerality of the imaginary identification by conjoining and holding discursive moments in a temporally expanded configuration. Depending on the angle from which one looks at it, this configuration is either the product or the producer of a subjective agent: the narrator. In this respect a narrative names its subject (e.g., Odysseus is the *hero* of the *Odyssey*) by incorporating it in a story that subsumes the subject's agency in the act of representing it, thus dividing it into the subject who speaks the story and the subject spoken in the story.

I will return to this division shortly, but I will begin with more general and more genuinely linguistic considerations. A.-J. Greimas and J. Courtès provide a serviceable definition of narrative as "a (more or less long) series of *states* between which are inserted transformations, that is reflexive, or transitive operations, insuring the passage from one state to another."[8] It is thus the function of narrative to articulate change by holding together in various configurations the notions of identity, difference, and time. As Tzvetan Todorov observes, the mediation of identity and change through time may be understood as the defining characteristic of narrative:

> Narrative is constituted in the tension of two formal categories, difference and resemblance; the exclusive presence of one of them brings us into a type of discourse which is not narrative . . . . The simple relation of successive facts does not constitute a narrative: these facts must be organized, which is to say, ultimately, that they must have elements in common. But if all the elements are in common, there is no longer anything to recount.[9]

Thus, any notion of change or transition implies a perception of the narrative subject as both self-identical and self-differing. Narrative *formally* represents change over time.

Narrative organizes *over time* the dialectic of the two poles of discourse, of *I* and *You*, whose interaction is essential to the emergence of the subject. While the oscillation of *I* and *You* in a conversation is ephemeral, the imitations of such oscillation in a narrative are collected and reconfigured within an always belated but ever anticipated synchrony. Thus, in a narrative, a subject proceeding through a series of states encounters and reencounters itself as other, as different in time. The speaking subject defines itself in its effort to come to terms with the series of "I's" that occupy the various positions along the curve of the plot. This movement of the subject is mediated by transitive predications that either relate subject to verb or join substance and accidents across the copula. For example, in the statement "Jack left school prematurely," Jack, the student, is joined to Jack, the dropout, through the verb, which asserts the identity of the two and places them in a temporal order with respect to one another. In the statement, "Jack is back at school," the predicate carries the return to school back across the copula, modifying an implicit earlier state of Jack. Thus, in the little narrative, "Jack left school prematurely, but he is back at school now," Jack is a student, drops out, and becomes a student again—perhaps older and wiser—but still, substantively, Jack.

The subject emerges as an agent through a reflection on the actions it has taken, is taking, will take, or can be conceived of taking within the narrative.

The opposition of *I* to *You* that obtains in active discourse may therefore be assimilated to the subject of narrative as the opposition of an *I* consequent to one action and an *I* consequent to an alternative action. The narrative voice continually interrogates its signifiers in the written text along the temporal sequence determined by the unfolding of the plot.

Although I have changed the terminology so as to insert this notion into a particular critical context, the relationship of subject to predicates in narrative that I am urging enjoys the authority of Aristotle and also may be derived from the familiar critical taxonomy devised in Northrop Frye's "Theory of Modes."

In the *Poetics* Aristotle argues that mythos is prior to ethos because character depends on action. Since character is defined within the plot, only a character consistent with the actions that he must undertake may be employed.[10] What stands behind this prescription is the fact that the network of predications which form the plot creates a "character effect," such that the character it determines would conflict with and ultimately supplant an incompatible character, created by description and imposed upon the plot. The truth of Aristotle's claim may be seen in the fact that when discrepancies between description and narration occur, readers generally discredit description and accept the character's actions as the index of his or her ethos. If we are told that character A is good and kind and has thrown his poor old mother off the roof, we invariably use the action to discredit the description unless we are given definite cues to do otherwise. It is this conventional response that allows us to deem a narrator unreliable. As I suggested in chapter 1, the history of the reception of Milton's Satan may be taken to illustrate the more complex possibilities that are opened by a disparity between the plot's character and the narrator's descriptions of his ethos.

In a similarly Aristotelian fashion, Frye's "Theory of Modes" uses the power of action of the hero as the criterion of modal classification: Particular mythoi require particular kinds of heroes. Conversely, the hero defines a specified plot structure by bringing into play a defined range of predicates.[11] Narrative relates an action, and the subject emerges within the range of possible actors. Just as certain verbs are restricted to certain kinds of subjects, certain plot structures assert lexical restrictions on the characters who may participate in them. Conversely, characters are known by their responses to the contingencies that befall them.

Of the various kinds of discourse in which a subject can inscribe, and thus come to know, itself, narrative is of particular interest because its plot structure necessarily discloses its characters' power of action; that is, narrative tells us what sorts of things can be predicated of a specified subject. Thus, the actions of men and women in narratives tell us something about the imaginative possibilities open — in a given time and place — to a writing subject creating and re-creating itself in discourse.

Insofar as a narrative develops any defined point of view — which is to say, insofar as it develops a "character effect" — it encompasses a mimesis of discourse in which the polarities of person, self and other, emerge. The reader's privilege of occupying the successive positions inscribed in the narrative is specifically extended by these mimetic elements, which invite him to appropriate (or be appropriated by) the specified subjectivity to which the notion of point of view is reducible.

Thus, narratives serve a cognitive purpose. By generating a narrative, a speaker or writer positions himself or herself with respect to the objects that he or she encounters; he or she extrudes himself or herself into a world perceived as exterior. As Taylor puts it:

> In order to have an identity, we need an orientation to the good, which
> means some sense of qualitative discrimination, of the incomparably
> higher. Now we see that this sense of the good has to be woven into
> my understanding of my life as an unfolding story. But this is to state
> another basic condition of making sense of ourselves, that we grasp our
> lives in a *narrative*. . . . Our lives exist also in this space of questions,
> which only a coherent narrative can answer. In order to have a sense of
> who we are, we have to have a notion of how we have become, and of
> where we are going. (p. 47)

In Benveniste's terms, the utterer inscribes his or her signifier(s) in the utterance. I refer here to the distinction between *énonciation* (uttering) and *énoncé* (uttered). The subject of the *énoncé* presupposes, and is necessarily belated with respect to, the subject of the *énonciation*. Lacan draws from this linguistic distinction a key element of psychic ontology, which I alluded to earlier in reference to the division of the subject into narrator and narratee on its entry into the Symbolic. For Lacan, the speaking subject becomes a constitutive blind spot, the empty place from which signification issues, but which cannot itself be subsumed within its own discourse.[12]

Narrative thus responds to specific demands that grow out of perceived discontinuities between self and world and between self and self, and the analysis of specified narratives may recover not only the exigent demands experience makes on their authors, but the general configurations of response available at the time of their composition.[13]

For an individual, the one serious answer to the question "Who are you?" is the story of his or her life. The literary record may be seen as another kind of life-story, one from which we may recover the dialectic of literary change and, perhaps, infer — tentatively and modestly — a relationship between that dialectic and the material world from which it speaks. To do so, it is necessary to consider the relationships between the writing subject and his or her surrogates in the story and between the reader and the text with regard to the cognitive functions of narrative.

In an essay called "The Storyteller," Walter Benjamin notes the special authority conferred on a story by its having reached an irreversible conclusion, observing that, "Not only a man's knowledge or wisdom, but above all his real life — and this is the stuff that stories are made of — first assumes transmissible form at the moment of his death."[14] This final authority, conferred by completion, is necessarily deferred to a place beyond the boundaries of experience.

But experience is itself structured with reference to an imagined end, a personal eschatology. Without resort to this proleptic ending, experience remains a disarticulate set of contingent events. Therefore, narrative is always constituted in an act of reflection — though this reflection may be from the point of view of a projected telos.[15] As this reflection captures the subject over which the net of narrative is cast, the subject, even of this anticipatory retrospection, escapes, receding into the memory of its own reminiscence. At any given moment, the constitution of a narrative represents an attempt to anchor this subject to its own ephemeral reflections — to establish its continuity over time — through the interpretation of a set of events, understood in relation to a proposed end. The subject of narrative is thus realized as the site of a desire, which would, as Peter Brooks describes it, "seem to be totalizing in intent, a process toward combination in new unities: metonymy in the search to become metaphor";[16] or, more colloquially, a desire to unify the this and that of temporal sequence by bringing them together under a single name. For example, the *Odyssey* is the story of Odysseus, whose adventures join under this name to inscribe within it the attribute "skilled in all ways of contending."

To exemplify the complex ways in which this process becomes self-conscious in the works within the purview of this study, we may consider how the narrative production of character through the gathering together of predicates becomes the thematic motive of the first book of *The Faerie Queene*. Referred to in the letter to Ralegh as a "clownishe younge man" appearing anomalously at court, Spenser's knight of holiness is, until canto x, identified to himself and the reader only as the Red Crosse Knight, after the design on the coat he wears. Brought by Una to the House of Holinesse for recuperation after his internment by Orgoglio and subsequent encounter with despair, he is, under the guidance of *Contemplation*, afforded a view of his future that secures also his hitherto lost past. Both past and future are explicated as elaborations of a newly revealed proper name:

> Then seeke this path, that I to thee presage,
>> Which after all to heauen shall thee send;
>> Then peaceably thy painefull pilgramage
>> To yonder same *Hierusalem* do bend,
>> Where is for thee ordaind a blessed end:
>> For thou emongst those Saints, whom thou doest see,
>> Shalt be a Saint, and thine owne nations frend
>> And Patrone: thou Saint *George* shalt called bee,
> Saint *George* of mery England, the signe of victoree.[17]

After having revealed to Red Crosse that his name is George and that he will realize his destiny as the *name* of English triumph, "the signe of victoree" (and I am reminded here particularly of the battle cry, "England and Saint George"), *Contemplation* doubles back on the story to explain the knight's origin and the origin of the name that will both determine and be determined by the life he will have led. Sprung "from the ancient race / Of *Saxon* kings" (1.10.65), Red Crosse was taken by a Faerie as a changeling:

> Thence she thee brought into this Faerie lond,
>> And in an heaped furrow did thee hyde,
>> Where thee a Ploughman all vnweeting fond,
>> As he his toylesome teme that way did guyde,
>> And brought thee vp in ploughmans state to byde,
>> Whereof *Georgos* he thee gaue to name. (1.10.66)

This story gathers a great deal under the name *Georgos* (from the Greek: γεωργός, husbandman). It tells us and the Red Crosse Knight that he is of royal stock and that his royalty has taken a detour through the soil, so that he may now begin to realize his destiny as a symbol, not only of English strength, but of the putative origin and support of that strength in the noblesse oblige of a landed aristocracy that cross-couples its ruling-class culture and the cultivation of its land (much as the term "breeding" is applied both to the production of the seigneurial class and the animal husbandry it pursues). It is in this strong sense that the life of the Red Crosse Knight can be constructed as the preparation for an insight that brings his nation and his name decisively together:

> O holy Sire (quoth he) how shall I quight
> The many fauors I with thee haue found,
> That hast my name and nation red aright,
> And taught the way that does to heauen bound?
> This said, adowne he looked to the ground,
> To haue returnd, but dazed where his eyne,
> Through passing brightnesse, which did quite confound
> His feeble sence, and too exceeding shyne.
> So darke are earthly things compard to things diuine. (1.10.67)

In narrative the set of exigencies that make up experience is naturalized and articulated as a function of the subject's continued progress through time, while, inversely, the subject derives his or her self-identity and self-consistency through his or her ability to render experience as a function of subjectivity. In this way the subject may appropriate his or her experience by finding a place for it in an ongoing story. The self projected in a narrative reduces the contingent to the significant by arranging for it a demand within his or her discourse.

Experience, then, is mediated by narrative. If we consider an event to be a potential semantic unit in the discourse of an emerging subject, we see a dialectical confrontation between semantic openness and closure, or between the immediate impact of the event and the potential revisions of it, as it is assimilated to a diachronically developing context. This dialectical confrontation of determined event and potential response establishes the semantic value of the event as a function of the subsequent travels of the subject through the discourse.[18] The vagaries of life within such semantic indeterminacy offer powerful challenges to our appropriation of subjectivity, holding over us the threat of alienation—exclusion from the verb—as the penalty for any failure to reduce contingency to coherence and design by fitting it into the syntax of the narratives we live.

Narrative is a cognitive tool precisely because it situates the subject in the world of his or her experience, which might otherwise remain inchoate, indifferent. This articulation, both spatial and temporal, reflects the narrative syntax that is the vehicle of its assimilation. And that syntax itself manifests the modes of predication that determine the subjects appearing in it.

There is, as Jonathan Culler notes, a "double logic" at work in every narrative, according to which plot is presented "as a sequence of events prior to and independent of the given perspective on these events, and, at the same time, suggesting by its implicit claims to significance that these events are justified by their appropriateness to a thematic structure."[19] The end of a given narrative may be construed either as a formal requirement, necessary to the completion of the story, or as an event which occurred earlier than the story and which forms a part of the material from which the story is constructed.[20] Saint George is the "signe of victoree" because he slays the dragon, and he slays the dragon so that he may become the "signe of victoree."

Culler makes the point that in fictional narrative "one logic assumes the primacy of events; the other treats the events as the products of meanings."[21] We may assume that events—be they of interior or external origin—enter an individual's personal narrative contingently, but the individual works to assimilate those events to a structure of meaning—to motivate them, as Viktor Šklovskij might have put it. Frequently events are themselves the products of their intended meanings. Take, for example, the events that organize a career. What student could motivate himself or herself through medical school without first imagining certain events—graduation, internship, practice—as necessary consequences of the story, which he or she constitutes in advance and that allows the interpretation of his or her actions through a series of provisional endings?

It is not difficult to see how the double logic of narrative reinscribes the semantic dialectic outlined above. Any addition to the world of experience or subtraction from it entails a revision of the story that presents our experience to us. To persevere in our self-identity we are charged continually to accommodate the autobiographies we project to the contingencies that befall us. This is as true of the presentation of the world in which we come to know ourselves as it is of the worlds given to us in literature.

Such large discursive formulations as Hegelianism and Marxism depend on a similarly enclosing vision of history completed; this vision, representing temporal sequence in a master narrative, enables these hermeneutic systems to evaluate each action or event in relation, respectively, to Spirit's ascension to absolute knowledge or the inevitable emergence of classless communism.[22] When events do not coincide with the meanings ascribed to them or do not occur as predicted by the story, the plot turns in an unexpected direction. This turn or trope is a syntactic-semantic operation bent on conserving meaning and warding off the disintegration of the story and the consequent disintegration of its subject. Even in the unfolding narrative that presents us to ourselves as heroes of a story, significance and event are dialectically linked yet irreducibly distinct aspects of the two poles of subjectivity inscribed in discourse. The crucial difference between the (usually) generic stories in which we cast ourselves, and through which we sometimes determine our actions and responsibilities as historical agents, and the Hegelian, neo-Hegelian and post-Hegelian master narratives is that while History presents no independently discernible historical agency, the provisional dialectic of the self does. That is to say, individuals often *act* in consonance with stories, which therefore — through these actions — become historical, regardless of the complex, shifting, and incoherent ways in which they do or do not correspond to some putative, extrasubjective, material or collective "reality."

If narrative bears the heavy social-psychological charge with which I have encumbered it, that is, the enabling of the self in its relationship to its objects by producing a substitute for experience that is the vehicle of experience, if as Benveniste remarks, "the characteristic of language is to produce a substitute for experience which can be passed on *ad infinitum* in time and space" (p. 53), we may now ask: What is the contribution of narrative itself as a formal, cognitive technique to the various articulations of human experience, and how, specifically, do literary narratives function toward this end? An answer to the second of these questions can be stated briefly; the answer to the first must be more elaborate.

2

Generically different literary narratives serve specifiable cognitive purposes. What they have in common is, invariably, some sort of closure, even if that closure is simply the blank space following an interrupted final line or the brief trail of dots indicating the absence of the ending, the ending in absence. Unlike the unendable narratives of our lives, literary narratives fix meaning by supplying endings through which the individual events they recount may be rationalized. Even a work of intentional indeterminacy is stabilized by its implicit elevation of indeterminacy to the level of theme. The narrative ending provides both a mimesis of the dialectic of vision and revision by which the contingent is rendered significant and the opportunity to test possible endings and evaluate the force they exert, retrospectively, on the events that have (apparently) led up to them. Thus, narratives may function as laboratories in which the dialectic of experience and significance may be arrested and examined at given moments in its progress.

The force and utility of narrative is not limited to the orientation of the individual with respect to a provisional eschatology and the meaning with which that eschatology invests the actions of his or her life. Discourse of any sort is a social product, dependent not only on the creation of a text but also on the innovative text's intelligibility to an audience large enough to maintain it as part of a continuing discourse, as living language. For a work to participate in the organization of the discourse of its time — either the time of its publication or subsequently — that work must be significantly relatable to the material world as it is constituted in the discourse of its day.[23]

A literary narrative may therefore be understood as an experimental organization and orchestration of several elements: the author's self-representation as it emerges in his discourse, the audience's concern with the experience embodied in the narrative, the language in which the narrative is cast, and the historical context determining the experience to be articulated, that is, the inchoate mass of exigent data to be rendered significant.[24] The specific narrative forms that emerge from this combination of elements may be seen as cognitive operations answering, with varying degrees of success, to the material historical situation that narrative attempts to know.

Foucault argued that discourse may be conceived as a "totality in which the dispersion of the subject and his discontinuity with himself may be determined."[25] I am suggesting that narrative discourse discloses not only the dispersion of the subject, but also its efforts to resolve, through story, its "discontinuity with [it]self," and that fictive narratives are thus historically situated approaches to the solution of this inherently unsolvable problem.

The relationship of the writing subject to his or her characters reflects this dispersion and discontinuity. Through a usually complex series of tropes the subject constitutes itself within the narrative in which it dwells. Narrative characters are surrogates of a historically situated author experimenting (with a partiality appropriate to his or her as yet, and perpetually, incomplete state) with a series of possible configurations. Each of these configurations brings its author into one or another determinate relation to his or her own indeterminate and always mediated exigent experience. Thus, literary history offers an approach to material history through the study of the vicissitudes of the subject internal to fictive discourse. One task of the literary historian is to analyze the constitutive role of narrative form in the representations of experience produced in a given epoch. Narrative, because it forms a more or less closed set, raises and resolves (always provisionally) the problem of relating events and objects within a significant design.

How then do narratives relate phenomena to each other, and how may narrative forms be categorized according to the relational modes they employ? The grammar of the language in which a narrative is cast establishes the modes of relationship within the sentence. In the Western languages (at least), this grammar enforces a logic of *predication*. Rhetoric develops the limited predicatory apparatus supplied by grammar into a complex dialectic of relational modes, and it is, therefore, rhetoric that provides the means of classifying the modes of relationship implicit in any given narrative.[26]

The analysis I propose will be less concerned with the self-conscious use of rhetoric as a strategy of persuasion than with the ways in which different rhetorical configurations relate characters to actions in particular narratives and the effect of these relational modes on narrative design. Therefore, I want to be especially attentive to the action of tropes that operate along the borderline between rhetoric and grammar. In order to map this borderline, I will draw upon Hayden White's studies in the tropology of historical and literary narratives and will follow his lead in adapting Kenneth Burke's four master tropes: metaphor, metonymy, synecdoche, and irony.[27] Broadly but logically defined, these four tropes provide a taxonomy for the possible relations of character to action in narrative.

Each trope represents a distinct structuring of elements within a narrative, and each generates a particular articulation of experience within literature.[28] A narrative dominated by metaphor is shaped by the relationships of analogy or similarity; one dominated by metonymy is shaped by the possibilities of substitution of terms in what often appears to be a causal series (effects substituted for causes and the reverse); one dominated by synecdoche relates parts to an inclusive whole; and one dominated by irony foregrounds the inadequacy of words to things, of appearance to essence. An infinite variety of narrative surfaces may thus be generated from a limited number of logical-linguistic operations, and the various narrative designs may be understood as ad hoc cognitive instruments for adapting these operations to the assimilation of a great variety of data. The resulting narrative form may be thought of as the result of a collaboration among the available modes of representation, the circumstances of the historical moment, and the speaking or writing subject who, as we shall see in chapters 3 and 4, fully appears only after and as delineated by his or her representation. A tropological analysis of a given narrative will raise the following questions: How are the four master tropes manifested in the work? How do they affect the sequence of narrated events? What does the interaction of tropes within a narrative tell us about the exigent experiences mediated by it?

Obviously, there are a great many more than four narrative paradigms, and it will be necessary to consider how tropes interact and combine to generate specific narrative strategies. Some further consideration of the tropes as relational modalities is thus prerequisite to developing procedures that formally pose the questions I have raised. Narrative is transitive discourse. The tropes contribute to an articulate account of experience by representing relations within narrative and motivating the transitions that are its primary requirements. A trope turns language from its presumed normative reference to an intralinguistic relation, from the material object to which a word purports to refer, to the materiality of the word itself. To serve its turn, a trope necessarily recalls and preserves a putatively "literal" usage. Were this not the case, the trope would be lexicalized and received as nonfigurative. Such lexicalized language is itself grounded in tropic strategies that have been effaced as the articulation of experience represented in them became identified with experience itself.[29] In a long view, such effacements are literary historical events.

Thus the organization of relationships among actors and objects in any discourse can be opposed to a different organization that represents an alternative configuration. For the purpose of understanding the internal relationships among the tropic strategies, it is necessary to bear in mind this production of an alternately troped (or "literal") text. This other text is always implied, even though the "literal" terms may be present only as determined absences. The four very broad categories of tropes I have proposed represent two alternative encodings of two logical alternatives. Metaphor and synecdoche create orders of inclusion. Metonymy and irony generate exclusive classes. I contend that narrative represents its putatively "literal" ground by configuring and reconfiguring various combinations of these primary figurations.

Synecdoche creates an explicit hierarchy by situating one thing as part of another. It is distinguished from the other tropes by the fact that it includes its "literal" term within a figure to which it is subordinated.[30] The opening of *Paradise Lost* provides an example:

> Of Man's First Disobedience, and the Fruit
> Of that Forbidden Tree, whose mortal taste
> Brought Death into the World, and all our woe
> With loss of *Eden*, till one greater Man
> Restore us, and regain the blissful Seat,
> Sing Heav'nly Muse. (1.1–6)[31]

In the phrase, "Of Man's first disobedience," "Man's" may be read as a synecdochic substitution for "Adam's." Because Adam contained within him the entire human race and thus acted for all mankind, what is predicated of Adam, specifically, may be predicated of mankind, generically. "Till one greater Man restore us" repeats the same procedure, substituting "man" not for the first, but for the second Adam. Again, the part of mankind assumes the power to act for the whole.[32] The two synecdoches establish the sinning Adam and the saving Christ as representatives included within the class *man*, and the lengthy narrative that depends from the several lines that develop these synecdoches at the opening of the poem elaborates this exchange of predicates as a series of (pre)historical events.

Within this frame, the poem explores in great detail the unity of the one and the many in Christ (as given by St. Paul) and the implications of the promise of a time after time, a totally resolved synecdochic unity when "God shall be All in All" (3.341). Significantly, the equations of Adam with man in the Fall and of Christ with man in the resurrection demark the two transitional moments in Milton's story. The perceived discontinuity of human individuals over the course of the world's history is resolved by a narrative that synecdochically and proleptically represents the continuity of Adam and Christ, Paradise and Heaven, past and future, death and life. The unpleasant shadow of a more discontinuous articulation of the world is inscribed within this enclosing figure and placed within the excluded category of the fallen.

The fact that for Milton the story may have been understood or felt as literal has no bearing on the impact of the trope on the form of the narrative. The narrative establishes a discontinuity between the disobedient "man" of the first line and the "greater man" of the fourth, so that both may be reunited — at the end of time — in an apocalyptic reduction of all difference. The rhetorical vehicle of this reduction is a synecdoche, the figurality of which is effaced, so that the apocalypse may be represented as self-evident truth. I wish to stress that, in practice, the supple combinatory possibilities of Milton's tropes do not simply determine the historiography of the Christian apocalypse, nor are they determined by it. The tropes facilitate a properly dialectical mediation of History, as given in the *grand-récit* of Christian theology, and as experienced in the exigent contingencies of everyday life. Provisionally identifying with various characters at various times in the narrative, the reader is situated and resituated within a lexicon of relational possibilities defined by the collaboration of exigent experience, theological presupposition, and the constraints of representation.[33]

Metaphor also establishes inclusive classes, occasionally where relatedness is not obvious. To take a famous example: when, in "A Valediction Forbidding Mourning," Donne compares lovers to twin compasses, the reader makes sense of the metaphor by constituting the class of items that seem to act independently, but are joined at a remote point. This class includes lovers and compasses. By transferring the predicates usually associated with one subject to another, metaphor invites us to search out the level of generality at which the transfer of predicates no longer appears impertinent. Thus, "my love is a red, red rose" unpacks as something like the "ruddiness, softness, smoothness, sweet odor, and ephemerality" characteristic of the rose may also be pertinently predicated of 'my love.'" As metaphor becomes more and more inclusive, it shades into synecdoche; the identity of two things is subsumed in the unity of all things:[34] "My love and a rose are one insofar as they mutually partake of and exemplify the universally pleasing attributes of ruddiness, softness, smoothness, and sweet odor, as well as a characteristically cautionary ephemerality." It should be noted, moreover, that in the metaphor "my love is a red, red rose," the other person, who is the object of my love, has already disappeared behind a metonymy of effect for cause, *my love* being the desire *in me* that she elicits. Thus, the metaphor comparing her to a rose further elides the difference between *us* by gathering us both under a set of shared attributions.

Because metaphor and synecdoche link objects intrinsically, they present a static picture of the world. One cannot *narrate* a wholly synecdochic or metaphoric articulation, although one could *describe* it. Rather, metaphor and synecdoche work to reduce the differing in time that is the mark of narrative. They reconcile differences and establish continuities.

Metonymy and irony, on the contrary, imply exclusive classes. The substitution of contiguous terms in a series relates two objects by specifying their difference, often with the implication that one may be reduced to the other, that one term is a function of the other. Thus, when I say that the "crown commands" a particular act, I reduce the man who gave the command to the functioning of the power inherent in his office. Irony, finally, excludes through a systematic negation, instructing the reader that what is asserted is specifically not the case. If all the tropes are shadowed by an implicit literality, irony shadows an explicit affirmation that is canceled as it is uttered. Irony signals a dissatisfaction with representation as such, and it motivates a recourse to the tropological lexicon from which a new and more responsive formulation may be sought. *Metaphor and synecdoche are thus the brakes of the tropological machine; metonymy and irony are its engines.* Metonymy and irony motivate the discontinuities that must be worked out over time, and they indicate syntactic chains of causation in which some things appear to be necessarily prior to others.

The four relational modalities represented by the tropes may now be assimilated to the moments of a dialectic: metaphor represents the identification of the other as another like the self, metonymy the succession of subjects differing from themselves over time, irony the simultaneous negation and preservation of self-identity that advances the dialectic to a new phase, and synecdoche the sublation of difference in the perceived homogeneity of subject and object.[35] Thus, the dialectical confrontation of antithetical tropes informs the progress of narrative innovation and provides the sense of continuity within change.[36]

To understand the operation of this dialectic within narrative, we may return briefly to Benveniste's linking of subjectivity in discourse to grammatical person. Insofar as narrative compels the relation of the subject to itself as it develops through an unfolding series of episodes, the *you* addressed is the *I* of a different time. Metaphor and synecdoche represent the self-identity of these temporally differing versions of the subject as achieved. They present the states between which the narrative moves: the subject presents itself to itself as similar in a specifiable way, as forming an inclusive class, or as a particular manifestation of a homogeneous whole. Irony and metonymy represent the transitive moments through which the subject passes in its search for self-identity. Thus, we can characterize a narrative by its tropes of transition and of closure. Because the initial trope of a story is always the closing trope of a previous story, initial and closing tropes need not be differentiated. In narratives of subtlety and complexity, these characterizing tropes will themselves be seen as emerging moments in a dialectic of representation that is implicit in the development of the plot; they will underlie and structure the mythos.

The subject emerges as the *grammatical* subject of the network of predicates it assumes at the (provisionally) terminal points in this dialectical process, the points at which an ironic destabilization is necessary to initiate new movement. New elements enter the field of representation through experience and the dialectical process moves to incorporate them in a revised plot, leaving behind the record of its successive attempts, inscribed in the adventures of its hero.

3

It may serve as an example to consider, in this light, the story that Freud tells "to specify the point in the mental development of mankind at which the advance from group psychology to individual psychology was achieved also by the individual members of the group." After the *omphagos* of the primal father (which Freud refers to as a "scientific myth"), the individual psychology of the brothers is submerged in the fraternal group: "the totemic community of brothers, all with equal rights and united by the totemic prohibitions which were to preserve and expiate the memory of the murder."

"But," writes Freud, "the dissatisfaction with what had been achieved still remained, and it became the source of new developments." The old state of things revived "on a new level," the brothers became family chiefs, heads of their own hordes. "And yet the new family was only a shadow of the old one;

there were numbers of fathers and each one was limited by the rights of the others":

> It was then, perhaps, that some individual, in the exigency of his long-ing, may have moved to free himself from the group and take over the father's part. He who did this was the first epic poet; and the advance was achieved in the imagination. This poet disguised the truth with lies in accordance with his longing. He invented the heroic myth. The hero was a man who by himself had slain the father — the father who still ap-peared in the myths as a totemic monster. Just as the father had been the boy's first ideal, so in the hero who aspires to the father's place the poet now created the first ego ideal.[37]

The myth of the primal father is superseded by the heroic myth. The story moves from the exclusion of the brothers, to the incorporation of the father, to the dissemination of the father, until, at last, the individual gives birth to him-self and his world. And, as one might expect of Freud, the plot is recapitulated as the metonymic decomposition of the primal identity of all in the father into the many brothers seeking the father function (as the personality under psychoanalysis is decomposed into the structured scenes of its complexes).

Freud may then act upon this retold story with a further revision: the ironic decomposition of the self into the subject and its specular ideal. The transi-tion from the group to individual consciousness is thus articulated in a series of tropic reconfigurations culminating in the release of the subject into a nar-rative, the hero of which is the surrogate of his own desire. And, is it not also fair to say that Freud's primal poet, creating "in the exigency of his longing" an ego ideal, also creates the medium in which he will encounter that longing and recognize it as his own? Insofar as fictional narrative imitates the cognitive process of narrativization, it is no accident that Freud's story of consciousness also becomes the story of story, of the birth of the poet.[38]

Examining the relationship of words to things in Western culture from the Renaissance to the present, Foucault found four distinct epistemological con-figurations (*épistèmes*).[39] According to Foucault, each of these configurations is separated from its predecessor and successor by a radical epistemological rupture. Thus, the Renaissance may be characterized as having organized its knowledge according to the criteria of similitude, the age of reason according to identity and difference, the nineteenth century according to succession and analogy, and our present age according to criteria necessarily invisible to us, as we derive our self-definition from it and breathe its intellectual ether as our lungs do air.[40]

Hayden White characterizes Foucault's epistemological epochs as themselves projections of various dominant tropic organizations, as rhetorics of classification.[41] In White's terms, Foucault's *épistème* of similitude becomes that of metaphor as the mode of encoding "the world of experience at that time." White further argues that a science "committed to the making of a complete list of all the *similarities* that might be conceived to exist among things in the world . . . is necessarily driven, by the logic of the listmaking operation itself, to an apprehension of all the differences that might exist among things" until the discourse articulated by metaphor or relation is succeeded by one controlled by exclusion or metonymy, "a mode of linguistic usage by which the world of appearances is broken down into two orders of being, as in cause-effect or agent-act relationships." A metonymic revisioning of the world accumulates a greater and greater number of such functional relationships until "the discovery that things not only differ from one another, but differ internally within themselves along the course of their life cycles" becomes the ground of "that temporalization of the order of things that Foucault ascribes to nineteenth-century consciousness." Synecdoche preserves the order of things by enclosing their diachronic development within a teleology that envisions a final and permanent synchrony with reference to which significance may be established. It is commonplace to characterize our present age as an ironic one, one in which the nineteenth century's synecdochic articulation of history and experience has collapsed under the weight of a rapidly increasing accumulation of knowledge, infused too quickly to be assimilated by the comparatively slow-moving rhetoric of cognition. Thus, White's trope of irony suggests the characterization of the modernist *épistème* that Foucault forbears.

White's recasting of the Foucauldian *épistèmes* as configuring rhetorics has the virtue of calling into question Foucault's insistence on their radical discontinuity. The transformation of one *épistème* into another may be seen to be the result of dialectical confrontation between antithetical tropes of articulation. Although a discourse may be dominated by a specific rhetorical configuration, it will not display this dominant trope exclusively. In fact, it seems likely that the confrontation of tropes within individual works plays a significant role in their narrative design. The movement from discourse in general to literary narrative in particular allows us to study finite units of discourse with identifiable transitive and closing configurations. Moreover, for the reasons I have argued, narrative confers a privileged access to the history of the emergence of the subject within and out of the constraints of discourse. If we see the narrative configurations of a work as, at least in part, the result of changes in the experience mediated by the work—that is as, at least allusively, referential—we have a method of analyzing the construction of narrative as a problem-solving activity through which subjective positions (though not the speaking subjects themselves) are represented.

The apparent formalism of tropological analysis thus returns to an appreciation of determined and contingent events mediated by the *combinatoire* of tropes. The story of this process of assimilation and adaptation is inscribed in the movement from stasis through transitional tropes to a trope of closure characterizing the canonical narratives of a given period: canonicity here being accorded to those works that are received within their contemporary literary traditions as transparent bearers of experience. If my speculations here are correct, periodization in the literary historical sense will reflect distinctive clusters of narratives using specifiable tropic strategies. This is so both because a large part of exigent experience is shared collectively among contemporaries and because the diachronic development of genres will have prepared similar rhetorical habits and conventions. Moreover, works representative of transitional periods will incorporate the history of literary change in the dialectical processes through which their narrative form emerges.

One's story as an individual in relation to society has already started before one realizes one's experience as one's own.[42] Culler's question as to whether narrative is framed to account for events or events generated to fit narrative is rendered moot by the impossibility of ordering or hierarchizing the two narrative logics. As conscious beings, we are born in and of story; we first encounter ourselves in a primal attempt to appropriate our own lives through acts of infantile autobiography. Thus, in the game of the *fort/da* reported by Freud in *Beyond the Pleasure Principle,* the child is already the subject of a story. He devises new events (his own access to subjectivity) to assimilate given contingencies (his mother's absences) and to render them, in his imagination, functions of his will. He finds himself already in a plot, of which he moves to make himself the hero.[43] This movement occupies the space, however restricted, in which the child becomes both the subject and an agent of history, for the precise choices he makes, the genre of narrative he writes, will combine the motivated and the unmotivated, the historical and the accidental, in ways that cannot be predicted. We will see in chapter 4 that the movement of time in this special space is a peculiar one; the child as subject and agent will be born belatedly with respect to these choices by taking responsibility for them and gathering them together under his "I."

The maternal absences he seeks to narrativize are already elements in another story, of which his mother is the subject. There are no given events without a formal vehicle of representation, and there is no purely formal narrative free of material content. There is only a developing context, the strands of which provide the substance of self and other. This context subjects experience to its own rules — semantic, physical, linguistic, logical — and the possibility of incorporation in a story according to these rules is the criterion governing production of the "reality effect." The "reality" of experience cannot be understood apart from its significance, which is never stable while the context continues to develop. Semantic closure is only complete when the story ends, and for any given subject the story can end only fitfully, provisionally, until the subject ends with it. Thus, the narrative process I have sought to outline here is installed, irremediably, in a mediatory position between experience and life, between knowledge and its object, the subject and its desire. All stories turn, and it is in the interstices that mark the turns that we may constitute a category of the "Real." A properly literary history will chronicle the *literary* forms in and through which this empty place of the "Real" is successively marked, situating, on the one hand, the trace of the pressure of the literary on the "Real" and, on the other, the trace of the pressure of the "Real" on the literary.

Chapter 3

Augustine and the Rhetoric of the Christian Ego

> *Annon tibi videtur imago tua de speculo quasi tu ipse velle esse, sed ideo esse*
> *falsa, quod non est?* (Does not thy image in the mirror appear to will to be
> thou thyself, but to be therefore false, because it is not?)
> — Augustine, *Soliloquia*
>
> I identify myself in language, but only by losing myself in it like an object.
> What is realized in my history is not the past definite of what was, since it
> is no more, or even the present perfect of what has been in what I am, but
> the future anterior of what I shall have been for what I am in the process of
> becoming. — Lacan, *Écrit*[1]

1

What passes between Augustine's and Lacan's proverbial moments in the
theory of identity? What story, if any, connects Augustine's assertion and fal-
sification of the image's will to be the thing it reflects and Lacan's assertion
that the self must forgo its desire to be immediately present to itself so that it
may become the retrospective object of the language it speaks and in which it
is bespoken? In the perspective of Lacan's theory of ego formation, these two
formulations mark a passage from the *Imaginary* through the *nom du père* to
the *Symbolic*—from the subject of an alienated image, through the name and
the "no" of the Father, to the subject of an expropriated word. It will be my
contention that, reconsidered as a passing from one more or less historically
determined literary inscription of the ego to another, that is to say, from a
literary historical perspective, the two passages mark in the temporal space
between them a turn from the subject of lyric to the subject of narrative.

In this literary historical passage the lyric "I," aspiring to present itself *ut
pictura poesis*, struggles to isolate the verbal sign from the linear and temporal disposition of language so as to gather its contingent differing over time
into an iconic presence. The passage imputing the appearance of will to the
image in the mirror comes from a work whose form and theme figure the
predicament of the temporal self in search of its eternal essence. The irony of

its title poses a question immediately pertinent to our discussion of the narrative and historical construction of the self: How is it that Augustine's two books of *soliloquies* are, in fact, *dialogues?* The *Soliloquia,* written immediately after Augustine's baptism at the age of thirty-three, and thus the first work of his new life, take the form of an inward dialogue that begins with a division of the self that is at once the cause and the effect of a movement toward self-knowledge. Augustine begins by telling the reader of an inward search. "I had been long revolving with myself matters many and various and had been for many days sedulously inquiring both concerning myself and my chief good, or what of evil there was to be avoided by me" (*Volenti mihi multa ac varia mecum diu, ac per multos dies sedulo quaerenti memetipsum ac bonum meum, quidve mali evitandum esset*), when "suddenly someone addresses me, whether I myself, or some other one, within me or without, I know not. For this very thing is what I chiefly toil to know" ("*ait mihi subito, sive ego ipse, sive alius quis extrinsecus, sive intrinsecus, nescio: nam hoc ipsum est quod magnopere scire molior*")(Starbuck, p. 537; Migne, p. 869). Augustine is henceforth metonmyically decomposed into two characters: A, who searches in and with himself, and R (Reason), who acts as A's interlocutor. The question concerning the falsity of the image in the mirror, spoken by R, is part of a complicated argument aimed at affirming the immortality of the soul seated in the mortal body, but what most interests me in the present context is the way in which Augustine's turn inward (*quaerenti memetipsum*), in search of what he might do to avoid evil and realize his greatest good, results in the sudden (*subito*) emergence of another voice, the interiority or exteriority of which cannot be established. This voice leads Augustine out of his interior revolvings (*volenti*) into the linear unfolding of an argument that situates the self whose image is reflected in the mirror as itself the image of God.

The splitting of Augustine into a Reason (*Ratio*), which he can clearly locate neither in the self nor in the logos, and a troubled voice that remains somehow in excess of the logos as given to it by Reason, figures in a specifically iconic (or Imaginary) encounter of the "I" that speaks and the "I" that is bespoken; that is, to use the terminology introduced in chapter 2, between the subject of the enunciation and the subject of the utterance. The failure of this lyric "I" to realize itself "*ut pictura poesis*" and thus to *be,* in the Platonic sense of persisting essentially outside time, is recognized in the very act of its own recuperation, as the subject comes to be represented as irreducibly double — entrapped in its own verbal mirror. As this experience of verbal entrapment becomes thematic, as the subject conceives a desire to tell the story of its own temporal vicissitude, it becomes the subject of narration, unfolding itself to itself in an anticipatory retrospection.[2] Since this *narrative* subject situates itself as the agent and patient of history, I propose to take the moments of its passage as episodes in a case history of history. The point of formalizing these moments in and as narrative is to reconsider the Augustinian and Lacanian discriminations of "the self," with which I began. In this way I hope to open a *historical* view of the determined relationship of psychoanalytic theorization, with its emphases on *seeing*, on providing a topography of the mind through spatial metaphors, to the verbal practices that have come to be encompassed by it.[3]

As I argued in chapter 1, this highly motivated coupling of literary history and the history of psychoanalysis may begin with Joel Fineman's description of the Shakespearean subjectivity effect. Arguing that psychoanalysis theorizes the practice of a specifically verbal (and Renaissance) subjectivity, Fineman explains how Shakespeare's "invention" of poetic subjectivity establishes a *necessary* connection between the "subjectivity effect" and the peculiar duplicity of a speech that presents itself as the falsifying trace of an ineffable truth, and he points out, with stunning precision, that the practice and theory of the subject of this constitutionally duplicitous speech "derive from the disjunctive conjunction of, on the one hand, a general thematics of vision and, on the other, a general thematics of voice," that is, a chiasmic joining and disjoining that insists on the difference between what is said and what is seen.[4] In this reading, the epideictic subject, which rescues itself from time by seeking and asserting its identity with the ideal that it contemplates and represents, holding "the mirror up to nature" that it may show "the very age and body of the time his form and pressure" (*Hamlet* 3.2.23–25), is decisively subverted by the frankly linguistic *I* of Shakespeare's Dark Lady sonnets: the poet-speaker who believes his love when she "swears that she is made of truth," while also knowing that she lies, and lies not only knowingly but punningly, speaking, as it were, with a forked tongue. "Therefore I lie with her, and she with me, / And in our faults by lies we flattered be" (sonnet 138).[5]

In recapitulating the movement from Augustinian to Lacanian conceptions of desire, I want to tell how the rhetorically duplicitous subject of Shakespearean desire is, early in its canonization, rescued from its verbal (and formal) indeterminacy through its subjection to a *narrative* conception of history. This movement from *eye* to *ear,* which displaces the unfolding of Truth from space to time, presupposes and enables the theorization of the historically specified, though durable, subject of Shakespearean desire. The temporal displacement and extension I propose will have the effect of softening Fineman's focus on the formal decay of epideictic *vision* in favor of a sharpened focus on an ideology of narrative bildung that emerges as a response to that decay. In this displacement, the epideictic ideal of *ut pictura poesis* yields to a series of scenes giving the appearance of motion: still life gives way to montage. In this more elongated view, the reception and canonization of the Shakespearean subject may be seen to be part of a development away from the visionary stasis sought by Augustine and toward the dialectical narrativity theorized by Lacan, in which the subject is posited as the momentary sum of its (historical) experiences: as specifically and determinately the subject *of* history.

In the present chapter this large project of explication will be represented by the description of two episodes, flanking on each side the Shakespearean invention of poetic subjectivity—two snapshots, if you will—in the literary history of the self: the influential inscription of an iconic ego in Augustine's *Confessions,* and its narrativization, that is to say, the narration of how the lyric subject becomes narrative, in Andrew Marvell's mower poems. While I will be considering the inscription of the Augustine ego in some detail, the discussion in this chapter of Marvell's revision is intended to serve only as a bridge to the literary history offered in part 2. In attempting to trace the formal vicissitudes of the Augustinian subject, I also will have occasion to advert briefly to Dante's *La Vita Nuova* and Petrarch's *Rime sparse,* as literally, signposts situated along the path between the Augustinian and Marvellian representations of the self in search of self-possession. The *literary* history traced through these world-historical moments may be described in rhetorical (or generic) terms as the presentation of the self in lyric and narrative, respectively, or, to recapitulate: the Augustinian (lyric) and the Lacanian (narrative) constructions of the self.

2

The Renaissance was one aspect of a social reorganization that, generally speaking, included a decline in the political power of an aristocracy grounded in military prowess and a diversification of the forms of wealth from which power might come. These and other changes placed new strains on the conventional idealization of man as the *Imago Dei*. In chapter 1, I proposed to focus on the experience of time as a way of bringing together the material and textual aspects of change in the practical experience of human agency. In accord with that plan, I want now to locate the trace of the pressure of exigent events, on the one hand, and formal predispositions, on the other, on literary representations of the self in relation to time. In particular, I shall be interested in signs of stress and revision with regard to the mastering of historical exigence in a world previously thought of as immutably *ordinatissima*—a world in which time is rewritten as a spatial arrangement everywhere and always bearing the discernible intentions of the divine architect. If man is to realize himself as the image of a God who transcends time, the irruption of the aleatory into the providential design of history must be either recuperated or suppressed. If, as I have argued, time in the Renaissance comes increasingly to be recognized as the medium in which significant human action occurs, we should be able to isolate the pressure of this irruption within the literary tradition. As we shall see, the self that comes to be characteristically represented in the narrative poetry of early modern England unfolds *in time* a relationship to the eternal that is far more dynamic than that of the conventional representations of the self preceding it. Narrative poetry in early modern England negotiates the incorporation of human agency into representations of a providentially ordered universe in which *apparent* contingency is *immediately* assimilated to a spatially articulated and always already perfected design.[6]

Everything that enters this construction is *immediately* meaningful. All elements of the design reveal and represent God's prior intention, and apparently exigent events join an already completed history as motives endowed with a fixed and essential semantic value. To appreciate the innovative force of this specular subjectivity, it will be necessary to picture the canonical mode of self-representation that precedes the modern one at some crucial moments during its long literary career. Thus, I begin my story with some details of Augustine's rhetorical strategy in the *Confessions* and its filiations within the epideictic literary tradition on which English literature drew.

A historical moment juxtaposes Augustine, son of an overbearing Christian mother and an urbane pagan father, flourishing in the dying moments of the Roman classical age, and the geographical and, in Augustine's case, domestic proximity of two cosmologies that are likewise his parents—the one offered by the mother church of Christ and the other by the urbane world of Augustine's pagan, Neoplatonic father. The critical conjunction between the personality of Saint Monica and the social role of the early church is evident in Peter Brown's characterization of the historical moment of Augustine's Carthage:

> The imagination of African Christians of the time of Augustine had become riveted on the idea of the Church. This Church was the "*strong woman*" [*Sermons*, 37.2, citing Prov. 31.10]. "It would not be decent for us," Augustine said, "to speak of any other woman" [*Serm.* 37.1]. In a land which, to judge from Monica, had a fair share of formidable mothers, the *Catholica*, the Catholic Church was The Mother: "One Mother, prolific with offspring: of her are we born, by her milk we are nourished, by her spirit we are made alive." (Cyprian, *de Unitate*, p. 5) [7]

As an instance of the literary historical state of Augustine's "family romance" and its presence in his writing, we may take, for example, the account in the *Confessions* of his abandonment of Monica at Ostia, which, as Charles Klegerman and others have noted, reenacts the abandonment of Dido by Aeneas. Aeneas abandons his *lover* to found Rome. Augustine abandons his *mother*, but only to be reunited with her in the mother church of the City of God, whose founding Aeneas Augustine shall become. The superposition of Aeneid-Augustine and Dido-Monica is further complicated by the depiction of Monica's guidance of her son in the *Confessions*, in which Andrew Fichter also sees an allusion to the Venus of the *Aeneid*. Thus, "The antithesis between Carthage and Rome which Virgil keeps so clearly in view from the outset of his epic collapses in the presence of the greater alternative Augustine envisions between the earthly and the heavenly cities." [8] Reading the allegory from the other direction, we also might see a promise of the collapse of the distinction between mother and lover in the heavenly city.

There is no need to retread at greater length the well-worn ground of Augustine's Oedipal exaltation of his mother, Saint Monica, and suppression of his father, Patricius, in the *Confessions* or the fluidity of his historical moment at the beginning of the establishment of state Christianity and the end of the Roman classical age. [9] I wish merely to call attention to the conjunction of these personal and social exigencies, which, combined with Augustine's creative and rhetorical skills, stands as a work of chance that vastly underlies the ensuing development of the world's material history.

It is altogether to the point of this study that we pause here, at the beginning, to appreciate the interweaving of personal, intellectual, and social histories that come together in the "Augustine" constructed by our retrospective (and to some extent, his anticipatory) glance, the inextricable combination of man and moment that conduced to the social hegemony of what remains to this day, in the deepest sense, his *personal* vision. Insofar as a properly *literary* history ought to remain committed to defending the ground of chance against the narrative enclosure of History — against, that is, the retrospective destiny monumentalized within a master narrative — it is worth remarking the oddness of chance that gave to Augustine a historical moment in which church and Mother might so easily meld, and gave to the moment an Augustine, who might so effectively and urgently meld them.

Against this very general background I want to elaborate more specifically Augustine's role in the formalization of a *literary* tradition from which the narrative of historical causation would — after long delay — evolve, and to call attention, in particular, to the serendipitous collusion of the rhetorical procedures exemplified in the *Confessions* and the exigent need in the early church for a temporal synthesis that would somehow unite the radical historicality of the Hebrew Scriptures and the emphatically eternal design given in the Christian testament.

Because the warrants for the divinity of Christ are drawn from their prophetic texts, the Hebrew Scriptures cannot be dispensed with, but their emphasis on the national history (and, by implication, destiny) of Israel do not sit easily alongside the universality and atemporality of fourth-century Christianity. The eventual synthesis, which Augustine played a leading role in bringing about, develops a Hellenized reading of the historical and historicizing Hebrew Scriptures as the means of appropriating them for an evangelical Christian church.[10] By submitting the continual intervention of God in the historical destiny of the nation of Israel to a structure of thought conditioned by the atemporal categories of Neoplatonic anamnesis, this reading transfers the meaning of mundane actions from the temporal and temporizing *metonymies* of cause and effect to the *metaphors* of a totalized pattern — from consequence to design. When a continued metaphor is elaborated in narrative, allegory occurs.[11] The force of this allegory is to stabilize the problematic relationship between the testaments and the cultures they represent within a far more general (and notably Greek) view of the human problem of orienting the self with respect to eternity. The interest in typologically grounded figures evidenced by Renaissance poets has generally (and correctly) been attributed to Protestant distrust of allegory. Insofar as typology functions to join Old Testament history to New Testament sense in a somewhat different way, consideration of Augustine's allegorical procedures will help us appreciate the degree to which the typology represented in Renaissance poems represents formal tensions and determinations as well as theological ones.

A formal analysis of a moment in Augustine's *Confessions,* during which the founding of the Christian ego becomes visible, will thus serve to illuminate the narrative structure of Renaissance texts — in which the temporal founding of what had to become a (super)natural ontogenesis is once again made visible. Augustine's new law purported to abrogate, yet retain, the older Mosaic laws by introjecting the lawgiver as Love and reinvesting that affection in the image of its introjected ideal. Without venturing to isolate any single historical cause, but rather invoking the complex of social changes to which I have already alluded, I will argue that the experience of daily life in the Renaissance brought into question the paternal authority of Augustine's representation of the law. Renaissance texts, therefore, record the contradictions made visible when the law undergoes a sea change before reinstituting itself in an ideologically altered form.

3

In the course of *describing* himself and his world in the *Confessions,* Augustine engages a rhetoric that conceals its own generative capability under the disguise of a historical representation. This commerce between the semiotic and the mimetic calls into view a specifically Christian ego, a version of the self that is brought into being wholly within a system of signs, yet represents itself as the accurate copy or reflection of an ontically prior and necessarily immutable original.

By the surrender of his own language to the Lord and the consequent representation of the self as *Imago Dei,* Augustine gives his word to an Other, who returns it to him as the object of Augustine's allegorical interpretation. The self discovered in this verbal reflection is displaced from the world of the senses and thrown into the symbolic space of a verbal mediation that is figured in the *Confessions* as the space between the surface of the earth and the infinity of heaven.[12] The crossing of man's words and God's Word in this space serves at once to demark and undermine the boundaries of human agency.

This mediation and demarcation situates the individual in relation to time and action, according to a specific narrative rhetoric, the story of which may be read in the seemingly supplementary thirteenth book.

In this last book of the *Confessions,* Augustine turns from the story of his beginning to a universalized story of *the* beginning with an extended meditation on the first chapter of Genesis, particularly as revised by the first chapter of the fourth Gospel. One problem that exercises his commentary is the meaning of the scriptural injunction given to creatures of water and air and repeated to Adam and Eve to increase and multiply (*crescite et multiplicamini*). Why, asks Augustine, is the injunction reserved to fish, fowl, and humankind?[13] Since herbs, trees, beasts, and serpents all propagate and preserve their kind according to their natures, human beings too could be expected to follow the law of kind. Therefore, to understand the Lord's words to Adam and Eve in a literal way (*proprie*) would imply that they were spoken with no particular intention ("*quia vacat hoc, quia inaniter ita dictum est*") (2.440). Because God does not speak promiscuously, an allegorical interpretation is required. The allegory that Augustine supplies depends on a proportional metaphor. The fish (*generationes aquarum*) represent words as material signifiers, while the birds who share the blessing, having emerged from the water to multiply under the heavens (*subfirmamento*), represent thoughts:

> *signa corporaliter edita generationes aquarum propter necessarias causas carnalis profunditatis, res autem intelligibiliter excogitatas generationes humanas propter rationis fecunditatem intelleximus.* (2.442, 444)[14]

> By corporeally pronounced we understand the generations of the waters: necessarily occasioned by the depth of the flesh, by things intellectually conceived we understand human generations, on account of the fruitfulness of reason.

Man speaks from the depth of the flesh, multiplying words in the body as fish multiply in the sea, and these words fly forth into the firmament, fly free of the body, as birds fly beneath the firmament, free of the sea creatures with which they were created.

In Augustine's version, God's command to be fruitful and multiply pertains not to sexual reproduction, which Adam and Eve will achieve in any event "according to their kind," but to the generation of discourse by the contingent association of *signans* and *significandum:*

et ideo credidimus utrique horum generi dictum esse abs te, domine:
crescite et multiplicamini. in hac enim benedictione concessam nobis a
te facultatem ac potestatem accipio et multis modis enuntiare, quod uno
modo intellectum tenuerimus, et multis modis intellegere, quod obscure
uno modo enuntiatum legerimus. (2.444)

And for this end we believe thee, Lord, to have said to both these kinds,
Increase and multiply. For within the compass of this blessing, I conceive thee to have granted us a power and a faculty; both to express
several ways that which we understand but one, and to understand
several ways, that which we read to be obscurely delivered but in one.

Thus, Augustine's allegorical interpretation of the injunction to increase
and multiply turns out to be the sanctioning allegory of allegory itself. Man is
defined by and through his ability to allegorize. Through this faculty, which
raises him above kind or nature, he enacts the divine injunction that he supplement the sexual generation of nature with the special generation of words
bestowed upon him by God at the creation. In this way the reproductive
sexual congress of Adam and Eve is subordinated as one among many imperfect repetitions of God's orignary Word. In Augustine's view it is precisely the
allegorical use of words that will allow man's words to return to their origin
in God's Word. Through this allegory Augustine sublimes thought from the
flesh to the unchanging world of spirit; in it God's (apparent) injunction to
sexual procreation becomes a signifier, the vehicle of a metaphor the tenor of
which is an injunction to verbal — as opposed to sexual — conception.[15]

In effect, Augustine's allegory of allegory ends by reversing the polarity of
the metaphor with which it began.[16] That is to say, the allegorization begins
when the sexual sense of "increase and multiply" is metaphorically read as
the vehicle of a broader reference to thought and speech. This sense is, at first,
presumed to be literal — and again, it is the superfluity of the literal sense that
evokes the allegorical interpretation (2.440). But, within the symbolic economy that Augustine establishes, we are asked to recognize sexual reproduction
as merely the concrete and material representative of God's meaning, which is
now, *literally,* to breed thoughts through speculation. There is more governing this inversion than a simple desire to suppress, displace, or Platonize the
iure divinio ground of sexual intercourse.

With reference to the ability of allegory to either extend a single conceit over time or condense a number of instances into a single structural moment, Fineman recognizes that some allegories are "concerned more with structure than with temporal extension." These may "make only the slightest gestures toward full scale narrative progress." For others, "such as picaresque or quest narrative, . . . figurative structure is only casually and allusively appended to the circuit of adventures through time." Still other allegories "blend both axes together in relatively equal proportions." As Fineman observes, regardless of its relative emphasis on narrative or figurative structure, what distinguishes allegory as a trope extended over time is that it must in some way relate time to structure:

> Whatever the prevailing orientation of any particular allegory, however, up and down through the declensions of structure, or laterally developed through narrative time, the allegory will be successful as allegory only to the extent that it can suggest the authenticity with which the two coordinating poles bespeak each other, with structure plausibly unfolded in time, and narrative persuasively upholding the distinctions and equivalences described by structure. ("The Structure of Allegorical Desire," TSE, p. 7)

Augustine's allegory of allegory thus places sexual reproduction on the level of the signifier. The force of this placement lies in the fact that it applies not only to the text of the divine injunction but to the activity enjoined therein. The observable fact that humankind extends its structure — its image — over time by physically reproducing itself points to, and finds its significance in, the encompassing and eternal structure ordained by God and instantiated by his Word. This structure must be recovered from the vicissitudes of time in the form of speculative discourse, which alone can apprehend the reproduction of the parents' image in the child as the allegorical representative of the originary moment in which man was created in the image of God. Thus, in Augustine's account, it is the ability to allegorize that connects men to Man (Adam, Christ) and men's words to the Word of God and beckons human agents in time to behave as *images* of God. The price of admission, so to speak, to this symbolic economy is a willingness to render the empirical experience of sexual procreation supplemental to the speculative task of verbal conceptualization.

Augustine's transformation of the apparently sexual injunction to increase and multiply into an allegorical authorization of allegorical language thus bears all the characteristics of what Derrida calls "the logic of the supplement": (1) It appears at the site of an excess of signification—God does not speak superfluously; therefore the identity of the injunction's repetition for birds and fishes and for humankind must be recast as difference, signaling not man's common lot with the beasts but the distinguishing characteristic that guarantees his dominion over them. (2) It installs a myth of origin within the signifying system, rendering that system prior to itself by substituting the originary (albeit belated) action of the *Word* for the sexual generation of humankind. (3) It adds to something (sexual intercourse, generation according to kind) by replacing and concealing it (negating sex and, as we shall see, writing in favor of speech).[17]

To grasp the shape of the rhetorical path along which Augustine transforms the apparently sexual injunction to increase and multiply into the supplement of a divine recognition of the linguistic identity of his earthly image, it is necessary to broaden the context to include Augustine's remarks on birds and fishes in the preceding chapter 23.

Two key words form the verbal bridges over which Augustine's allegory crosses from the sea of the fifth day of creation to the dry land of the sixth. The simpler of these crossings is "*profunditatis.*" The analogy of the depths of the sea to the depths of the flesh is a commonplace of early Christian rhetoric: as the sea surrounds the fish, the flesh surrounds the soul (*anima vivens*). But Augustine also uses a second bridge to connect corporeal signs to things mentally conceived. This second, and divinely instituted, joining of *signans* to *signatum* arrests the unrestrained allegoresis that is threatened by the emancipation of the sign. Returning the gift of words to the Word, this rhetorical bridge converts a potentially pathological logorrhea to the logocentric speculum in which the image of God is (verbally) disclosed. This recuperative motion ultimately frees language from nominalism by structuring the flow of signifiers according to an a priori pattern.

On the fifth day God blessed the creatures of the sea (*pisces et coetos*) and the fowls that fly over the earth. Augustine's word for fowls (and that of the early Latin Bibles) is not *aves* but *volatilia,* a substantivized form of the adjective derived from *volare,* to fly. In chapter 23, Augustine has recourse to the birds and fishes to allegorize God's grant of dominion over the other creatures to newly created man (Gen. 1:28). Man receives this dominion because he alone judges, approving what is right and rejecting what is wrong. His judgment is exercised in taking the sacraments of the church, receiving Christ (*"ille piscis . . . , quem levatum de profundo terra pia comedit"*; "that Fish . . . , which taken out of the deep, the devout earth now feedth upon") (2.436), and in the use of language — properly subordinated to Scripture:

> *in verborum signis vocibusque subiectis auctoritati libri tui, tamquam sub firmamento volitantibus, interpretando, exponendo, disserendo, disputando, benedicendo atque invocando te, ore erumpentibus atque sonantibus signis, ut respondeat populus: amen* (2.436).

> in the expressions and sounds of words, subject to the authority of thy book (like the fowls as it were flying under the firmament); namely, by interpreting, expounding, discoursing, disputing, praising and praying unto thee with the mouth, expressions breaking forth with a loud sounding, that the people may answer, Amen.

The birds (*volatilium caeli*) are thus the material signifiers of man's words, which erupt from the body to fly under heaven (*sub firmamento volitantibus*) when man expounds, discourses, disputes, praises, or prays under the authority of God's words in Scripture. The analogy is made on the level of the signifier. The use of the substantive and participial forms of *volare* for birds and words, respectively, validates the notion that words escape the sinful flesh to return in prayer to the Word, whose gift they are.

Sanctioning, and pointing to, this entire construction is a divinely instituted sign, the acronym ΙΧΘΥΣ, derived from the Greek appellation, Jesus Christ Son of God Savior. The *fish* (*ille piscis*) alluded to above is thus, in the Greek letters, the sign of Christ who exists sinless *"in huius mortalitatis abysso velut in aquarum profunditate"* ("in the abyss of our mortality, as in the depths of the sea.")[18] The allegorical interpretation of the passage in Genesis extrapolates from the mediating function of Christ as the Word in the flesh to the fish as his material signifier in the sea. Presumably, God has written this pun into the Greek language to point the way to a necessary, metaphoric closure, as he has enjoined our sexuality so that it may be displaced (sublimated?) into a conceptual productivity.

The flow of signs in this system is contained and returned upon itself by its inscription within a primal semiosis which is — in structural terms — its exact duplicate: the generation of the logos (coeval with the Father in Augustine's view) and its subsequent incarnation in the mortal flesh. The logos is generated as word or material signifier in two registers — once and always in eternity as the efficient cause of creation and again as punctually inscribed in that creation so as to form of it the Book of Nature. The Holy Scriptures stand, as it were, midway between these two inscriptions of the Word. The words of the Word — and, allegorically, its history as narrated in the Gospels — contain the totalized narrative in terms of which historical events are to be understood.

At a singular and unrepeatable point in history the Word itself is incarnated, enters the world as corporeal signifier, and unifies sense, sign, and concept, multiplicity and unity, time and eternity. But this unity is merely exemplary. Because of the depth of the flesh, that is the imperfection of fallen man, the at-one-time-present transcendental signified retreats into a *metonymically* multiplying chain of signifiers in which meaning is merely potential and from which it must be recovered through the double movement of allegorization and containment.

In Augustine's reading of Genesis, the multiplication of signs and thoughts is a blessing because man, existing in time and interpreting history and the material creation presented to his senses can (potentially) reconstruct the plenitude of meaning that was available before the descent into the flesh and repossess, if only momentarily, the Word disseminated in the words. However, such a reconstruction necessarily leads one out of the flesh and out of time, raising the question of the efficacy of words uttered in time, which Augustine had articulated in Book 11:

> *quis tenebit cor hominis, ut stet et videat, quomodo stans dictet futura et praeterita tempora nec futura nec praeterita aeternitas? numquid manus mea valet hoc aut manus oris mei per loquellas agit tam grandem rem?* (2.232)

> Who now shall so hold fast this heart of man, that it may stand, and see, how that eternity ever still standing, gives the word of command to the times past or to come, itself being neither past nor to come? Can my hand do this, or can the hand of my mouth by speech, bring about so important a business?

This simultaneous recognition of, and turn away from, time figures forth a subject that recognizes itself as the image of eternity in time and remains

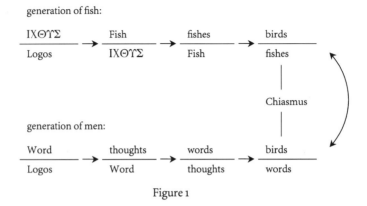

Figure 1

committed to moral action in a world of only apparently contingent events.[19] Augustine's rhetoric joins two distinct chains of signs (see fig. 1). In each chain the signifier of the previous concept becomes the concept of the succeeding sign. Thus, in the chain of signifiers developing the generation of fish, the acronymic, ΙΧΘΥΣ, serves at once to signify the Logos, incarnate as Jesus Christ, Son of God, Savior, and the corporeal fish. But this dual signification leads Augustine to reverse signifier and signified, appropriating the fish that may be observed in nature for use as corporeal signs (material signifiers) of the divinely instituted sequence of phonemes that names them. The image or concept *fish* now refers not to the sea creature but to the Greek letters by which it is named. Because the *word* for fish points to Christ, the corporeal image of the fish (represented by the fish itself or, more to the point, its icon) comes to signify the word.[20] The signifier becomes iconic because its function as a sequence of sounds evoking an associated image is displaced in favor of an *analogy* between the image that it evokes and the attributes imputed to Christ. The concept of the sign ΙΧΘΥΣ is thus allegorized as a metaphoric sign of the Christ, whose proper name is enfolded within its letters. Moreover, the mediating association that draws us first from the word *fish* to the concept *fish* and then from the fish to Christ is carried not through the sound but through the anagrammatic insistence of the *written letters*.[21]

Augustine's interpretive leap (a leap made considerably more manageable by the rhetorical bridging of the gap it crosses) consists in bringing together the scriptural account of the creation of the birds and fishes on the same day and the analogy of the sea to the flesh, so as to join fish to birds at the end of the chain of metonyms representing the generations of the sea and birds to words at the end of the chain representing the generations of men. Understood as a twisted chain of metonymic displacements, originating and terminating in metaphor, Augustine's allegory of the injunction to "increase and multiply" also serves as the bridge over which we cross between the Augustinian and Lacanian formulations with which this chapter begins.

I made the claim, at the beginning of this chapter, that the Christian ego is, in some sense, the product of a commerce between the semiotic and the hermeneutic in Augustinian allegory. We are now in a position to observe that commerce at the precise moment in which Augustine *reads* the multiplication of birds enjoined in the hexameron back into the "generations of men." The production of signs in each chain is accomplished by the absorption of a contiguous concept into the signifying chain. The logos, the sign of the Father, generates by its momentary presence a world of signs behind which it withdraws. It is in this way that an atemporal, idealistic, and—following a path rhetorically identical to that followed by the reading of *fish*—iconic notion of the Father comes to appropriate the discourse of the historically present, but explicitly unrepresentable, God of Israel.[22] The ethical discourse in which the people of God retain the presence of God by adhering to his written laws is transformed by the introjection of the lawgiver as the speaking subject within the subject. Self-presence is thus mediated as the word, speaking in time from beyond time.

The chain of signs beginning with the generation of fish is joined to the chain beginning with the generation of men through a chiasmus, which interrupts the production of figures by maintaining *volantia-volatilia* as a single primary signifier with a dual signification, thus concealing the discontinuity of body and spirit, nature, man and God. The sense of trope as turn is literal here. It is the chiasmus, the sign of the cross, and the semantic folding back of a pivotal word that rescue discourse from the contingent (and linear) paths of historical contiguity and return it to its source in the now introjected logos.[23] The chiasmus thus prefigures within its semantic fold the *putatively actual* infolding of time and eternity in the incarnation, when the Word made flesh will experience the death of the flesh so as to finally and conclusively impose its meaning on history, thenceforward to be viewed as already completed. The Passion of Christ will then historically enact the abrogation of history itself.

In terms of the rhetorical tropology I outlined in chapter 2, we can now characterize Augustine's crucial allegory of allegory as a narrative with metonymy as its trope of transition and metaphor as its trope of closure.[24] It is distinctive, however, for the intralinguistic level at which its metonymies are driven—each sign in its allegorical chain dialectically appropriating the concept of a contiguous sign—and the intricate conjunction of corporeal observation, scriptural interpretation, and phonic association brought into play in order to authorize the metaphoric ratio: birds are to fish as words are to thoughts.

Augustine's allegory disguises this semiosis as a hermeneutics, purporting to interpret a language of God that it rhetorically generates. Therefore, within the Augustinian ideology of the *Imago Dei* the scheme of chiasmus disappears behind the representation as history of the moments of the creation and the Passion. The joining of words to birds reiterates the joining of souls to bodies, of logos to flesh. Into the chiasmic space of this analogy Augustine inserts the icon, the image of God. Thus, his autobiography ends, appropriately enough, with the production of the self in words. The midwifery of the pen brings forth the *anima vivens* in its detour through time. Man's signifier, like Christ's, is divided between a temporal incarnation and an eternal inscription in the Book of Life. Access to that eternally signifying script is for a time blocked by the depth of the flesh, but under the authority of Scripture this bar can be crossed and the being of man's becoming disclosed.[25] The unchanging icon is thus discovered at the center of a speech that has been, so to speak, folded over on itself.

In making the allegorical nature of language the subject and sanction of his allegorical reading of the hexameron, Augustine recognizes that the desire for and the danger of unrestrained allegoresis—the threat that brings the containing (and apocalyptic) narrative into play—is immanent in the words themselves. The metonymic generation of signs, the kind of phonic contiguity exemplified in Augustine's representation of the generations of the sea and of men, respectively, is formally endless. As John Freccero observes of the *Confessions:*

> The Word, the silence that subtends the system, grounds both desire and language. In its absence, however, both threaten to become an infinite regression, approaching ultimate satisfaction and ultimate significance

as an unreachable limit. This is probably most clear in terms of Augustinian desire, which is insatiable in human terms. Each of the successive desires of life are in fact desires for selfhood, expressed metonymically in an ascending hierarchy of abstraction: nourishment for the child, sex for the adolescent, fame for the adult. In an Augustinian world, there is no escape from desire short of God.[26]

The iconic Word, that is, the Word taken from its phonic context and used metaphorically as the image of God, acts as a counterweight against the proliferation of linguistic associations. In this way the installation of the Word-out-of-time at the beginning of both generations serves to bend the arrow of time into a circle—to subsume time within structure. God, we are told, "is an intelligible sphere whose center is everywhere and circumference nowhere."[27] The divine Word, now understood as the atemporal image of the faculty of speech itself, contains and presides over the temporal *unfolding* of the words of men, collecting them into a perfect and timeless structure. Because human access to the being of the Word is through the words of Scripture, the written text, the book between covers, understood as a synchronic system in which meaning resides, mediates between the temporal words of man and the unchanging image divinely revealed.[28] Thus, within the circle of Augustine's rhetoric, man's relation to the present speech of an interior Word is mediated by his relation to the inscripted words of the Holy Scriptures.

To appreciate how pervasive this underlying rhetorical configuration is in generating the crucial narrative moments of Augustine's text, we can now consider the articulation of the "supplementary" commentary of *Confessions* 13 and the autobiographical narrative that precedes it, tracking the ways in which the metonymies that drive Augustine's narrative transitions are assimilated to *writing* and the metaphors that arrest the narrative in favor of a view of the self *sub species aeternitatas* are assimilated to *speech*. To accomplish this, I am going to try to reconstruct as carefully as possible the transitional rhetoric of two representative episodes in the *Confessions,* one recounting the conversion experience that is the turning point of the narrative, the other concluding the subsumption of the narrative within the supplement, that is, the climactic account of Augustine's conversion through the mediation of a written text in Book 8 and the use of *the book* as a metaphoric vehicle to express the division of the dry land from the sea in Book 13.

4

Augustine's account of his conversion in Book 8 of the *Confessions* is anticipated by a series of conversion narratives. "In the text of the *Confessions*," as
Freccero remarks, "conversion is always a literary event, a gloss on an anterior
text."[29] Drawing attention to the power of these precedent stories to inspire a
repetition *in fact,* Augustine tells how after hearing Simplicianus's account of
the conversion of Victorinus, he was moved to imitate Victorinus and complete his own conversion: *"ubi mihi homo tuus Simplicianus de Victorino ista
narravit, exarsi ad imitandum: ad hoc enim et ille narraverat"* (1.422; "So soon
as thy man Simplicianus had made an end of his story of Victorinus, I was all
on fire to be imitating of him: yea, this was the end he told it for").

However, at this point — and with the model of the converted sinner, Victorinus, before him — Augustine's conversion is impeded by a divided will:
*"ita duae voluntates meae, una vetus, alia nova, illa carnalis, illa spiritalis, con-
fligebant inter se, atque discordando dissipabant animam meam"* (1.424; "Thus
did my two wills, one new and tother old, that carnal, and this spiritual, try
masteries within me, and by their disagreeing wasted out my soul"). Finding
himself painfully suspended between these contradictory desires, Augustine
comes to understand his present experience as an illustration and confirmation of something he had *read:*

> *Sic intellegebam me ipso experimento id quod legeram, quomodo caro con-
> cupisceret adversus spiritum et spiritus adversus carnem: ego quidem in
> utroque, sed magis ego in eo, quod in me approbabam, quam in eo, quod
> in me improbabam. ibi enim magis iam non ego, quia ex magna parte id
> patiebar invitus quam faciebam volens.* (1.424)

> Thus came I to understand (myself affording me the experiment) what
> I had sometimes read: how the flesh lusteth against the spirit, and the
> spirit against the flesh. I myself was in both; yet of the two, in that rather
> which I approved of in myself, than in that which I disallowed. For in
> this, I was now no more; because much of it I suffered rather against my
> will, than did it with my will.

We can see in this moment of intricate internal division, this shadow play of
being and nonbeing, doing and suffering, the same division of the carnal and
spiritual, natural and divine, that underlay the division of the generations of

man from the generations of the sea. And we can see the same movement toward an authorizing word, the matching of experience and something read.

The experience of division is brought to consciousness by a story—that of the conversion of Victorinus—and it is interpreted according to a story—the war of the flesh against spirit and spirit against flesh. As he had with the joining of birds to thoughts in his allegorical reading of Genesis, Augustine again employs a chiasmus to figure the general law that underlies the crucial ambivalence of the self as the subject and object of its own experience: "*caro concupisceret adversus spiritum et spiritus adversus carnem.*" The freedom of Latin word order allows Augustine to visually reproduce the enclosure of the spirit within the flesh by placing *caro* and *carnem* around the chiasmus of *spiritum et spiritus.* The iconic presentation of the written words to the eye parallels the encircling repetition of lust and flesh as presented to the ear, while syntactically the paired exchange of nominative *caro* and accusative *carnem* and accusative *spiritum* and nominative *spiritus* enforces the oscillation of the subject between his "old" and "new" wills. The effect of the chiasmus is to signal the eternity of a timeless structure, as it is *literally* carved from the linear succession of syllables.

That which is experienced and the ego that experiences it are thus received as the empirical confirmation of two narrations: "*me ipso experimento id quod legeram.*" The Christian ego appears at the spot where the two ends of the hermeneutic circle are (chiasmically) entwined, and the self—understood only in and through its moment of understanding—escapes from action *into* (self-) knowledge: "*id patiebar invitus quam faciebam volens.*"

To complete his (self-)analysis of an individual who, because he is the site of conflicting and powerful forces, finds that he does what he knows he does not wish to do, Augustine localizes the aspects of the divided self as two distinct wills issuing from two separate origins. The self that is the subject of the spirit wars against the flesh, and the self that is subjected to the flesh wars against the spirit, because each is subjected to a law that contradicts the other:

> *frustra condelectabatur legi tuae secundum interiorem hominem, cum alia lex in membris meis repugnaret legi mentis meae, et captivum me duceret in lege peccati, quae im membris meis erat. lex enim peccati est violentia consuetudinis, qua trahitur et tenetur etiam invitus animus, eo merito, quo in eam volens inlabitur. miserum ergo me quis liberaret de corpore mortis huius, nisi gratia tua per Iesum Christum, dominum nostrum?* (1.426, 428)

> I in vain delighted in thy law according to the inner man, when another
> law in my members rebelled against the law of my mind, leading me
> captive in the law of sin which was in my members. That law of sin
> now is the violence of custom, by which the mind of man is drawn and
> holden even against its will; deserving to be so holden, for that it so will-
> ingly slides into that custom. Wretched I therefore, who could deliver
> me from the body of this death; but thy grace only, through Jesus Christ
> our Lord?

Augustine's mind is now God's, but the concupiscence of the flesh holds it cap-
tive to custom. Body and mind are separated as were sexual reproduction and
speech in our first example, and, at this stage of the conversion, the mind cries
out from the body, as the fish (ΙΧΘΥΣ) cries out from the depths of the sea.

Augustine continues for a time in this distraught condition, until God ar-
ranges for him to hear yet another conversion story. This one is told by Ponticianus, an African, and an official of the imperial court, who, while visiting
Augustine and Alypius on some forgettable business, discovers that Augustine has been reading the Epistles of Saint Paul. This discovery leads them
to discuss two subjects that — as it will turn out — encompass Augustine's immediate destiny: conversions and the monastic life. Ponticianus tells of two
court officials, men of affairs (*agentes in rebus*), who, while walking outside
the walls of Milan (then the imperial capital), happen to chance upon a small
house inhabited by Christians, where they find a little book of the life of Saint
Anthony. Reading this book, they are converted; subsequently, they give up
all secular employments and dedicate themselves to the service of God.

This tale of conversion by a book is the final preparation for Augustine's
own reenactment of the by now generic conversion narrative. It becomes a
mirror in which he finds himself:

> *Narrabat haec Ponticianus. tu autem, domine, inter verba eius retorquebas*
> *me ad me ipsum, auferens me a dorso meo, ubi me posueram, dum nollem*
> *me adtendere; et constituebas me ante faciem meam. . . .* (1.438)

> These things Ponticianus narrated. But you, lord, between [among?]
> his words, turned me back toward myself, carrying me from behind
> my back, where I had placed myself, while I was unwilling to observe
> myself; and set me before my own face. . . . (my translation)

Spoken by Ponticianus, but divinely directed at Augustine, this story prepares Augustine's mind for its final revolt against the subjugating law of the members:

> *et si conabar a me avertere aspectum, narrabat ille quod narrabat; et tu me rursus opponebas mihi, et inpingebas me in oculos meos, ut invenirem iniquitatem et odissem. noveram eam, sed dissimulabam et cohibebam et obliviscebar.* (1.438)

> And if I went about to turn mine eyes off from myself, he went on telling his tale; and thou thereupon opposedst my self unto myself, and thrustedst me ever and anon into mine own eyes, to make me find at last mine own iniquity, and to loathe it. I had heretofore taken notice of it; but I had again dissembled it, winked at it, and forgotten it.

Schooled by the conversion stories of Victorinus and the two *agentes in rebus*, Augustine is able to project the two sides of his internal conflict as two temporally opposed points of view, seeing in his present the loathed life of the unconverted self—*as it would appear*—to the converted self. In this way an intolerable paralysis of indecision is converted into a narrative event, having a before and an after—and, indeed, yielding a happy ending. The vehicles that carry the self across this event were already encountered in the story of the *agentes in rebus*. They are, famously, a voice and a book.

> *et ecce audio vocem de vicina domo cum cantu dicentis, et credo repetentis, quasi pueri an puellae, nescio: "tolle lege, tolle lege." . . . repressoque impetu lacrimarum surrexi, nihil aliud interpretans divinitus mihi iuberi, nisi ut aperirem codicem et legerem quod primum caput invenissem. audieram enim de Antonio, quod ex evangelica lectione, cui forte supervenerat, admonitus fuerit, tamquam sibi diceretur quod legebatur, . . . et tali oraculo confestim ad te esse conversum. itaque concitus redii in eum locum, ubi sedebat Alypius: ibi enim posueram codicem apostoli, cum inde surrexeram. arripui, aperui et legi in silentio capitulum, quo primum coniecti sunt oculi mei: non in comissationibus et ebrietatibus, non in cubilibus et inpudicitiis, non in contentione et aemulatione, sed induite dominum Iessum Christum, et carnis providentiam ne feceritis in concupiscentiis. nec ultra volui legere, nec opus erat. statim quippe cum fine huiusce senten-*

*tiae, quasi luce securitatis infusa cordi meo, omnes dubitationes tenebrae
diffugerunt.* (1.462, 464)

Whenas behold I heard a voice from some neighbour's house in a sing
song voice, saying and I believe repeating, as it were of a boy or girl, I
know not: "Take up and read, Take up and read". . . . Whereupon re-
fraining the violent torrent of my tears, up I gat me; interpreting it no
other way, but that I was from God himself commanded to open the
book, and to read that chapter which I should first light upon. For I had
heard of Anthony, that by hearing of the Gospel which he once chanced
to come in upon, he took himself to be admonished, as if what was read,
had purposely been spoken unto him . . . and by such divine oracle that
he was presently converted unto thee. Hastily therefore went I again to
that place where Alypius was sitting; for there had I laid the Apostle's
book whenas I rose from thence. I snatched it up, I opened it, and in
silence I read that chapter which I had first cast mine eyes upon: Not
in rioting and drunkenness, not in chambering and wantonness, not in
strife and envying: but put ye on the Lord Jesus Christ; and make not
provision for the flesh, to fulfil the lusts thereof. No further would I read;
nor needed I. For instantly even with the end of this sentence, by a light
as it were of confidence now darted into my heart, all the darkness of
doubting vanished away. (Watt's translation, slightly modified)

Earlier in Book 8, the reader has learned, along with Ponticianus, that Augustine has been reading the Pauline Epistles. Within the narrative, some considerable time elapses between the discovery of the text and the conversion.
What, then, makes this moment, this reading, decisive? The conjunction of
three elements: the mysterious voice, which *breathes* the presence of God into
the writing he has inspired, the perceived relevance of the text (Romans 13:13–
14) to Augustine's personal circumstances, and the apparent absence of *human*
intention in the discovery of the passage: "*arripui, aperui et legi in silentio capi-
tulum, quo primum coniecti sunt oculi mei.*" The law in the members, which
had not been subdued by the scripted laws of the Hebrew covenant, is finally
subjugated to the voice that speaks the law within, personally, at (and perhaps
to) the origin of the generations of men.[30]

Crucial to Augustine's construction of these three elements, that is, to his
fashioning of a performative conversion narrative, are the generic conversion

stories that form its anticipatory context in Book 8 of the *Confessions*. When, after much painful delay, the voice bids him *"tolle lege,"* he is in the position of reading a story he has already followed, and so, too, is his reader.[31] The anticipatory conversion narratives allow Augustine to encounter his own experience as though it were already retrospective. They (pre)structure experience in the form of a narrative representation.

This crucial narrative motif, itself the story of a divine cause and its historical effect, does not open Augustine's text to history. On the contrary, it establishes an iterative pattern of divine intervention to which the only apparently historical event is subjected. The visit of Ponticianus, the reading of the Pauline Epistles, the story of the *agentes in rebus* are no longer to be taken as the random events of a mundane life, but as messages from a voice that finally reveals itself to be, in fact, unembodied. It is both in respect of the ultimately unembodied nature of the voice of God and of Augustine's immediate need to free himself from the injunction to increase and multiply (so that he may "make not provision for the flesh") that Augustine takes particular note of the indeterminate gender of the childlike voice from the neighbor's house (*"quasi pueri an puellae, nescio"*).

When this voice commands Augustine to take up and read, he is to read not just the passage in Paul but the series of events that lead up to its call. This is confirmed by his crucial reference to the story of Antonius, on the basis of which he decides to retrieve the Epistles and read — as if it were intended for him — the first passage on which his eye alights. His reading of this passage is thus predetermined by the expectation that he too will be converted. The voice, then, that answers Augustine's internal subjection to two mutually contradictory laws is emphatically and insistently a voice *outside* (*"vocem de vicina domo"*). This voice, whose essence is repetition, calls Augustine to foreclose the unfolding history of his earthly life, to reduce the difference between the laws of the members and of the spirit by turning (*"conversare"*) from his engagement in their conversation to a fixed attention on the timeless alterity of the voice that calls him.

Having examined Augustine's conversion by and to the book, I want to return briefly to his reading of Genesis in Book 13 to consider his use of the book as metaphor in yet another episode of differentiation; this time to figure the difference not between humankind and nature, nor between the spiritual and corporeal aspects of a single man, but between God and his image.

Interpreting the creation of the firmament and the separation of the dry land from the waters, Augustine generates an elaborate allegory in which the spirit, Scripture, the waters, and the body are once again joined in an eternal structure within which the narrative of worldly actions is contained and rendered (eternally) representative. In this allegory, the firmament, under which the birds and thoughts of the generations of fish and men will fly, is revealed to be the divine words of Scripture:

> quis nisi tu, deus noster, fecisti nobis firmamentum auctoritatis super nos in scriptura tua divina? caelum enim plicabitur ut liber, et nunc sicut pellis extenditur super nos. sublimioris enim auctoritatis est tua divina scriptura, cum iam obierunt istam mortem illi mortales, per quos eam dispensasti nobis. et tu scis, domine, tu scis, quemadmodum pellibus indueris homines, cum peccato mortales fierent. unde sicut pellem extendisti firmamentum libri tui, concordes utique sermones tuos, quos per mortalium ministerium superposuisti nobis. namque ipsa eorum morte solidamentum auctoritatis in eloquiis tuis per eos editis sublimiter extenditur super omnia, quae subter sunt, quod, cum hic viverent, non ita sublimiter extentum erat. nondum sicut pellem caelum extenderas, nondum mortis eorum famam usquequaque dilataveras. (2.402, 424; my emphasis)

Who except thou, O our God, made that firmament of the authority of divine Scripture to be over us? As 'tis said: *For the heaven shall be folded up like a book;* and is even now stretched over us like a skin. For thy holy Scripture is of more eminent authority, since those mortals departed this life, by whom thou dispensedst it unto us. And thou knowest, O Lord, thou knowest, how thou With skins didst once apparel men, so soon as they by sin were become mortal. Wherefore hast thou like a Skin stretched out the Firmament of thy book, that is to say those words of thine so well agreeing together; which by the ministry of mortal men thou spreadedst over us. For by their very death is that solid Firmament of authority, in thy sayings set forth by them, stretched on high over all that be under it; which whilst they lived on earth, was not then so eminently stretched out over us. Thou hadst not as yet Spread abroad that heaven like a skin; thou hadst not as yet everywhere noised abroad the report of their deaths.

As we have seen, the soul lies in the body as the fish lies in the sea, the words of prayer fly forth under the firmament as the birds fly free of the sea, and the desire of the spirit to fly free wars against the concupiscence of the flesh and the law of the members; we now see that the analogies and oppositions between the words and the birds, the birds and the fish, the spirit and the flesh, are signifying practices bound together by the book that enfolds within its closure the inscripted words of an eternal Word. The firmament, which is also a book, marks the boundary between time and eternity; for above the firmament, outside the fold of Scripture, angels, reading, as it were, from another book, praise God eternally. This other book is the face of God:

> *non clauditur codex eorum nec plicatur liber eorum, quia tu ipse illis hoc*
> *es et es in aeternum, quia super hoc firmamentum ordinasti eos, quod*
> *firmasti super infirmitatem inferiorum populorum, ubi suspicerent et*
> *cognoscerent misericordiam tuam* temporaliter enuntiantem te, qui
> fecesti tempora. (2.406; my emphasis) [32]

> Their book is never closed, nor is their scroll folded up: seeing thyself art
> this unto them, yea, thou art so eternally; because thou hast arranged
> them above this Firmament, which thou hast settled over the infirmity
> of the lower peoples: where they might gaze up and learn thy mercy,
> *which declares in time thee that madest times.*

The book, then, divides the temporal from the eternal as it divides the angels, who contemplate the unchanging face of God, from mortal men and women, who, themselves made in the image of God, must find that image, inscribed (literally) within this temporal flow of words. The book itself, as physical object, comes then to figure the peculiar temporal predicament of humankind, which is to live along the boundary between time and eternity, as it is precisely reflected in the dialectic between the unfolding story and the completed design experienced by the reader of narrative. For the angels, who live eternally in the presence of God, God's book is never closed (*non clauditur codex*), but for humankind, eternity remains folded into time, a closed book, until one hears the timely call to "take up and read."

In the remainder of this chapter I want briefly to evoke some exemplary moments in (1) the disintegration of the iconic reflection of the face of God understood by Augustine as the image of God given to God's image in the form of an iterative pattern to be abstracted from the flow of words; (2) the replacement of the subject delimited by that image with the subject of a self-conscious reflection on frankly duplicitous verbal processes of self-representation; and (3) the subsequent emergence of the subject as subject of history through a transfer of historical meaning from the lost origin of the past to the anticipated consequences of historical events, constrained and circumscribed within a narrative closure.

5

> Who now shall hold fast this heart of man, that it may stand, and see, how the still-standing eternity speaks [*dictet*] the times past or to come, itself being neither past nor to come? Can my hand do this, or can the hand of my mouth through speaking [*manus oris mei per loquellas*] bring about a thing so great? (2.233) [33]

In the eleventh book of the *Confessions*, Augustine, remarking the difficulty of his task, asks how a man, who is himself subject to a heart that "flieth about in the past and future motions of things," can use words to bring others to see the events of history as *spoken* from a place that is itself outside time. Augustine's "*Quis tenebit . . . ?*" is, of course, the answer to its own question. For the *Confessions* is the story of the coming to be of the man who will undertake the task, and the question—with its evocation of the "still-standing eternity"—aims to draw its readers out of the flux of time by showing them the timeless design that governs its own production. In short, the answer to Augustine's question is the story of the voice that speaks it. Moreover, the question asserts a relationship between eternity and event that is already given in the relationship between the "I" who speaks this text and the "I" represented within it.

On the one hand, Augustine conceives the words issuing from the hand of his mouth to be the translation of a *vision* into the temporal medium of language. Thus, the speaking "I," which is, like the logos, also a seeing eye and a making hand, is the still point from which the spoken "I" issues. But, unlike the logos, this voice issues from a mortal body. It therefore is subject to desires generated elsewhere, while the written words—the work, as Augustine puts it, tightening the association with the logos, of the tongue of his pen ("*lingua calami*")—achieve, if only latently, the atemporal synchrony of a narrated design. The "I" that stands in the fold between the *nunc stans* of eternity and the motions of the heart, the motions of bodily desire, is also folded within its own discourse. What begins as an assertion of the priority of eternal design over temporal discovery becomes, as well, a covert demonstration of their reversibility. If the things of this timely world can be rendered signifiers of the concepts of the spirit (as, for example, Augustine renders sexual procreation a signifier for the generation of prayers), so, too, can the concepts of the spirit come to point toward the things of this world.[34]

Such reversibility inheres in narrative generally. Insofar as narrative configures episodes that follow one another in time as a chain of causes and effects, it projects time as the medium in which causation occurs. But narrative causation exists in a supplementary relation to narrative design. Plot does not simply recount cause; it elicits cause. Narrative discovers its chain of causes as the pattern that emerges, at the end, as having been necessary to the execution of a design. Because narrative transposes and defers meaning from an originating action to its more *or less* predictable consequences, we may, in this context, consider the illusory unfolding of its plot as the Other of lyric's in-folding of creating and created selves.

To contain this reversibility of temporal cause and eternal design, to assert always the priority of an originary and atemporal order, Augustine must suppress his own role as mediator between the timeless design of God and the timely desires of the body. He must identify himself so fully with the spoken "I" of his text as to represent its origin as God's own plan, the very plan whose revelation is also its end, both temporally and causally; his allegory must end where it begins. For Augustine, the achievement of re-creating the self is this reorientation of the self to the uncreated. This is why the *Confessions* becomes, in its final books, a commentary on the opening chapters of Genesis. The voice created in the conversion narrative turns back from the narration of its experience to a reiteration of the creating voice of the logos. As the *Confessions* is a book folding over Augustine's life and folded under the overarching firmament of Scripture, self-creation is narrated within the fold of creation itself.

Always already inscribed within the relation of lyric to narrative, Augustine's problem and the rhetoric it elicits are, from the beginning, literary. It is, therefore, unsurprising that, as the subject of the *Confessions* passes into Dante's conversion story, the tension between the self speaking itself in time and the self presumed to speak the uncreated divine, now reenvisaged across the narrative links and embedded lyrics of *La Vita Nuova* as a tension between narrative and lyric experiences of time, should come to define as well the speaker of epideictic lyric. This speaker must unfold in sequential language a pattern that is beyond time, yet from which particular events necessarily issue. He tells a story that cannot reach its end, because its end is its cosmic beginning, as the end of Augustine's allegory of allegory is the origin of words in the Word. The subjective agent who fashions his or her timely actions in anticipation of such an extension from and return to the origin is, in this respect, coeval with time itself.

Consider, for example, the literally proleptic vision that ends *La Vita Nuova*:

> *Appresso questo sonetto apparve a me una mirabile visione, ne la quale io vidi cose che mi fecero proporre di non dire più di questa benedetta infino a tanto che io potesse più degnamente trattare di lei. E di venire a ciò io studio quanto posso, sì com'ella sae veracemente. Sì che, se piacere sarà di colui a cui tutte le cose vivono, che la mia vita duri per alquanti anni, io spero di dicer di lei quello che mai non fue detto d'alcuna. E poi piaccia a colui che è sire del cortesia, che la mia anima se ne possa gire a vedere la gloria de la sua donna, cioè di quella benedetta Beatrice, la quale gloriosamente mira ne la faccia di colui qui est per omnia secula benedictus.*[35]

After this sonnet a miraculous vision appeared to me, in which I saw things that made me resolve to say no more about this blessed one until I could write more worthily of her. And to come to this, I work as much as I can, as she truly knows. Therefore, if it would please Him through whom all things live that my life continue a few more years, I hope to say of her that which has not been said of any woman. And then may it please Him who is lord of grace, that my soul may rise to see the glory of its lady, that is, the blessed Beatrice, who gloriously looks on the face of Him who is blessed throughout all ages.

This passage refers us back to the opening of *La Vita Nuova* where we are told that the *libello* draws from the "book of memory" ("*del libro de la mia memoria*") material found under the rubric "*Incipit vita nova*" (1); but, from the perspective of our present literary history, the passage inevitably refers forward as well—to the realization in the *Commedia* of the "*mirabile visione*" left unnarrated at the close of *La Vita Nuova*. As it happens, the date of the final chapter of *La Vita Nuova* is a vexed issue for Dante studies, with one group of scholars reading the passage as a prophecy later fulfilled and another group attributing it to a retrospective revision.[36] For our purposes, however, whether Dante, in fact, lived his new life in the ten or so years that separate the composition of *La Vita Nuova* and the *Commedia* in anticipation of his concluding return to an originary vision or whether he restructured those years retrospectively as having been so lived is less important than the collusion between narrative structure and subjective agency offered in and by Dante's conversion narrative. Like Augustine's *Confessions,* the story of the beginning of Dante's new life represents conversion *literally* as a narrative turn, and, again like the *Confessions,* turns on the pivot of a saving word, Beatrice's "*salute.*"

Alongside these similarities there are, however, three important differences between the construction of Augustine's conversion narrative and Dante's:

(1) Although Dante's conversion, like Augustine's, includes the strategic intervention of a voice (Beatrice's "*salute*") and a book ("*del libro de la mia memoria*"), the position of the book and the voice with respect to the narrator is differently articulated. In Augustine's text the voice and the book, though not entirely exterior to the narrator, are clearly presented as interventions through which God turns Augustine back upon himself ("*retorquebas me ad me ipsum*"). In *La Vita Nuova,* the book, and the voice in which it is found, has migrated inward. Thus, the crucial passage is not found in God's enfolding Scripture, or in an immediately symbolic determination of the things of this world, but in the "*libro de la mia memoria.*" From this book, in which experiences are recorded, the narrator fashions the smaller book ("*libello*") that is *La Vita Nuova,* within which poems (presumably written at or close to the time of the events they record) give lyric representation to an "I" corresponding to the time of the narrative, while in the prose framework a narrating "I" turns back upon its former selves so as to assign to the lyric moments meanings that would not have been available when they occurred.[37]

(2) The thematic structure of the *Confessions* forms around the conflict of corporeal and spiritual desire: the law of the members and the law in the soul. Thus, in the climactic moment of conversion, the injunction to "make not provision for the flesh" turns Augustine "back to himself" by turning him from carnal to spiritual investments. This turn, subsequently enforced by the dismissal of his mistress, is rhetorically enacted in the allegorical reading of "increase and multiply" as pertaining not to flesh but—literally—to spirit

(the inspiring breath of God returned in the words of men). In sharp contrast to Augustine's indeterminately gendered and vaguely situated voice from a neighbor's house, Beatrice is and remains, even in Paradise, an embodied female form. Because Beatrice remains a woman, the displacement of carnal to spiritual appetites effected by Augustine's allegory of allegory manifests a very different kind of temporal presence in Dante's text. The punctual moment of conversion by the book is replaced by the iterative and laborious process of conversion in the book ("And to come to this, I work as much as I can").

The subject of Dante's desire does not turn away from its corporeal object to seek the truth of its own heart; on the contrary, it seeks its truth as it is reflected in her. Taking a few more steps on the bridge from Augustine to Lacan, we might say that Dante seeks the desire of Beatrice; but because Beatrice's desire is for God, Dante's desire returns to him transmuted into spiritual yearning. Seeing in Dante's desire for Beatrice the intersection of two lacks—both are incarnate but neither is the self-signifying Word—we might say that he wants what she wants. In psychoanalytic terms, Beatrice signifies the catalytic location of a transference. In his relation to her, Dante reenacts and completes the archaic exchange of the maternal (corporeal) object for the law of the (spiritual) Father. As we shall see, this mediation of spirit through praise of an embodied woman who is both desired and lacking leads to a narrative articulation of subjectivity significantly different from Augustine's mediation of the incarnate Word. Augustine's narrative seeks to end at the beginning, returning literally in Book 13 to the Word of God; Dante's "little book" remains at the level of the sign. To approach this distinction and appreciate the underlying rhetorical difference between the *Confessions* and *La Vita Nuova,* it will be useful to consider the different relations to the symbolic implied by Augustine's use of the Greek ΙΧΘΥΣ to render the perceived world of nature a unitary signifier of divine will and the insistence of the letter in the name Beatrice.

(3) The focus of the lyric and narrative recollections of *La Vita Nuova* is Dante's reaction to Beatrice, who, because her name is formed from a common noun, figures in the *libello* as both a person and a personification. Here, the static symbolic structure according to which Augustine finds Christ in the letters of the word ΙΧΘΥΣ is set in motion as an agent that lives up to her name. Because she is Beatrice and she is *beata* (blessed), she comes, in the end, to enjoy the sight of him *"qui est per omnia secula benedictus."* Thus, as a

figure of narrative, incorporating in her name and her actions an ethos and a mythos commensurate with it, Beatrice can move through the text conferring that which she is. In contrast to Augustine's *Imago Dei,* which remains at the boundary of time, as what Freud might term an ideal ego, Beatrice enters and resides within the narrative frame, incorporated in memory as an ego ideal.[38] By replacing Augustine's originary *Imago Dei* with the memory and anticipation of Beatrice as the temporal poles of his narrative, Dante substitutes an identification with the signifier, *Beatrice as beatitudine,* for Augustine's captivation by the image. This splitting of the narrative "I" between an originary image and an anticipatory identification with its signifier is textually performed by the splitting of Beatrice into the proper noun designating the young female person who figures in the early part of Dante's book of memory and the signifier of the beatitude she comes to personify. The closing prolepsis of Dante seeing Beatrice seeing the one *"qui est per omnia secula benedictus"* is thus an iterative representation of the epideictic function itself: Dante, having attained a certain beatitude, will have been able to produce the signifier that will point to Beatrice who, by personifying beatitude, will have pointed to God, the *"sire de la cortesia"* from whom all beatitude devolves. In the way in which in this tableau the name of Beatrice comes to insist upon itself, to introduce a hesitation over the word as signifier between itself and its denominative function, we may observe what Fineman has identified as the paradox of epideixis, that it can only praise its object by implicitly praising itself.[39]

One notable filiation, then, of the tension of Augustine's paradoxical need to speak or write in time so as to open the view of what lies beyond it is the desire of epideictic lyric to behold its own origin, to present in words outside the body the predestining, yet untraced, mark of the divine within it. For Augustine, the seeing, speaking, and making logos that lies folded within the visible cosmos also enfolds the cosmos within its unending self. Similarly, the seeing, speaking, and making of the motionless, yet migratory, *heart* of the lover becomes both the beginning and the end of the epideictic subject, his interior and ineffable essence and the exterior and visible product of his art.

Thus, through the representation of Beatrice, Dante will place in Love's hand *una cosa la quale ardessa tutta* [a thing that was burning everything], that he and we may obey Love's imperative to "*Vide cor tuum* [see thy heart]" (p. 4). Harrison remarks with respect to this burning heart that:

The heart introduces through metonymy the narrator's presence in the dream. Except for this heart, Dante is altogether absent from the vision. His real presence is as the spectator outside the vision for whom the scene plays itself out. But within the dream, he figures only in and through the emblem of his passion. He sees himself metonymically condensed, as it were, in the figure of a heart burning in the hand of the terrifying lord. (p. 25)

I would make the additional observation that the metonymy of the burning heart for the subject absent from his own vision is doubled by the play of *cor* and *cosa* in Dante's report of this memory. The disappearance of the *cor,* which Dante is enjoined to *see,* under the periphrastic *cosa* of his narrative precisely denotes the empty place of origin out of which and around which the tale of the new life will be generated. This initiating vision alerts us to the fact that the passing moments and the trembling of the heart recovered in "this little book of memory" are to be seen against the background of fated hours and the mastery of Love — *sub species aeternitatis.* Thus *cor,* which is Dante's only representative in the vision, is only an undetermined *cosa* until the intervention of the exteriorized lord of Love names it in the imperative mode.

Paradoxically, however, the eternal heart, revealed to the eye of history as the still point through which Time is spoken, can only write itself out as writing itself. Through the poet's decision to "speak no more," the burning heart of *La Vita Nuova* comes to figure the poet of the new life and the new style and, proleptically, even the poet of the *Commedia*'s beatific vision. In contrast, the lyric moments of Petrarch's collection organize themselves around, and so reveal, a name, which they must obsessively repeat.[40] In Petrarch, as the reference to "scattered rimes" in the opening sonnet indicates, the epideictic vehicle, that is, the woman, who is the support of his poetic activity, is reflected more candidly back to the poet himself than is Dante's Beatrice, who is always also a signifier of God's grace; the narrator never achieves the metaphoric identification with the object of his praise that allows Dante to fall silent while working toward his own beatitude. As a result, the subject and object, praiser and praised, of the *Canzoniere* are scattered along the metonymic defiles of a disseminated desire.[41]

When Dante locates the advent of his new life in the encounter with Beatrice, he invokes what is already a narrative construction of the self. The lyric moments represented by the poems are found in an early part of memory, when there was not yet much written in the book, but they are recovered retrospectively by a narrative "I" who has learned at least something of their meaning ("*sentenzia*") and who is able to assert his continuity with the narrated "I" whose experience he interprets. Petrarch, on the other hand, tells us that the *Rime sparse* contain "*il suono / di quei sospiri ond' io nudriva 'l core / in sul mio primo giovenile errore, / quand'era in parte altr' uom da quel ch' i' sono*" ("the sound of those sighs with which I nourished my heart during my first youthful error, when I was in part another man from what I am now").[42] Where Dante presents the continuity and unity of a *libello,* Petrarch offers the scattered rhymes of a scattered self. To continue the analogy to psychoanalytic transference: Dante remembers and works through; Petrarch repeats.[43]

Doubtless there are contingent and personal differences peculiar to the lives and temperaments of Dante and Petrarch that would, if they could be specified, account in part for the formal and thematic differences between their works. Some of these are perhaps recoverable; one is almost certainly Petrarch's need to distinguish his work from that of an overshadowing predecessor. But I want now only to point to the formal implications of their respective objects: to ask, in a sense, "what's in a name?" The beatitude of Beatrice comes from God, "the lord of graciousness," and she mediates that divine gift to Dante by embodying it in visible form. She cannot be described because, as a signifier of God's grace, when she is seen properly she is not, finally, seen at all. The perfection of epideixis, she shows not herself but the way to that which stands above her. Thus, there is no blazon in *La Vita Nuova.* Laura, on the other hand, figures not the affect she evokes or transmits but a reaction to it. She calls forth praise, and — as Petrarch's story develops — the praise she figures is that praise which is specific to poets, the praise of the laureate crown. Within the circuit thus established there is no effective moment of transcendence because the poet who praises and Laura, the praise who is praised, are both finally absorbed into the poetry of praise that their collaboration produces. If he praises her, he praises her as she appears in his praise, and thus he praises himself for his ability to replicate her. Moreover, if, like Dante, he falls silent, then there is no praise, and Laura, effectively, disappears.[44] In the formal terminology established in chapter 2: "Beatrice," which unites a person and her attribute, performs and illustrates metaphor, while "Laura," which unites a cause and its effect, performs and illustrates metonymy. The former figures the inclusion of Beatrice in her beatitude; the latter figures the exclusion of Laura from the praise, which reproduces and exceeds her.

Thus, in the *Canzoniere* the heart and the name that Love has written on it coalesce, not through an anticipated identity, but in and through the temporal acting out of the anagrammatic fate schematically explicated in Rime 5:

> *Quando io movo i sospiri a chiamar voi*
> *e 'l nome che nel cor mi scrisse Amore,*
> *LAU-dando s'incomincia udir di fore*
> *il suon de' primi dolci accenti suoi;*
>
> *vostro stata RE-al che 'ncontro poi*
> *raddoppia a l'alta impresa il mio valore;*
> *ma "TA-ci," grida il fin, "ché farle onore*
> *è d'altri omeri soma che da' tuoi."*
>
> *Così LAU-dare et RE-verire insegna*
> *La voce stessa, pur ch' altri vi chiami,*
> *o d'ogni reverenza et d'onor degna;*
>
> *se non che forse Apollo si disdegna*
> *ch'a parlar de' suoi sempre verdi rami*
> *lingua mor-TA-l presuntuosa vegna.*

> When I move my sighs to call you and the name that Love wrote on my heart, the sound of its first sweet accents is heard without in LAU-ds.
>
> Your RE-gal state, which I meet next, redoubles my strength for the high enterprise; but "TA-lk no more!" cries the ending, "for to do her honor is a burden for other shoulders than yours."
>
> Thus the word itself teaches LAU-d and RE-verence, whenever anyone calls you, O Lady worthy of all reverence and honor; except that perhaps Apollo is incensed that any mor-TA-l tongue should come presumptuous to speak of his eternally green boughs.

Just as the name of Beatrice anticipates and encloses the beatitude that she is and confers, the name of Laura teaches the voice that calls it to praise and revere her. Laura, however, personifies not the beatitude that enables praise but the praise itself, and the praise she elicits, being a matter of words, leads not to the Word from which her attributes descend but to the letters out of which her praise is assembled. This sense of linguistic entrapment is present not only in the decomposition of Laura into the syllables of her name but in the deployment of certain acoustically related words. For example, the insistence of the sibilants and nasals in *impresa* (l. 6), *insegna* (l. 9), *stessa* (l. 10), *degna* (l. 11), *disdegna* (l. 12). Thus, in line 6, the redoubling of strength for the "high task" (*impresa*) of praise is shadowed by the *segno* or courtly lover's favor (*impresa*) that is the product of the enterprise and that becomes, in a sense, Petrarch's coat of arms (*impresa*).[45] In line 9 the verb form *insegna* (*insegnare*, to teach) shades into the noun *insegna*, again, a badge, a sign, a coat of arms, and in line 10 the same voice (*la voce stessa*) that is taught by the calling of Laura may unweave or unravel (*stessere*) as the possible scorn of Apollo (*disdegna*) in line 12 unravels the reverence and honor of which Laura is worthy (*degna*) in line 11.

This sort of counterreferential stuttering becomes thematic in the twenty-third canzone, when a similar collusion of temporal event and transtemporal denotation again (and more dramatically) reduces the unfolding of the sequence to the iteration of a name that figures the absorption of the speaker in his own emblematic and allusive utterance:

> I'dico che dal dì che'l primo assalto mi diede Amor, molt' anni eran passati, sì ch' io cangiava il giovenil aspetto, e d'intorno al mio cor pensier gelati fatto avean quasi adamantino smalto ch'allentar non lassava il duro affetto;
> lagrima ancor non mi bagnava il petto né rompea il sonno, et quel che in me non era mi pareva un miracolo in altrui Lasso, che son? che fui? La vita el fin, e 'l dì loda la sera; ché sentendo il crudel di ch' io ragiono infin allor percossa di suo strale non essermi passato oltra la gonna, prese in sua scorta una possente Donna ver cui poco giamai mi valse o vale ingegno o forza o dimandar perdono; ei duo mi trasformaro in quel ch' i' sono, facendomi d'uom vivo un lauro verde che per fredda stagion foglia non perde.
> (ll. 21–40)

I say that since the day when Love gave me the first assault many years had passed, so that I was changing my youthful aspect; and around my heart frozen thoughts had made almost an adamantine hardness which my hard affect did not allow to slacken:
no tear yet bathed my breast nor broke my sleep, and what was not in me seemed to me a miracle to others. Alas, what am I? what was I? The

end crowns the life, the evening the day. For that cruel one of whom I speak, seeing that as yet no blow of his arrows had gone beyond my garment, took as his patroness a powerful Lady, against whom wit or force or asking pardon has helped or helps me little: those two transformed me into what I am, making me of a living man a green laurel that loses no leaf for all the cold season.

Quis tenebit cor hominis? The laureate who would show his heart in letters becomes (is effaced by) the name he mimes; the *laurel* crown that encircles his head effects his metamorphosis into the root-bound object of his own desire, and, with a particularly keen insight into the psychology of obsession, Augustine's spirit surrounded—literally—by flesh ("*caro concupisceret adversus spiritum et spiritus adversus carnem*") is metamorphosed into Petrarch's heart surrounded—literally—by frozen thoughts ("*d'intorno al mio cor pensier gelati*"). The poet, who in this poem is driven through the metonymies of his desire as through the text of Ovid's *Metamorphoses,* is finally reduced entirely to writing a cold, dead [*fredda*] thing, written out on a leaf [*foglia*] of paper, as in the illustratively metonymic, "Would you hand me my Petrarch; it's on the shelf?" [46]

The history of the literary subject passes from the lyric Imaginary into the Symbolic through the insistence of this Petrarchan letter, but the Petrarchan subject continues to be taken for an image and so gets stuck in a hieroglyphic stasis that leads in the direction of the emblem, of Herbert's picture poems, of Pound's mystification of the Chinese ideogram, and of a certain deconstructive tendency to privilege metonymy over metaphor in the interest of an untenable rigor regarding the divisibility of the signifier. [47] As Harrison argues, it is Dante's substitution of an anticipatory silence for the apocalyptic closure of Augustine's reabsorption into the Word, rather than Petrarch's discovery of the insistence of the letter, that stands in the line of development whereby the essential or ideal lyric "I" is finally foregone and replaced by another "I," which knows itself to be the (necessarily belated) subject of history. [48] As the subject of a narrative of (historical) causation, this latter "I" identifies itself with the ever self-differing and self-deferring accumulation of its temporal experiences. What Petrarch represents and what so captivated the subsequent poets of "Petrarchism" was the intrusion of language into the imaginary field, the moment of the paternal "no," and the sense of loss incurred when the goal of a perfect representation, a representation in kind, is relinquished. The originary ideal that had been sought in the captivated reflections of the poet's face in the poem's representation of his mistress's eyes, the paralyzing coming together of subject and object in the mirror of the poem must then be transmuted to the writing of temporal experience on the poet's face, as he remakes and masters the natural world through his actions in time.

6

The duration of this passage from the subject of lyric Truth (which struggles to deny its extension in time) to the subject of narrative history (which represents the self as the protagonist of the story of its acts and choices) is marked by a number of curious literary forms that, like *La Vita Nuova,* the *Rime sparse,* and the English sonnet sequences, combine narrative and lyric or assemble lyrics into implicit narratives. These poems differ from the sonnet sequences, however, in that they relinquish the desire to encounter and reify the origin of the speaking voice in favor of a rhetoric that highlights and explores the internal division of a self conceived of as suspended between an originary essence and the story of its accumulating worldly experiences. Where Augustine had imagined life outside the Book as a spastic de-cadence, these poems tend to reinscribe the exigencies of temporal succession as yet another supplement of the lost origin.

Andrew Marvell is, to my mind, the most thematically reflective practitioner of these hybrid forms. Therefore, to conclude my synoptic narration of the literary emergence into history of the subject of historical narrative, I will at this point anticipate the discussion of Marvell in chapter 6 by briefly examining the narration of time in the mower poems. This group of four poems plays out (and plays with) the coupled stories of humankind's doubled division from nature and the homogeneous cycles of time that nature presents: the variations of night and day, the recurrent succession of the seasons, the seasonal rhythms of agricultural work. In the mower poems the reflexive compulsion to repeat that defines the characteristic curve of Petrarchan desire through the ideal eye of an unattainable love is projected and disrupted by the literary historical play of genres. The georgic mower, a worker in a rapidly industrializing agriculture, finds himself subjected to a pastoral desire that serves only to underline his dispossession from an already nostalgic pastoral otium.[49]

In "The Mower Against Gardens," the planting of the formal garden is but one facet of the business of agriculture (whose industrial face is meticulously described in the meadow sequences of "Upon Appleton House"). This appropriation of seed and soil to the representation of human will and imagination repeats the Fall even as it moves technologically to overcome the Fall's effects:

> Luxurious Man, to bring his Vice in use,
>   Did after him the World seduce:
> And from the fields the Flow'rs and Plants allure,
>   Where Nature was most plain and pure.
> He first enclos'd within the Gardens square
>   A dead and standing pool of Air:
> And a more luscious Earth for them did knead,
>   Which stupifi'd them while it fed. (ll. 1–8) [50]

The corruption of Nature, here represented in the aesthetic space of the Garden (a georgic shadow cast over the aestheticized arcadia of pastoral), culminates when the seed's unfolding of its originary essence is betrayed by and into the historical world of a human agency attained through the enclosure and manipulation of nature's bounty. I call this manipulation narcissistic because the design of the formal garden and its hybrid plants points away from nature and its putatively divine source and toward the artifice of its human creator. As the epideictic poem inevitably subverts its object by doubling it, pointing not to her, but to the poet's skill in representing her, the formal garden appropriates nature as the sign of the gardener's skill. The Augustinian metaphorics of the Book of Nature, in which God is read out of his creations, is thus implicitly defeated by a human agency that appropriates nature to signify itself. This reading would seem to place too heavy a load on Damon's rustic back, except that it brings us very close to the generative core of Marvell's pervasive reflection on the ways in which the human subject at once contains and is contained within its perceptions and conceptions, especially his preoccupation, as in "The Garden," with the human mind as that part of nature which contains the concept of nature entirely within it. If man as the image of God is part of a natural order that signifies God, then the appropriation of nature as an image of human agency is a diversion or curving of the image back on itself—that is, an idol.

Damon's evocation of the supplementary excess added by man's manipulation of a divinely perfected nature culminates in a curious reversal of Augustine's desexualization of procreation. Floral hybridization figures, for Damon, the insinuation of perverse human desire into the reproduction of nature "according to its kind." Man deals:

> between the Bark and Tree,
> Forbidden mixtures there to see.
> No Plant now knew the Stock from which it came;
> He grafts upon the Wild the Tame:
> That the uncertain and adult'rate fruit
> Might put the Palate in dispute. (ll. 21–26)

This betrayal of destined kind to the historical exigence of human will is reflected in the fate of the hybrid flowers and the hybrid poem, which puts in dispute the difference between pastoral and georgic decorum: "The Pink grew then as double as his Mind; / The nutriment did change the kind" (ll. 9–10). A divinely ordered and orderly Nature, which had once contained man's experience, is now contained by it, transformed by his work into the doubling mirror of his doubled Mind, and so transformed, not coincidentally, by an improvident nutriment. Thus, man's seduction of the flowers with a "more Luscious Earth" repeats Satan's seduction of humankind with an apple, and Damon's very topical complaint is immediately recontextualized as a contemporary iteration of the fall of nature consequent to the Fall of man.

This categorical ascription of meaning to the luxury of hybrid gardens is a delicate pivot in the distribution of the poem's moral and satirical investments. On the one hand, Damon, as Protestant preacher, deploring the ornamentation of the garden as unwholesome and self-involved, is too facile. Damon's recapitulation of the Fall narrative is too much the articulation of an unexamined habit of thought to be taken seriously as a reduction of contemporary social life to universal pattern, especially, as Damon himself seems too self-involved to be listening closely to his own language. But on the other hand, the rhetoric of seventeenth-century Protestant commonplaces that draws Damon's complaint against contemporary tastes into the recapitulating *grand récit* of the Fall casts its shadow across the contemporary landscape.

The strictures against "enclosed" gardens exceed the confines of Damon's soliloquy and extend to more politically potent forms of *enclosure,* until the garden becomes, as it had in Shakespeare's history plays, a synecdoche of the nation.[51] In typically Marvellian fashion, Damon's garden is a small thing that encloses a larger one within it: the taste for hybrid flowers in the garden instances, not analogically but literally, the ethos of the market that surrounds it. In this new and perennially falling world, the "natural" stability of use value is sacrificed to the situational fluctuations of exchange value. The positive value of usefulness, which expresses a relation between the consumer and his or her need, is overtaken by a relative value, set by a disembodied market in which all things are measured against each other and the specificity of need is submerged in the generality of desire.[52]

Man's narcissistic interest in his own aestheticized creation, in turning upon itself, turns away from the God-given bounty that sustains it, encountering, in Damon's garden, a figure of its own excess in the specificity of a peculiar historical example:

> The Tulip, white, did for complexion seek;
>   And learn'd to interline its cheek:
> Its Onion root they then so high did hold,
>   That one was for a Meadow sold. (ll. 13–16).

The lines refer to the "tulip mania" of 1634–37, when "the bulbs were sold in Holland by weight like precious stones: a bulb of 10 grammes is recorded to have fetched 5,500 florins, i.e. 550 times the value of a sheep." [53] The metonymic slide from tulip bulb to meadow, from florins to sheep, unpacks the transposition of desire to its object and the inability of the object to support the desire invested in it. The historical moment indicated in Marvell's poem is thus made to evoke in miniature an economic and social history of the mid-seventeenth-century: the increase in aggressive agricultural technology, the enclosure movement, the displacement of agricultural workers, the gradually developing Protestant tendency to identify the accumulation of material goods and moral good.

The "natural" voice of pastoral never names itself in this poem, although implicitly Damon presumes to speak with it when he rebukes "luxurious Man," the "third person," who is neither the mower nor his dialogic partner. The allusion to the tulip as an exchange value marks a precise moment in the poem's articulation of Damon's subjectivity.[54] In the poem, the *art* of gardening derived initially from man's desire to procreate and see his desire: "to bring his Vice in use," where "use" has the force of "increase" in the sense of *usury*, and in the more candidly sexual sense embedded in the *uxor* phonically implicit in *luxurious*. But through the inflated exchange value of the tulip bulb, we cross (synecdochically) from an economy of the image to an economy of the sign. We pass from man's desire to see his image reproduced in a subjugated nature that visibly testifies to his presence, that is, in its simplest terms, man's desire to leave his mark on the world, to the circulating signifiers of his desire in the endlessly proliferating exchange of goods.[55] The exchange of the tulip's "onion root" for a meadow is explicitly a moment in which the answer to a literal need, the food that the meadow might produce, is sacrificed in the interest of a metaphorical, if conspicuous, consumption. As a georgic worker who exists for himself in contradistinction to the shepherd whose socially productive sheep the meadow would have nourished, Damon's inability or refusal to speak the first person figures antithetically doubled meanings: on the one hand, the unity of the mower and the uncorrupted nature he seeks to represent and, on the other, the suppression of productive labor as it is congealed (to use Marx's term) in the tulip bulb's inflated exchange value.

Thus, the self-involvement of "luxurious Man" leads to the alienation of the desire he had sought to make visible, as it had been briefly made visible in Dante's burning heart before being disseminated into the insistent letters of Petrarch's "frozen leaf." Man's coming "between the bark and tree" perversely reenacts Augustine's allegorical unsexing of the injunction to increase and multiply, substituting a violent imposition of the will for sex and its pleasures:

> And in the Cherry he does Nature vex,
>> To procreate without a Sex.
> 'Tis all enforc'd; the Fountain and the Grot;
>> While the sweet Fields do lye forgot:
> Where willing Nature does to all dispence
>> A wild and fragrant Innocence. (ll. 29–34)[56]

In the end, after his strenuous if largely unconscious and implicit excursus into the politics of the garden in contemporary social life, Damon sidesteps the alienating implications of a subjectivity suppressed under the exteriorized collectivity of the "market," forgoing his "I" in favor of a determinately indeterminate "us": "we mowers" but perhaps, also, "you (reader) and I, (Andrew Marvell, the MP from Hull, that Yorkshire nexus of commerce and agricultural 'improvement')":

> And *Fauns* and *Faryes* do the Meadows till,
>   More by their presence then their skill.
> Their Statues polish'd by some ancient hand,
>   May to adorn the Gardens stand:
> But howso'ere the Figures do excel,
>   The *Gods* themselves with us do dwell. (ll. 35–40)

The nostalgia for classical form, expressed in the enclosed garden and in the neopastoral poem that represents and condemns it, is here melded to the nostalgia for the relief from georgic labor, for a time when fauns and faryes tilled the meadows, giving them nature's form rather than man's. But as they are recognized, both nostalgias are *disfigured* by Damon's opposition of the idolatry of ornamental statues ("howso'ere the *Figures* do excel") to the dwelling of the gods. Thus topical narration is again enclosed within the universal narrative of the Fall.

In "Damon the Mower," the mower is dispossessed from the natural world of a lost pastoral Arcadia, not by the "graft" of modernity, but by the lyrical desire inspired by Juliana. The third-person frame of the first three stanzas places Damon within a sunburned pastoral landscape that mirrors his emotional state and names Juliana as the cause of the "unusual Heats" that scorch mower and meadow alike. In the fourth stanza the mower's "I" finally emerges at the borderline between the exterior and interior heats:

> Tell me where I may pass the Fires
> Of the hot day, or hot desires.
> To what cool Cave shall I descend,
> Or to what gelid Fountain bend?
> Alas! I look for Ease in vain,
> When Remedies themselves complain.
> No moisture but my Tears do rest,
> Nor Cold but in her Icy Breast. (ll. 25–32)

Once again the subjectivity implied by the mower's "I" is strenuous. It emerges at the border between internal and external fires, but the agency it represents is the faculty to imagine and to desire an escape from the very heat that has generated it. "When Remedies themselves complain," they do not remedy because they speak. Moisture and coolness are attributes of things, but within the context of pastoral complaint, which defines the boundaries within which Damon speaks, and therefore is, the mower's tears and Juliana's icy breast are no longer, in themselves, things at all. The remedy of "things" has been sacrificed so that "things" may speak, signifying the mower's sorrow and Juliana's scorn. Thus, the mower's "I," which is his signifier, comes out, so to speak, only by imagining and desiring its withdrawal. It comes out offering itself in dialogue to an absent "you," who is in turn the source of its distress and whose desired presence it cannot endure. Its essence is to disappear, and the mower's complaint, like those of Dante and Petrarch, sets before the reader its struggle with the paradoxical task of *showing* that thing—its momentary self—which by its nature disappears.

Damon's strategies in this struggle are mapped out in the ensuing stanzas. In stanza 5 he sends Juliana tokens, metonymies of himself, that are also metaphors: the harmless snake, the visibly changeable chameleon, and honey-tipped oak leaves. The demand for recognition made through these tokens is implicitly a demand that his figures be read, that these things be understood metonymically—as coming from Damon—and metaphorically—as making visible his harmless, variably hued, sweet, and poetic nature. When both these demands are refused ("Yet Thou ungrateful hast not sought / Nor what they are, nor who them brought" [ll. 39-40]), when his signs remain things and "you" refuses to sustain the discourse of his "I," Damon appeals, in stanzas 6 and 7, to his existence in a sphere beyond dialogue. Shifting from the first to the third person ("I am the Mower *Damon,* known / Through all the Meadows I have mown" [ll. 41-42]), he asserts that he is recognized by nature if not by Juliana—the morn moistens him with dew (an uncomplaining remedy), the sun licks off his sweat, and the dew collected in the cowslips bathes his feet. Still, nature cannot interpellate him as subject; it cannot ask the "who are you?" to which Damon's "I am the Mower Damon" would be a reply.[57]

Damon's interpellation as mower remains pre- or protosubjective so long as he mystifies his relation to the grass as belonging to the natural (Imaginary) rather than the social (Symbolic) order. The absence of Juliana—around whom he loops his desire in the hope that it will be returned to him in the form of a question from her, "Who is my desire?," to which he may answer,

"I am"—maintains him in the state of self-absence or alienation in relation to his desire to be the object she desires. This alienation, which precipitates his identification with the subject of pastoral complaint, supports his quasi-natural interpellation as the mower and enables the neopastoral discourse of the poems. Her presence, paradoxically, makes present the estrangement of his desire and renders that interpellation and its discourse insupportable.[58] As Dante's miraculous and unspeakable vision of Beatrice finally elicits silence, the coming of Juliana is presented as an iteration of death—although, of course, the similarity of structures does not preclude or minimize the vast difference in tone between the witty and ironic mower poems and the engaged intensity of *La Vita Nuova*.

Damon moves closer to a community of symbolic discourse when he compares his work favorably to that of the "piping Shepherd." The final line of stanza 7 grounds this symbolic union in a prototypical commodity exchange through which the exchange value of georgic and pastoral laborers become comparable: "And though in Wooll more poor then they, / Yet am I richer far in Hay" (ll. 55–56).

But in stanza 8, apparently still desiring and not obtaining a reciprocal interpellation from Juliana, Damon turns to an interrogation of his own image as he imagines it would appear in Juliana's eye. He seeks to see that he is not "so deform'd to sight" by looking in the curve of his scythe, which reflects his face as the crescent moon reflects (but partially) the sun: "If in my Sithe I looked right; / In which I see my Picture done, / As in the crescent Moon the Sun" (ll. 57–60).[59]

This curious image of an image in which Damon appears to rely on a mirror that reduces a circle to a crescent, and, moreover, on an image whose traditional association with death will be confirmed in the poem's final line ("For Death thou art a Mower too"), disrupts the lyric "I" of the poem, leaving us to wonder about the author's attitude toward his character. Does Marvell appear here, giving Damon an unapt simile, so that the character may speak more than he knows? The image of the image in the scythe is a partial one. It is as much of the sun as the crescent moon may hold, and, as such, it represents with astonishing precision the transitional tension between epideictic metaphor and narrative metonymy, between Augustine's vision of an unchanging eternity, perceived by man as folded into time, and the curve of a temporal movement, along the edge of a sharpened blade, through life to death.

It is, moreover, yet once more removed from the object to which it points. The image of the sun in the crescent moon, pointing to the image of the mower in the scythe, points to the image presumed to be returned to the mower from the eye of Juliana, and, as such, the "deformity" it seeks to rectify is implicit in the scorn with which she has responded to Damon's wooing. Thus, the partiality of the sun's image in the crescent moon, transferred to the deformation of the mower's image in the scythe, figures the subjectivity—in the modern sense—of his image in Juliana's eye, the affective bias (in this case, scorn) of her response (or nonresponse) to him. The self-destructive incorporation of this subjectivity, which subsumes Damon's imaginations both of Juliana and himself, is figured in the use of the verb "glance" to convey the action of the scythe when the mower mows (harvests) himself:

> While thus he threw his Elbow round,
> Depopulating all the Ground,
> And, with his whistling Scythe, does cut
> Each stroke between the Earth and Root,
> The edged Stele by careless chance
> Did into his own Ankle glance;
> And there among the Grass fell down,
> By his own Scythe, the Mower mown. (ll. 73–80)

The wounding glance of the scythe, which here figures time as well as death, once again makes literal a metaphoric captivation by the visual glance—the glance that glancingly observes Juliana or Laura or Beatrice glancing back.[60] The administration of this glancing cut is temporally complex. Stanza 9 ends in the very Petrarchan lyric present, "Sighing I whet my Scythe and Woes" (l. 72). Stanza 10, however, reintroduces the third-person frame and the past tense of retrospective narrative. The sequence of verbs is "threw . . . depopulating . . . does cut . . . did glance . . . fell . . . mown." While, in conformity to the present tenses of the previous stanza, "depopulating," "does cut," and the verbal adjective "whistling" impart an iterative presence to the motion of the scythe and the mower, the preterit verbs "did," "fell," and "mown" retrospectively specify the narrative moment in which the iterative mowing issues in a temporally determined event, the self-wounding of the mower.

No longer captured and preserved from time by the loop of contemplation, the mower's "I" is mown by his own device: "For She my Mind hath so displac'd / That I shall never find my home" ("The Mower to the Glo-Worms," ll. 15–16). Where the mower's mind "was once the true survey / Of all these Meadows fresh and gay; / And in the greenness of the Grass / Did see its Hopes as in a Glass" ("The Mower's Song," ll. 1–4), his (rhetorical) desire is now subjected to the vengeance of time in which "Flow'rs, and Grass, and I and all, / Will in one common Ruine fall" (ll. 21–22). In the refrain of "The Mower's Song," the commensurability of the mower's work on the grass and Juliana's work on the mower recalls the allusion in "The Garden" (l. 40) to Isaiah's "all flesh is grass," while the evocation of the common ruin, in the same poem, looks forward to the complex origins of "Upon Appleton House."[61]

Given the familiar etymology of "Ruine" as a nominalized form of the Latin verb *ruere,* to fall, we may see in Damon's revenge yet another version of the mower mown. The "common Ruine," that is, the Fall, precedes historical time, which issues from it. Having fallen with Adam, humankind and nature, "Flow'rs, and Grass, and I and all," will continue falling until they have fallen into the ruin with which history — that is their fall — begins.

Such a reading of these lines would appear too precise, too precious, were it not reiterated by the peculiar tense sequence of the poem's refrain. The refrain in stanzas 1–4 reads: "When Juliana *came,* and She / What I do to the Grass, *does* to my Thoughts and Me" (my emphasis). Having once come in the past, Juliana, like the Fall, becomes the manifest *vision* of the present. Damon's captivated thoughts are cut short, returned always to her foregone image, until his inattention to his work joins him to the grass — in "one common ruine."

But in the poem's final stanza:

> And thus, ye Meadows, which have been
> Companions of my thoughts more green,
>   Shall now the Heraldry become
> With which I shall adorn my Tomb;
>   For Juliana *comes,* and She
> What I do to the Grass, does to my Thoughts and Me.

Imagining the death of the mower's "I," Damon foretells that what he had seen and cut, the Meadows, will be that by which he is seen, the heraldry that will adorn his tomb. But when the mower's eye sees that the companions of his green thoughts may now only be spoken to mark the place where he had been, "Juliana comes." Rather like Freud's grandson, who, in *Beyond the Pleasure*

Principle, replaces his mother with a spool, desire, speaking at last the present tense of the "common Ruine," has replaced Juliana with Damon's imagination of her, mastered her absence by bringing her into the timeless present of the lyric, and so, ironically, Damon seizes his own subjectivity by imagining her image of him.[62] In that moment, however, lyric time also knows itself as the representative of the glance it incorporates as its generative core—the glance that announces the moment of death.

Marvell's peculiarly self-enclosing metaphors remark the rhetorical supplement out of which Petrarchan desire is crafted. Recognizing that the poetic self is always a precisely rhetorical excess, proclaiming its identity with the mimed ideal from a temporally situated, yet unrepresentable, point outside the mimesis, Marvell turns the figure of metaphor over on itself to enfold the radically exigent aspect of history in the *remarkable* moment before its formalization as narrative. Thus, he catches and meditates on the historically determined moment in which the poetic subject is constrained by the New Science, the new technology, the market economy, the immense, largely unnameable, and not at all unified or homogenous forces of material culture—made synecdochically present in and through the allusion to the great tulip mania—to pass from the image of its self-presence into the unfolding recesses of its implacable sentences.

Part Two ∽

And thus it was: I writing of the Way
And race of Saints in this our Gospel-day
Fell suddenly into an Allegory
About their Journey, and the way to Glory;
In more than Twenty things, which I set down:
This done, I Twenty more had in my Crown;
And They again began to multiply,
Like sparks that from the coals of Fire do flie:
Nay then, thought I, if that you breed so fast,
I'll put you by your selves, lest you at last
Should prove *ad infinitum,* and eat out
The Book that I already am about.

Chapter 4

Spenser and the Metonymies of Virtue: A Case of History

1

In the first scene of *Othello,* Roderigo asks why, if Iago truly hates the Moor, he would choose to follow him. Iago replies in part:

> I follow him to serve my turn upon him.
> We cannot all be masters, nor all masters
> Cannot be truly follow'd. . . .
>
> . . . . .
>
> It is as sure as you are Roderigo,
> Were I the Moor, I would not be Iago.
> In following him, I follow but myself;
> Heaven is my judge, not I for love and duty,
> But seeming so, for my peculiar end.[1]

Shakespeare is not the principal subject of this chapter. His presence, here at the beginning, will be the first of several deferrals along the road to a discussion of *The Faerie Queene.* This delay in getting to the text is neither altogether strategic nor stylistically elective. Rather, I will be following the theme of deferral, or belatedness, in the early modern period (in Shakespeare, Tasso, and Spenser) and in our own (in psychoanalysis and the historicist critique of psychoanalysis). I will be arguing that a specifiable and unavoidable structure of deferral is integral to Spenser and to the historicist and psychoanalytic contexts through which I will be viewing *The Faerie Queene.* In a peculiarly thematic way, the multiple deferrals evident in my own critical path exemplify — even as they seek to explain — why it is that both Spenser and his critics sometimes seem to have difficulty getting to the Spenser.

I begin, then, with these lines from *Othello* because of the exemplary way in which Iago uses the spatial/temporal metaphors of following, turning and ending to relate the *social* categories of master and servant to the *psychological* categories of self and other. Recent historicist scholarship might see something broadly characteristic of Renaissance culture in Iago's notion of a psychic self partially independent of the social order and able to manipulate that order by moving around in space and time.[2] Iago follows Othello only "to serve his turn upon him," and although this inverted service, in which the master serves the servant's turn, serves Iago's "*peculiar* end," it also *exemplifies* how some masters are (un)truly followed. Iago's logic and experience have taught him that a servant who knows how to turn while seeming to follow comes, through his service, into possession of his own identity as master: "In following him, I follow but myself."

In turning from the attempt in chapter 3 to construct a historical bridge between Augustinian and Lacanian constructions of the ego to an attempt to follow the turns of Iago's service, I also hope to serve my own peculiar end, which, in this chapter, is to explore the implications of what I take to be a historically and formally determined resemblance between the turns and ends of Spenser's Renaissance narrative and those of the psychoanalytic case history. The point of such an exercise is neither to elicit from Freud, Spenser's meaning, nor to identify the ways in which Spenser's meaning must exceed or elude Freud's interpretive procedures. It is rather, to understand the peculiar intimacy of Renaissance narrative practice and psychoanalytic interpretation by locating both within the same literary, historical (that is, literary *and* historical) event, and, by so doing, to begin to move from the lyric snapshots offered in Part 1 to the episodic and retrospective narrative history of Part 2. By opening a parenthesis that begins with Spenser and closes with Freud, I hope to establish a context of retrospection in which the snapshots may be sequentially arranged as episodes in a narrative literary history. The aim of this narrative is to illuminate some of the relationships of continuity and difference that inhere between *The Faerie Queene* and what may be constructed as its literary and historical contexts *and* to support a continued reflection on the relations between the causal or determinative aspects of history and the contingent and aleatory elements out of which history is fashioned and which history comes, finally, to occlude.

The immediate critical context for what may seem at first an arbitrary procedure is an exemplary episode in the recent efforts of Renaissance studies to be historical. In chapter 1, I indicated in general terms what I take to be the

limitations of the New Historicism. I propose now to focus on the New Historicist assertion that its understanding of the appearance of human agency as
the subject of culture is somehow inherently more historical than the understanding by psychoanalysis of the human agent as the subject of an individual
and exigently acquired unconscious — a claim, then, in the most general terms
that one methodology is more historical than another. The New Historicist
argument is made in Stephen Greenblatt's influential essay, "Psychoanalysis
and Renaissance Culture." Greenblatt begins with a general observation: "in
the study of Renaissance literature and culture: an image or text seems to invite, even to demand, a psychoanalytic approach and yet turns out to baffle
or elude that approach."[3] The putative origin of this invitation and bafflement
is, he believes, the incompatible presence in Renaissance texts of two distinct
mediations of identity, which Greenblatt finds exemplified in the records of
the contested identity of Martin Guerre.[4] In Greenblatt's reading, the court at
Toulouse in its efforts to determine which of two bodies properly corresponds
to the name and person of Martin Guerre comes ultimately to construct the
subject in question as the object of a network of communally recognized social
relations and obligations, while the imposter, Arnaud du Tilh, through the
appropriation of memories that he had acquired from various village interlocutors, vests identity in the subject's possession of his own experiences,
memories, and desires.[5] The contradiction in this case between externally
derived and subjectively assumed notions of identity leads Greenblatt to conclude that because "psychoanalysis is at once the fulfillment and effacement
of specifically Renaissance insights: psychoanalysis is, in more than one sense,
the end of the Renaissance" (p. 210).

In this view, psychoanalysis is the end of the Renaissance because it takes
for its subject precisely the historically self-possessed individual who has been
regarded traditionally as the product of the Renaissance and, more recently,
as the agent of Renaissance self-fashioning. By theorizing (seeing whole) the
subject of possessive individualism, psychoanalysis completes and thus ends
the Renaissance construction — in and as history — of just such a subject. Articulating a late stage in the "slow, momentous transformation of the middle
term [joining body and name] from 'property' to 'psyche' " (p. 221), psychoanalysis marks the fulfillment of the Renaissance invention of the subject as
ego and then reinscribes Renaissance history as the necessary expression of
the ego created by these very events. Greenblatt concludes from this that

psychoanalysis depends on and is thus controlled by the material history of Renaissance culture, which precedes and enables it:

> The consequence, I think, is that psychoanalytic interpretation seems to follow upon rather than to explain Renaissance texts. If psychoanalysis was, in effect, made possible by (among other things) the legal and literary proceedings of the sixteenth and seventeenth centuries, then its interpretive practice is not irrelevant to those proceedings, nor is it exactly an anachronism. But psychoanalytic interpretation is causally belated, even as it is causally linked: hence the curious effect of a discourse that functions *as if* the psychological categories it invokes were not only simultaneous with but even prior to and themselves causes of the phenomena of which in actual fact they were the result. (p. 221)

Thus, in Greenblatt's view, psychoanalysis follows the Renaissance only to serve its turn upon it, and this turn is a metalepsis in which the Renaissance text appears (paradoxically) to repeat and fulfill its own psychoanalytic theorization. Because Greenblatt recognizes and values the explanatory power deriving from what he takes to be the peculiar historical intimacy of psychoanalysis and Renaissance culture, he calls on psychoanalysis to "redeem" its "causal belatedness" by historicizing its own procedures and thus becoming a properly historical criticism (ibid.). What would such a historicization entail? Greenblatt's expressed concern is with "psychological categories," but he assumes that these categories are made possible by barely specified "legal and literary proceedings," which, I suspect, he would identify as "material history." However, the evidence he adduces suggests the contrary as well. The court at Toulouse seems to be as baffled by Arnaud du Tilh's assumption of Martin Guerre's psyche as psychoanalysis may be baffled by the social exigencies of Renaissance culture. Might we more accurately imagine a situation in which both the court and its belated interpreter are adjusting their respective procedures, in which neither psychoanalysis nor Renaissance text reaches its end independently, in which, in fact, the ends that they reach are simultaneously and interdependently structured? What I am asserting here is that the New Historicist's appeal to "material history" — manifest in this case in the court's administration of laws — and the psychoanalytic categories that seem to make the success and the failure of Arnaud's imposture less inexplicable are equally belated, because both articulate an underlying structure that is too general to be identified with either of them — and which belatedly and retrospectively supports them both.[6] For me, then, it is not a question of the priority of psyche to history, but of the contemporaneous appearance of psyche and history as a literary historical event. The duration of this event is defined not simply by the narration of deferral or belatedness in Spenser (and his predecessors) but, as we shall see, by the specific way in which Spenser's narrative is thematically conscious of the structural deferral deployed within it.

Thus, I reiterate my definition of the literary historical moment as something that occurs when a specifiable rhetorical structure also comes to be taken as the order of things, and I would be inclined to distinguish, at least in a preliminary way, the deferrals of, say, the *Odyssey* from those of *The Faerie Queene* on the basis of the fact that the rhetorical structure of the former has become what one might call the grammar of the latter. What in one is a way to tell a story has become in the other the story that must be told. My interest is thus less in arguing about the claims to historicity of the New Historicism and psychoanalysis than to argue that a seriously historical consideration of the dialectic of invitation and bafflement noted by Greenblatt renders the accusation of belatedness impertinent. Historical analysis in this case identifies and describes a structure of deferral shared by Renaissance and psychoanalytic narrative that is the ground of the "belatedness effect" in both.[7] In this view, both psyche and history emerge as *literary* categories.

In an approach less preemptive than Greenblatt's, Joel Fineman relates psychoanalytic theories of desire to the appearance in the Renaissance of what Fineman calls the poetic "subjectivity effect," that is, to the appearance, especially in Shakespeare, of characters who seem to possess psychological "depth" or "interiority."[8] Fineman discusses the mutual implication of Renaissance practice and psychoanalytic theory in, among other places, an extraordinary essay, "The Sound of O in *Othello:* The Real of the Tragedy of Desire."[9] Through an intense consideration of acoustic inscriptions in Shakespeare's language, that essay corroborates, yet significantly displaces, Greenblatt's argument. Fineman locates the connection between Renaissance culture and psychoanalysis in a formally elaborated literary practice rather than a vaguely asserted set of historical events:

> As to whether we should see in Othello and Shakespeare the corroborating proof or evidence of Lacan's theorizations about subjectivity or,

instead, whether we should see in Lacan's theorizations an epiphenomenal consequence of the powerful literary subjectivity effect Shakespeare
invents toward the end of the English Renaissance: given the historical
force of the sound of O in *Othello,* I say the latter and call him, Lacan,
Shakespearean. (pp. 158–59)

Calling Lacan a Shakespearean is not exactly the same thing as calling
psychoanalysis belated with respect to Renaissance culture. Psychoanalysis
for Fineman, is "an epiphenomenal consequence" not of exigent changes in
the administration of the law of property in the Renaissance, but of a specific
linguistic practice. Of course, it can be asserted that this linguistic practice
itself arose out of (or in some complex relation to) exigencies of Renaissance
life. But the importance of Fineman's displacement is that the relation between psychoanalysis and Renaissance texts is understood to be just that: a
relationship between forms of writing.[10] The appearance of this relationship
in the Renaissance and its persistence into modernity are no less historical
than the archives of the court at Toulouse.

As we have seen, the metalepsis whereby, according to Greenblatt, psychoanalysis posits as causes of Renaissance texts categories that are in temporal
fact their products is already thematic in Marvell's trope in "The Garden" of
writing as the cause of desire:

> *Apollo* hunted *Daphne* so,
> Only that She might Laurel grow.
> And *Pan* did after *Syrinx* speed,
> Not as a Nymph, but for a Reed.[11]

Greenblatt, however, lacks the doubled irony of Marvell's lines, which refer
to literary not historical events and are thus *literally* true. The point here is
not a contention over whether or not psychoanalysis is belated with respect
to Renaissance culture but the significant fact that *belatedness* as such is, from
a formal point of view, the determining structure of psychoanalysis and Renaissance culture. Along with Shakespeare and Marvell, Freud and Lacan can
be said to share a certain understanding of desire that resides in — is mediated
by — language.

Fineman establishes a *necessary* connection between the "subjectivity effect" and the peculiar duplicity of a speech that presents itself as the falsifying

trace of an ineffable truth. Like Hamlet's "actions that a man might play" (1.2.84), this speech undermines its own referentiality by pointing to a silent interior truth that it cannot adequately represent. Fineman points out, with characteristic precision, that the practice and theory of the subject of this constitutionally duplicitous speech "derive from the disjunctive conjunction of, on the one hand, a general thematics of vision and, on the other, a general thematics of voice," that is, a chiasmic joining and disjoining that insists on the difference between what is said and what is seen ("Shakespeare's Ear," TSE, p. 224). This disjunctive conjunction registers a relation of dialectical negation existing between time and structure, between, for example, the synchrony of the visual frame and the sequential unfolding of the sentence ("The Structure of Allegorical Desire," TSE, pp. 3–31).

The narrative literary history that I propose softens Fineman's focus on the formal decay of epideictic *vision* and sharpens the focus on an ideology of narrative bildung that emerges in response to that decay. In this history the epideictic ideal of *ut pictura poesis* yields to a series of scenes giving the appearance of motion. Still life gives way to montage; the spatial aspect of Iago's turn shades into the temporal as the *end* with which he begins, his purpose or intention, is subsumed in the *end* that he achieves, that is, the tragic denouement.

In this view, slightly more elongated than Fineman's, the reception and canonization of the Shakespearean subject—which is also the subject of psychoanalysis—may be seen as part of a development away from visionary stasis and toward a dialectical narrativity in which the subject is posited as the momentary and provisional sum of its (historical) experiences. In such a view, the tension between vision and voice is recuperated within the structure of narrative as the temporal difference between plot as unfolding action and plot as retrospected design.

Othello offers something like an emblem of this dialectical narrativity. Iago follows Othello in the wars and serves his turn upon him by telling a story that Othello will follow to a *méconnaissance* of Desdemona's return of his desire. As Othello's ancient, Iago bears the general's ensign so that he follows Othello precisely *by* preceding him. Acting out in space and time the trope of his character, he carries the signifier that his leader follows as he makes his name in battle. But in the story that he, Iago, the bearer of Othello's sign, tells and Othello follows, Iago's "peculiar end" turns out to be the temporal end of Othello and Desdemona as well: the generically tragic end of *Othello*.

Iago's *end* refers to an act of narration that combines the senses of subjective intention and temporal closure with the trace of a sexual connotation. This connotation, faint at the beginning, acquires a retrospective force as we move through the text until it is unmistakably disclosed in 3.3.410–26, when Iago, for his own "peculiar" purpose, proffers to Othello an intensely homoerotic fantasy in which Iago plays the part of Desdemona:

> I lay with Cassio lately,
> And being troubled with a raging tooth,
> I could not sleep.
>
> . . . . .
>
> In sleep I heard him say, "Sweet Desdemona,
> Let us be wary, let us hide our loves";
> And then, sir, would he gripe and wring my hand;
> Cry, "O sweet creature!" then kiss me hard,
> As if he pluck'd up kisses by the roots
> That grew upon my lips; then laid his leg
> Over my thigh, and sigh'd, and kiss'd, and then
> Cried, "Cursed fate that gave thee to the Moor!"

Whose fantasy is this?[12] Iago predicates his awareness of Cassio's dream on the pain of "a raging tooth." But this (falsified or imagined) pain with which the fantasy begins is soon transferred to Othello, as its substantive effect, and the chiasmic exchange of pain and pleasure, pleasure and pain that Iago's story brings about, is soon refigured as the famous exchange of "marriage" vows between Iago and Othello at the end of the scene. Moreover, to the degree that the dream of an *illicit* sexual pleasure with Desdemona is and always was Othello's, Iago's words return to Othello an inverted representation of his own desire.[13] Whatever its thematic resonance in the play, from the point of view of structure we are justified in seeing in this strange hint of a sadistic and homoerotic desire—passed between Iago, the storyteller, and Othello, his devoted listener and the tragic hero of the story he tells—the final element in the figuration of narrative implicit in Iago's post as ancient. If Iago follows by going first, and Othello leads by following his precedent, then the indeterminate provenance of the fantasy that passes between them, with the result that Iago is advanced from sign to placeholder and wife ("Now art thou my lieutenant." "I am your own for ever" [3.3.479–80]), is the strictly narrative desire that drives each of them through the text — that is, the desire to get to the bottom of things by getting to the end of a story.

With this Shakespearean opening supplying a retrospective context, I propose in this chapter to reconsider the relations between psychoanalysis and Renaissance culture. By considering the coming together — in thematic extension and formal principle — in a late sixteenth-century narrative of a similar nexus among intentional, temporal, sexual, and generic ends, and the re-appearance of that nexus in the narration of the psychoanalytic "case history," I propose to open a set of nested boxes, embedding the Freudian "ego" in the Shakespearean character and the Shakespearean character in Spenserian allegory. By this roundabout maneuver, I hope to identify the literary historical moment of *The Faerie Queene* as an episode along the way to the determinately narrative subject that psychoanalysis represents to us as the subject of a case history — in which, typically, the structure of a particular psyche is disclosed by the accumulation of interpretable data over time. It is neither coincidental nor arbitrary that a brief detour into the evolution of the psychoanalytic case history will take us back into the question of how the successive synchronicity of a sequence of snapshots can be reconstructed as the diachronically consequential episodes of a narrative history.

2

A case history, medically speaking, is the story of an illness.[14] In reading (or constructing) the case history of an illness, we follow the turns of its symptoms and treatments until we reach an end, be it recovery or death. As we follow the plot to its comic or tragic denouement, we are usually guided by generic markers that signal the turns (e.g., the fever breaks or continues to rise; a symptom responds to treatment or it does not). A psychoanalytic case history is the story of a story.

Lacan remarks, near the beginning of his first seminar, that the novelty of psychoanalysis lies in the analysand's assumption of the story elicited and constructed in the analysis as his own.

> The subject's centre of gravity is this *present synthesis of the past which we call history.* And it is in that that we trust when it is a matter of keeping the work [of analysis] going. That is what is presupposed by analysis from its beginnings. Henceforth, there are no grounds on which to

prove that it is refuted at its end. In truth, if it isn't like that it is absolutely impossible to see anything *novel* [*nouveau*] in analysis.[15]

The irrefutable "truth" of analysis is not to be found in its correspondence
to a sequence of exterior events—a putatively material history—but in the
analysand's recognition of himself or herself as the subject of its "present synthesis of the past." The subject is thus constituted as the site of a division between a narrating voice (subject of the enunciation) and a narrative character
(subject of the utterance) in relation to the synthetic narrative generated in the
analysis. The "truth" of the analysis lies in and is validated by the analysand's
identification with his or her story to the extent that he or she feels a continuity
with a past that leads up to and beyond the present. The Freudian alternative
of remembering or repeating, in which what is not remembered is obsessively repeated, is central to this conceptualization of analysis.[16] Generically,
an analytic case history, which is the story of the emergence and acceptance
of a story, begins with symptoms that opaquely act out gaps in the history of
the analysand. As the analysis succeeds in overcoming the resistances offered
by repression, the symptoms are replaced by their corresponding memories;
the associated trauma is finally experienced and remembered rather than repressed and repeated. The narrative of narrative given in the psychoanalytic
case history differs fundamentally from the Augustinian allegory of allegory
discussed in chapter 3 insofar as psychoanalysis subordinates its return to the
origin (the repressed traumas that need to be remembered as narrative episodes) to a release from repetition. Where the Augustinian ego realizes itself
by surrendering its agency to the will of God, the psychoanalytic ego realizes
itself by seizing its agency from the subject's ability to manipulate his or her
own past. As befits allegory, the Augustinian ego seeks its end in its beginning
by converting metonymy to metaphor. The psychoanalytic ego, as the subject
of a generic narrative of historical causation, seeks to convert metaphor (the
symptoms signifying immemorial traumas) to metonymy (temporally unfolding episodes). The literary history that unfolds between these antithetical
constitutions of the self is itself the story of the displacement of meaning from
origin to end. When Iago tells Roderigo that all masters cannot be truly followed, that he serves to serve a turn, and he grounds this conviction on what
he has seen, he implies that people are what they make of their experiences.
Generals and servants are not constrained to play the roles they started with.

When, in the denouement, Othello looks for Iago's cloven hooves (5.2.286), he returns to an Augustinian conception, seeking Iago's motives in a hellish origin, just as he will shortly return to his own origins to repeat an earlier episode and "smote" the "malignant turk" he sees himself to be (5.2.351–56).[17]

There is, perhaps, a certain etymological and historical interest across the linguistic lines between French original and English translation in the relation between the destiny of the kind of narration described here and Lacan's conviction that what is "novel" in psychoanalysis is precisely the privilege accorded the closure of the analytic session as specifically the scene of a narration. This closure follows from the fact that the "truth" at issue is not the correspondence of the narrative to extralinguistic events but rather its adequacy to the affects circulated through the transference, its ability to balance action and emotion. Generically, this is also the sort of truth we expect from a novel. Analysis thus reenvisioned as a linguistic procedure, a form of writing, which follows out the route by which, as Lacan put it most provocatively at the end of the seminar on "The Purloined Letter": "a letter always arrives at its destination," discovers a truth that is and always has been literary, even generic.[18]

When we move, as we are now prepared to do, from Greenblatt's assertion of belatedness to the more pointed accusation that psychoanalysis, as a structure of belatedness, can only repeat the precedent texts it studies, we see that the testy defensiveness with which Lacan enforces the identification of analytic and literary "truth" turns out to be warranted, for it is precisely by asking what is novel in psychoanalysis—that is, by way of questioning its quasi-generic closure—that Lacan's most formidable adversary begins "Le Facteur de la Vérité":

> What happens in the psychoanalytic deciphering of a text when the latter, the deciphered itself, already explicates itself? When it says more about itself than does the deciphering . . . ? And especially when the deciphered text inscribes in itself *additionally* the scene of the deciphering? When the deciphered text deploys more force in placing onstage and setting adrift the analytic process itself, up to its very last word, for example, the truth?[19]

Greenblatt's discomfort with the tendency of psychoanalysis to represent its own categories as the "causes" of Renaissance history is here broadened from a historical to a theoretical doubt. The question of what is novel in psychoanalysis becomes the question: if, in a text, psychoanalysis finds itself, what other than itself can it find? Can the psychoanalytic case history do anything other than repeat the plot dictated by its genre? Does psychoanalysis help us to remember the literary history of the Renaissance subject or to repeat it?

Thus far we have seen that a psychoanalytic *perspective* on *The Faerie Queene* requires a glance, from Freud to Spenser, from the twentieth century to the sixteenth, and that what falls under the view of such a retrospective perspective is retrospection itself, the realization of a metalepsis of the origin as belatedness. Analysis claims to be therapeutic insofar as it transfers the structuring experiences of early childhood from the immortal present of the unconscious to the ordered retrospection of a spoken (and speakable) tale, a *tensed* narrative of desire, which, having become (more or less) conscious, restores and confirms the agency of its protagonist. The efficacy of this transference determines the progress from repetition to remembrance.

The psychoanalytic narrative of narrative given in the case history as the story of the coming to be of a transference that opens the future — *Wo Es war, soll Ich werden*[20] — by working backward to discover a lost origin is the inverted double of the history it elicits. Early on, in his introductory remarks on the presentation of Dora's case history, Freud represents this inversion as an exigence of publication rather than an analytic structure. Although he has "not yet succeeded in solving the problem of how to record for publication the history of a treatment of long duration, . . . two circumstances have come to [his] assistance" with regard to the presentation of Dora's case. First, "the treatment did not last for more than three months." Thus, this first case history was made possible by its exigent closure; its brevity urged its recording, so that the *psychoanalytic case history is at its inception a genre of fragments,* which is to say, a genre that evokes and exploits the immanent tension between a promised totality and its functional absence. Second, "the material which elucidated the case was grouped around two dreams, (one related in the middle of the treatment and one at the end)."[21] Thus, Dora's *action* in suddenly breaking off the analysis certifies her subjectivity, yet it lies outside the narrative that the analysis sought to construct, providing a closure, as it were, from outside, from a present beyond the immanent development of the tale.

The events recorded in this case history emerge *as events* only retrospectively, comprising not the chronicle of discovery but the discovery of design, the emergence of the significant as a missing element within the structure that constitutes its meaning by holding a place empty for it. "The case history itself was only committed to writing from memory after the treatment was at an end, but while my recollection of the case was still fresh and was heightened by my interest in its publication" (p. 10).

Because Dora has terminated the analysis, the first dream can be recognized as its middle and the second dream as its end. These posterior positionings privilege the dreams as the nodal points around which the elements of the analysis can be organized into an imbricated narrative and, consequently, a causal design. Freud tells us, furthermore, that the "present synthesis of the past" represented by this design has been largely abstracted from the analytic process by which it was produced (pp. 12–13).

Organized by a narrative whose events may only be defined because its fragmentary nature enforces its closure, and distilled from the timely sessions in which the presence of its history was produced, the case becomes history when, as in the recounting of a dream, the disparate elements are subjected to a secondary revision.[22] Thus, Freud reports of his report of Dora's analysis that "Nothing of any importance has been altered in it except in some places the order in which the explanations are given; and this has been done for the sake of presenting the case in a *more connected* form" (p. 10; my emphasis).

So, the "truth" spoken by Dora's many symptoms, strung out over years of life and then recapitulated in three months of analysis, emerges all at once when the symptoms are replaced by a story whose power resides in its ability to integrate each symptom as the letter of an autobiographical text, that is, to provide the etiology of the symptom in the form of a narrative of historical causation. Freud, in presenting a case history, is to construct a narrative in which Dora's symptoms legibly designate the traumatic episodes: to elicit from his patient a story that will discover and maintain a transtemporal identity, punctuated, as it were, by the rigid designator of the proper noun "Dora."[23] Had she *followed* him (followed his reading) in the metonymic transfer of that noun from the static determination of her metaphoric symptoms to the history synthesized in the analysis, he indeed would have served his turn, either for or upon her. The story told in the analysis would have become hers, as Iago's fantasy became Othello's, though not necessarily with so negative a result.

When, in the case history of the "Wolfman," Freud encounters the future persistence and retrospective organization of the past as an element of the analysis itself rather than its rhetorical disposition, he formulates it as the psychoanalytic principle of *Nachträglichkeit*—deferred action.[24] Freud constructs a chronology of the Wolfman's childhood in which the trauma of the primal scene, witnessed at eighteen months of age, remains latent in the form of mnemic traces until a symbolic structure has been acquired that allows it to come to light in the four-year-old's recurrent dream. This structure is at first iconographic, represented by the Wolfman's drawing of a tree full of strangely foxlike wolves. Freud completes the "reading" of the past by unfolding from the iconic details of this dream and its pictorial representation a narrative history of the patient's early years (pp. 39–47).

Thus, the latent dream thoughts represented by the four-year-old child's dream are always already belated. They cannot be thought outside the symbolic structure in which they first become manifest, but once thought, insofar as they disclose the very particular organization of the polarities of mother, father, and child according to which the child's symbolic universe is structured, they are seen to be the traumatic *cause* of the very structure in which they are first thought. Generalizing this account, we might say that psychoanalysis begins with the opaque disfigurements (symptoms, abnormalities, the "turn" served by a false ensign) of the present and works back to originary events, so as to understand what these recondite memorial markers will have meant, when, in the precipatory moment that ends their latency, they come to be unfolded within the signifying structure that they will have determined.[25] This *nachträglich* turn, in which the past is inscribed within the future it determines, also exemplifies the "belatedness" that Greenblatt ascribes to psychoanalysis.

For Lacan, this temporal inversion of experience and design marks the constitutive temporality of the speaking subject to which psychoanalysis pertains. "What is realized in my history is . . . the future anterior of what I shall have been for what I am in the process of becoming."[26] Thus, in his account, *Nachträglichkeit* is not only the form but also the theme of psychoanalysis; to disclose the content of the Wolfman's dream is to establish the frame in which it may be told. Under the name and in the form of the "transference," it is the generic process that produces and informs that "present synthesis of the past which we call history," which is, for Lacan, the self-validating product of psychoanalytic experience. From this perspective we may see in the belatedness of which Greenblatt complains not the anachronism of psychoanalysis with respect to Renaissance culture, but the constitutive belatedness of the (Renaissance) psyche with respect to itself.

3

Turning at last — after multiple deferrals whose mimetic relation to the construction of Spenserian narrative is not entirely adventitious — from Freud's comments on his case histories to Spenser's letter to Ralegh, we see that the *nachträglich* construction of a narrative is also — and within a similarly self-validating closure — Spenser's procedure and theme. His relation to (and of) the tale in *The Faerie Queene* anticipates psychoanalysis in its project of prospective retrospection.

> For the Methode of a Poet historical is not such, as of an Historiographer. For an Historiographer discourseth of affayres orderly as they were donne, accounting as well the times as the actions, but a Poet thrusteth into the middest, euen where it most concerneth him, and there recoursing to the thinges forepaste, and diuining of things to come, maketh a pleasing Analysis of all.[27]

In view of this uncanny congruence of theme and method, I propose to outline a Spenserian / Freudian *story* of the formation of the ego in and through desire's quest for the always deferred trace of its effaced (and constitutively barred) origin. In this reading, *The Faerie Queene* appears as an interminable (and incomplete) effort at representing — in practice — the "I," both historically specific and specific in its historicity, that will become the subject of Freud's theoretical analysis.[28] At this point we may begin to see in greater detail the substantive structural relationship that underlies Greenblatt's observation that Renaissance texts seem to demand and then to baffle psychoanalytic interpretation by asking: When psychoanalysis finds itself in Spenser's text, what has it found? Or, again still more broadly, What is *novel* in analysis?

Like the remarks prefacing Freud's presentation of the Dora case, the proems to the books of *The Faerie Queene* articulate — as a distinction between memory and fantasy — a certain anxiety about the relationship of representation to experience. What is represented is true *if it is remembered* as opposed to invented:

> Right well I wote most mighty Soueraine,
> That all this famous antique history,

> Of some th'aboundance of an idle braine
>   Will iudged be, and painted forgery,
> Rather then matter of iust memory,
>   Sith none, that breatheth liuing aire, does know,
>   Where is that happy land of Faery,
>   Which I so much do vaunt, yet no where show,
> But vouch antiquities, which no body can know. (Book 2, Proem 1)

The subject who remembers these memories is precarious, emerging at the spatio-temporal junction of retrospected *famous* antiquities that are at once vouched for but unknown and the anticipated rebuff of "some" who will have judged the matter of the book to be the superfluity of an "idle braine." Bracketed by the "Right well I wote" of anticipated rejection and the "which no body can know" of a baffled retrospection, the narrator of *The Faerie Queene* represents his text as, in a sense, the signifier of his own unconscious, especially, insofar as he certifies its authenticity by his inability to identify its sources. He speaks on the authority of what is famously incognito, known well by being unknown.[29]

The probable warrant for Spenser's dichotomy of "iust memory" and "th'aboundance of an idle braine" is the distinction made, among other places in Plato's *The Sophist,* between the icastic and the phantastic imaginations. This distinction figured largely in the continental debate over the *Orlando Furioso* and, at the time Spenser wrote, was playing or was about to play an important role in Tasso's *Discorsi del poema eroico.*[30] The icastic faculty imitates things that are, whether or not they may be sensed, while the phantastic faculty "imitates" nonexistent things (Tasso, 29). Thus, what I have called the unconscious of *The Faerie Queene,* the unseen sources in which "iust memories" are read, would have been construed by Renaissance readers as the intelligible but suprasensible realm of Platonic anamnesis. Tasso argues in contrast to Mazzoni that "Poetic imitation is thus rather icastic than phantastic: and even if it were the work of phantasy, it would be in the sense of an intellectual imagination which cannot be differentiated from the icastic." As proof that "the poet's subject is rather the true than the false," Tasso adduces an argument "derived from the teaching of St. Thomas":

> The good, the true, and the one are interchangeable, and the true is the good of the intellect. . . . Evil, therefore, not being in nature, must be

founded in goodness or some good thing, since no entirely wicked or evil thing can exist. In the same way, every multiplicity is based on unity, nor is there any multiplicity which does not participate in unity; and every falsehood is founded on truth. (Tasso, p. 33)[31]

Truth then inheres in being and the icastic sign is true, because, while it cannot be the thing to which it points, it testifies to the existence of the unseen thing it represents. Since it is of the nature of phantasy sometimes to induce us to take the false for the true, on what can Spenser base his claim to *know* that his "antique history" is "the matter of iust memorie" and thus icastic imitation (the false — because noncoincident — picture of a true thing) rather than "painted forgery" (the true picture of a false — because nonexistent — thing)? How does his allegorical sign certify that its meaning is other than itself? How does it cede its being to that which it represents?

Augustine, Thomas Aquinas, and Tasso provide an answer from within the rhetoric of the Christian ego as instituted in Augustine's *Confessions.* The evidence of the sense generates a linked chain of contiguous signs disclosed sequentially in time, but recuperable at every instant through metaphoric reference to a structured whole. Each term in this signifying chain is doubly articulated, joined by cause, effect, or simple contiguity to its neighbors in the metonymic chain and by similitude to its metaphoric origin and terminus.

Thus, to review the Augustinian examples offered in chapter 3. In the thirteenth book of Augustine's *Confessions,* the divine Word originates a signifying chain when the injunction to Adam and Eve to increase and multiply threatens to be an empty repetition of the command to the land creatures that they be "according to their kind." This moment of creative excess in which the *nous* of the divine Word spills out into time as an instance of divine speech that must be recognized as at once temporally directed and sensible, yet universal and intelligible, provokes Augustine first to join it by similitude to the previous instruction to the birds and fishes, and then to follow the birds and fishes back to the logos, which generates both words and things. Man thus arises as subjective agency when, and to the extent that, he refuses the explicit interpellation of the divine words, which refusal would leave him, like the fish, drowned in the sea of concupiscence. By making no provision for the flesh, the converted Augustine returns the divine words to their origin in the Word — something, which he accomplishes by casting his speculative autobiography in the form of prayer, addressing the book not to its human reader but to a divine "thou."

The allegory of the birds and fishes, we will recall, recapitulates Augustine's conversion by a randomly chosen but divinely appropriated passage from the Epistles of Paul in an action of reading that brought together the metonymic reiteration of a generic conversion narrative and the metaphoric ascription of a voice in the street—the voice of a neighbor boy or girl—to a divine vocation to "take up and read." What I have called (generically) the Augustinian ego is, then, the "I" that emerges in the fold between time and eternity, the "I" that—through linguistic and conceptual processes that it construes as both within and beyond itself—answers to the call of the eternal as it is mediated by the contiguous signs encountered in the world of the senses and obeys the voice of an unknown child because it is the voice of God. This "I" constitutes itself as the point at which the contiguous metonymies of the signifying chain yield the metaphoric identity of all words in the divine Word.[32] The constitutive agency of the Augustinian subject is historical precisely in the sense that it posits itself as that temporal point at which, and through which, what seems random, contingent, or merely anecdotal in the becoming of the sensible world is taken up into the universal truth of being.[33]

The truth that Tasso claims for icastic imitation resides precisely in the ability of the soul to "remember" what the senses never saw and to reproduce that memory in others through the mediation of sensible signifiers, what Tasso refers to as signs having "the power to perfect" (*Discourses*, p. 32). Thus, the imitative arts are true insofar as they conduct the spectator through the material signs out of which they must be constructed to an ineffable and universal truth, which he or she always knew without knowing it.

Tasso spells out the mechanics of this double articulation of sensible and intelligible meaning in the "Allegory" prefacing the *Gerusalemme Liberata:*

> *Heroicall Poetrie* (as a liuing Creature, wherein two natures are co-nioined) is compounded of *Imitation* and *Allegorie:* with the one she allureth vnto her the mindes and eares of men, and maruellously delighteth them; with the other, either in vertue or knowledge, she instructeth them. And as the heroically written *Imitation* of an *Other* is nothing else, but the patterne and image of humane action: so the *Allegorie* of an Heroicall Poeme is none other than the glasse and figure of humane life.[34]

Like the chain of metonyms comprising the generation of fishes in the thirteenth book of Augustine's *Confessions,* the narrative of connected actions in the heroic poem is presented to the senses: "*Imitation* regardeth the *Actions* of man subiected to the outward senses, and about them being principally imployed, seeketh to represent them with affectuall and expressive phrases, such as liuely set before our corporall eies the things represented." But, like the history of Israel narrated in the Bible, the imitated actions, subject to rules of coherency and probability in terms of their relation one to the other, are further appropriated as the signifiers of an ineffable signified: "On the other side, *Allegorie* respecteth the passions, the opinions and customes, not onely as they doe appeare, but principally in their being hidden inward; and more obscurely doth express them with notes (as a man may say) misticall, such as only the vnderstanders of the nature of things can fully comprehend." Thus, the constitutive duplicity of the allegorical sign—the truth of which depends on its not being itself—opens an interior or "inward" space that belongs at once to the reader and the text, or to the always belated coming together of the reader and the text within the unity of "the nature of things."

In some ways the Renaissance proposes to handle icastic poems the way that Freudians handle dreams—as repositories of material signifiers that may be traced through other, associated signifiers to a memory that has remained unthought because it cannot be directly represented. Like dreams, these poems only give up their latent truth if their superficial falsity is first recognized. Their claim of truth lies not in the mimesis of action, but in the metaphoric realization of that action on another scene. There is, therefore, a determinately negative relation between the mimetic and the conceptual in allegory so conceived; truth only emerges when the former gives up its pretense to represent anything other than the figural vehicle of the latter.[35] The resistance internal to allegory is thus the resistance of the real, the exigent detail that exceeds or escapes conceptual assimilation and yet remains as a determined and determining textual element.[36]

Two additional points are noteworthy here. (1) Since the truth disclosed by the allegorical reading of a heroic poem is universal and eternal and that disclosed in the latent content of a dream is an unconscious and therefore timeless thought, in both poem and dream the latent or allegorical content surfaces in the *literary* present tense: The *Gerusalemme Liberata*'s Goffredo always, right now and forever, "stands for *Vnderstanding,* & particularly for that vnderstanding, which considereth not the things necessarie, but the mutable and which may diuersly happen, & those by the wil of God," and the foxy wolves in the Wolfman's dream always and forever manifest the witnessed "coitus a tergo" of his parents. (2) Given this unfolding of time into a timeless present, the "truth" of both dream and poem depends upon the unity and coherence that corresponds to the presence of all the relevant elements in a single picture; that is the projected moment of "truth" occurs as a lyric transumption of narrative. Recalling the terms established in chapter 2, we can say that "truth" appears when metaphor puts the brakes on the metonymic engine.

4

The memories in Spenser's dream book, like those in Freud's, include *introspections* of archaic events that have become audible only after the residues of a future history have been appropriated to their representation and the result has been subjected to a secondary revision that lends them narrative coherence. The promise of this coherence is present in, but formally outside, the structure of the tale. The letter to Ralegh indicates that Spenser's text begins (like Iago) with the pursuit of an end: "the generall end . . . of all the booke is to fashion a gentleman or noble person in vertuous and gentle discipline" (p. 167), but it also (infinitely) defers the implementation of this program by launching the phantom twelfth book as the place in which all the narrative episodes and maddening *entrelacements* leading to the formation of "a gentleman *or* noble person" will be resolved.[37] This resolution, which marks the aim and the desire as well as the temporal *end* of the tale, comprises a return to the origin of desire in the court of Gloriana.[38]

Choosing as its originary scene an earthly (albeit a Faery) rather than a heavenly court, Spenser's narrative is less ambitious but more politically pointed than Augustine's or Tasso's. Augustine's conversion represents a moment that he answers as a man; it is, at least in theory, a turn away from the earthly city of the pagans to a heavenly Jerusalem that will remain comfortably beyond the temporal confines of the text. Spenser's narrative is ostensibly constructed to interpellate explicitly a gentleman and implicitly an English gentleman who will have come to build Jerusalem "in England's green and pleasant land." Spenser's obvious engagement with the political affairs of his day leads to a diffusion of allegorical containment. Rather than gathering the narrative action into an epiphanic moment of conversion, the allegory of *The*

Faerie Queene proliferates on a vertiginously multiplying number of "other scenes": the dynastic alternatives represented by the queen's manipulation of her suitors, the Irish rebellions, the reformation of the Church of England, the imperial opportunities offered by and reflected in the continental wars of religion, the national and international consequences of the trial of Mary, Queen of Scots come readily to mind.[39]

Augustine's conversion is presented as a completed action relative to the writing of the *Confessions. La Vita Nuova* and the *Rime sparse* represent the deaths of Beatrice and Laura, respectively, as past relative to the present of the narrative "I." In the *Gerusalemme Liberata,* Tasso self-consciously subordinates the Ferrarese politics of the dynastic theme to the epic action, completed and suitably remote in time and place, of the siege of Jerusalem.[40]

The Faerie Queene, on the contrary, with Spenser's insistent interaction with unfolding events during its long time of composition, just as self-consciously and insistently represents its allegorical recuperation of apparently contingent action as that which will have been completed rather than as that which has already occurred. This failure of closure is made thematic by the extravagantly proportioned fantasy poem described in the "Letter to Ralegh," with its promise of originary scenes that will not be found in any conceivably executable version of the poem. Thus, the letter to Ralegh performs a function precisely identical to that performed by Freud's prefatory comments on the case history of Dora: it constitutes what is to follow as *necessarily* a generic fragment.

The literary historical consequence of this enforced and thematic fragmentation is that the unfolding, temporalized "I," moving along the defiles of a metonymic desire, is reinscribed within the putatively allegorical scenes of the poem. Narrative escapes its allegorical containment and breaks out on the allegorical "other scene" itself. Allegory depends on a rejection of narrative as representation. The reader must understand that the meaning of the text cannot be found simply in its mimesis of action. In *The Faerie Queene,* however, the mimesis of historical events erupts onto the allegorical scene. Actions imitated on the literal level represent on the allegorical level not timeless concepts but more and different historical actions. If, as we saw in chapter 2, metonymy is the engine that drives narrative forward and metaphor the brake that brings it to a close, we might say that Spenserian allegory suffers from recurrent brake failure. Each time that metonymy reappears to interrupt allegorical closure, it requires a new metaphor and another level of allegory to negate it.

Within the metaphorics of the microcosm and the macrocosm common-place in the sixteenth century, Gloriana's court stands in for God's. There, the (metonymic) origin of the narrative is to be revealed in the assignment of quests, and the quests themselves are to be given their (metaphoric) origins as semantic ascriptions through the performance of which each knight will come to read his proper name in the face of the maternal potentate who stands, as we shall see, both behind and in front of *The Faerie Queene:*

> Then pardon me, most dreaded Soueraine,
>> That from your selfe I doe this vertue bring,
>> And to your selfe doe it returne againe:
>> So from the Ocean all riuers spring,
>> And tribute backe repay as to their King.
>> Right so from you all goodly vertues well
>> Into the rest, which round about you ring,
>> Faire Lords and Ladies, which about you dwell,
> And doe adorne your Court, where courtesies excell. (Book 6, Proem 7)

But this hierarchical reciprocity is present in the poem only as a determined absence. Spenser's narrative goes beyond denying its reader the scene of fulfillment in Gloriana's court to an almost delirious subversion of the possibility of such fulfillment.

Standing over against the promise of a unified and unifying Truth — the unspeakable truth of and about the dreaded sovereign — held out by this never to be completed race to the mythic origin are three very different originary scenes (or traumatic figures): the stripping of Duessa in Book 1, the simile of the Hermaphrodite that ends Book 3 (and the text) in the 1590 edition and is suppressed in subsequent editions, and Calidore's intrusion on Colin Clout, interrupting the text decisively in Book 6. Each of these imaginations of the origin coincides with a strategically important terminus: the end of Duessa's deception, which marks *The Faerie Queene's* first major closure — putatively marking the end of the Red Crosse Knight's divagations among the illusions of Archimago; the end of Scudamour and Amoret's separation — in which the quest of chastity seems — for a moment — to culminate in marriage; and the end of the poet's song, when the appearance of Colin Clout signals the precipitate and unsuccessful superposition of the courtly and the pastoral. As we follow *The Faerie Queene,* each of these apparent endings turns out to be only a pause, revealing the empty space that the tale is generated both to conceal and hold open, that is, the space of the subject, posited in the irreducible gap between the telling and the tale, the subject of "this present synthesis of the past." Following the temporality of the *nachträglich,* I will comment on these scenes in reverse order so as to delineate with an increasing generality the primal scene(s) on which Spenserian desire is propped and the strategically determined absence around which the tales of *The Faerie Queene* loop.

5

Approximately midway in its journey to the fictive origin in the court of Gloriana, the narrative of *The Faerie Queene* confronts the fictionalized origin of its fiction in the authorial alter ego, Colin Clout. At the beginning of Book 6, canto 10, we find Calidore, Spenser's knight of courtesy, "Vnmyndfull of his vow and high beheast" (1.3). This dereliction is first laid to his fixation on Pastorella, but in this canto the attraction of Pastorella is also transumed into a generalized disenchantment with the court, which is now, for the first time in *The Faerie Queene,* marked by "shadowes vaine / Of courtly fauour, fed with light report" (2.6–7). This sudden disenchantment is attributed partly to the positive attractions of pastoral life and of Pastorella, but also, as we learn rather suddenly and without narrative preparation, to Calidore's having witnessed what would appear to be a staging of the poem's primal scene:

> For what hath all that goodly glorious gaze [at court]
>> Like to one sight, which *Calidore* did vew?
>> The glaunce whereof their dimmed eies would daze,
>> That neuer more they should endure the shew
>> Of that sunne-shine, that makes them looke askew.
>> Ne ought in all that world of beauties rare,
>> (Saue onely *Glorianaes* heauenly hew
>> To which what can compare?) can it compare;
>> The which as commeth now, by course I will declare. (6.10.4)

In and through Calidore's encounter with Colin Clout, the allegorical register established by the figure of the courtiers in a ring around Elizabeth in the proem to Book 6, which one might otherwise expect to be completed by a memorial representation of Gloriana's court, is abruptly reinscribed as a figure of the origin of the tale in the poet's *erotic* fantasy. The survival of this fantasy—as a content of the unconscious—depends on its concealment from the allegorical world it creates.

> [Calidore] durst not enter into th'open greene,
>> For dread of them vnwares to be descryde,
>> For breaking of their daunce, if he were seene;
>> But in the couert of the wood did byde,
>> Beholding all, yet of them vnespyde.
>> There he did see, that pleased much his sight,
>> That even he him selfe his eyes enuyde,
>> An hundred naked maidens lilly white,
> All raunged in a ring, and dauncing in delight. (6.10.11)

At the center of the rings within rings that dance on Acidale, where "They say that *Venus*, when she did dispose / Her selfe to pleasaunce, vsed to resort" (9.1–2), we find neither Elizabeth nor Gloriana, but Colin Clout and his shepherd lass (ll. 15–16); that is to say, the image of Spenser and the image of *his* desire.

> All they without were raunged in a ring,
>> And daunced round; but in the midst of them
>> Three other Ladies did both daunce and sing,
>> The whilest the rest them round about did hemme,
>> And like a girlond did in compasse stemme:
>> And in the middest of those same three, was placed
>> Another Damzell, as a precious gemme,
>> Amidst a ring most richly enchaced,
> That with her goodly presence all the rest much graced. (6.10.12)

Implicitly, it is on this image of the shepherd lass in the "middest" of the Graces that the poet's image of the desired Queen is modeled. The tableau of poetic generation on Mount Acidale performs the allegorical task of a return to the origin by recapitulating the image of the Queen radiating grace to the ringed throng of courtiers in the proem to Book 6; but, by virtue of its strategic reversal of direction, this representation of the origin is markedly eccentric to that presented in the epideictic proem. For now it is the Queen, who is, in effect, an allegory of the shepherd lass.

For Bellamy, this scene figures Spenser's inability to write the Queen's proper name. Insofar as Elizabeth is the putative origin of *The Faerie Queene*, she exceeds the text and cannot be comprehensively represented by her surrogates within it. Referring to 6.10.4, Bellamy observes that because:

> nothing in worldly "false blisse" (10.3.8) can compare to the vision Calidore is about to witness, except the "heauenly hew" (which is not to say the face) of Gloriana, a sight beyond compare. . . . the lesser vision "beyond compare" engulfs the superior vision "beyond compare," challenging the reader to an almost impossible sorting out of a *mise en abyme* of non-originary comparison. ("The Vocative and the Vocational," p. 15)

The undecidable question of Gloriana's relationship to Elizabeth — as either a surrogate within the text or a "metonymic displacement of Elizabeth whose alterity threatens to subsume the originary 'Faerie Queene' " — signals for Bellamy "a fall into writing which cannot control the ever-shifting referentiality of the elliptical 'Faerie Queene' " (ibid.).

It is, however, important to recognize that Spenser's *mise en abyme* is, in fact, a precisely determined indeterminacy. In language that explicitly recalls the scene on Acidale, Spenser makes clear, in *Amoretti* 74, that there are, in fact, not one but three Elizabeths who together account for the origin of poem and poet:

> Most happy letters fram'd by skilfull trade,
> with which that happy name was first desynd:
> the which three times thrise happy hath me made,
> with guifts of body, fortune and of mind.
> The first my being to me gaue by kind,
> from mothers womb deriu'd by dew descent,
> the second is my souereigne Queene most kind,
> that honour and large richesse to me lent.
> The third my loue, my liues last ornament,
> by whom my spirit out of dust was raysed:
> to speake her prayse and glory excellent,
> of all aliue most worthy to be praysed.
> Ye three Elizabeths for euer liue,
> that three such graces did vnto me giue.[41]

Bellamy's evocation of a deconstructive "fall into writing" too quickly covers over the salient historical fact that, for Spenser, the "Proper Name of Elizabeth," shared by Spenser's mother, wife, and queen, was overdetermined de facto as well as de jure, and that its "coincidental" repetition provides an occasion that vocatively and uniquely calls him, Edmund Spenser, to an analytical exploration of the erotics of epideictic comparison.

The acuity of that analysis lies not in the general case of a "fall into writing," but in the specifically situated indeterminacy that Spenser encounters in the concrete task of naming names. I argued earlier that the signal peculiarity of Spenser's allegory is its tendency to reinscribe narrative on its allegorical scenes. It is a corollary of that argument that the dissemination of Elizabeth as character in *The Faerie Queene* is reflected on the other side of the linguistic mirror by the dissemination of the proper noun itself. The episode on Mount Acidale recognizes not the absence of the queen's proper name, but its constituent superfluity. The trace of *différance* that Bellamy discovers in the persistent differing and deferring of the queen's name is, in my view, of less interest than the specifically supplementary and determinate form of this particular "fall-into-writing," which signals the eruption of a strictly historical contingency (the coincidence of Elizabeths in Spenser's life) into the allegorical landscape of *The Faerie Queene*, and, insofar as *The Faerie Queene* remains a canonical example of dynastic romance, into the subsequent history of allegorical representation.

Historicized in this way, the frustration of Colin Clout on Mount Acidale may be seen to figure the inability of (Spenser's) allegory to define another scene on which the historically (and thus exigently) situated voice of its author is transumed into the divine Word of universal meaning. The return of Colin Clout and the consequent reinscription of the division between court pastoral and country georgic marks—in the most homely way—the ironic moment of Spenser's inability to unify England and its destiny by speaking its national voice.

The sense of closure, represented on Mount Acidale as a collapse of the fiction that returns us not to the ultimate origin of the divine word but to its proximate origin in the exigent experience of an author who is situated on the colonial periphery and trying unsuccessfully to locate a British Troynovant that transcends and enlarges English London, derives in part from the multiply recursive presentation of the episode. As the appearance of Colin Clout on

Mount Acidale evokes an image of Spenser's career by returning us to what we now constitute as its early phase, a resonance in the language recalls Spenser's representation of the prehistory of *The Faerie Queene*. In a phrase whose latent eroticism becomes retrospectively manifest in Book 6, the "Letter to Ralegh" tells us that, unlike the historian who is the subject of chronology, the "Poet thrusteth into the middest, euen where it most concerneth him." When Calidore reaches Acidale and penetrates the ring of naked maidens, he finds the graces in their *midst* and the shepherd girl in the *middest,* where she is placed "as a precious gemme / *Amidst* a ring." In stanza 14, we are told again that she stood in the *midst* of "this goodly band." In stanza 15, when the girl in the middle is identified, we are told that the "faire one, / That in the *midst* was placed parauant, / Was she to whom that shepheard pypt alone, / That made him pipe so merrily, as neuer none" (ll. 6–9). Five times in thirty-six lines, we are given the word. Here, in what would be — according to the outline given in the "Letter to Ralegh" — the middle of the first half of *The Faerie Queene,* the poet appears, indeed, to have thrust into the middest to discover what most concerns him.[42] And what does he discover? Not the Fairy Queen, not the universal virtue Magnanimity, not the epideictic model of the perfect gentleman, not, in fact, any kind of gentleman at all, only himself: "Poore *Colin Clout* (who knowes not *Colin Clout?*)" (16.4).

This terminally original encounter of the narrating and narrated subjects exhausts the story, leaving behind the trace of a despondent authorial identification; when Colin breaks his pipe and the poem ends in the "middest," the dark shadow of the nymph "out of *Dianes* favour," who "Sat downe to rest in middest of the race" (1.7.4.9, 1.7.5.4), is cast across the text. Does this faintly recollected identification of the frustrated piper and the nymph, whose sloth polluted the fountain from which the Red Cross Knight drinks the water of lassitude, as faintly suggest a similarly debilitating inducement to lassitude latent in the text that flows from Colin's muse through Spenser's pen? If so, then the reader's experience ironically performs and reduplicates Calidore's withdrawal into pastoral, and the degree to which this irony becomes thematically conscious determines the outcome of what might with some precision be termed a transference: either the reader, in the historical present of the reading simply *repeats* the frustrating impasse of Colin and Calidore on Acidale — in which case the poet, as subject of a negative transference, remains (as Spenser apparently did) "out of *Dianes* favour" — or the reader *remembers* (as Calidore seems not to remember) the political history of pastoral representation. From the literary historical point of view I have sought to establish, insofar as the episode on Mount Acidale inverts and complicates the intertwined myths of a pastoral and courtly origin it deploys, the curious appearance of the poet in the act of composition, at what is functionally the end of *The Faerie Queene,* marks the collapse of Spenser's dynastic-epic narrative as also the collapse of allegory as the narrative form of epideictic mimesis.[43]

As we have seen, in Augustine, Dante, Petrarch, and, parodically, in Marvell as well, epideictic mimesis, in its variously stressed forms, relies on metaphor to arrest and assign meaning to the metonymic chain of narrative events. Such metaphorical closure is explicitly and thematically at issue on Mount Acidale. Calidore, who has seen the fairy queen, is dazed by a sight to which nothing in the world can *compare.* "(Saue onely Glorianaes heuenly hew / To which what can compare?)" The story of the Augustinian "I" is compressed into this self-consciously self-defeating parenthesis recounting the collapse of epideictic mimesis as a poetry of (metaphoric) comparison reaching toward that which is incomparable: nothing in the world compares with what Calidore sees, except the structurally incomparable and determinately absent Gloriana.[44] As Lacan would predict, however, the speaking subject's desire returns to him in an inverted form. Queen Elizabeth's power figures (as an allegory of) the power of the gaze with which the shepherd girl (presumably Elizabeth Boyle, Spenser's wife and the recipient of the *Amoretti* and *Epithalamion*) returns Colin Clout's captivated desire, as, indeed, the return of Colin Clout returns the reader to the opening lines of *The Faerie Queene:* "Lo I the man, whose Muse whilome did maske, / As time her taught in lowly Shepheards weeds" (Book 1, Proem 1–2).[45]

When Calidore, whose "courtesy" inscribes the set of "legal and literary proceedings" that determine the court in its blank and irreducible objectivity, and who, "rapt with pleasaunce, wist not what to weene," comes out of the woods and reveals himself, Colin is bereft of his imaginations:

> They vanisht all away out of his sight,
> And cleane were gone, which way he neuer knew;
> All saue the shepheard, who for fell despight
> Of that displeasure, broke his bag-pipe quight,
> And made great mone for that vnhappy turne. (18.2–6)

Is it too farfetched to see in the encounter on Mount Acidale—across the thousands of intervening lines—an inverted recapitulation of the proem to Book 2? In the earlier verses the poet addresses his sovereign audience anticipating the dispersal of what he well knows ("Well I wote") by courtiers who will not accept as "matter of iust memory" things which "no body can know." On Acidale a vision of the poet, in the privacy of his memory, is dispersed by an errant courtier who "wist not what to weene." The unbridgeable gulf between Colin's world and Calidore's, emphasized in Calidore's blank incomprehension of what the shepherd poet knows, appears in the text as clearly as it must have appeared by 1596 that Elizabeth, the queen, would become, in fact, neither wife nor mother.

Calidore's apology at once mourns the dispersal of Colin's fantasy constellation and—marking Colin's passage into the Symbolic order (of courtesy), which Calidore represents (and from which he attempts to flee)—solicits the recuperation of desire's ring in the form of an ordered history or tale. This tale (which, as we shall see, materializes as a *tail* in the stripping of Duessa) serves to cover the empty and obscene space left by the irruption of history into the Imaginary, figured (for Colin) by Calidore's unmotivated and contingent presence:

> Right sory I, (saide then Sir *Calidore,*)
> That my ill fortune did them hence displace.
> But since things passed none may now restore,
> Tell me, what were they all, whose lacke thee
>   grieues so sore. (20.6–9)

If Colin is interrupted, as I take him to be, in the act of composing the tale that Spenser proposed in the proem to Book 2, to read out of "iust memory," while preemptively anticipating that "some" will judge it "th'abundance of an idle braine," his reply—"Not I so happy, . . . / As thou vnhappy, which them thence didst chace, / Whom by no meanes thou canst recall againe" (20.1–3)—encompasses the failed closure of *The Faerie Queene* in a moment of radically uncertain retrospection. For we still do not know ("no body can know") whether the tale bracketed by the "not happy I" of its speaker and the "unhappy thou" of its audience is, in fact, "matter of iust memory" or "th'abundance of an idle braine."

The momentary interruption on Mount Acidale is decisive because in it the not happy Spenser-Colin follows courtesy, the mistress he serves, to the point at which he occupies her gaze and turns to discover his unhappy self. Like his earlier interruption of Calepine and Serena, Calidore's discovery of Colin acts out the contradiction implicit in the quest of the Knight of Courtesy to bind the Blatant Beast, which is — as an embodied *dis*courtesy — the transgressive product of the court itself — the falling out as opposed to the falling in of its many self-interested and opportunistic voices. The allegory is ironic. Calidore, who has been sent to subdue the beast of slander, seems unable to move about the countryside except as the embodiment of the court's intrusion into the intimate lives of its subjects, an intrusion which by its nature makes public what ought to remain private and thus releases the uncanny beast that Calidore seeks to suppress.[46] The fact that Calidore's courtesy offers protection precisely against its own violation — protection, that is, against the scandal incurred by violating its own hypocritical codes of conduct — is wryly dramatized in the episode of Aladine and Priscilla, when Calidore courteously protects Priscilla from the scandal of her interrupted sexual encounter with Aladine by swearing on his knighthood to the equivocation that covers it up (6.3.18).[47]

On Mount Acidale, suddenly seeing himself from the place where Calidore sees him, Colin discovers that in following the legend of courtesy, Calidore, the subject of the narrative, has served his turn upon Colin, the pastoral narrator. Calidore, at this point, has abandoned his quest for the blatant beast in favor of a return to Pastorella. But, as in literary historical fact, this return serves only to contaminate the bucolic with the courtly.[48] Spenser's elaboration of this contamination goes beyond the commonplace.

The discovery on Acidale discloses to Colin that the superimposition of court and country proceeds inextricably in both directions: his imaginings of Elizabeth Regina are also his imaginings of Elizabeth Boyle. The epideictic ambition to fashion a georgic gentleman for England's court is elided by an inevitable, yet contingent, collapse into the personal. The Immerito, who set off to make his name in and through *The Faerie Queene,* returns home as Colin Clout, ironically no longer exactly "vnkent": "who knowes not *Colin Clout?*" But the turn of his return is a double one, for, when, in the encounter of Calidore and Colin, the court finally comes face to face with its poet, the poet serves his turn upon the queen, revealing that in following her, he too follows but himself.

The recursive dynamism of this tropic structure may be seen in the fact that

Colin fashions his sovereign queen out of an image of his love, the woman whom love has fashioned as his proper queen. Colin's fashioning of Elizabeth is thus an instance of the reciprocal fashioning that Louis Montrose describes in "The Elizabethan Subject and the Spenserian Text":

> The historical subject, Elizabeth Tudor, was no more than a privileged agent in the production of the royal image. At a fundamental level, all Elizabethan subjects may be said to have participated in a ceaseless and casual process of producing and reproducing "The Queen" in their daily practices. . . . But she was also rather more systematically and consciously fashioned by those Elizabethan subjects who were specifically engaged in production of the texts, icons, and performances in which the queen was variously represented to her people, to her court, to foreign powers, and (of course) to Elizabeth herself. (pp. 317–18)

I would stress, however, that the return of Colin Clout on Mount Acidale goes one subversive step beyond Montrose's formulation. As Harry Berger has argued, rather than simply participating in the fashioning of the queen, the episode on Mount Acidale represents — in fairly acute clinical detail — the very process of fashioning itself.[49] Spenser's representation of Colin in the act of representing opens the queen herself to the contingency of the anecdote, as exemplified in this instance by the role played by a historically determined other woman (Elizabeth Boyle) in the construction of the royal image. Generically, the pastoral, in which a courtly poet assumes the guise of a shepherd whose songs figure the complexity of court life under the cover of a nostalgic simplicity, returns to its sender in an inverted form — mediated, moreover, as a generic negation about which we know the Renaissance to have been self-conscious.[50] Montrose's text, then, does not explicate Spenser's so much as repeat it, for Spenser and Montrose observe the textualization of Elizabeth Tudor at precisely the same level of thematization. Spenser, Freud, and Montrose are in this respect contemporaries.

The encounter of Renaissance text and psychoanalytic interpretation, then, is not, as Greenblatt argues, a case of "causally belated" psychoanalytic categories inscribing themselves as the causes of "the phenomena of which in actual fact they were the result" (p. 221), but of the reinscription in the terms of a theoretical discourse of what the Renaissance, through its own revision of classical genres, had in this instance already understood.

If something of the relation between desire and the tale is disclosed on Mount Acidale, the nature of that desire is further elucidated by the 1590 close of Book 3. The reunited Scudamour and Amoret embrace such that:

> Had ye them seene, ye would haue surely thought,
>> That they had beene that faire *Hermaphrodite,*
>> Which that rich *Romane* of white marble wrought,
>> And in his costly Bath causd to bee site:
>> So seemd those two, as growne together quite. (3.12.46.1–5 [1590])

The figure of the Hermaphrodite makes an ambivalent comparison to the embracing lovers. On the one hand, it is a figure of married bliss (man and wife become one flesh) with its promise, always crucial in *The Faerie Queene,* of generation. This aspect of the image will reappear importantly in the idol of the crocodile wrapped around the lower body of Isis in Book 5, canto 7, the sexual content of which is released in Britomart's ensuing dream (5.7.13–16).[51] But, on the other hand, the Ovidian original to which it points recalls not the fertility of married love, but impotence resulting from female sexual aggression.[52]

Looping through Ovid, the allusion to Salmacis returns to *The Faerie Queene* at 1.7.4–5, disclosing the source and identity of the slothful nymph "out of *Dianes* favour," whose enervating waters leave Red Crosse vulnerable to Orgoglio.[53] Thus, the end of the 1590 *Faerie Queene* anticipates the return to the middest enacted in the end of the 1596 version, when Colin breaks his pipe on Mount Acidale. To recapitulate the career of this recursive allusion in *The Faerie Queene:* Salmacis's name is elided in the Orgoglio episode to emerge later under a peculiarly performative metonymy — she comprises one-half of the resulting hermaphrodite — when Hermaphroditus is named at the end of Book 3. This belated metonymic denomination is then canceled in the 1596 version where, as I have argued, the concluding return to the nymph who sat down in the midst of the race is deferred to the discovery of Colin Clout on Mount Acidale. Left unnamed in 1596, Salmacis's spectral presence adds one more self-referential determination to the unnamed fourth grace, whom I earlier identified with the three Elizabeths, two of whom, Elizabeth Spenser and Elizabeth Boyle, have some successive claim to be merged — of one flesh — with the body of the poet.

Content to leave this possibly Oedipal conflation in the shadows of over-determination and return to the realized text, we may note that, although the fact that Amoret and Scudamour are "grown together quite," fits well with the figure of Adonis installed within the Mount of Venus "Ioying his goddesse, and of her enioyd" (3.6.48.2), the Ovidian intertext reminds us that Adonis is himself the sex-avoidant child of an incestuous union.[54] The segue at the end of 3.6, from the Garden of Adonis to the story of the sexually terrified Florimell and the maternally inhibited Marinell, encloses the love of Scudamour and the exemplary Amoret ("of grace and beautie noble Paragone, / . . . / . . . th'ensample of true loue alone, / And Lodestarre of all chaste affectione" [3.6.52.2–5]) on both sides with tales of incest, sexual avoidance and piercing wounds.

Thus, while the figure of Adonis installed beneath the Mount of Venus ("in the middest of that Paradise" [3.6.43.1]) may be integrated into the larger tale as manifesting the procreative ethos of the Garden of Adonis, it also merges uncomfortably with the counterimage in the Bower of Bliss of Verdant sleeping with his head in the lap of Acrasia, "his warlike armes, the idle instruments / Of sleeping praise" (2.12.80.1–2), while her snowy breasts "Few drops, more cleare than Nectar, forth distild" (2.12.78.4).[55] Seen in this context the figure of the hermaphrodite forms part of an intertextual series of repetitions in which a too close union of man and woman results in the feminization of the man. Britomart fits all too well in this line of aggressive women, and her dream in Isis' Church may thus be understood as a fantasy of release from the obsessive repetition of the pattern. Neither the crucial variation of Britomart's masculinization (as a questing knight), nor the symbolic wounds she receives from Gardante (3.1.65) and Busyrane (3.12.33) save Artegall from his near fatal brush with emasculation at the hands of her evil double, Radigund.

It should be clear by now that in anticipating Freud's narrational form, Spenser also anticipates his content. The anaclitic propping of the fecund genitality of the Garden of Adonis on a disabling regression to the Oedipal object is stipulated with striking precision both by the Pietà pose of Verdant in the arms of Acrasia and by the bliss / blesse pun in the lines that immediately follow the allusion to the Hermaphrodite:[56]

> That *Britomart* half enuying their blesse,
> Was much empassiond in her gentle sprite,
> And to her selfe oft wisht like happinesse,
> In vaine she wisht, that fate n'ould let her yet
>   possesse. (3.12.46.6–9 [1590])

On a purely formal level, fate cannot allow to Britomart the ambiguously blessed wound of bliss because to do so would prematurely end the story. Spenser's narrative, however, like that of psychoanalysis, goes a step further to suggest that the destiny of desire is, in fact, not its fulfillment but an impasse.[57] The subject of desire is, after all, a desiring subject. When the story of its desire ends, the characters that peopled that story are reduced to "senceles stocks in long embracement" (3.12.45.9 [1590]). Becoming allegorical emblems (metaphors), they are removed from the metonymic chain of signifiers out of which the story emerges. In Spenser's dream book, as in Freud's, the (imaginary) origin of this desire in the rupture of an originary unity with the mother figures forth the last — or rather, the first — origin of the tale.

Thus, desire is realized as a witch, a shape changer, the external projection onto another of an archaic image. Spenser introduces her early on. And true to her name, Duessa enters the tale as a doubled double. The double of Una, she joins the Red Crosse Knight in company with "a fit false dreame, that can delude the sleepers sent" (1.1.43.9). Through the mediation of this dream, she is not just an image or simulacrum of Una, but, more specifically, the corruption of the *Red Crosse Knight's image of Una,* his fantasy of Una's desire. Thus, Una is always already doubled in precisely the way that, within a certain constitution of desire, *the* Woman (who in Lacan's notorious formulation does not exist except as a symptom of male desire) always doubles and subverts masculine subjectivity — because *women* exist both in and for themselves *and* as the objectified ideal of male desire:[58]

> [Archimago] all this while with charmes and hidden artes,
> Had made a Lady of that other Spright,
> And fram'd of liquid ayre her tender partes
> So liuely, and so like in all mens sight. (1.1.45.1–4)

Thus, from our Spenserian/Freudian perspective, we may understand desire's endless errancy as the loop described by the immemorial past as it empties out and appropriates the present. In Spenser's tale, the invaginating nature of this loop is explicitly and emblematically figured by the loop of Venus's desire enclosing Adonis beneath its mount and the proliferating narrations of an engulfing return to "maternal" origins that interminably defer the ultimate return to the Court of Gloriana. Thus, Spenser's tale and Freud's most originally disclose, as the origin of a subject irremediably divided from the

desire that generates its actions, that particularly empty space which the Eliza-
bethans sometimes called "nothing," a space at once concealed and revealed
by the tale: "a foxes taile, with dong all fowly dight" (1.8.48.4), or, as Freud, put
it, delicately appropriating a dead tongue, "*inter urinas et faeces nascimur.*"[59]

6

What, then, is the relationship of Spenser's dream book to Freud's? I have
tried to present my argument in a way that resists applied psychoanalysis,
the notion that Freud's story can unlock the "true" or "deep" or "repressed"
meaning of Spenser's. Such an application would remain tautologically de-
scriptive, as diagnostics always do.[60] Rather, it seems to me that Freud does not
explain Spenser so much as repeat him, (re)allegorizing in a theoretical discourse the temporal predicament of human agents when they are conceived in
the historically specific way in which they are mediated in Renaissance narrative. Spenser's Renaissance text represents as narrative practice the explicitly
verbal and implicitly narrative subjectivity that Freud would later theorize.

To repose Derrida's question: what is *novel* in psychoanalysis is thus its
retroactive repetition of the origin of that historical subject — self-consistent,
yet changing in response to its accumulated experiences — that will become
the subject of the novel. From the standpoint of literary history, we can say that
those pressures — formal and social — that canonized the Shakespearean char-
acterology of psychological depth were already at work in Spenser, troping
the dynastic romance toward an endlessly repeating and highly self-conscious
reflection on the metaphoric relation between its theme of generation and its
metonymic mode of narration. Spenser and Freud may thus be taken to represent two historically determined moments in what Adorno and Horkheimer
call the dialectic of enlightenment: Spenser's allegory — insofar as it demystifies the "romance" of "chilvaric" and pastoral desire — releases the individual
"I," at a distance from itself, into a georgic agency through which a gentleman
may aspire to cultivate his world and himself without ceasing by his labor to
be a gentleman. Freud sees the rationalization of nature thus accomplished as
a self-limiting historical process and, by arresting its narrative, returns to the
site of an impasse: the irreducible gap between reason and passion, on the one
side, and the (unrealized) perfection of formal cause and the radical contingency of the historical "event," on the other.[61]

Recalling Greenblatt's demand for a historicized psychoanalysis, we should note that Spenser's narrative also offers and records a resistance to History that is itself historical. What I mean by this is that the exigent and contingent events which Spenser encounters are insistently recorded in *The Faerie Queene* as details that return the text from the allegorical to the mimetic narrative. Insofar as they resist meaning, persistently and dynamically exceeding the allegorical denominations under which they are pinned, these events stand outside of and in a supplementary relation to the destined dynastic History that is the text's avowed and public intention. They are that which History, understood as a retrospective explanation of present things in terms of prior causes, must necessarily leave out, the dissonant details of the dream which — in the cause of narrative coherence — are eliminated by the secondary revision. What are the consequences of this anecdotal openness to the contingent and the noncausally motivated detail for the representation of the self as historical agent?

In chapter 7 we will have occasion better to appreciate the homology between Spenser's narrative subject and Freud's by comparing them both to the intervening subject of Miltonic narrative. For the present purpose of assessing the effects on narrative agency of the resistances to and of history in *The Faerie Queene,* it will be useful to look to the comparison of Spenser and Milton conducted in Gordon Teskey's important essay, "From Allegory to Dialectic: Imagining Error in Spenser and Milton." [62] Teskey makes a fundamental distinction between the two poets' narrations of error: "In Spenser, error is represented *diagetically,* in all the various forms offered by narrative romance. In Milton, error is represented *dialectically,* as the negation of all that is good" (p. 9).

As one might expect, the crucial difference in terms of narrative construction is that the diagetical allegory, lacking a principle of dialectical negation, also lacks the discovery of character through and as negative agency. Milton's epic narration turns and returns on two reciprocally negative moments. The Fall, as the negation of human agency, calls forth the Incarnation, which, as the negation of that negation, opens the way to a restored human agent who seizes control of history by internalizing the paired moments of the Fall and the Incarnation and — in the second chance thus obtained — insistently re-enacting the choice of God's will, which it construes as a negation of its own corrupted appetite. Teskey provides a succinct description of the different representations of narrative agency, or character, entailed by the presence or absence of dialectical negation:

> While the whole structure of Milton's epic turns on one catastrophic act of negation, Spenser's large network of stories is designed to explore nuance and complexity in our ordinary moral experience. Thus moral deviation in *The Faerie Queene* is the condition of the narrative as a whole, and the turns and counterturns of romance are easily identified with error. In the prelapsarian world of *Paradise Lost,* however, error must be set apart from existence and restricted to a category of things that are *not*—perversity, paradox, and negation—so that the narrative will remain uninfected. These isolated regions of negation in the Miltonic narrative cannot be wandered into like the adventures encountered by errant knights of romance: they must be entered by deliberate choice. As a result, the freedom to negate produces a phenomenon that is almost entirely absent from *The Faerie Queene:* an internalized moral consciousness that seems perfectly unconstrained by its story. (pp. 9–10)

I want to briefly consider the temporal relationships of character to action articulated respectively by the exterior determinations of Spenserian diegesis and the interior negations of Miltonic dialectic. Both Spenser and Milton make use of the fact that the word *error* holds in suspense the punctual notion of a mistake or misrecognition and the temporal and spatial dilation of *errancy,* or wandering, retained in its verbal root. For Milton, this suspension between two meanings is resolved temporally along the divide of the Fall, so that prelapsarian *error* signifies innocent wandering, but postlapsarian *error* cannot escape the implication of an epistemological fault. Through the choices they make, Milton's characters determine the events in which they participate.[63] They conceptualize choice punctually, in terms of the alternative consequences that may follow an action. The loss of innocence suffered by the word *error* and the activity of wandering it might have previously implied is thus moralized as an example of the way in which the error of the Fall instantaneously and precipitously transfigures the world. Spenser's characters, on the other hand, discover sequentially the events that call upon them to act. Where Milton's characters generally confront one thing *or* another, Spenser's are apt to encounter one thing *after* another.

Teskey sees the interiority of Milton's characters and the lack of interiority in Spenser's characters as resulting from the former's use of narrative as the "vehicle" and the latter's use of narrative as the "instrument of meaning":

> [Milton] preserves an inviolable space between the constraints of the story he must tell and the apparent freedom of his characters not to engage in its action. In *Paradise Lost,* only a choice can be perverse, never an event in itself. In *The Faerie Queene,* however, where the narrative is not a vehicle but an instrument of meaning, no long speeches are given by the characters to explain why they act as they do. . . . For the Spenserian knights, who are, in effect, what they do in the story, there is no Cartesian sanctuary where Reason can sit back and choose. (p. 10)

Milton, then, represents history as determined by reasoned choice, while Spenser represents choice as continually emerging from history. For Spenser, choices are selected from the menu, so to speak, that exigently comes before his knights. For Milton, choice determines history; for Spenser, history determines choice. Where narrative is the vehicle of meaning, meaning is confirmed by the retrospective design in which the choices can be evaluated and judged. Where it is an instrument of meaning, meaning is constructed along the way and with a certain enforced provisionality. Teskey observes that the "exclusion of complexity by reversion to an original cause allows Milton to focus on the general psychology of choice (assuming only two possible choices) without interference from the practical circumstances of everyday life. Milton's aim is to justify, Spenser's to fashion" (p. 10). I would add that to justify is to narrate again, to follow the story for a second time, and only after having been privileged with "things invisible to mortal sight." It is, in brief, the second reading which — superimposing error on errancy — turns the past into History. Theodicy is thus justification of God by God, that is through the assumption of the point of view of an interiorized eternity. Spenser's aim of fashioning is more modest; it implies not understanding but a certain practiced readiness; it prefers practice to theory. Thus Milton's epic refers all choices metaphorically to the choice offered by the sole prohibited tree, while Spenser's knights wander metonymically among an open-ended catalog of trees (*FQ* 1.8–9). Milton returns all the events of his poem to the point of view of the Spirit who was present from the first (*Paradise Lost* 1.20), while Spenser, finally and candidly, embeds his narration in the exigent circumstances of his own timely life.

Milton's narrative desire thus yearns toward the moments of renunciation when subjective agency is manifested as a return of the individual will to the universal will of God. In those moments action closes down around the renunciatory "No." For example, in the fifth book of *Paradise Lost* (ll. 803–76) Abdiel says no to Satan, and in *Paradise Regained* Jesus again says no to Satan. The typology of the single just man that joins Abdiel's *no* to Jesus' marks out an Augustinian containment of desire. At strategic points along the line of metonymies traced out by what appear to be historical circumstances, the transcendental *no* of renunciation traces a metaphoric circuit back to the origin of action in the Father's primal prohibition. To exercise the will is to renounce the forbidden fruit. Augustine makes "not provision for the flesh"; Jesus, at the climax of *Paradise Regained,* takes no action but to say and stand.

Spenser's knights, by contrast, wander in search of positive attributes. They are called upon to intervene in urgently unfolding situations, and they always exceed their onomastic determinations because these situations entail subsequent situations that call on them differently. Because, following the *Nicomachean Ethics,* Spenser conceives of virtue as habit, and because he continues to understand the efficacy of his narrative in terms of epideictic mimesis, he must fashion a gentleman by unfolding in varying situations the habits of virtue.[64] In terms of the underlying rhetoric that structures his narrative, his knightly virtues are always one thing or another because the actions predicated of them support one thing or another, and they cannot be unified or terminated because the contexts of action that manifest their virtue lie along chains of signification subject to unlimited metonymic extension. At best they are like Odysseus, whose cunning requires a second voyage to prolong and renew its habitual expression.

It is this constraint of linear narrative to predicate of a character one thing or another that results in the tendency, noticed by Teskey, for "a deviant loop of episodes in romance very often [to] open with some indication that the character to deviate has split into two parts . . . , as if the only way to indicate that digression from the main action constitutes moral deviation from the self is to show a split in the integrity of that self" (p. 12).[65] As Teskey points out the manifestation in romance allegory of internal deviation (deviation from the self) as narrative doubling—division into a true and a false self—conditions the interpretive paradigm according to which allegorical meaning is developed:

The tendency of romance to release uncontrolled adventures from a moment of duplication provides an opportunity that no sensible interpreter will let pass. For the doubling of images gives the interpreter a place to take hold of narrative error and to impose on it, at least momentarily, a clear opposition from which a more general statement of meaning can be raised. Yet the structure can never be made sound. For whereas interpretive doubling works by a logic of opposites that cannot be brought together as one, narrative duplication proceeds by shearing off some part from the whole and allowing that part to wander until it is reunited again with its source. (p. 12)

When, in variations of the Augustinian loop described in chapter 3, Dante and Petrarch desire virtues that are reflected into the self, the lyric moment aligns the beatitude of Beatrice or the praiseworthiness of Laura with that which the poet ultimately locates in himself. In the enclosing narratives of *La Vita Nuova* and the *Rime sparse,* the deaths of Beatrice and Laura mark the moment when narrative gives way to interpretation, for from that moment on the contemplation of the epideictic moment is no longer divided between memorial introspection and narrative observation. Dante desires to be blessed and finds his blessing in a renunciation of praise until Beatrice leads him to the common origin of all that is praiseworthy, until he may himself enjoy her blessedness. At that time he will write of blessedness not as a character distinct from himself but as inwardly experienced. Petrarch desires to praise and becomes synonymous with the praise he produces, thus collapsing narrative into description. In the one case the narrative terminates with the expectation of a metaphoric identity of subject and object; in the other, with the metaphoric transumption of a plaintive disappearance of the speaking subject into the verbal object he has produced. Spenser's virtues, however, remain disjoined from the metaphoric moment that would unite them. Rather, the unity of knightly virtue, the magnanimity Arthur is to offer — that is, the peculiar specialization of the Arthur character as a narrative subject somehow expected to reverse the process of metonymic doubling through a metaphoric absorption of each thing into everything — already suggests a certain pressure in the direction of the dialectical narration that we have, following Teskey, identified as Miltonic.

In *The Faerie Queene,* Arthur appears at the negative moments in the onomastic dialectic of the knightly virtues. For example, he restores the Red

Crosse Knight so that he may be conducted by Una to the House of Holiness, after and as a negation of his unholiness with Duessa (which in narrative terms is also an un-wholeness—realized in Archimago's temporarily successful assumption of the Red Crosse Knight's identity). Thus, Arthur typically enters the narrative precisely as the negation of the negation that mediates the Red Crosse Knight's recognition of himself as Holiness. Similarly, Arthur shows up to restore Guyon and lead him to the House of Alma only after Guyon's experience of intemperance in the Cave of Mammon (and it is worth noting that the intemperance of Guyon is itself negative; he is weakened not by the temptation of wealth but because he intemperately goes three days without food or drink). As the attempted synecdochical presentation of a Virtue that contains and encompasses all other virtues, Arthur moves through *The Faerie Queene* as the dialectical moment of the negation of the negation so that each of the metonymic knightly virtues that he putatively exemplifies may come to self-knowledge historically, through the experience of its Other, as in the overarching discovery of knowledge through negation in the Fall. The ideal(-ego) enters history (as the ego-ideal) only by losing itself, only, that is, through the mediation of the negative. The failure of dialectical sublation in *The Faerie Queene* is, I am arguing, the failure to effect a transfer across the character of Arthur—like the transfer Augustine effected across the ambivalent signifier *volentilia* in his allegorical reading of the injunction to increase and multiply, or alternatively the one effected by Milton's temporalized suspension of *error*—from the open circuit of meanings deriving from the mimetic narration of errancy (the chain of significations entailed by metonymy) to the totalized symbolic of allegory (the metaphoric reinscription of each temporally unfolding episode as the iteration of a universal moral truth). The impasse that calls forth this failure appears clearly in the comparison. The pun on *volentilia* works only so long as the word remains a metaphor at the limit of the narrative, designating *birds* on the literal level and *words* on the allegorical. If Augustine were to do as Spenser does and reinsert this metaphoric limit as the subject of yet another allegorical narration, he would find that as narrative agents his *volentilia* would fairly quickly tend to become one thing (birds) or another (words). From the reversed angle of critical vision afforded by literary history, however, we can just as well say that the failure of metaphoric closure in *The Faerie Queene* constitutes precisely its success in remaining open to the space and time of the anecdote—which is to say, its success in representing a reflection on its own historicity that allows it to engage the construction of history as one of its themes.

This opening to history may be located precisely in the redoubling of the putatively dynastic couples: Saint George and Una, Arthur and Gloriana, Artegall and Britomart. I cite these names in a specifically hierarchical order. The unity of holiness and the true church ought to define and include the marriage (and dynastic generativity) of the two ideal monarchs; through the internalization and emulation of these ideal monarchs, the unity of government within the concept of holiness ought to enter history as the dynastic union of Britain and Faery Land to issue from Britomart and Artegall. Gloriana and Arthur would then be middle terms by which the substantive goodness of heaven, from which all good depends, would be mediated to the dynastic couple, whose power of action is defined by their efforts to institute the ideal on the historical ground. This is not, however, what occurs in Spenser's text. Instead, the scandal that always haunts this traditional hierarchy of concept and act — the possibility of reading the metaphors in the other direction, of seeing the historical as the ground rather than the reflection of the universal, is realized in the (formally) endless proliferation of exigently associated details.[66]

In the backward glance across the pages from Freud to Spenser, enlightenment may perhaps be seen to run its course: from the rationalist demystification of chivalric ideology to the enlightened demystification of reason itself. This course may be understood (retrospectively) as the career — in the marketplace — of a commodified history identified in and packaged as the *nachträglich* narrative of historical causation.

What remains to be decided is whether in this reading, we, as reader-analysands, place the psychoanalytic reading in the position of "the subject who is supposed to know." To ask this question is to ask whether or not the psychoanalytic repetition can effect for us a transference relation that, like Calidore's interruption of the tale, allows us to move from a dualistic relation to the text, a relation in which fantasy is infinitely reallegorized, perpetually reenacted *on another scene,* to a dialogic position from which we may perceive that "Truth" arises always through the mediation of a third term: that Calidore, as disenchanted representative of queen and court, must come between Colin Clout and his shepherd lass (as he had earlier come between the joying and enjoying of Serena and Calipine) and that Colin, as narrator of the queen's tale, must himself produce the very court from which that gentleman disturbs his fantasy.[67] Such a displacement from content to form, from mis-recognized thing to recognition of the symbolic structure in which the necessary *méconnaissance* takes place would fulfill—probably as best we can—Freud's chiasmic joining of ego and id *over time,* "*Wo Es* war, soll *Ich werden.*"

7

One last retrospection, returning us to our beginning in the juxtaposition of Shakespeare's fiction and the true story of Martin Guerre, will provide an example of just such a chiasmus of thing and structure. At the end of the main action of *A Midsummer Night's Dream,* but before its dark Ovidian repetition in the *Pyramis and Thisbe* of the rude mechanicals, Theseus and Hippolyta engage in a famous and fascinatingly gendered controversy over the meaning of a tale, which is also, in this case, the interpretation of a midsummer night's dream. This interpretive discourse begins when Hippolyta remarks apropos the tale of the lovers who have been discovered asleep outside the Athenian walls: "'Tis strange, my Theseus, that these lovers speak of," to which the Duke replies dryly and with a certain diagnostic pomposity:

> More strange than true. I never may believe
> These antic fables, nor these fairy toys.
> Lovers and madmen have such seething brains,
> Such shaping fantasies, that apprehend
> More than cool reason ever comprehends.
> The lunatic, the lover, and the poet
> Are of imagination all compact.
> One sees more devils than vast hell can hold;
> That is the madman. The lover, all as frantic,
> Sees Helen's beauty in a brow of Egypt.
> The poet's eye in a fine frenzy rolling,
> Doth glance from heaven to earth, from earth to heaven;
> And as imagination bodies forth
> The forms of things unknown, the poet's pen
> Turns them to shapes, and gives to aery nothing
> A local habitation and a name.
> Such tricks hath strong imagination,
> That if it would but apprehend some joy,

> It comprehends some bringer of that joy;
> Or in the night, imagining some fear,
> How easy is a bush suppos'd a bear. (5.1.1–22)

Theseus's categorical view is strikingly paradigmatic: fancy apprehends, reason comprehends. Imagination grasps, brings in; reason surrounds and holds together, and when, following its desire, imagination would grasp joy, it misapplies reason to create also agency, "some bringer of that joy."

Curiously, however, Shakespeare's verse would seem to know something that Theseus' words miss, to know, in fact, what Hamlet knows: that "there are more things in heaven and earth, Horatio, / Than are dreamt of in your philosophy" (*Hamlet* 1.5.165–66). For the glance of the poet's *eye* discovers something voiced but not exactly said, a metrical ambiguity that appears beyond cool reason to complete a chiasmus when the poet: "Doth glance from heaven to earth, from earth to heaven." To the eye and to the modern ear, this would be a hypermetric line. But, of course, in the sixteenth century "common disyllables that show an intervocalic *th, v,* or *r,* will often [but not always] be treated as monosyllables. . . . Presumably, poets heard such intervocalic consonants as less than fully formed."[68] Experienced readers of Shakespeare will therefore scan "heaven" as a monosyllable, thus producing a regular pentameter line. Still, something remains of the elided, I am tempted to say the repressed, *v,* a momentary recording of the transaction that folds two syllables into one, and this something is in play in the resonance we may detect between the content of Theseus' speech and the remark with which George Wright concludes his discussion of ambiguous syllables in *Shakespeare's Metrical Art:* "To write ten-syllable lines that have, in a sense, eleven or twelve syllables (or eleven and a half) is to crowd the air with meanings only half-spoken, partly concealed. The hypermetrical half-syllables imply that, just as the line contains more in the way of syllables than the meter promises, so too in the meanings conveyed by the words there is more than meets the ear."[69]

It is Britomart's sister, Hippolyta, the defeated Amazon about to wed the "reasonable" Theseus, who accommodates the excess in the lovers' tale, which perhaps also remains hidden in the textual unconscious of Theseus' speech. Precisely by *following* the story through its repetitions, she recognizes the *novelty* of an intersubjective subscription in the lovers' speech to the *truth* that resides in their "present synthesis of the past," and, with a "but" (which is not an end), she marks its empty place:

But all the story of the night told over,
And all their minds transfigur'd so together,
More witnesseth than fancy's images,
And grows to something of great constancy;
But howsoever, strange and admirable. (5.1.23–27)

In Hippolyta's honor I want to return, finally and fancifully, to the return of Martin Guerre. We know that the details of this case, as recorded by Jean de Coras and Guillaume Le Sueur in 1561, caught the attention of such a literary historical character as Montaigne. Suppose for a moment that Coras's *Arrest Memorable* also came into the hands of Edmund Spenser, who, as he evidently had with other "historical" material, found it to his purpose to insert a version of the story of Martin Guerre into *The Faerie Queene;* say, for example, in Book 3, adjacent to the story of Malbecco and Hellenore, where it might well serve as another elaboration of the contradictory relations of love and mastery—one in which the young Martin's presumed impotence in the early years of his marriage to Bertrande supplies a male counterpart to the sexual terror that afflicts Amoret.[70] How, then, might this episode be read?

The appearance of Arnaud as second Martin and his subsequent call to account for his crime of usurpation would, I think, be understood as an example of the familiar Spenserian technique of allegorical doubling. Along with the usurpations and doublings of Red Crosse by Archimago, Una by Duessa, the Snowy by the False Florimell, Arnaud's simulacrum of Martin would be seen to realize allegorically some deviation internal to Martin's character. By way of identifying this deviation and placing it in the narrative of *The Faerie Queene,* no competent interpreter would fail to note the significance of the name *Guerre* in this story of a man who disappears from the struggles of his domestic life, goes to war, and returns with the experience of combat written visibly on his body. The precise meaning of Martin's amputated leg would probably evoke controversy: some would find it impossible to disconnect the returned Martin's wound from a symbolic economy that would include his earlier impotence, his having disappeared after (and presumably as a result of) a bitter quarrel with his father, his defeat in court of the imposter Arnaud, and his belated assumption of his place as head of the Guerre household. Critics of this sort might read Martin's wound as symbolic of the castration he had to accept before he could accede to social potency. Others, following Greenblatt, might find such a "Freudian" reading of Martin's wound tempting but reductive and appropriative, refiguring in a newer discourse what the text has self-consciously figured in its own. Few, I think, would contend that the wound was simply adventitious, a narrative detail without narrative motive; though some historicists, having found Spenser's source in Coras, might account these details evidence of a tendency on Spenser's part to incorporate undigested historical material in his narrative, material which remains in excess of (and a distraction from) the allegorical design. Even these skeptics, however, would see in Spenser's use of the story an allegorical evocation of the relations of affection and mastery as they are played out between son and father, husband and wife, state and subject.

Read on this very general level, Martin Guerre's story also might be taken to represent — in *The Faerie Queene* — something fairly specific about the relationship of the two Martins to the desire of the wife, Bertrande, who, in the story, seems to play a key role in mediating the identity of the first Martin to the second. Her circular passage from Martin to Arnaud and back to Martin would be an interesting contrast to the linear descents of Hellenore and Malbecco. Finally, a reader with literary historical interests might wish to connect the emulations and usurpations of Martin and Arnaud over the construction of Bertrande as wife to the general case of rivalrous male constructions of female desire. This literary historical context might include, for example, the constructions of Desdemona's desire that pass between Iago and Othello.

So, we are left with a determined difference between the historical and the literary reading of the "facts" of the case of Martin Guerre, the former admitting of coincidence, the latter of an obligation to discover meaning. At what point in time — in, so to speak, the history of the history of Martin Guerre — does this difference between the historian's tale, presumably the work of cool reason, and the poet's tale, which "apprehends more than cool reason comprehends," occur? Is it only, and anachronistically, after Freud, or was it perhaps the eminently reasonable Jean de Coras who first perceived "something of great constancy" in the agreements and discrepancies among the stories told by the principals and interested parties in Artigat and so took the unusual step of publishing his history of this case, this *Arrest Memorable?* Does, in fact, a question arise even as to which of these two interpretive protocols was likely to have been used by Martin Guerre and his associates before the fateful encounters at the court in Toulouse? Would it be anachronistic to imagine a day on which Martin Guerre, wherever he was, imagined his return, anticipated one rather than another ending to the story, and acted so as to bring about what he anticipated?

Read as what we are today called upon to call history — that is — as the record of what happened — the Martin Guerre story simply does not tell us anything about the 'meaning' of Martin's name or his missing leg, or, for that matter, of the conversations between Arnaud and his, that is, Martin Guerre's, wife, Bertrande, which Natalie Zemon Davis believes to be the "cause" of Arnaud's success in assuming the identity of Martin. But read as fiction — as something signifying an enunciating "I" as its necessarily absent cause, those details cry out for interpretation. The interpretations they elicit may be, strictly speaking, from a historical-causal point of view false, which is to say that on the evidence they cannot be shown to have caused anything narrated in the story; but from an analytical, critical point of view, speaking now of narrative rather than historical truth, they — like Shakespeare's not entirely silent intervocalic "v" — remain, and so, too, in a sense that is *nachträglich* but not, in Greenblatt's usage, belated, does the truth of their interpretation. This truth, which in fact was always already latent in the causal story — the narration of bare facts — with which we began, is the irrefutable "truth" to be found in the individual's recognition of himself or herself as the subject of its "present synthesis of the past." The subject and its truth emerge precipitously in the moment when the unfolding of events turns from a terminal point that is both provisional and proleptic to a reflection on itself as unfolded meaning. This psychoanalytic truth is also Spenser's truth. It is, formally speaking, this subject and its truth, joined to each other at the moment of a halt, a *memorable arrest,* in which the subject remembers itself as the subject of its own past, to which Spenser refers when he invokes "matter of just memory" and cites, in the proem to Book 2, those things that, like the recently discovered lands of the American continent, seem always to have been there but only belatedly remembered.

Chapter 5

Refiguring the Remains of the World in Donne's *Anniversaries:*
Absolute Monuments to Absolute Knowledge

1

To understand better the force of lived experience in literary history and the
force of literary history in the lived experience of the Renaissance, I propose to
examine in this chapter the cognitive force of one particular set of rhetorical
configurations: a group of interrelated representations of the self that derive
from the analogy of macrocosm to microcosm. In particular, I want to examine the literary historical moment represented by the use of this analogy in
some poems by John Donne, but first I want to place my reading of Donne in
the context of a more general discussion of the ways in which the dialectic of
rhetorical tropes outlined in chapter 2 supports the microcosm-macrocosm
analogy.

Dynamically poised between metaphor and synecdoche, the analogy of
macrocosm and microcosm insures the homogeneity of self and the symbolic
system within which self acts. It puts the subject into one or another picture of the world by putting the world into the subject. The metaphors and
allegories generated by the analogy of macrocosm to microcosm reach synecdochic closure when the analogy assures that each and every perceived object,
if viewed correctly, will be seen to reproduce a cosmic totality. Although it is
not possible to quantify the degree to which historical human agents actually
constructed self and world according to the paradigms implicit in a dialectical
progression of rhetorical tropes, the breadth of social institutions, practices,
and representations informed by a few self-consistent rhetorics testifies to the
cognitive force of such paradigms. The historical force of the analogy of the
macrocosm to the microcosm is apparent, for example, in such socially significant metaphors as the "body politic" and the incorporation of the church
in Christ.

I intend to show that the ground of the analogy of macrocosm and microcosm is — in rhetorical practice — *an iterative set of metonymies of genus for species and species for genus;* in this set of metonymies the *species* is literally what appears, what may be seen, and *genus* is a concept or category of thought into which the species may be assimilated. For example, the elaborate allegory of the body in the House of Alma in Book 2 of *The Faerie Queene* uses the regulatory systems of the body to evoke a generic notion of regulation, which extends over an open-ended range of activities, cosmic, political, and social as well as physiological. The metonymic substitutions of genus for species and species for genus *become metaphoric* when the substitutions are accorded ontological force, so that, for example, physical evidence of self-regulation on the level of the species also becomes evidence of categorical self-regulation. This metaphoric identification of regulation at different levels becomes synecdochic when all evidence of regulation is understood to manifest a single regulatory principle — divine providence, for example.

The work performed by this rhetoric relates to one of the crucial philosophical problems of the Renaissance: How to relate the particular to the universal so as to produce an intelligible world by uniting appearance, which is understood to be time-bound, and thought, which seeks the stability of a truth outside time.[1] The intelligibility of a world still understood according to an idealist principle, and thus conceiving of truth as a verisimilar reproduction of an ideal that remains always self-identical and comprehensive, resides in the ability of the subject to locate each particular that it encounters within the concept proper to it. Particular individuals appear as unintelligible *things* until they are subsumed under concepts.

Literary history records — in its details — both the struggle to *see through* particulars to the categories in which they may be made intelligible and the (literary) performances through which the resistance of *things,* encountered as particulars within an increasingly assertive unfolding of temporal events is staged. In earlier chapters we have seen how Augustine's allegorical interpretation of the injunction to increase and multiply uses a metaphoric identification of birds and words to assimilate sexual procreation to the production of thought in human speech and to assimilate thought to the expression of a timeless and eternal logos. We also have seen how Spenser's metaphoric identification of timeless fairyland and timely England collapses back into the irreducible particularity of Colin Clout when *The Faerie Queene* stages the scene of its own composition.

Taken together, these two cases exemplify how the dialectic of rhetorical tropes — on the level, for example, of the deployment of metonymy and metaphor in the analogy of microcosm and macrocosm — draws exigently appearing phenomena into preexisting systems of symbolization, while at the same time it preserves, as a determined excess of the signifier, the exigence of the signifying or symbolic thing itself. Human speech returns God's word to the logos in the form of spoken prayer, but it also stands apart from God as human speech. Colin Clout stands for the poet in the text, but he also stands out as the poet of the text.

Take for another example this exchange between Hamlet and Gertrude in act 1, scene 2:

> HAMLET Ay, madam, it is common.
> QUEEN   If it be,
>   Why seems it so particular with thee? (ll. 74–75)

The scene begins with the entry of the court. Claudius assumes the chair of state with an awkward speech about the nearness of the old King's death and the new King's marriage. The speech is clearly intended to put the scandal of his accession in the past and to move forward into the new reign. Following this declamation, Claudius enacts his supersession of old Hamlet by turning to immediate and urgent business of state, dispatching an embassy to Norway for the restraint of Fortinbras. But throughout the scene the visible anomaly of Hamlet's mourning clothes, by which he is recognized before he speaks, stands out as a resistance to Claudius's rhetoric of succession. The quoted exchange follows the Queen's request that this anomaly be resolved:

> Good Hamlet, cast thy nighted color off,
> And let thine eye look like a friend on Denmark.
> Do not forever with thy vailed lids
> Seek for thy noble father in the dust.
> Thou know'st 'tis common, all that lives must die,
> Passing through nature to eternity (1.2.68–73).

Gertrude's effort may be thought of as a plea to Hamlet to get the dust of the father he cannot see, the father who no longer is there, and who was Denmark, out of his eye so that he might see more clearly the "father" ("my cousin Hamlet, and my son —," 1.2.64) who is there and who is in this scene particularly concerned to assert himself as *Denmark.* The ocular adjustment Gertrude seeks from Hamlet is preliminary to getting Hamlet's ostentatious mourning out of the court's eye.

Gertrude's "common" is doubly articulated. Sententiously, it seeks to help Hamlet let go of his father by subsuming the old King under a generic "father" whose death is the "common" fate of "all that lives." Hamlet's duty in this particular instance is to comprehend the exigence of his father's (untimely) death as an instance of an eternal pattern. But also, and more particularly, Gertrude's "common" merges Claudius and King Hamlet under the categorical roles "Father" and "Denmark" in an effort to ease the substitution of the former for the latter.[2]

Hamlet's dry response repeats Gertrude's "common" in a way that discloses the contextual specificity of its meaning, disrupting Gertrude's philosophically sanitary opposition "common/particular" by shadowing it with the alternative opposition, "common/refined." In this way, Hamlet deflects Gertrude's "common" away from universalizing philosophical discourse and back onto the seamy particulars of her behavior. He resists the assimilation of the scene to a generic moment of perfunctory mourning and succession and insists instead on the sordid particularity of a circumstance that remains in excess of the generic performance.

The inexpressible difference between an inassimilable and unique event and the iterative categorical performances through which the event is marked cues the thematics of Hamlet's repetition of "seems" in the following line. When he responds to Gertrude's "Why seems it so particular with thee?" with, "Seems, Madam? nay it is, I know not 'seems.' " Hamlet employs his technique of strategically displaced repetition exactly as he had with "common." But the difference between Gertrude's neutral use of "seems," as a synonym for "appears," and Hamlet's redeployment of "seems" to effectively assert a mutual exclusion between what *appears* and what *is* opens an ontological rift. Metonymy is asserted over metaphor. Things that *seem* alike cannot *be* the same. A few lines later, when he identifies "seeming" with "playing" and rejects the denotative value of "actions that a man might play" (1.2.84), the play, *Hamlet*, threatens to disappear all too precisely into the chasm between seeming and being.

Hamlet sees in his displacement of "seems" from Gertrude's neutral "appears" to his own "pretends" not a contingent slippage in language, but a structuring opposition in fact. What appears *cannot* be true *because* it may be played. If the truth is "that within which passes show" (1.2.85), it would seem that the truth of a thing cancels its appearance. But the appearance remains and is, finally, all there is, "the play's the thing / Wherein I'll catch the conscience of the King" (2.2.604–5).

For there to be a Hamlet, there must be a *Hamlet*, a play of actions that point to the elsewhere, the other stage, where action plays out as truth. Hamlet articulates the complicated connection between the appearance and disappearance of truth within a rhetoric that is still based on the mimetic interplay of ideal and speculum, original and simulacrum, and in which truth is in the concept discovered in the mind, not in what appears to the eye. Fineman's discussion of the coming together of metaphor and mimesis in epideictic poetry explores the way in which the visual element inherent in idealist mimesis engages the poetic image as the material representation of the idea:

> Before it means anything else, "idea," *idein,* means "to see," and this
> originary visual image colors in specific ways both the physics and the
> metaphysics of a poetics that thinks itself toward an ideal, whether
> we think of the *eidola* or *simulacra,* the likenesses, of Stoic optics, the
> *eidei* or essences of Plato's Forms or Ideas, or the "species," realist or
> nominalist, of medieval scholasticism (from *specere,* "to look at").[3]

The poem, then, serves up the immaterial idea in the realm of the senses. The reader is enabled to "see" the idea as materially present in metaphor:

> Such "ideas" are, so to speak, materialized in the poetry of praise. They
> are present as things or artifacts the very physicality of which is thematically exploited, explicitly remarked, as though through this physicality
> it were possible to instantiate the rhetorical logic of an idealizing poetics based on effective force, the "actuality," of likeness—whether this
> poetics is exemplified by the way it understands mimesis as an exercise
> of iconic imitation that offers vivid pictures of that which it presents,
> or by the way it understands figure as a genericizing and essentializing
> metaphoricity by means of which, as Aristotle said of metaphor, poets
> "see the same" (*to homoion theorein estin.* (ibid.)

"Species" in this sense — that which may be seen — crosses over immediately to, permeates, overlaps with, the particular, which is sensed, in opposition to the genus, which must be thought. By examining in a formal way the rhetorical structure that sustains the analogy of macrocosm to microcosm, I hope to show the dialectical mediation — in time — of species and genus. This mediation will, in turn, mark a literary historical shift from a poetics of vision to a poetics of voice.

2

The versions of the self we have seen in Augustine, Dante, Petrarch, and Spenser may be formalized as a set of dialectical transformations in the rhetoric of the Christian ego set out in the *Confessions*. Returning briefly to Augustine's allegorical reading of the injunction to Adam and Eve to increase and multiply, we will recall that he rejects a literal reading of this phrase as superfluous, because, acting "according to their kind," Adam and Eve would have procreated without it. On the assumption that God does not speak superfluously, Augustine offers an allegory of allegory, in which the phrase is read as granting man "a power and a faculty, both to express several ways that which we understand but one, and to understand several ways, that which we read to be obscurely delivered but in one." [4]

Referring to a slightly more elaborated version of the diagram of this allegory offered in chapter 3 (fig. 2), we can see that the signifying chains corresponding to the generation of fish (AB) and the generation of men (CD) are each generated in accord with the same metonymic principle. The concept (signified) of each sign in these chains is the material signifier of the sign immediately preceding or succeeding it in the chain.

In the generation of fish (AB): AB_1 IXΘΥΣ enters the chain at the left as an acronymic name of the logos, reducing the acoustic image /icthys/ to a purely visual indication of the deity. The attendant excision of the signified /fish/ stands as the primal repression — both material (syllabic sounds reduced to visual inscriptions) and conceptual (the effacement of the concept fish) — that initiates Augustine's allegory of allegory. Following this initial repression, *fish,* which had been canceled as concept or category, returns as material signifier (AB_2). The thing itself, as it were — the fish which one takes from the sea — reenters signification with an acquired transparency, as an index pointing

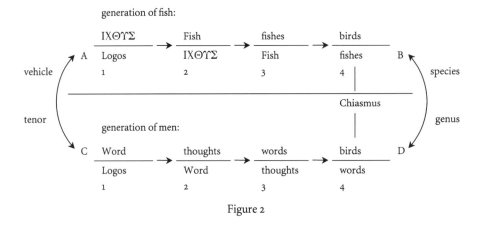

Figure 2

through the acronym inscribed in its Greek name to the logos itself. Signification thus passes through the *fish,* eliding the thing and the concept, the fish or the thought of fish, in favor of a generalized affirmation of the designedness of the natural (visible) world. In the final link of this chain the category derived from the association in AB_3 of the particular and observable fishes and the conceptual genus fish, understood as a symbolic manifestation of the logos written out in the natural world (AB_4), mediates the conceptualization of the birds as an alternative appearance of the logos. Under this concept, the literal contiguity of the horizon — that is, the spatial contiguity of sea and sky — motivates the categorical continuity of birds and fishes.[5]

In the generation of men (CD): CD_1 similarly enters the chain as a primal repression, but in a crucially reversed direction. Whereas AB_1 elides the word as acoustic material by placing the common noun signification of /icthys/ behind or under the acronymic insistence of its letters, CD_1 restores the Word as a metonymic substitution for the incarnate God who speaks it. Thus, AB_1 and CD_1 may be understood as reciprocal metonymies articulating the relationship of genus to species: if we are to hear the word as referential discourse, as logos, we must lose sight of its material support; if we are to see or hear the Word as material presence, we must forget the self-variations over time that allow it to be heard. Thus, reading the diagram from left to right, as though each sign were the temporal successor of the one before it, we encounter a

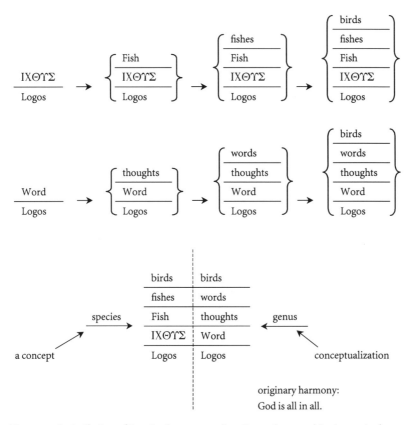

Figure 3. Assimilation of Species (appearance) to Genus (concept) in Augustine's Allegory of Birds and Fishes

series of metonymic appropriations by which various material supports are assimilated to a signifying system.

Figure 3 shows in more detail the generation of the signifying chain through metonymic appropriations. The appropriation of contiguous signs is arrested only when the dual signification of *volatilia* cross-couples *birds* in one chain and *thoughts* in the other. By following this rhetoric in such detail, I hope — with the patience of the reader — to catch the belated moment of the emergence of *the thing* as the material ground of signification. As we saw in our discussion of the returns of Martin Guerre and Colin Clout, this moment is belated because the thingness of the thing, the exigence of its blank materiality, appears only in contrast to the signifying function that fails to exhaust it.[6] It is, in a sense, excreted by the symbolic system it seems to precede. Things are made visible, configured as objects of cognition, as they become the signifiers of preceding concepts or the concepts of preceding signifiers.

Respecting this constitutive belatedness, we note that when the chains are read back from the metaphoric chiasmus to their initiating figures, the metonymies become metaphors. In this case the proportional metaphor, birds are to fish as thoughts are to words — arrived at by the assimilation of birds and thoughts, as two species within the broadly defined genus of "flying things" — is formally reflected back through the chains, retrospectively organizing a series of signs based on genus-species metonymies that metaphorically signify logos (designedness, Heideggerean *collection*).[7] Whatever else this dialectic of prospective metonymies and retrospective metaphors may be — and it may be a lot — it is the formal structure of the macrocosm-microcosm analogy, and it authorizes the discovery of the same lexicon of repeating relations on different levels. Things becoming present as things remain *uncollected* (supplementary to logos) until the formal structure is revised by its retrospective conversion from metonymy to metaphor.[8]

Generalizing from the example of Augustine's allegory of the birds and fishes, it is possible to express the generative configuration of signs that produces the Augustinian ego in purely formal terms. Figure 4 indicates the rhetoric of metonymic generation and metaphoric arrest as a cognitive mode that organizes the things given to the senses as particulars as also the material signifiers of intelligible generic concepts. The signs in each column are articulated vertically by metonymy and horizontally by metaphor. For example, S_3 on the left — the position of "fish" in Augustine's allegory — is, by metonymy, the concept derived from the material object above it and, by metaphor, the vehicle for the concept S_3 in the righthand column — the position occupied by "thoughts" in Augustine's allegory.[9]

As we saw in chapter 4, *The Faerie Queene* tropes this tropic structure by becoming thematically aware of its reversibility. The metaphoric closure of *The Faerie Queene* is disrupted by the collapse of the distinction between metonymic vehicle and metaphoric tenor so that metonymy reappears inside the metaphoric recuperation of exigent events — as meaning. Because Spenser's text allows its readers to see Fairy Land as a reflection of their temporal history as well as envisioning history as a reflection of the (never fully) moralized

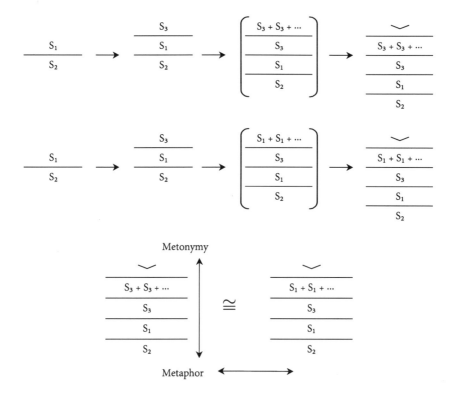

$\smile$ = the switch word that metaphorically joins the signifying chains.

Figure 4. Generalized Rhetoric for Metaphoric Assimilation of Metonymic Chains

landscape of Fairy Land, the sublimation of the particular into the genus, which forms the decisive climax in the Augustinian scheme, becomes instead a recursive motif. This recursive patterning finds its fullest expression in the specter of the "nymph out of Diane's favor" haunting Calidore's discovery of Colin Clout on Acidale. The unvoiced name of Salmacis serves to indicate a crease where the narrative's endings fold over onto its putative origins. The subject of the narration (Spenser) and the narrated subject (Colin) coincide precisely at the point where the project to fashion a gentleman or noble person iteratively partakes of (gives way to and becomes identified with) the waters of lassitude.

The punctual and iterative emergence of the scene of writing in *The Faerie*

Queene reverses the tenor and vehicle of the extended metaphor that comprises its allegory so that the allegory becomes the vehicle for the discovery of the story of the self in relation to its allegorical desire. In the unstable cognitive world determined by Spenser's rhetoric, metonymy is never successfully contained by a metaphoric or synecdochic closure. Rather, the (allegorical) scenes of the poem are continually referred back to the embodied voice of a historically situated narrator. Thus, the pressure of history leaves its trace in the metaphoric brake failure marked by the returns to the scene of writing in *The Faerie Queene.*

When we turn from the narrative ambition of Spenser's epic romance to the lyric and occasional voice of John Donne, we encounter this trace in another form. The expectation of a metaphoric resolution that converts the exigent to the meaningful remains, but the failure of that expected closure is ironically realized as the failure of representation itself. The confrontation of generic form and historically exigent particular emerges as theme, and the metaphorics of the macrocosm and microcosm are seen to offer the positive assertion of being only from within their own linguistic negation.

3

In recent scholarship Donne has been called variously a "coterie" poet, a social conservative, and the neurotic victim of his own religious apostasy.[10] These speculations signal the return of a personal and materially situated Donne from a repression shaped by the confluence of the formal reticence of the New Critics and the ghastly hyperbole and puzzling duplicity of Donne's own self-presentation. Interestingly enough, however, these more recent social, political, and psychological historicizations of Donne also invite a renewed attention to form. Having demystified and contextualized Donne's "wit," we are now in a position to meaningfully resuscitate the category under which his poems were successfully revived early in the twentieth century—that is, to think again about Donne as a Metaphysical poet.

While the epithet "metaphysical," scornfully but critically applied by Johnson and admiringly bestowed by Eliot and the New Critics, has, historically, been used to describe Donne's style, the term is aptly used in its strong sense—pertaining to the science of first principles and the ultimate nature of reality or being—to describe the intellectual work carried out in many of Donne's poems.[11] I shall be particularly concerned with a reading of Donne's *Anniver-*

saries, supported by readings of two philosophically related poems, "Aire and Angels" and "A Nocturnall upon S. Lucies Day." I shall argue that these poems treat of a timely tendency to forgo metaphysics—the futility of which they metaphysically explore—in favor of epistemology, that is, to shift the focus from the world to be known to the knowledge of the world. However, to say that in calling these poems metaphysical I want to push past the critical tradition, almost as old as the poems themselves, that uses the term to refer to a set of stylistic affectations (e.g., the conceit, argumentative tone and form, appropriation of esoteric scientific, alchemical, and Scholastic vocabularies, use of the unexpected comparison) and to consider the poems as instruments of a serious philosophical inquiry is not to tell the whole story. I also want to seek the rhetorical ground on which the distinction between style and content becomes obscure, and style itself becomes metaphysical in the strong sense. This ground, which is in a given historical moment more or less conscious of the ways in which rhetoric configures *being,* constitutes the metaphysics of Donne's metaphysical style, the use of style as a primary mode of philosophical elaboration.

I say this because to understand the philosophical content of these poems — at the level on which that content is deployed as rhetoric—is also necessarily to historicize them. To understand the ways in which they are at once metaphysical and historical is to bring to bear a properly mediated understanding of the extrinsic pressures of material history on the intrinsic development of intellectual history at the turn of the sixteenth century. Such an understanding will help us achieve an exemplary aim and a general one: to step outside the fallacious dichotomy that has reinscribed the poet's retrospective and expedient disjunction of Jack Donne and Doctor Donne as a disjunction of a ludic, conventional, masking Donne and an ambitious, neurotic, obsessive Donne, and, procedurally, to step outside the dichotomy that has needlessly separated material and intellectual historiography into an extrinsic determinism and an intrinsic idealism.[12]

The *Anniversaries* are obscure poems. Critics faced with their obscurity have resorted to a number of esoteric readings. The reading I shall propose is, on the contrary, a literal one. To read the *Anniversaries* as what the text says they are—the diagnostic postmortem of a dead world and a contemplation of the soul's progress to a better one—is to allow that their themes include a philosophically serious account of a dislocated subjectivity in the garden of epideictic verse.[13] To say that they record the substitution of an epistemological meditation for a thwarted metaphysical meditation is to say that they are thematically aware of an inability to accommodate in a single metaphysics the universe and the subject who knows it. To say that the style they deploy is irreducible to, yet inseparable from, the thematic statement which they encompass is to refuse the displacement of the ideal object intrinsic to the poem by the extrinsic circumstances that stand in a determined relation to it.

The details of the *Anniversaries* tell something of the story of the historical moment in which their dislocated subjectivity, always in excess of its own knowledge, begins to be established as a rhetorical norm. The self produced by the rhetorical configuration that emerges from their confrontation with "new philosophy" speaks as an inward stranger. Always appraising itself from the position of another, it insistently repeats an originary undoing: "For all assum'd unto this Dignitee, / So many weedlesse Paradises bee, / Which of themselves produce no venomous sinne, / Except some forraine Serpent bring it in" (*First Anniversary* ll. 81–84).[14] In the *Anniversaries* (and elsewhere), Donne tracks the production of the self constituted specifically as difference, as that which is *not* (and cannot be) represented adequately, and offers an intellectual historical retrospection of some of the material conditions that underlie its appearance. This self appears precisely in the space opened by the failure of metaphysics that Donne's poems metaphysically identify.

Thomas Willard remarks the precise descriptions given on the title pages of the 1612 edition of the *Anniversaries*: "The world is 'represented' in the *First Anniversary*, whereas the soul is 'contemplated' in *The Second Anniversary*. The first is a mimesis, an imitation of the world that is passing; the second is a noesis, an insight into the life of the world to come."[15] The relationship between them, then, parallels that between species and genus, imitation and understanding, in the analogy of microcosm and macrocosm. The movement from representation in *The First Anniversary* to contemplation in *The Second Anniversary* may be understood as a movement inward that is also a fall from metaphysical ontology into the beginnings of a critical epistemology. One *represents* an object, but to *contemplate* is necessarily to place oneself, one's knowledge, in relation to the object and to observe the effect of that relation on the self. As we shall see, for Donne, contemplation ultimately situates the object inside the self, possessing it as one's own knowledge. The burden of my argument includes an attempt to understand how it comes about that this rejection of being in favor of knowing gives rise to both the historical method and the epistemological-subjective tradition around which history is formed.

4

By 1611 Donne had lived through a number of social, economic, and religious developments that, taken together, mediate his exigent circumstances and an event in intellectual history — an epistemological cusp.[16] That year, in response to a commission from the wealthy father of a recently deceased fourteen-year old girl, Donne produced an enduringly anomalous poem, *An Anatomy of the World*. A year later, this poem became known as *The First Anniversary* when it was published together with *The Second Anniversary: The Progres of the Soule*. Asked to commemorate the death of an entirely undistinguished young girl, whom he had never met, Donne presents himself with a question about remainders, about what is left when something crucial is subtracted from one's world.[17] Adopting the conceit that a certain world could not survive the death of the girl, whom he figures, generically, as "she," he works over the world's remains, paradoxically asserting the value of a dissection that no one will remain alive to study.

"Shee, shee is dead; shee's dead: when thou knowst this, / Thou knowest how drie a Cinder this world is" (*Anatomy*, ll. 427–28). What, beyond the paying of a commissioned compliment, does it mean to link "her" death and the reduction of the world to ash? Although not formally deployed as a refrain, the formula "Shee, shee is dead, shee's dead; when thou knowest this, / Thou knowest . . ." appears five times in the 475-line poem, and a variation of it is picked up beginning at line 81 of the *Second Anniversary*: "Shee, shee is gone; shee is gone; when thou knowest this, / What fragmentary rubbidge this world is / Thou knowest. . . ." Through these eccentric refrains, the reportage which comprises the bulk of the *Anatomy* is represented as adding up to a series of grim conclusions: the world is "a trivial thing," "a lame cripple," "a monster," "a wan ghost," and "a drie cinder." But in each case it is not precisely the world that has changed but our knowledge of it: what "thou knowst" when "Thou knowest this." "Her" death is a *sign* by which a more cosmic death is known. It is the symptom of this greater death but not the cause.

Donne's hyperbolic lamentations elicit a familiar anecdote, recorded by Drummond of Hawthorden in his *Conversations* with Ben Jonson. As the story goes, when Jonson complained of "Donne's 'Anniversary' " that such an extravagant poem about a teenage girl was "profane" and that "if it had been written of the Virgin Mary it had been something," Donne replied that "he described the idea of a woman, and not as she was."[18] Jonson's remarks on *An Anatomy of the World* and Donne's response to them indicate that in 1611 the superimposition of experienced cause and rhetorically assimilated result that produced — as a literary historical event — a subject that understood itself to be the subject of its own knowledge was not yet completed. Jonson and Donne could not at first agree on the "prior reality" to which Donne's poems "referred." If, as Donne indicated to Jonson, "shee" is not to be mistaken for Elizabeth Drury, but is rather to be understood — by a metonymy of the genus for the species — as "the idea of a Woman," then we can understand Donne's poem as a meditation on the use to which an idealized and generic "shee" has been put in the poetic (and, by a brief extension, the intellectual) life of his times.[19]

To better understand "her" function, before proceeding to a discussion of the generic "she" who stands in for or points to the "idea of a woman" in the *Anniversaries,* I want to turn first to a curious and poignant transition appearing in a letter that Donne wrote in April 1612 while he was in Paris with Sir Robert Drury, and then to a reading of a lyric among the *Songs and Sonets,* "Aire and Angels." In the letter, addressed to "Sir G. F.," Donne writes:

> I am yet in the same perplexity which I mentioned before, which is, that I have received no *syllable,* neither from herself nor by any other, how *my wife* hath passed her danger, nor do I know whether I be *increased by a child or diminished by the loss of a wife.*
>
> I hear from England of many censures of *my book* of *Mistress Drury;* if any of those censures do but pardon me my *descent in printing anything in verse . . .* , I doubt not but they will soon give over that other part of that indictment, which is that I have said so much; for nobody can *imagine* that *I who never saw her,* could have any other purpose in that, than that when I had received so very good *testimony* of her worthiness, and was gone down to print verses, *it became me* to say, not what I was sure was just truth, but the best that I could *conceive;* for that had been a new weakness in me, to have praised anybody in printed verses, that had not been capable of the best praise that I could give.[20]

Here, where the relation between the subject who writes and the "I" represented in the writing is nearly immediate, we may note the curious linguistic crossing of two women, Anne Donne and Elizabeth Drury. Donne's abandonment of his pregnant wife, from whom he has had "no syllable," in order to seek fortune with Drury, crosses over his "descent in printing anything in verse," also to seek fortune with Drury. Donne's mind, passing in this letter from writing, the "syllables" of his wife, who may or may not be living, to writing, his printed "book of Mistress Drury," who is not living and whom he never saw, traces an anaphoric chiasmus: Writing / Anne Donne < > Elizabeth Drury / Writing. In this exchange he cannot know whether he "be diminished by the loss of a wife" or "increased by a child," diminished by the descent to print or increased by the imagination — absent the life of Elizabeth Drury — of the idea of a Woman, the best he could conceive.[21]

By way of emphasizing the interpenetration of poetic trope and lived world, before returning to the generic "she" of the *Anniversaries,* I am going to trace a similar pattern, as it appears in more abstract, sententious, and generic form in "Aire and Angels." Before leaving the passage from the letter, however, I make special note of the total coexistence in it of abstractly formal pattern and clearly felt grief.

In "Aire and Angels," in a very different mood, Donne affords us a less contextualized and, therefore, less restricted view of the relations of masculine desire, imagination, and woman as he understands them. This view indirectly illuminates the relations of universal, particular, and signifier that underlie and enable the chiasmic exchange and appropriation of idea, woman, and poem exemplified in the letter to Sir G. F.

> Twice or thrice had I lov'd thee,
> Before I knew thy face and name;
> So in a voice, so in a shapelesse flame,
> *Angells* affect us oft, and worship'd bee;
>   Still when, to where thou wert, I came,
> Some lovely glorious nothing did I see.
>   But since my soule, whose child love is,
> Takes limmes of flesh, and else could nothing doe,
>   More subtile then the parent is,
> Love must not be, but take a body too,
>   And therefore what thou wert, and who,
>   I bid Love aske, and now

That it assume thy body, I allow,
And fixe it selfe in thy lip, eye, and brow.
　　Whilst thus to ballast love, I thought,
　　And so more steddily to have gone,
With wares which would sinke admiration,
I saw, I had loves pinnace overfraught,
　　Ev'ry thy haire for love to worke upon
Is much too much, some fitter must be sought;
　　For, nor in nothing, nor in things
Extreme, and scatt'ring bright, can love inhere;
　　Then as an Angell, face, and wings
Of aire, not pure as it, yet pure doth weare,
　　So thy love may be my loves spheare;
　　　　Just such disparitie
As is twixt Aire and Angells puritie,
'Twixt womens love, and mens will ever bee.[22]

As with the *Anniversaries,* the meaning of this poem is obscure.[23] I offer here one possible and self-consciously schematic reading, turning on the double articulation of a phrase that hovers over but never occurs in the poem: "my love." "My love" joins within it the speaker and the addressee of the poem: the poet's Love (desire), which emanates from within and of which he purports to have been aware before he allows it to "assume [her] body" (l. 13), and the girl who, for a time, embodies that desire and makes it visible.[24]

This precisely missing phrase is most closely approached — by a metonymy of genus for species — in the bawdy reduction of both "loves," to the punning genitality of line 25, "So thy love may be my loves spheare."[25] I contend that whatever else may be going on in the poem, "Aire and Angels" is about the noncoincidence of these two desires: desire understood, to use Lacanian terminology, as a "lack in being," (*manque-à-être*), as that which the man seeks *because* he cannot see it — cannot see the place from which he sees — and desire understood, as Lacan's *objet petit a,* that is, as an object that metonymically supplies desire's lack, an object that acts simultaneously as the putative cause and the representative of his desire and is known only as that which, like the phrase "my love," necessarily slips away.[26]

In terms of the dialectic of rhetorical configurations sketched out in chapter 2, the metonymic conflation (in line 25) of desire as it appears in the aroused phallus and as the more general and idealized notion of Love is *ironic*, not because it provokes a cynical reading, but because of the way it undoes or deconfigures the sublation of body by spirit that the poem's Petrarchan trappings lead us conventionally to expect.[27] Donne's irony precisely reverses the direction of the displacement of reference that we saw in Augustine's reading of the biblical injunction to "increase and multiply" as an injunction to allegory.[28] Where Augustine rubs off the disparity between words and birds, prayer and sexual insemination, by abstracting from species to genus until a metaphorical equivalence can be invoked, Donne analogizes the disparity "'Twixt womens love, and mens" as a disparity between air and angels, figuring both terms of the analogy in the copulatory coming together of the male thing and the female "nothing": "when, to where thou wert, I came, / Some lovely glorious nothing did I see."

In arguing that the poem makes this reduction, I am aware that the language of "So thy love may be my loves spheare" is also the language of an established angelology, within which the poem's speaker may refer to his love as the angel that gives motion to and is manifest within a cosmic sphere.[29] My point is literary historical and empirical. In a lyric reinscription of the intrusion of history into allegory in Spenser's narrative, the spiritual analogy of "Aire and Angels" cannot (as we read in the poem's critical history, which now includes the reading I have just offered) efface or accommodate the carnal reading. Each and every time the bawdy puns on "nothing," "love," and "spheare" are heard, the carnal scene asserts itself, even from within the idealist scene that would replace it; the Petrarchan pinnace is found to be once more overfraught.[30]

The poem stages, then, the coming together of desire and its object *as* the coming together of spirit and body. But the lyric also implicitly narrates the brief time of their apparent coincidence and their inevitable separation, representing them as a chiasmic crossing in the poet's imagination of a necessarily and multivalently generic Love and the exigent appearance of a particular girl, who comes (for a time) to embody and particularize that Love — who comes, that is, to be the material vehicle through which "my love" may be visibly expressed, but only as "some lovely glorious nothing." This chiasmic pattern of exchange, doubled by the chiasmic exchange of the analogy of angels, which seems (but only apparently) to pertain to woman in the first stanza and to man in the second, binds this poem to the pathos of Anne More as absent syllable in the letter to Sir G. F., on the one hand, and to the conceit of the never seen Elizabeth Drury in the *Anniversaries,* on the other. In short, and eliding much detail, the poet loves before he meets the beloved, but his love is a feeling without a corresponding image, shape, or sound. The presence of this love, which is neither wholly within nor exterior to the speaker, may be inferred from a slight disturbance in the air, as the presence of angels may be inferred — adventitiously — in a voice or the flicker of a flame.

Assuming that the opening of the poem uses "the vocabulary of love theory that the Renaissance elaborated out of Plato's *Symposium,*" in which the female beloved "figures as the source and agent" of the speaker's love for her, Janel Mueller concludes that the speaker's two or three instances of loving before he knew the face or name of the beloved represent the early stages of the infatuation ("The Play of Difference," pp. 86–87). My more literal reading sees the paradox of the opening lines as a reflection of the disjunction between male love and female object that is the poem's theme. The angel does not change from female to male. It is at first the male's desire that is elicited by but precedes the female object. The girl allows the man to become aware of this desire, which he recognizes as his own even though it comes to him as though provoked from the outside. The allure of this desire is, precisely, its nonsignifying character, its appearance as a sort of hole in a world otherwise saturated by meaning. This perceived lack in the signifier ("Some lovely glorious nothing did I see") is explicitly understood to be a lack of material, of signifying matter (*res*). When "my love" (male desire) becomes "my love" (the beloved woman), his desire becomes visible in her; he becomes the subject of a desire that reaches around her. *His* angel inseminates *her,* and she returns his desire to him in reciprocating form ("thy love" as "my loves spheare"). But woman fails as the *matter* in which male desire is actualized. His penis overfreights her pinnace. Desire reappears ("Wee dye and rise the same," "The Canonization," l. 26). The lack in the signifier reappears as a surplus of signifier ("Ev'ry thy haire for love to worke upon / Is much too much"). The speaker now reconstructs himself as lover — that is, as subject of a love that constitutively overbears its female object (species), who returns to the status of nonsignifying matter. This reading gives more force to the speaker's assertion that love is his soul's child (l. 8), seeing in it the implication that the woman is the empty vessel in which the child grows to visible proportions. In this respect, the voice and flame in line 3 recall the indeterminate "voice from some neighbor's house" (*vocem de vicina domo*) that urges Augustine to "take up and read" in the climactic scene of the *Confessions* (l. 464). Donne's seeing the woman, like Augustine's reading the book, is felt as a constitutively belated recognition, the correlative matching of some indeterminate sensible thing and an interior development seeking expression.

When the poet encounters the girl, he restages the legendary first recognitions of Beatrice and Laura. She is the object of his love, which is to say that the preexisting, objectless, immaterial, and generic desire he felt is retroactively reconstituted, misrecognized as love of this particular girl. As Hegel might put it, the subject's love has passed over into its object, where it may be recognized and encountered — and, most importantly, sublated and repossessed — as "my love."[31] Insofar as the lyric encounter is staged as an iteration of the literary historical encounters of Dante and Beatrice, Petrarch and Laura, the retroactive restructuring of desire represented in it extends also to the restructuring of the literary historical tradition that structures the encounter and is ironically undone by it. The subsequent failure of the encounter with the unnamed girl to stabilize and contain "my love" also marks the failure of the Augustinian — Petrarchan tradition to sublime spiritual from bodily love.

The poet's undifferentiated love, which was, at first, the idea of love, of himself as lover, *appears* divisible when lodged in the *parts* of the beloved, "thy lip, eye, and brow." But, in a wry reversal of the Augustinian-Petrarchan passage of the subject through a recalcitrant and scattering object (*Rime sparse*) to reunion in a transcendental subjectivity, Donne's male love appropriates and inhabits the woman's body as an angel appropriates and thickens air, so as to make itself both visible and divisible, only to reencounter itself as a persistent excess. As I suggested earlier, in the seventeenth century this passage of the subject through its object would have been thought of in terms of an Aristotelian epistemology of species and genus.[32] According to this conception, the particular, or species (that which appears to the senses), is strictly unintelligible because it is unique. To be understood, the object given to the senses must be mentally shorn of its distracting accidents and actively joined to its appropriate *idea*. What is outside must be joined to what is inside so that thing may correspond to mind, the wit conform to the object.[33] Having established the woman as the species through which the man's idea of Love becomes, for a time, grossly visible, "Aire and Angels" wittily performs and describes the operation of cognition as the *disparity* between gross (particularly carnal) and refined (ideally generic) readings of the same words. The disparity between the corporeal vehicle, for example, the syllables of his wife that Donne misses or the descent into print that he regrets in the "Letter to Sir G. F.," on the one hand, and the conceptual signified — the child by which he may be increased, or the idea of a woman "the best he could *conceive*" embodied in the printed poem — on the other, is further elaborated in the diagnostic thematics of the *Anniversaries*. The death of Elizabeth Drury is transmuted into the death of the idea of a woman, the generic "shee," who stands for a certain making visible or incarnation of "the best he could conceive."

5

Returning now to the "shee" of *The Anniversaries,* we may best understand "her" as a certain kind of "sign." To assess the literary historical event figured by her passing, it will be helpful to give this "shee," for the moment, an equally generic but historically more determined name. Recalling the thoughtful commentary on Petrarchism implicit in the folds of "Aire and Angels," let us call her, as Joseph Hall does in his commendatory poem for the *Second Anniversary,* Laura — that is, the generic female, fictive and chaste, who stands as the cynosure of the tradition that had informed European, epideictic verse from *La Vita Nuova* onward.[34] To see "her" in this way is to realize the inanity of Jonson's response; the poem marks the impossibility, in 1611, of effectively writing either the Virgin Mary, or her iterative surrogate. It marks, that is, a determined historical estrangement of woman as species and Woman as genus.[35] In short, Donne uses the death of Elizabeth Drury as an occasion on which to represent the failure of (Petrarchan) love portrayed in "Aire and Angels" as a historically mediated event.

The generic denomination of the "shee" of the *Anniversaries* as Laura permits two questions to arise, one historical, the other theoretical: (1) Why — in 1611 — has "Laura" died? What are the contemporary conditions of her inviability? and (2) What (metaphysically and epistemologically speaking) has changed with her death? What crucial function had she played for all those years — in fact and practice? To explain the importance of this question, Donne asserts an enduring relationship in *An Anatomy of the World* between the dead world and a succeeding world, neither born nor created, but constructed by its own creatures:

> For there's a kind of world remaining still,
> Though shee which did inanimate and fill
> The world, be gone, yet in this last long night,
> Her Ghost doth walke; that is, a glimmering light,
> A faint weake loue of vertue and of good
> Reflects from her, on them which vnderstood
> Her worth. (ll. 67–73)

Two things intrigue me in this passage: (1) the experience — the feeling — of a world that has become inanimate or soulless and yet persists, and (2) the persistent reflection in this world — as a ghost or spirit — of that which had made it live — the ghost's persistence as the reflection of that which is no longer there. The first of these interests engages the sense of familiarity or recognition that this persistence of the lost spirit has today.[36] Is there some useful analogy between Donne's experience and the peculiarly persistent nostalgia for the present, the reception of the present as something already past, indicated by the post- of postmodern?[37] My second question is more historical, or, perhaps, literary historical. Is the "wan ghost" that persists in a dead world a premonition of the (Romantic) *Geist* that goes on to become the elusive Spirit of modernity?

A preliminary reading of the ghostly play of this spirit (if that is what it is) in this passage and this poem may perhaps be mapped in Donne's use of the word *inanimate* as a verb in line 68. The *OED* indicates that the common usage of *inanimate* as an adjective meaning "lifeless" (literally without soul) was well-established in 1611. Probably less well-established was its now obsolete use as a verb of opposite import, for which the *OED* records Donne's 1610 *Pseudo-Martyr* as the earliest instance.[38] The shift of accent from the second to the fourth syllables triggers a semantic antithesis by moving between two homophonic Latin prefixes: the expected *in-* meaning negation (as in *in-sincere, in-soluble, in-capable*) shadowing Donne's use of *in-* as a preposition (*in-side, in-ternal, in-spire*). If *shee* is the soul of the world when *in* it, the world becomes soulless when she is *not*. Thus, the soulless world, which is the subject of Donne's *Anatomy*, is that which obtains in her absence, when she is not *in* place, except that she is, because of her walking Ghost, in place—as disembodied spirit, or, in the current cliché, the presence of an absence—realized verbally as the preposition of a negative particle—where *nothing* holds its place. The afterworld left behind by Elizabeth Drury is thus defined by a relation of spatial eccentricity between soul and world.

Thus, the "world remaining still," which she "did inanimate and fill," is in its decay not exactly still or inanimate, and Donne's *Anatomy* hovers between postmortem and vivisection. Willard relates this ambiguity to the controversy between Vesalian (Galenic) and Paracelsian physicians: "Donne uses the word 'anatomy' in contrary ways" to describe "a procedure and a body, apparently alive but feared to be dead."

> The Paracelsian doctrine is there, at least in the balm and perhaps in the related virtues, but Paracelsian medicine saves no one. No physician can draw down the heavenly influences to generate a perfect remedy, herbal or mineral. For the correspondences of heaven and earth have disappeared. What began as a Paracelsian anatomy of a world sufficiently dead for a Vesalian autopsy becomes, it seems, a Vesalian dissection of the Paracelsian world of correspondences. But even the Vesalian approach fails, for it does not clarify the functions or relationships of things, as Vesalians attempted. Quite the contrary, it points out that functions are arbitrary and relationships have been forgotten.[39]

At stake in this controversy was (among other things) a distinction between a functional taxonomy that is profoundly visual and a system of correspondences that can be grasped only intellectually, through the familiar metaphorics of the microcosm and the macrocosm, as may be seen in the following excerpt from the popular Paracelsian text of Oswald Croll:

> The Foundation of this Physick is according to the agreement of the lesser World Man with the greater and externall world, as we are sufficiently instructed by Astronomy and Philosophy, which explaine those two Globes, the superiour and inferiour . . . : And therefore it is necessary to accommodate the disposition of the great World as of a parent to the little World as to the Son, and duly compare the Anotomy of the World with the Anotomy of Man. . . . [40]

The "Anotomy" endorsed by Croll is conceptual, not visual, and the relation between the macrocosm and the microcosm is explicitly understood to be that of the visible to the invisible.

> The externall world is the figure of Man, and Man is an hidden world, because visible things in him are invisible, and when they are made visible then they are diseases, not health, as truly as he is the little world and not the great one: And this is the true knowledge, that Man may Microcosmically be known and visibly and invisibly or magically. (ibid., p. 25.)

In making an anatomy not of a man but of the world, Donne exposes to view the correspondences between the parts that replicate on one level correspondences that inhere cosmically. But when these correspondences become visible, they become visible only as symptoms. To see what is inside, it is necessary to kill the organism. One sees the parts and in seeing them sees only where the whole was but is no longer.

A passage from *The Second Anniversary* (ll. 157–218) illustrates the point. After a series of imperatives, in which the soul in its progress from the body to heaven is admonished not to see but to "think" the elements visualized in the anatomy, the speaker shifts to the third person (l. 189) to describe the progress of the soul after death. The soul

> At once is at, and through the Firmament.
> And as these stars were but so many beades
> Strunge on one string, speed vndistinguish'd leades
> Her through those spheares, as through the beades, a string,
> *Whose quicke succession makes it still one thing:*
> As doth the Pith, which, least our Bodies slacke,
> Strings fast the little bones of necke, and backe;
> So by the soule doth death string Heauen and Earth,
> For when our soule enioyes this her third birth,
> (Creation gaue her one, a second, grace,)
> Heauen is as neare, and present to her face,
> As colours are, and obiects, in a roome
> Where darknesse was before, when Tapers come. (ll. 206–18; my
>   emphasis)

Only the swiftness of the soul's progress after death preserves the visual image of correspondence, figured when the planets on one level and the spinal cord on another are joined to the image of beads on a string. This process of figuration must be carried out conceptually, because to anatomize is to break the string and lay out the pieces, thereby missing the motion, which is the point. Seeing things one after another in "quick succession" may reveal the design that makes one thing of many, but only insofar as that succession leads to the beatific vision in which the presence of heaven supplants objects and colors with the unimaginable sight of design itself, of pure form.

In a similar leap from temporal succession to eternal immediacy, within the tradition of epideixis epitomized by Petrarch's praise of an unattainable woman whose name means praise, a fantasy of female perfection serves as a visible form that conducts its lover to the contemplation of a disembodied virtue, from which, like Plato's philosophical soul, he "catches sight of the immortal."[41] In this transaction the praiser, the praised, and the praise are each to become the mirror of the other and thus become one.

The lost world whose postmortem Donne conducts is a world in which a visible *she,* taken as the inspiring object of an anatomical blazon, could fill with an excess of apparent meaning: a self-signifying universe. *She* could do this because the universe given to the senses was thought of — within the rhetoric of the macrocosm and the microcosm — as ontologically homogeneous. The totality of its form could be read in every region of its content. Thus, the ideality of the woman also identified the ideality of the world. In charting what remains of this world when *her* presence is reduced to memory, to a thing that is, like Lacan's *objet a,* known and experienced only as lost, Donne's *Anatomy* retrospectively places this transcendent universe in relation to an extensive and collapsing web of "visible" supports.

Donne traces the symptoms following from the loss of this figural woman — the idea of whose physical and moral beauty stands in for the Idea itself. He anatomizes specifically the world as it had been organized — in and before the Renaissance — by a certain cultural aspiration put into play through what Slavoj Žižek calls the "sublime object" of ideology — that is, a mute desire mediated by a fantasy that retrospectively structures reality itself.[42] Unlike the embodied woman of "Aire and Angels," the fantasied idea of woman would be able to actualize "my love" in just such a purely formal object.

For Donne and his time the sublimation of this object is failing. As the literary conventions of Petrarchan epideixis become increasingly visible as such, the experience they had mediated fades from view. The visible letter kills, and the spirit flees.[43] Intuiting that "shee," not Elizabeth Drury, but her letter in the text of the world, our generic "Laura," is a fetish that "conceals the lack ('castration') around which the symbolic network is articulated" (Žižek, *Sublime Object*, p. 49), Donne is momentarily in a position to name the constituent elements in that network, to see them as mere things in the moment when they are about to vanish into or beneath a reconstituted symbolic web. The antithetical superimposition of adjectival and verbal forms of *inanimate* near the beginning of *The First Anniversary* captures precisely this insistence of the desublimated letter. For the *inanimate* may only be construed as *dead* in relation to its previously having been experienced as alive. The apodictic horror of the postmortem arises — literally — in the superimposition of negation (*in-*) on a merely *pre*positional presence (*in-*). Writing from a time when one sublimation has been, so to speak, put under erasure and another has not yet taken hold, Donne encounters the repressed, the excess that cannot be accommodated to the symbolic system, the thing with no corresponding concept — returning, as Žižek puts it, from the future (*Sublime Object*, pp. 55–58). It is this future that we share and in which Donne's idea of a woman is misrecognized as one or another symbol.

The corpse in *An Anatomy of the World* is thus the remains of a universe in which intelligible truth could be *embodied* in poetic sublimations of *things,* because the natural world was given to the senses in forms *immediately* available for appropriation as signifiers. To put this another way, we might say that an Imaginary intellectual universe, structured by idealized but still embodied forms, passed into a universe in which meaning was irreparably disjoined from substance. In this "world remaining still," things signify only through a double mediation in which they are subjected to (and disembodied by) the Other of a virtual symbolic order. To be accepted into this order, they also must cease to be things. Their sheer material existence is absorbed by a symbolic significance that is necessarily elsewhere. Elizabeth Drury has died — as, indeed, Beatrice and Laura had died before her — but her death structures these earlier deaths as autonomous repetitions. Whereas the deaths of Beatrice and Laura are decisive in the literary texts of Dante and Petrarch — textual events that become metalyptically formative of their authorial personae — the death of Elizabeth Drury resists symbolic incorporation. Because her death does not signify and cannot be made to mean, it retrospectively hollows out and empties these previous literary sacrifices.

Donne lived in and complained about a world in which a developing technology was *de-signing* a "natural" world that had seemed to have been, from time immemorial, *designed*. With the "infictable" death of Elizabeth Drury, "Laura" stops supporting the desire for design and marks instead the materialization of the Real, which exceeds it and from which, if I may use the Lacanian term, the subject *ex-sists*.

A famous passage in *An Anatomy of the World* illustrates this eventual existence. When, among other material disruptions, the mediation of Galileo's optics deprive humankind of the Idols of the Cave and Mind, Donne catches the systemic character of the ensuing disruptions:

> And new Philosophy cals all in doubt,
> The Element of fire is quite put out;
> The Sunne is lost, and th'earth, and *no mans wit*
>   Can well direct him, where to looke for it.
> And freely men confesse, that this world's spent,
> When in the Planets, and the Firmament
> They seeke so many new; they see that this
> Is crumbled out againe to his Atomis.
> 'Tis all in pieces, all cohaerence gone;
> All just supply, and all Relation:
> Prince, Subject, Father, Sonne, are things forgot. (ll. 205–15; my
>   emphasis)

When the Ptolemaic universe offered the "eye" a cosmos of concentric spheres, the Book of Nature was a relatively easy read. The journey from the visible circle to the infinite God whose nature it signified was a short one. The intervention of the telescope to greatly complicate and disturb this picture did not simply extend the range of the human eye; it displaced and disembodied that eye so that with vision isolated from the person and given over to a measuring instrument, incapable of intellect or desire, man found himself no longer to be "the measure of all things," no longer a little world.[44]

"Her" disappearance thus marks the inviability in 1611 of a cosmology that organized *vision* around "natural" forms that also offered themselves *immediately* as symbolic representations. The circular orbits of the Ptolemaic planets traced lines in phenomenal space to outline the abstract conceptual being of a God whose center is everywhere and circumference nowhere. Within this visually organized *relation,* the world cohered around "She that had all Magnetique force alone, / To draw, and fasten sundred parts in one" (ll. 221–22). She was the subtle knot that held the beads together on the string. As the conventional and visual embodiment of a sublimed and subjected desire, "Shee" is also the sign of significance itself, the assurance that things (history) have meaning:

> She whom wise nature had inuented then
> When she obseru'd that euery sort of men
> Did in their voyage in this worlds Sea stray,
> And needed a new compasse for their way;
> Shee that was best, and first originall
> Of all faire copies; and the generall
> Steward to Fate; shee whose rich eyes, and brest,
> Guilt the West Indies, and perfum'd the East;
> Whose hauing breath'd in this world, did bestow
> Spice on those Isles, and bad them still smell so,
> And that rich Indie which doth gold interre,
> Is but as single money, coyn'd from her:
> She to whom this world must it selfe refer,
> As Suburbs, or the Microcosme of her. (ll. 223–36)

Donne thus diagnoses "Laura's" signifying function as that of the object beyond—missing in its perfection—around which the relation of self and world are organized—"Who could not lacke, what ere this world could giue, / Because shee was the forme, that made it liue" (*The Second Anniversary,* ll. 71–72), and he diagnoses the malady that afflicts her: The natural world, which is, with the help of instruments, beginning to be seen in its denatured complexity, does not signify; or worse, it signifies precisely that it lacks *immediate* meaning. Henceforth, this lack will be supplied not—as in Petrarchan epideixis—by the *pictura poesis* of the blazon, but by the speaking subject's newly constituted memory of loss, the "wan ghost" of full meaning understood as (visualizable) presence. What had been at the center of the universe now resides outside it, an absence present as the eccentric *voice* of memory. No longer simply what it is, the world becomes what we know of it.

Persisting in the best idealist tradition, the memory that defines this subject seeks and achieves an identity with the world it has introjected. The Aristotelian epistemology behind this impulse toward identity is elaborated by Edward Tayler:

> In Donne's entirely traditional formulation in *The First Anniversary*, the process begins when "to our eyes, the formes from objects flow" (316), which is to say that the *species sensibilis*, the sensible species, flow from the girl to our eyes where they are impressed on the organs of sense, then channeled within through the agency of the bodily 'spirits' to become expressed species or sensuous representations. Yet she remains unintelligible, incomprehensible. Passing though the *sensus communis*, the expressed species of the girl is once again impressed, on this occasion in the glass or mirror of the imagination where for the first time "she" becomes available to the intellect. The understanding functions under two aspects, the passive and mirrorlike *intellectus possibilis*, and the active, lamplike *intellectus agens*. The active intellect illuminates (Plato's trope used, desperately, by Aristotle) the sensuous image of the girl, making it possible for the first time to comprehend the object in and through the image of the object discerned in the fantasy (or the memory). In other words, the active intellect expresses the intelligible species from the image of Elizabeth Drury "as she was" and impresses it upon the passive or potential intellect, where it is actualized as an expressed intelligible species. The object known and the knower are now identical: "it is both the object and the wit." The knower now possesses, in what Aristotle calls the Place of Forms, "the Idea of a Woman and not as she was." (pp. 32–33) [45]

The characteristics of the sensuous image itself are important in this process, because to the extent that the sensuous image presents insistent details or, in Aristotle's terminology, accidents that cannot be accommodated to the intelligible idea, the mediation of world and intellect fails, "the object and the wit" remain heterogeneous. Thus, I take it that *The Anniversaries* record not the death of Elizabeth Drury but the death of the Idea: the intellect's increasingly frequent failure to render intelligible the sensuous images of contemporary life. *An Anatomy of the World* dissects the corpse of meaning, identifying and marking the pathological insistence of a world that has begun to present sensuous images full of resistant details. In this world, species is estranged from genus, and with this estrangement the link between the macrocosm and the microcosm becomes instead the site of an impasse where "quick succession" fails to "make it still one thing." In a strategic and preserving reversal of Petrarch's *laurete Laura,* in which praise, praised, and praiser become one, Donne anatomizes a world that has itself become the site of a disembodied and lacking spirit: "Shee, shee is dead; shee's dead: when thou knowst this, / Thou knowst how wan a Ghost this our world is" (ll. 369–70).

What remains of "the world remaining still"? A mediating *voice,* of indeterminate origin, comprising a remembered spirit and an always already archaic form. The poem's final lines are a commonplace, made mordant by the renewed precision with which it is employed:

> Nor could incomprehensiblenesse deterre
> Me, from thus trying to emprison her.
> Which when I saw that a strict graue could do,
> I saw not why verse might not doe so too.
> Verse hath a middle nature: heauen keepes soules,
> The graue keeps bodies, verse the fame enroules. (ll. 469–74)

If in the modernity to come of "the world remaining still," the Word embodied in comprehensible design is lost; words remain. Although these words cannot imprison the incomprehensible particular within its genus, they persist as the monuments of *things* that — by becoming visible — have disappeared.

Immediately before these lines, in a curiously disproportionate allusion, Donne compares his office as commemorator of Elizabeth Drury to that of Moses in Deuteronomy 31.16–22, where God, foreseeing that the Israelites will break his covenant, commands Moses to write down a song to be learned and repeated by the Children of Israel ("teach it to the children of Israel: put it in their mouthes") (Deut. 31:19; KJV):

> if you
> In reuerence to her, doe thinke it due,
> That no one should her prayses thus rehearse,
> As matter fit for Chronicle, not verse,
> Vouchsafe to call to minde, that God did make
> A last, and lastingst peece, a song. He spake

To *Moses,* to deliuer vnto all,
That song: because he knew they would let fall,
The Law, the Prophets, and the History,
But keepe the song still in their memory.
Such an opinion (in due measure) made
Me this great Office to inuade. (ll. 457–68)

This remembered and repeated song, which predicts the future lapses of
Israel and their consequences (Deut. 32), supplements by repeating that which
will have been forgotten: "The Law, the Prophets, and the History." Some
three or four years after the publication of *An Anatomy of the World,* Donne
would comment that, as a song to be learned and repeated, the Song of Moses
would find its special efficacy in causing the Israelites to hear the words of God
issuing from their own mouths.

> And God himself in that last peice of his, which he commanded *Moses* to
> record, that Heavenly Song which onely himself compos'd, (for though
> every other poetick part of Scripture, be also Gods word, and so made
> by him, yet all the rest were Ministerially and instrumentally delivered
> by the Prophets, onely inflamed by him; but this which himself cals a
> Song, was made immediately by himself, and *Moses* was commanded
> to deliver it to the Children; God choosing this way and conveyance
> of a Song, as fittest to justifie his future severities against his children,
> because he knew that they would ever be repeating this Song, (as the
> Delicacy, and Elegancy therof, both for Divinity and Poetry, would
> invite any to that) and so he should draw from their own mouthes a
> confession of his benefits, and of their ingratitude.) [46]

Song or verse "hath a middle nature," substituting the materiality of words
—rhythm, meter, the historical dimension of etymology—for the lost particularity of the thing in its exigence; it mediates in memory between the dead
weight of the incomprehensible thing on the one hand and the intuition of its
unspecifiable meaning on the other. The song in Deuteronomy prepares the
Israelites for a momentous loss, the death of Moses, and a momentous gain,
the entry into the promised land. The embodied lawgiver who has brought
them out of bondage will disappear, and the nation will possess its promised
land only so long as it sings his song. With the passing of Moses as the *visible*
embodiment of the community's connection to God through the Law, the re-

iteration of the song will bear witness against the Israelites and unify their world around its shared idea.

In *An Anatomy of the World,* verse is the descent into writing that mediates the absent syllables of a known woman, who may have been (eventually would be) lost in childbirth, and the "idea" of a woman never known, "the best he could conceive." The story told in and by this descent into writing is the story of the passing of vision, the object of the Petrarchan gaze, into voice, the passing, that is, of the homogeneous spatial repetitions of macrocosm and microcosm into the linear reiterations of memory.[47]

6

This coordinated movement from vision to sound and from presence to memory is recapitulated in the opening of *The Second Anniversary.* A series of strikingly interwoven similes represent the afterlife of the world in the year since Elizabeth Drury's death, first as subjectless motion ("But as a ship which hath strooke saile, doth runne, / By force of that force which before, it wonne" [ll. 7–8]), then as subjectless sound ("as Ice, which crackles at a thaw: / Or as Lute, which in moist weather, rings, / Her knell alone, by cracking at her strings" [ll. 18–20]). Mediating between the similes evoking visible motion and those evoking sound is the evocation of a beheaded man, so charged with detail that it threatens to overwhelm the conceit:

> Though at those two Red seas, which freely ran,
> One from the Trunke, another from the Head,
> His soule be saild, to her eternall bed,
> His eies will twinckle, and his tongue will roll,
> As though he beckned, and cal'd backe his Soul,
> He graspes his hands, and he puls vp his feet,
> And seemes to reach, and to step forth to meet
> His soule. . . . (ll. 10–17)

Continuing the simile of the ship and the sea that precedes it, the man's blood forms two seas on which the soul has sailed. The motion of the dead tongue effects the transition to the following similes of subjectless sound by representing the voice as visual: the rolling tongue, which we see but cannot hear because it is cut off from breath, indicates the vain attempt to retain the soul by *calling* it back.

Donne next compares the counting of days after the death of Elizabeth

Drury to the counting of days before the creation of the sun, thus establishing
the present similes as *nachträglich* or retrospective constitutions of a past that
can only be known as lost. He then resumes the image of an overwhelming sea,
comparing the death of Elizabeth Drury to the flood, and identifying memory as the motion that remains when what is present to the senses is washed
away. The poet entrusted with her memory is then situated in the position of
the beheaded man who would call back his soul:

> Yet a new Deluge, and of Lethe flood,
> Hath drown' vs all, All haue forgot all good,
> Forgetting her, the maine Reserue of all;
> Yet in this Deluge, grosse and generall,
> Thou seest mee striue for life; my life shalbe,
> To bee hereafter prais'd, for praysing thee,
> Immortal Mayd, who though thou wouldst refuse
> The name of Mother, be vnto my Muse,
> A Father since her chast Ambition is,
> Yearely to bring forth such a child as this. (ll. 27–36)

Reversing the image of the rolling tongue as a vision of sound, the memory of
the poet, like the beheaded man beckoning to his soul, seeks to retain the soul
of the world—that is, the envisaged idea of Elizabeth Drury—in the form of
a subjectless sound, a sound that issues at once from his mouth and her disembodied soul. Thus, as promised by the allusion to the Song of Moses at the
end of *An Anatomy of the World,* Donne enacts an ironic parody of the moment in which Augustine escapes the flesh (as though a fish escaping the sea!)
when in prayer the word of his mouth returns to its original in the heavens of
the divine Word.

The words of *The Progres of the Soule* are virgin births that will bring into
the future the saving grace of an originary past:

> These Hymes may worke on future wits, and so
> May great Grand-children of thy praises grow.
> And so, though not Reuiue, enbalme, and spice
> The world, which else would putrify with vice.
> For thus, Man may extend thy progeny,
> Vntill man doe but vanish, and not die.

> These Hymns thy issue, may encrease so long,
>
> As till Gods great Venite change the song. (37–44) [48]

The vision of Elizabeth Drury, whom Donne had never seen but of whose worthiness he had received "so very good testimony," passed into print in 1611. When in 1612 *An Anatomy of the World* becomes *The First Anniversary*, the "immortal Mayd" is refigured in the *Second* as the inseminator of the poet's feminine muse. He is, in turn, the womb of procreatively male "hymes," which will provoke in the hearers an "hydropique" thirst for the eschata on the one hand and the reduction of present experience to story on the other: "And vnto thee, / Let thine owne times as an old story be" (ll. 49–50).

In a final concentration of the coupled passage from vision to voice and from syllable to print, the present hymn, that is, *The Second Anniversary*, figures the departed soul of Elizabeth Drury as, herself, a book:

> Shee, who in th'Art of knowing Heauen, was growen
>
> Here vpon Earth, to such perfection,
>
> That shee hath, euer since to Heauen shee came,
>
> (In a fairer print,) but read the same:
>
> Shee, shee, not satisfied with all this waite,
>
> (For so much knowledge, as would ouer-fraite
>
> Another, did but Ballast her) is gone,
>
> As well t'enioy, as get perfectione,
>
> And cals vs after her, in that shee tooke,
>
> (Taking herselfe) our best, and worthiest booke. (ll. 310–20)

Heaven is now what Elizabeth Drury knows, and we are invited to know it by knowing her. But that knowledge is mediated in the form of the book that she has become, which is no longer available on earth. It is precisely in accord with Freud's understanding of the uncanny as the return of the repressed that just at the point when the soul's progress from earth to heaven is completed, we encounter in an inverted form the figure of the ballasted and over-freighted vessel that had carried the erotic weight of "Aire and Angels." [49]

In that poem, we recall, the speaker had sought to ballast Love, only to find that he had "loves pinnace overfraught." When his love had taken "limmes of flesh," the particular woman in whom he had invested love could not support the weight of his idealizing desire: "Ev'ry thy haire for love to worke upon / Is much too much." In "Aire and Angels" the corporeal grossness of this figure

asserted an ineradicable corporeality that resisted idealization. Used in a reverse direction in *The Progres of the Soule,* the figure turns on a punning
quibble on the word "waite" that converts the *avoir du poids* of the corporeal
particular to a rejection of the passage of time. The knowledge that Elizabeth
Drury had acquired on earth, which would have sunk "another" (as, for example, love had sunk the girl in "Aire and Angels,"), "did but Ballast her";
so that unwilling to *wait* for greater *weight* of knowledge, she took herself to
heaven, where the object does indeed become the wit, but only at the cost of
removing both object and wit to another place, outside time.

From a literary historical perspective, the "shee" of the *Anniversaries* figures the generic Laura of the Petrarchan tradition, and the poems narrate her
departure from the world. In them, the passing of Laura marks the resistance
of the corporeal world, as it was observed in 1611–12, to the use of an idealizing
figure to render in microcosm a totality of meaningful relations. Thus, Donne
tells in these poems the literary historical story of the transformation of this
generic Laura from a timely proof of coherence to a memory of lost coherence, and he evokes the experience of meaninglessness and desolation "shee"
leaves behind: "shee tooke, / (Taking herselfe) our best, and worthiest booke."

The removal by death of the ideal woman — of Beatrice, of Laura — is a standard feature of the epideictic tradition, as is the aspiration of the poet to join
her in heaven. But the removal of Donne's "shee" differs from its antecedents. For one thing, it occurs not in the middle of the story, as do the deaths
of Beatrice and Laura, but at once at the beginning and the end. Whereas
the earlier examples present a progression in the understanding of the subject
from corporeal to spiritual, the death of Elizabeth Drury is presented as both
the cause and the culmination of the *Anniversaries.* In bald summary: Elizabeth Drury dies and the world, whose soul she was, dies with her (*First Anniversary*). The postmortem performed on the remains of the world discovers
only that the remains of the world are without meaning. In the *Second Anniversary,* we leave the dead world behind and instead accompany its departed
soul on her progress to heaven. We learn again from this journey that the corporeal world she leaves behind can speak only its own meaninglessness. The
meaning implicit in the design of the world has been absorbed by Elizabeth
Drury, and we can no longer read it in her because she has gone to heaven.
The world is dead because she has left it and she has left it because, having absorbed its meaning — hydroptiquely sucked down the "balme" — she under-

stood it to be dead. The peculiar temporal structure in which her death is both the inception and the climax of the poem tells us that we are not dealing with a woman who comes, like Beatrice and Laura, to symbolize an ideal but with the idea of that ideal woman, a figure of the figure, its function and its failure.

The book that Elizabeth Drury has become remains, however, in yet another uncanny image, a curiously fleshy book:

> Shee, who left such a body, as euen shee
> Onely in Heauen could learne, how it can bee
> Made better; for shee rather was two soules,
> Or like to full, on both sides written Rols,
> Where eies might read vpon the outward skin,
> As strong Records for God, as mindes within. (ll. 501–6)

Certainly, these lines explicitly assert the epistemological theme of sensory particular and intelligible genus that runs through the *Anniversaries*. But insofar as this book also remains "shee," the double articulation of "skin" as both the written-on page and the human skin her soul has left behind—coming exactly at the moment when corporeal "shee" is to be fully transubstantiated into incorporeal knowledge—has a contradictory impact. The metaphor of the "both sides written Rols" asserts "her" corporeality in the very moment of her transformation into a celestial book. If we set out to distill universal meaning from timely corporeality, it is the meaning that effervesces and the meaninglessly corporeal with which we who remain here on the dead earth are left.

We have seen the figure of the book folded over us and marking the boundary between time and eternity before, at the conclusion of Augustine's *Confessions:*

> Who except thou, O our God, made that firmament of the authority
> of thy divine Scripture to be over us? As 'tis said: For the heaven shall
> be folded up like a book; and is even now stretched over us like a skin.
> For thy holy Scripture is of more eminent authority, since those mor-
> tals departed this life, by whom thou dispensedst it unto us. And thou
> knowest, O Lord, thou knowest, how thou With skins didst once ap-
> parel men, so soon as they by sin were become mortal. Wherefore hast
> thou like a Skin stretched out the Firmament of thy book, that is to say
> those words of thine so well agreeing together; which by the ministry
> of mortal men thou spreadedst over us. For by their very death is that

solid Firmament of authority, in thy sayings set forth by them, stretched on high over all that be now under it; which whilst they lived on earth, was not then so eminently stretched out over us. Thou hadst not as yet Spread abroad that heaven like a skin; thou hadst not as yet everywhere noised abroad the report of their deaths. (2.403, 5) [50]

As in Donne's figure of the "both sides written Rols," this book articulates time and eternity as verso and recto of a single page. On the far side, angels, reading, as it were, from the other side of the book, praise God eternally. "Their book is never closed, nor is their scroll folded up: seeing thyself art this unto them, yea, thou art so eternally; because thou hast arranged them above this Firmament, which thou hast settled over the infirmity of the lower peoples: where they might gaze up and learn thy mercy, *which declares in time thee that madest times*" (2.407, my emphasis).

In Augustine's text, the book as physical object figures the temporal predicament of humankind, living along the boundary between time and eternity. For the angels, God's book is never closed (*non clauditur codex*), but for humankind, eternity is folded into time, a closed book, until one hears the timely call to "take up and read." When the call is heard, eternity is joined to time in the unity of God's eternal Word and the words issuing in time from the mouth of the Christian who experiences the scriptural words as his own, who lives, as it were, in God's "skin." To read a script is to revoice in temporal sequence what has been folded into a spatial synchronicity.

Donne's trope goes a step further, however. Augustine's revelation comes in time, and, like an allegory, it seeks to connect each temporal moment with the eternal synchronicity that lies putatively beyond writing. The soul of Elizabeth Drury, on the contrary, "not satisfied with all this waite," becomes itself the book. Donne suddenly collapses the two metonymic chains of Augustinian allegory so that the timely outside "where eies might read" is but one face of the skin/page. The heavenward or angels' side, which cannot be read with the eyes but must be understood by the mind is the other. Three points are salient: (1) That part of Elizabeth Drury that had been available to the senses, and which had functioned, like Laura, as the visible representative of an ideal perfection, is reimagined after the apotheosis of her soul, as offering a script to be read rather than a beauty that might be seen and felt prior to conceptual mediation. Recalling Donne's comparison of Moses' office as the singer of the divinely composed song of memory at the end of Deuteronomy and his own office as singer of anniversary hymns, we might say that she must be voiced before she can be thought. (2) The metaphor of the "both sides written Rols" cross-couples the chains of signification generated by the visual appearance of her body and her soul's intellectual knowledge of God—the skin offered to the eyes and the mind to the understanding, which, in turn, cross-couples the relation of the body's surface to its interior—a proper subject of anatomy, and a support of the microcosm/macrocosm analogy—with the relation of time to eternity; and (3) The skin written on both sides figures at once the unity and the division of these realms. By substituting the literal image of an open book for the unseen and unseeable depths of the generic ideal woman— "that within [her] which passes show"—Donne repeats with a difference Augustine's sublimating allegory of the injunction to increase and multiply as the faculty of using one word to mean many things and many words to mean one thing. Whereas Augustine's allegory subordinates sexual procreation, as a means to persist over time, to intellectual creation, as a means to join eternity to time, Donne radically separates time and eternity; either the carnal overfreights the spirit, as in "Air and Angels," when desire disappears into the body of the girl, or the spirit overfreights the carnal, as in the *Second Anniversary,* when the soul in pursuit of spirit disappears from view and can no longer serve as the support of desire. One can see one side of the page or the other but not both at once—like the two sides of a coin.

> nor wouldst thou be content,
> To take this, for my second yeeres true Rent,
> Did this Coine beare any other stampe, then his,
> That gaue thee power to doe, me, to say this. (ll. 519–22)

The coin is made specie by the image stamped upon it. Its value is extrinsic, and its usefulness depends entirely on its convertibility into other specie. The accidents that mark the history of any particular coin are necessarily effaced by the symbolic system of exchange in which it is realized as the cypher of a purely abstract value. God imprints his truth on the skin of Donne's book, and Elizabeth Drury's rent is paid. She is now fully and only "the best he could conceive." We will not *see* her again.

7

> But as the Heathen made them seuerall gods,
> Of all Gods Benefits, and all his Rods,
> (For as the Wine, and Corne, and Onions are
> Gods vnto them, so Agues bee, and war)
> And as by changing that whole precious Gold
> To such small copper coynes, they lost the old,
> And lost their onely God, who euer must
> Be sought alone, and not in such a thrust,
> So much mankind true happiness mistakes;
> No Ioye enioyes that man, that many makes.
> Then, soule, to thy first pitch worke vp againe;
> Know that all lines which circles doe containe,
> For once that they the center touch, do touch
> Twice the circumference; and be thou such.
> Double on Heuen, thy thoughts on Earth emploid;
> All will not serue; Onely who haue enioyd
> The sight of God, in fulnesse, can thinke it;
> For it is both the obiect, and the wit.
> This is the essentiall ioye. . . . (*The Second Anniversary*, ll. 425–43)

All joys must be understood as aspects of one essential joy, all sights comprehended in the sight of God; all true coins must bear the imprint of the king and
thus stand not for themselves as specie but, synecdochically, for the entirety of
the royal treasury whose adequacy and integrity they represent. I have argued
that the figure of the ideal woman—we have called her, generically, Laura—
functions in the epideictic tradition extending through Dante and Petrarch
to Spenser and Donne as a temporal stand-in for the sight of God, making
visible in the harmony of her parts the ineffable quality of the divinity that
shines within her. She is constructed so as to lead the mind from the unity of
her many good features (hair, lips, skin, eyes, bosom) to a desire to unify the
soul of the lover and the soul of the beloved and thence to an understanding of the unity of all enjoyment beyond time. Through figures such as Laura,
the analogy of the microcosm to the macrocosm that supported the essential homogeneity of (corrected) earthly and divine enjoyment opened a road
from time to eternity. But these figures were adapted to a world where the

object given to the senses was constructed so as to accommodate an appropriate meaning within the symbolic order. Planets moved in circles; virtue was blond. Donne's *Anniversaries* bear witness to the fate of Laura as this world of divine design passed into a messier world of ad hoc discovery and the chaos of newly discovered things. The poems are thus a monument to the memory of God's visible and immediately recoverable presence in the things of this world. But as a monument they mark not a living presence but the remains of something that has passed from presence into memory.

If the sight of God is "both the object and the wit," what happens to the wit when the object disappears into memory? Tayler observes rightly that Donne's most salient characteristic is his obsessive desire for an identificatory union that may be (in descending order): the ecstatic moment of the beatific vision; the intermediate "union of the form of the object and the intelligible 'idea' in the mind"; or, the one that occurs during sexual intercourse (ll. 128–29). What remains is the question of whether or not this union (these unions) takes place. Does Donne represent for his reader the achievement of union or the sliding and inherently frustrating moments of nostalgia for an origin that can only be known as lost, because the desire for it is the effect of its loss? Does not the subject, as projected in the epideictic tradition from Augustine through Dante and Petrarch to Spenser and Donne, speak from the very place where union does not occur?

This nonoccurrence is marked in different ways in *The Faerie Queene*, where the subject of the poem and the subject in the poem collide on Mount Acidale in a shortcircuit that returns the reader from Colin Clout in Book 6 to the nymph, "who sat downe in the middest of the race," in Book 1, and in the *Anniversaries*, where the loss of a dependably idealized image, like that of Laura, becomes the theme of an earnest contemplation of *nothing*. In the Spenserian shortcircuit, metonymy, used to represent exigent cause and effect, persistently resists the metaphoric resolution anticipated by a poetics of allegorical vision. The object continually exceeds the wit. As the progress of instrumental mathesis and technologically aided observation accumulates observed details, more and more newly observed things resist the reduction of their being to concept in the process of imaginary ideation. The encounter with this resistance leads Donne also from metonymy to metaphor, along the established path of the analogy of macrocosm and microcosm, to the discovery of an excess of signification. But where Spenser sought to recover this excess by "looping" it back into his narration, Donne's pursuit of the subject in the moment of lyric meditation enters into an ironic questioning of mimetic representation itself.

In perhaps his most enigmatic and moving poem, "A Nocturnall upon S. Lucies Day, being the shortest day," Donne gives expression to a moment in which the resistance of the phenomenal thing appears finally to reveal the void beyond or behind the veil of vision. The death of a beloved woman, perhaps Anne Donne, opens a hole in the world of meaning through which is glimpsed a nothing, that leaves the speaker literally dead to the world.[51] Whereas Elizabeth Drury, whom Donne had never met, is just a logical operator, always already an idea, the loss of the fully individuated and therefore incomprehensible woman mourned in the "Nocturnall" leads to a negative adequation of the object and the wit. The object, not as idea but as incomprehensible individual, has departed, leaving an empty place comprehended in the genus *nothing*. The wit having comprehended this idea of nothing and conformed to it has become, strictly speaking, what is left over: "every dead thing." The coin of memory has two sides: the mental image of what has been lost and the emptiness of the space and time where once it was. The speaker of the "Nocturnall" stares into this empty space, and the analogy of macrocosm to microcosm is written ironically as an analogy of whole to hole.

Having come to see in the absence of his love the positive appearance of nothing, that is, the empty place where a meaningful object is required but lacking, the poet is "Of the first nothing, the Elixir grown" (l. 29). The difference between nothing and the elixir of nothing is the difference between species — that which, in this instance, paradoxically does not appear — and genus, the concept of nonexistence as such. Nothing appears as the empty place, the hole or black stain, left where "she" — who had embodied the ideal and integrated the microcosm and the macrocosm within the frame of a self-contained subject and object — has disappeared. This appearance of nothing presents itself as meaningless in a specified historical context, but as the "elixir" of nothing its resultant subject comprehends it under the genus of meaninglessness — restoring in the negative the homogeneity of the macrocosm and microcosm; the experience of meaninglessness in temporal life bleeds into an empty and meaningless cosmos.

This lack of meaning, once discovered, extends itself into time. The world, which is now reduced to a memory of the speaker, returns to "the first nothing" that preceded the creation. The metaphoric accommodation of the object and the wit is ironically completed in the extinction of the desire that had been at once the cause and consequence of the encounter in "Aire and Angels":[52]

> Were I a man, that I were one,
> I needs must know; I should preferre,
>   If I were any beast,
> Some ends, some means; Yea plants, yea stones detest,
> And love; All, some properties invest;
> If I an ordinary nothing were,
> As shadow, 'a light, and body must be here. (ll. 30–36)

The woman in "Aire and Angels" had facilitated the speaker's encounter with his "love" by showing him the shape and substance of desire; the loss of the woman in the "Nocturnall" results in the extinction of this desire by which the subject knew himself to be a man.

When the poet of the "Nocturnall" says that if he were something rather than nothing, he would "some properties invest," he recalls the "love" of the speaker of "Aire and Angels," which returns to his eye after a detour through the "lip, eye, and brow" of the beloved. Staring into the void left by death, the poet of the "Nocturnall" visualizes none of the accidental properties that seemed to arouse the desire in which he encountered himself as subject. Thus, the final lines of the stanza negate the inanimating relation of air and angels. If the speaker were "an ordinary nothing" like a shadow, there would necessarily be a corresponding light or body of which he would be the effect, an angel to thicken and animate his air. But there is none and he is none. The limit of the metaphoric transumption of metonymy has been reached. The subject of memory becomes memory and thus becomes a monument to its own passing:

> The world's whole sap is sunke:
> The generall balme th'hydroptique earth hath drunk,
> Whither, as to the beds-feet, life is shrunke,
> Dead and enterr'd; yet all these seem to laugh,
> Compar'd with mee, who am their Epitaph. (ll. 5–9)

The *Anniversaries* and the "Nocturnall upon S. Lucies Day" thus exemplify the ironic moment in the dialectic of rhetorical configurations underlying the *visionary* tradition of idealist epideixis; that is, the tradition that aspired to imitate *ut pictura poesis.* Turning in the next two chapters to two poets immersed in the revolutionary politics of the mid-seventeenth century, we will see a profoundly narrative subject emerge from the lyric stasis of idealist mimesis. This narrative subject articulates a far more dynamic — I am tempted to say, historicizing — engagement with its far less stable world.

Chapter 6

Authoring the Boundary: Allegory, Irony, and the Rebus

in Marvell's "Upon Appleton House"

Thus far we have seen how the poetics of visionary imitation articulates a subject at the junction of time and eternity in writings by Augustine, Dante, and Petrarch. In *The Faerie Queene* and Donne's *Anniversaries,* we have seen that subject reach an impasse that is both formally and historically determined. In the remainder of this study I want to trace the emergence from this impasse of a poetic character that construes itself as the subject of a narrative of historical causes. As this subject situates itself at the boundary of an unrecoverable past that must be constructed in memory and an anticipated future that must inform and structure present action, there is a concomitant letting go of visionary mimesis in which allegory gives way to narrative. The distinction that I now wish to invoke between allegory and narrative concerns the representation of time. Allegory attempts to mediate an unfolding sequence of events and a timeless design in which the truth of those events inheres; narrative understands meaningful design as something retrospectively discovered. In rhetorical terms, while it may tell a story by propelling itself through a series of metonymies — as does *The Faerie Queene* — allegory continually situates its meaning in a metaphor. The narrative of historical causes also becomes meaningful through metaphor, but only after deferring meaning to the end of a series of causally implicated episodes that become metaphoric only retrospectively. Allegorical acts tend to be interpreted essentially, their meaning established atemporally. Narrative acts are interpreted contextually, according to their consequences. Thus, allegory presents the expression of character, while narrative presents its development.

We have already noted the temporal complications that Marvell introduces into his lyrics. In chapter 1 we adverted to Marvell's "The Garden" for an example of a parodic reading backward that posited the "destined" achievement of present effects as the causes of the earlier events from which they issue: "*Apollo* hunted *Daphne* so, / Only that She might Laurel grow. / And *Pan* did after *Syrinx* speed, / Not as Nymph but, for a Reed" (ll. 29–32). At the conclusion of chapter 3, Marvell's mower poems served to exemplify the narration of a subject conscious of its exclusion from the time of its own narration. In this chapter I want to turn to Marvell's long poem, "Upon Appleton House, to my Lord Fairfax." Addressed to and celebrating Marvell's patron, Thomas Fairfax, the poem's meditation on the alternatives and availability of the active and contemplative lives is informed and made timely by Fairfax's recent resignation from the command of the parliamentary army in protest of the proposed Scottish expedition. As a country house poem in which the poet seriously addresses his patron on a matter of national as well as personal importance, "Upon Appleton House" will afford us an opportunity to examine in some detail the contextual pressures and the rhetorical mediations engaged in the reconfigurration of allegory as narrative.

Beyond the more or less immediate political concerns circulating around Fairfax's resignation, Marvell's poem incorporates, through its depiction of the Nun Appleton estate as a working farm, a larger social, historical context. In the seventeenth century a growing mastery of "second causes" reformed agriculture and, together with the development of a European market economy, transformed and redistributed economic powers.[1] By 1688, ideas of progress and accumulation would displace older ideas of stability and the patrilinear descent of land that no longer answered to the material organization of social life.[2] In the transition, traditional views of the social and political world were challenged by the incipient perspectives of an emerging alternative symbolic order. However, the ideological competition that occurs during such a transition is not, by its nature, perceived or recorded as such. The civil wars fought across England also were fought within individuals, who also experienced the divisions in their social world as inward divisions of the self.

As a modern developer of the land and a general of the parliamentary army, Marvell's patron epitomizes the seventeenth-century modernizer caught between a temperamental and an intellectual attachment to the rising burghers on the one hand and a historical attachment to the traditions of the landed gentry on the other.[3] This tension registers in Marvell's poem through the conservative conventions of the country house topos, as they are most especially exemplified in Jonson's "To Penshurst," on the one side, and through a careful attention to the working of the land at Appleton House, on the other. Where Jonson's poem asserts the association of the Sidneys and the Kentish land as nature: the estate's walls "reared with no man's ruin, no man's groan" (l. 46), the fish running freely into the net, the partridge "willing to be killed" (ll. 30 and 38), the assimilation of the Sidneys to the trees in the references to Gammage's Copse and Sidney's oak, Marvell's evocations of agricultural labor (the reapers) and technology (the flotation of the meadow) emphasize Fairfax's intensive working of the land. Where Jonson represents Penshurst as an ancient and self-sufficient manor, Marvell represents the bustling activity at Appleton House as commercial farming. Where Jonson works to assert the perpetuity of the Sidneys on the land, concealing the Henrician origins of their holdings, Marvell makes the acquisition of the estate at the dissolution of the monasteries a central element of his poem. Finally, where Jonson represents Sidney as "dwelling" on his estate, Marvell represents Fairfax as having (questionably) withdrawn to his.[4]

A. D. Cousins compares the opening lines of "To Penshurst" and "Upon Appleton House" so as to isolate the "main difference" between the two accounts of country houses. For Cousins this difference is Marvell's emphasis on a Calvinist idea of "Christian moderation as a shaping principle of both architecture and life":

> "Upon Appleton House" is at once an appropriation and, theologically as well as politically, a comprehensive rewriting of the country house poem. . . . Through its description of the great house (lines 1–80) and then in its account of Fairfax's ancestry and of the man himself (lines 281–368), Marvell's country house poem represents Fairfax not as primarily courteous and charitable, nor as an epitome of the virtues . . . , but as virtually embodying the Calvinist idea of moderation — in fact, as an embodiment of Protestant heroic virtue. Having thus characterized Fairfax, the persona goes on to develop the poem as an apology for the general's retirement from public life.[5]

The argument I will develop suggests that Cousins sees settled issues (Calvinist moderation, Protestant heroic virtue, the general's retirement) precisely where the poem's hybrid form allows it to be experimental, probing, and finally indeterminate.

In another recent and densely historical view of the poem, Nigel Smith recognizes just these qualities:

> A truly liberated subjectivity, perhaps imaginable in the more immediate aftermath of the demolition of monarchy, would result in the renunciation of all forms of formalistic restraint, in a freeing of narratives, of prosody, and the political valency of one's material. Such a poem is Marvell's "Upon Appleton House." In its praise of Fairfax, it is of course a history of the Reformation. . . . Yet at its most arresting moments, "Upon Appleton House" manages to suspend a directed political meaning (or it forecloses a singular reading) but also arguably, makes us forget that we are under the bondage of verse.[6]

I hope to show, however, that it is precisely the counterpoise of "formalistic restraint[s]" that enables Marvell to think radically in verse.

As an English loyalist who may have, for a time, supported the king and flirted with the Roman church, and who would later represent the merchants of Hull in Parliament, Marvell, like Fairfax, may well have felt himself suspended between a dying past and an immature future.[7] In "Upon Appleton House" he obliquely treats Fairfax's decision to resign his command rather than lead Parliament's expedition against the Scots by embedding a parallel moment of choice in an evocation of Fairfax's estate and a recapitulation of his family history. This parable of withdrawal and action in William Fairfax's acquisition of a bride and the estate is juxtaposed both with the present Fairfax's withdrawal from parliamentary politics and with the marriage of his young daughter. Thus, the historical episode serves as a reference point for the intertwining of the past in the domestic and the political, the private and the public present.

John Rogers has considered the opposition of the political and the domestic theaters of human action in "Upon Appleton House" in some detail.[8] Reading back from Marvell's remark in *The Rehearsal Transpros'd* (1672) that the parliamentary cause was "too good to have been fought for," he sees Marvell in 1651 questioning the efficacy of human action. Finding in the Hewel episode of "Upon Appleton House" (ll. 537–52) a "narrative of political wish-fulfillment," Rogers contends that "in a fantasy alternative to the real facts of the English Revolution, Marvell's fable of the oak and hewel imagines a bloodless overthrow of the state, as if Fairfax, in his hewel-like retirement, devoted solely to the values of the household, had without the least trace of aggression or violence purged England of its corrupt monarchy" (l. 60). Rogers sees in this putative rejection of human historical agency, the passivity of a seventeenth-century vitalism precipitated in response to the growing turn toward Cartesian mechanism and exemplified in the work of Winstanley. Within this context, the intention of human agents and the anthropomorphic God of Calvinist voluntarism are elided in favor of a historical agency immanent in nature itself. It seems to me, however, that Marvell's poems in general and "Upon Appleton House" in particular are as continually aware of the inextricability of the domestic and the political as they are of the inextricability of the human and the providential. The principal interest of my argument is the poem's rhetorical representation of the temporal predicament of amphibious humankind, resident in timely and eternal media.

As we saw in the structural belatedness of narrative meaning in *The Faerie Queene* and the postmortem perspectives of Donne's *Anniversaries,* this predicament forces on humankind a *nachträglich* construction of the self. Marvell's awareness of the necessity to choose and act from within this structure of deferral and anticipation provides the point from which he views Fairfax's retirement. With Fairfax's military career suspended, and without a male heir to extend the family tradition, the Fairfaxes broke the entail on Nun Appleton and Bolton Percy so that the inheritance would pass to the children of their young daughter, Mary.[9] The choice of a husband for Mary would then settle the destiny of the Fairfax family in a new line and a new name. Thomas Fairfax's decision to end his military service to Parliament and the settlement of the Nun Appleton estate on his daughter's heirs may thus be viewed as paired choices. Marvell's narrative of Fairfax's family and political affairs mirrors these mirror-image choices with a lyric evocation of the poet as he moves between the poles of social engagement — celebrating his patron, tutoring Fairfax's daughter, commenting on his master's decision to withdraw to his estate to sit out the remainder of the civil wars — and contemplative withdrawal at Nun Appleton.

I should like to examine the rhetoric through which Marvell pairs the historical narrative of the Fairfax family and the contemplative lyric of the poet-tutor and to suggest that the organizing tropes of "Upon Appleton House" constitute a seventeenth-century effort to represent an inward division of the self as a discontinuity in the relationship of individual action to providential design, choice to destiny, during a period of material historical change. My formal analysis of "Upon Appleton House" seeks to describe the articulation of politics on and in poetic form, to show how the political choices of Fairfax and Marvell presuppose determined relations of self to history—the realization of individual acts in and as the destiny of England—that are at once formed in and reflected by literature, so that historical and literary experience each become the other's mirror, and the distinction between the original and its image is rendered moot.

In our discussion of Donne we saw how the new science created one set of problems for the assumption in visionary mimesis that truth inheres in the adequacy of representation to object represented. Despite the increased difficulties that they experienced in doing so, men in the mid-seventeenth century still expected to find nature's nature reflected in the literary mirror. But, as the social consensus decayed, the image found in the literary mirror became blurred, doubled, and unstable. The world of innocent speculation that gives Mary Fairfax "for a Glass the limpid Brook, / Where *She* may all *her Beautyes* look" (ll. 701-2) coexists, in Marvell's more sophisticated experience, with a flowing river whose serpentine folds are "a *Chrystal Mirrour* slick; / Where all things gaze themselves, and doubt / If they be in it or without" (ll. 636–38).[10] The formal accommodation of these newly tendentious "reflections" is a problem at once political and literary, and the peculiar engrafting of narrative and lyric in Marvell's poem thus records a struggle to refigure the self as a historical actor by refiguring its relations to received literary traditions.

"Upon Appleton House" joins innocent to experienced speculation through a dialectical mediation of allegory and irony. The allegory is constituted in this instance through a continuing reference to a specified precedent text. Because allegory locates meaning in a time or place other than that of the narration itself, the interpreter of an allegorical text must pass through the narrated events to discover a prior truth concealed behind or beneath them. Allegory thus reduces history to signification.[11] By irony, I understand the momentary dismantling of the illusion of continuity between world and representation. Allegory conducts its reader to a realm of universal and atemporal truth, while irony makes present the moment of representation itself, calling attention to itself as a figure by denying the *literal* truth of what it says. Thus irony reverses allegory by reducing signification to the inscription of a historically present voice.[12]

Allegory projects the world of innocent speculation. In its mirror, the marriage of Isabel Thwaites to the first Lord Fairfax and the consequent rise of Appleton House and the Fairfax line out of the ruins of the nunnery specify a precedent text that glosses the meaning of the impending marriage of Mary Fairfax as the founding of a new and, at least, equally illustrious line. We cannot say whether Mary's 1657 marriage to the odious George Villiers, second duke of Buckingham, was anticipated when Marvell wrote his poem, but if any major aristocratic marriage was envisioned, the new line would certainly have invited thoughts — at least among the principals — of a reinvigoration of England through the marriage of the best of the old and new orders. When Buckingham returned from exile (without Cromwell's permission) in the summer of 1657, Mary Fairfax had been betrothed to the Earl of Chesterfield and the banns had been twice published, but the match was broken off in Buckingham's favor. Buckingham brought to the match a high title, and Fairfax was in a position to do him good too — by restoring to him lands, which Fairfax held in sequestration, and interceding on his behalf with Cromwell.

As Cromwell and the council suspected, there may have been political and family motives behind the match. Mary's mother, Lady Vere, was an outspoken supporter of a Presbyterian accommodation with Charles II, as was Buckingham on the Royalist side, and the Fairfaxes may have been looking to help Buckingham promote the settlement and to enjoy an enhanced position in a restored Presbyterian monarchy.[13]

Against this complex and tumultuous background, the allegory of "Appleton House" thus defeats time and historical change by asserting an eternal cycle of Fairfacian fair doings. However, the poet's ironic self-presentation disrupts this timeless story and makes present the historical and contingent scene of its writing; it reverses the temporality of allegory to suggest that the family's future will determine the significance of its past. Displacing meaning from an originary act to its eventual consequence, Marvell's oscillation from allegory to irony projects character alternately as the iteration of an a priori essence and as the result of accumulated historical experiences. The allegorical character expresses his inborn essence in varied situations; the ironic character discovers and revises his meaning through such situations. He is the prototypical self-made man. Where allegory tends to be iconic, irony, depending as it does on the perceived difference between represented and representation, is ostentatiously verbal.

Marvell mediates iconic representation and verbal allusion by a variety of the rebus, which Geoffrey Hartman defines as "a special form of the emblem representing words by things . . . [in which] the text is projected by the picture or action of a particular stanza."[14] I use the term rebus to refer not only to a pictorial pun on the sound of a word but also, more broadly, to a general class of figures, the comprehension of which requires an intermediary pictorial step.[15] The rebus uses words to evoke a picture, which, at the moment of perception, refers itself to a second verbal text. This second text provides a necessary gloss according to which the meaning of the figure's occurrence in the poem is revised. The rebus, then, requires a double reading in which the developing narrative of the poem is juxtaposed to and reread within an alternative context through the device of a pictorial mediation.[16]

Paradigmatically, the second context to which the rebus points us and which it imposes as a gloss on the events narrated in the poem is a scriptural one. By alluding to scriptural texts as he does, Marvell transfers narrated events from their local, "historical" contexts to a providential narrative that subsumes and interprets them. Thus, the poem "contains great things in less" by progressively revealing that mundane, human actions are signs in a divine discourse. The movement from the historical to the providential demystifies the lived drama of human life by subsuming contingent and apparently meaningless events within a completed narrative that discloses their ultimate meaning. The subsequent reading of the providential back into the historical discloses the divine intention in everyday life.[17] The rebus is, therefore, a particular, literary species of the scriptural *type,* and the term rebus may be taken with its Latin signification. The figure shows us that "Truth" is inscribed not only in the verbal revelation of Scripture but also *in the things* of this world — as illuminated by revelation. The same need to assert a renewed continuity of past and present and a new understanding of historical action during a period of radical social change underlies both the politics of the doctrinal ascendancy of typological hermeneutics in the Reformation and the poetics of the rebus. However, as we shall see, Marvell's use of the rebus goes a step further to become finally thematic, turning back on itself to examine the implications of its own structure. In so doing, it also necessarily questions the very typology it seems at first to support and exemplify. The rebus refers to scriptural revelation, as it were, to derive authority, but it refers to it explicitly as script, playfully questioning the implicit history of the biblical text itself.[18]

The rebus is inherently unstable. Its perception as a rebus brings about its dissolution as a picture. Oscillating between a verbal decoding in which meaning is disclosed, in time, through reference to an absent, prior text, and a moment of pictorial presence that is not yet meaningful, it mediates between the allegorical and ironic responses to man's complex experience of time. The two phases of interpretation appear in Marvell's poem as a dialectical sequence of allegorical reference and ironic self-reference, promising but always deferring a synthesis of destiny and choice. The world of experience is negated yet preserved as significant in relation to an immortal and perfected design that is always present as design but whose material realization is perpetually deferred. This design does not designate individual human acts; it elicits and evaluates them. That is to say, human freedom consists in the temporal gap between the choice and its consequences. It is from this complex temporal position that decisions such as Fairfax's must be made.

The characteristic oscillation of the rebus between ironic and allegorical speculation structures "Upon Appleton House" according to the relationship of meaning to visible or audible signs implied in the poem's sixth stanza:

> *Humility* alone designs
> Those short but admirable Lines,
> By which, ungirt and unconstrain'd,
> Things greater are in less contain'd.
> Let others vainly strive t'immure
> The *Circle* in the *Quadrature!*
> These *holy Mathematicks* can
> In ev'ry Figure equal Man. (ll. 41–48)

The citation of short but admirable lines refers at once to the architectural moderation and grace of Appleton House and the octosyllabic couplets of "Upon Appleton House." The moment in which the signified of "Lines" slips from the estate to the poem is ironic because the word "Lines" at the same time asserts and cancels a historical referent, reminding us that we are not observing Appleton House but reading a verbal description of it.

Referring at once to Vitruvian architectural harmonies and the noble numbers of metrical composition, "*holy Mathematicks*" allows both poem and building to equal—let us say, to represent—man, to be the signature of poet or builder.[19] Thus, the famous Vitruvian figure of a man inscribed in a circle within a square succeeds where others "vainly strive t'immure / The *Circle* in the *Quadrature*."[20] Traditionally the circle stands for eternity and the square for earth or the world. Man—earth inhabited by soul—squares the circle and mediates the mundane and the divine.[21]

A similar route may be followed referring "Lines" to the poem itself rather than to the architecture of the house. The poem's stanzas of eight lines of eight syllables each form the figure of the square that Puttenham associates with the earth and the *hominem quadratum* of Aristotle's *Ethics*.[22] The squares of the poem contain the humble spirit of the poet as the modest vault of Appleton House contains the spirit of Fairfax. Further, as Maren-Sofie Røstvig has shown, the square stanzas of "Upon Appleton House" are arranged into circles of numerologically significant repetitions.[23] The material presence of the poem may thus be seen as pictorially representing the mediation of earth and heaven or, in narrative terms, of history and Providence.

The thematic circularity of the poem, which extends the microcosmic self-reference of the stanzaic structure to the narrative whole composed by the little squares, may be observed in the figure of the fishermen in the final stanza. The use of the epithet "*Tortoise-like*" (l. 773) for the "rational *Amphibii*" at the end of the poem sends the reader back to "the low-roof'd Tortoises [who] dwell / In cases fit of Tortoise-shell" (ll. 13–14) at the beginning and suggests that the meaning of this curious image is to be found endlessly replicated in the preceding text. The salmon fishers represented at the poem's close are amphibious because man belongs to both earth and heaven and because fishermen move between the elements of earth and water. Each visual representation—the squared circle, "the low roof'd Tortoise-shell," the salmon fishers—functions as a rebus to organize as pictorially present the truth that is revealed in the temporal unfolding of the poem, a truth that emerges, epiphanically, from the repeating patterns to be found *in the things* of Appleton House. Through the mediation of this "holy mathematics," the poem remains mimetic—imitating the architectural forms—squares, circles—of the house it celebrates, but it does not remain visual. Rather, the squares and circles must be perceived conceptually, mathematically, before the analogy of form and content can be recognized.

The allegorical narrative of the Fairfax estate is joined to the ironic lyric of the poet in the act of composition by the same holy mathematics that join the poem to the thing it describes through a common architecture. By obscuring the boundary between the verbal and the pictorial, the rebus represents a mediation of the boundary between the temporal and the eternal. The poet occupies this borderline or amphibious position when he retreats into the natural world of Fairfax's park, where *"Natures mystick Book"* appears as a *"Mosaick"* of light and shadow formed by the sun shining through the leaves (ll. 577–84). Given Marvell's fondness for using *light* as a vehicle for God's presence in his material creation, we may read "In this light *Mosaick*" as "informed by the unmediated presence of the Holy Spirit." Thus, the poet reads the light in the light of the light.[24] But, while the celestial light makes the mosaic pattern on the trees and ground, it is the poet's "Phancy" that weaves the leaves into "Strange *Prophecies.*" In doing this the fancy is informed by the light Mosaick of the Scriptures themselves, for it is only by calling on his previous knowledge of Moses' light that the poet can recognize in nature what *"Rome, Greece, Palestine,* ere said."[25] These earlier texts supply the meaning of nature and history by disclosing their ends, in both the logical and the temporal senses. In this way they contribute to one History that consumes, "Like *Mexique Paintings,* all the *Plumes"* — that is, the pens of all earlier writers.

The rebus places the poet in a mediate position between what his senses perceive and what his intellect knows of a providential history conceived of as already completed. His fancy weaves the impressions of the moment into the already given design of scriptural history, and his poem, itself a light mosaic, represents the dialectical synthesis of sense and Scripture that lies at the center of eschatological thought.[26] In this way the poetics of the rebus extend the restrained allegory of typological hermeneutics from biblical texts to the unfolding text of political choice.[27] Despite its theoretical neatness, in practice this process is tense and risky. For the poet on the borderline is at once a historical subject and the subject of history. He is enjoined to undertake historical acts, the rectitude of which are secured precisely by his insight into a transhistorical design. Like the reader of a rebus he must find truth as it emerges — fleetingly — from the midst of things.

The politics of Marvell's poetic practice may be understood in the light of Barbara Lewalski's observation that Protestant exegetes modified the medieval emphasis on Christ as "the antitype who fulfills all the types *forma perfectior"* to shift the "emphasis from *quid agas* to God's activity in us [and] . . . assimilate the pattern of individual lives to the pervasive typological patterns discerned in Old and New Testament history."[28] Beyond and behind the doctrine of biblical literalism to which it is commonly attributed, this shift in hermeneutic practice bespeaks an understanding of the Christian subject as a narrative character who exists on the border of time and eternity and makes judgments and choices in time so as to actively fulfill his providential destiny.[29] Destiny should be understood, however, not as the inexorable acting out of a divinely written script, but rather as the result of a collaborative improvisation in which individual players choose lines that will have proved more or less harmonious or discordant depending on how well they heard, understood, and anticipated God's music.[30]

Eschatological thought as deployed by Marvell—with its articulation of prospective and retrospective points of view—is the doctrinal manifestation of a narrative conception of the subject. In "Upon Appleton House" the amphibious poet is situated on the borderline between his lived experience and a predestined but unrealized Providence that interprets it. By relocating the meaning of temporally unfolding events in an eternally present design, the poet's fancy re-presents the perspective of pictorial (metaphoric) presence and textual (ironic) *différance* projected by the rebus as the point, moving in space and time, where the Christian ego is provisionally formed and re-formed. Thus, the (ex)stasis of the Augustinian ego, caught at the moment of its conversion from metonymy to metaphor, is set in motion by an ironic disfiguring of allegory. The reader's progress from a diachronic series of episodes to a grasp of the synchronic design of the narrative reproduces within the representation the sublation of history into eternity that is the goal of the moral life.

As the rhetorical shuttle of "fancy's" loom, Marvell's rebus performs a textual function analogous to the one called for by Hobbes in his description of Fancy as the faculty answerable at once to memory (history) and precept (design):

> Time and Education begets experience; Experience begets memory; Memory begets Judgement and Fancy: Judgment begets the strength and structure, and Fancy begets the ornaments of a Poem. The Ancients therefore fabled not absurdly in making memory the Mother of the Muses. For memory is the World (*though not really, yet so as in a looking glass*) in which the Judgment, the severer Sister, busieth her self in a grave and rigid examination of all the parts of Nature, and *in registring*

> *by Letters their order, causes, uses, differences, and resemblances;* Whereby
> the Fancy, when any work of Art is to be performed, findes her materials
> at hand and prepared for use, and needs no more then a swift motion
> over them, that what she wants, and is there to be had, may not lie too
> long unespied.[31]

Both fancy and judgment are grounded in memory, which is, itself, grounded
in experience. Fancy, as a synthetic faculty, picks up the threads of experience
and weaves them on the loom of judgment. The fabric thus woven assimilates new experience to the pattern of previous experience as threads might
be added to a cloth. Fancy's work is as good as the framework that judgment
supplies, as good as the design according to which new threads are incorporated into the fabric.

Like Marvell, Hobbes identifies a historical failure of the precepts of "Moral
vertue," which must be supplemented by a specifically structural or architectural Fancy:

> But so far forth as the Fancy of man has traced the ways of true Phi-
> losophy, so far it hath produced very marvellous effects to the benefit
> of mankinde. . . . Whatsoever commodity man receive from the ob-
> servations of the Heavens, from the description of the Earth, from the
> account of Time, from walking on the Seas, and whatsoever distinguish-
> eth the civility of *Europe* from the Barbarity of the *American* savages,
> is the workmanship of Fancy but guided by the Precepts of true Phi-
> losophy. But where these precepts fail, as they have hitherto failed in
> the doctrine of Moral vertue, there the Architect, *Fancy,* must take the
> Philosophers part upon herself.[32]

For Hobbes, the architect either assembles materials out of experience, according to precepts supplied by philosophy, or he discovers these precepts
where philosophy has failed to provide them. Hobbes's Fancy is to poetry
what the architect is to building, and, to a surprising degree, the language of
the materialistic Hobbes remains in touch with that of the Neoplatonic tradition of the Renaissance.[33]

Similarly, Marvell's fancy creates a verbal architecture in accord with the
precepts of the holy mathematics to join spirit to matter in and through the
composite or amphibious nature of man. Fancy both discovers and consti-

tutes a divine design, which is revealed at once in Scripture and in nature. That two such politically different figures as Hobbes and Marvell should inscribe the same set of ambivalences around "Moral vertue" suggests to me that we have reached the rhetorical substrate of the ideological conflicts between them, the boundary of what could be thought in and immediately after the English revolution.

The dialectic of allegory and irony conveyed by the rebus in Marvell's poem—which we may now understand as a figure of the dialectic of completed design and temporal sequence—represents the paradoxical temporality of eschatological thought, which determines present action not by prior cause but by subsequent fulfillment. The moments of pictorial fullness in the poem are also necessarily moments of linguistic transparency. The putative autonomy of the sensory image conceals the ongoing, constitutive activity of the poet's fancy and creates an emblem that becomes meaningful only when it is restored to the narrative. Thus, the meaning of Appleton House cannot be indicated without the excursion into the history of the estate and the Fairfax family on the one side and the prophecy of Mary Fairfax's future marriage on the other. "As Beasts are by their Denns exprest," Fairfax's moral character is expressed in Appleton House; reciprocally, Appleton House can speak only as an allegorical representation of the history of the Fairfax line. *Signans* and *signatum*, vehicle and tenor, type and antitype are, in practice, reversed. While the tortoise's life is determined by his shell, the narrative of "Appleton House" confirms the easier belief that the Fairfax shell is determined by the family's character. The final cause of the tortoise's shell is not his ecological niche and certainly not his choice, but the choice that the Creator has made, in advance, for the tortoise's participation in creation as a whole. Its role as a sign of the divine order is its destiny. But no one invests the tortoise with much capacity for moral choice. Since its actions are merely iterations of its nature, it resides on the side of the pictorial, lacking the extension into speculative time afforded by the faculty of speech; consequently, it participates in but lacks history.

Something more is expected of Fairfax and his poet. The reversal of sign and referent noted in Marvell's poetic practice playfully discloses the undecidability of destiny and choice and of man as creator and as creature within the temporal predicament of the subject. The serious implication of this playful design is the representation of a self that is known to be destined—or more precisely, a self that expects, at the end of time, to have been destined—but is experienced as radically indeterminate. This oscillation of perspective between an indeterminate present and an anticipated destiny parallels the ironic and allegorical polarities of Marvell's poetics on the one hand and the context in which moral choices — such as Fairfax's withdrawal from his military command — must be made on the other. The very instability of the rebus affords a privileged view of the formation of a new political actor. Suspended between allegorically iconic and ironically verbal conceptions of the self, the poetics of the rebus superposes the newly emerging Cartesian subject, whose self-awareness is the arbiter of certainty within which all things are contained, and the older understanding of the subject as one who is under the authority of an other.[34] Marvell's amphibious subject contains and creates his destiny by anticipating his role as a character in a narrative always already produced under the authority of a divine author.

The notion that history unfolds within a transcendent design has specific implications for the individual attempting to evaluate the moral character of his acts. Marvell explores these implications as they pertain to the Fairfax family and, in more interesting ways, as they affect the poet in the act of composition.

The evaluation of Fairfax's withdrawal from his command waits upon the unfolding of consequent events. Since these events are already complete from the perspective of Providence, the ethics of the withdrawal are determined but not yet fully knowable. Thus, as with Donne's dismantling of the homogeneity of microcosm and macrocosm, moral agency shifts from an *ontological* questioning of visionary adequacy to an *epistemological* questioning of the subject's anticipation of the consequences of his or her actions. A parallel case in the poem is the justification of the earlier Fairfax's violent "liberation" of Isabel Thwaites from the Cistercian nuns: "Yet, against Fate, his Spouse they kept; / And the great Race would intercept" (ll. 247–48). The weak justification of the legal warrant is given divine assent by a reading of posterior events that could, at best, only have been hoped for by William Fairfax. Proleptically denominating Isabel Thwaites "his Spouse," Marvell's sentence codes the outcome of William Fairfax's action as its cause. Noting Marvell's conflation of the "rescue" and marriage in 1518 and the acquisition of the property at the dissolution of the nunneries in 1542, Michael Wilding remarks that "the collapsing of twenty-four years into 'one instant' is a strategy of legitimizing William's onslaught on the nunnery, integrating his action with this historical process." As it turns out, William's act will have been "an act of revolutionary Protestantism, rescuing from the Catholics a woman whose descendants will be champions of Protestant reform" (*Dragons Teeth*, p. 147–48). Moral validation is subsequent to the act—necessarily so, given the processes of eschatological thought. But Marvell's ironic appreciation of the present moment does not allow the problems of eschatological ethics to escape unnoted.

Consider the episode near the end of the poem when the Fairfaxes, by choosing a mate for Mary, will "make their *Destiny* their *Choice*" (l. 744). The imagery is of sacrifice: "Whence, for some universal good, / The *Priest* shall cut the sacred Bud" (ll. 741–42). The indeterminacy of the future is emphasized by the linguistic indeterminacy of the vague "some universal good." The loss of possibility implicit in choice becomes, from a temporally reversed point of view, the achievement of destiny.

Like the shadowy patterns of the leaves that the poet reads in the light mosaic, the still virgin Mary is a cipher of limitless potential meanings, subsuming, as do Mexique Paintings, all potential assemblies of the material at hand:

> *She* counts her Beauty to converse
> In all the Languages as *hers;*
> Nor yet in those *her self* imployes
> But for the *Wisdome*, not the Noyse;
> Nor yet the *Wisdome* would affect,
> But as 'tis *Heavens Dialect*. (ll. 707–12)

"Heavens Dialect," in this passage, remains *meaning-in-potentia* until time renders it readable: "Till Fate her worthily translates, / And find a *Fairfax* for our *Thwaites*" (ll. 747–48).

The depiction of the halcyon flying across the darkening horizon with which Marvell marks Mary's entrance into the poem provides a rebus of Mary's temporal predicament, which is, in turn, the predicament of the Marvellian subject, suspended between his own moment of moral choice and an always deferred higher authority:

> The viscous Air, wheres'ere She fly,
> Follows and sucks her Azure dy;
> The gellying Stream compacts below,
> If it might fix her shadow so;

> The stupid Fishes hang, as plain
> As *Flies* in *Chrystal* overt'ane;
> And Men the silent *Scene* assist,
> Charm'd with the *Saphir-winged Mist*. (ll. 673–80)

Like the halcyon, Mary moves along a borderline between light and dark, knowledge and ignorance. This border is now revealed to be the present, always moving, yet, in a deeper sense, always still, always the single point between an irreversible past and an unpredictable future. Temporal "virginity" freezes the narrative and threatens, like Keats's Grecian Urn, to "tease us out of thought." An emblem, abstracted from its narrative context, leaves us hanging in the air like stupefied fish, waiting for the inevitable and necessary splash back into temporality and narrative.

The identification of Mary and Isabel implies a corollary identification of the garden retreat with the nunnery and emphasizes the responsibility of the self to its historical context, the individual to the race.[35] The implicit comment on Fairfax's retirement is clear, if complex. The retirement itself is a historic act that will be revealed, at a later date, to have been either a humble recognition of and submission to Providence or a proud and vainglorious attempt to withdraw from what will turn out to have been God's already written narrative. Fairfax's action is at once freely taken and part of the plan, and his moral character will be disclosed in and through a subsequent history that extends to the apocalypse. Only then will the significance of any world-historical episode be fixed. Moral virtue is the ability to recognize the pattern as it develops, to discover one's destiny in time to choose it, and thus to construct one's life as a narrative text. One might add, however, that insofar as Fairfax accepts this equation of his own ethos and the accumulating sum of his freely taken actions, he has already invested his destiny with the rising bourgeois class and broken with the agricultural past that Appleton House might be taken to represent, a predestination through choice reflected in the poem by the emphasis on such modern agricultural practices as the flotation of the meadow.

The belief that one's present acts become legible only when understood as signs in an incompletely known text, existing in an impenetrably alien atemporal matrix, engenders a sharp discontinuity between the self as subject of one's acts and the self as subjected to the transcendental totality of Providence. This discontinuity is explored within "Upon Appleton House" in at least two episodes. In stanza 71, the poet's reading in the book of nature momentarily suggests a simple continuity between nature and its human observer. But in the following stanza, the poet acquires the mute language of the natural world, and he and nature become fixed in a discourse that is likened to a trap: "And where I Language want, my Signs / The Bird upon the Bough divines; / And more attentive there doth sit / Then if She were with Lime-twigs knit" (ll. 571–74). The retreat into nature is also a retreat into a discourse of fixed gestures, a slippage from human language to natural signs.

Like birdsong, these signs are limited to a timelessly repeated self-assertion. Unable to refer beyond the situation of their production, such signs recall the ironic reduction of meaning by the assertion of a here and now that cannot be identical with the present of the text but that refuse the allegorical assertion of a meaning which is elsewhere than the text. The language of the retreat into nature recalls that of "The Garden," where the solitary nature lover reduces the social and historical symbolism of "the Palm, the Oke, or Bayes" (l. 2) to literal self-reference: "Fair Trees! where s'eer your barkes I wound, / No Name shall but your own be found" (ll. 23–24). Nature's time, measured in "The Garden" by a sundial of flowers, is cyclical, an endless, seasonal succession. Such a temporality of repetition looks back to the agrarian world that supported the hegemony of landed aristocrats, ideologically identified with the English soil they controlled economically. But Marvell's Protestant poetics again silently predestines the reader to a representation of the self in which man's responsibility is to act within the linear time of irreversible events until history is subsumed in eternity.

By weaving together the observations of experienced life and the prophetic text of Scripture, man discovers the "holy Mathematicks" of divine architecture. Thus, in stanza 73, to which I have alluded, "Phancy" begins to weave "strange" or new prophecies. The poet escapes the pictorial stasis of his "lime-twig" discourse with nature and, having recourse once more to human language, resumes his narrative. By assimilating the images of nature to the narrative patterns of revelatory verbal texts, the *"Prelate of the Grove"* preaches, in words, his own incarnation as a sign — the flesh made word — not in Nature, but in a poem, a lesser thing in which the greater is contained. The rhetoric of his incarnation is the textual representation of a man whose actions make and are made by history as a poet's words make poems, by whose form they are constrained.

Man's amphibious nature as the producer and product of his own history, as the chooser of an already chosen destiny, and as the image of an *invisible* God is dramatized by the disjunction of the author *of* the poem and the author *in* the poem in the episode of the slain rail.

> But bloody *Thestylis,* that waites
> To bring the mowing Camp their Cates,
> Greedy as Kites has trust it up,
> And forthwith means on it to sup:
> When on another quick She lights,
> And cryes, he call'd us *Israelites;*
> But now, to make his saying true,
> Rails rain for Quails, for Manna Dew. (ll. 401–8)

Thestylis at once illustrates and parodies the use of typological metaphor; she supplies the reference to the biblical text, the extension of the biblical context to the historical present ("he call'd us *Israelites*"), and the typological substitution that fulfills the prophecy ("Rails rain for Quails, for Manna Dew"). The poem first presents the death of the rails as contingent, but Thestylis's comic apology re-presents it as destined.

Thestylis, moreover, addresses the poet in the act of composition, appropriating to her interpretation the authority to "make his saying true." This momentary representation of the struggle for authority between the intentions of an author and the seemingly independent life of his created world is the textual image of the tension between individual choice and providential destiny. In the moment that Thestylis asserts the literal truth of the poet's world, she reduces the poet to a figure in it, passing him through the looking glass of verbal speculation: "Where all things gaze themselves, and doubt / If they be in it or without" (ll. 637–38). Presumably, in Marvell's Providence, God, like the poet, copes with the timely observations, interpretations, and actions of his creations.

But more dramatically still, when the fictionality of the poem's narrative surfaces in Thestylis's claim that her actions confirm rather than reflect the poet's characterization, the materiality of language represents the surplus of destiny over choice, as the typological fulfillment of the text takes place only on the level of the signifier, as a phonic play on words: "Rails rain for Quails, for Manna Dew."[36] The providential hand guiding this substitution is the attraction of a rhyme, and the difference between type and antitype is precisely the phonemic difference r/q. Here we may recall, yet again, Augustine's more straightforward assertion that the anagrammatic pun on the Greek ΙΧΘΥΣ and the appellation of Christ is a divine inscription in the language that may serve as the basis of an allegorical reading of the injunction to "be fruitful and multiply" (*Confessions* 13.22–24). Thestylis's paronomastic reproduction of Exodus surfaces as the ironic and negative moment of *allegoresis*. By foregrounding the dependence of typology itself on an association made only on the level of the signifier, it puts in question the Augustinian institution of allegorical interpretation by repeating it as parody.[37]

The typological shuttle between diachronic experience and synchronic design — between history and Providence — is mirrored in and by the linguistic shuttle between a diachronic series of sounds and a synchronic system of phonemic differences. Thus, the oscillation between space and time, between pictorial and verbal text, between description and narration in Marvell's poem can be seen as an (ironically) allegorical representation of the way that the self both produces and is produced by its language on one level and its history on another. As Paul de Man puts the general case:

> The reflective disjunction [of the subject] not only occurs *by means of* language as a privileged category, but it transfers the self out of the empirical world into a world constituted out of, and in, language — a language that it finds in the world like one entity among others, but that remains unique in being the only entity by means of which it can differentiate itself from the world. Language thus conceived divides the subject into an empirical self, immersed in the world, and a self that becomes like a sign in its attempt at differentiation and self-definition. ("Rhetoric of Temporality," p. 196)

The escape of the writing self from the rebus of language that can never fully and "literally" contain it graphically depicts the problematic relationship of self to time that is the burden of much of Marvell's poetry. The dialectic of icon and sign, image and word, established in "Upon Appleton House" is the rhetorical strategy through which the poem contains the poet, but which also, necessarily, allows him to escape. The image is rectified by the word, the word made full by the image. The poet creates the poem that includes but does not contain him, as God created a universe that includes but does not contain him. Man is an amphibium — *in* this world but not contained by it. But his existence beyond the world must be read in a book whose time is irreducibly other; each of his actions in this world is a sign in the as yet unreadable portion of that book, to be judged retrospectively by whether or not it fits the rebus that joins him to eternity. The question of withdrawal from worldly affairs — of Fairfax's withdrawal from the commonwealth government or the poet's withdrawal into the *locus amoenus* of the garden — is inscribed within this charmed (and charming) circle.

"Upon Appleton House" is neither a lyric nor a narrative poem, dedicated neither to the ironically textual presence of the poet's absent voice nor to the allegorical incorporation of that absent voice into a literary utopia in which its presence is ensured by its self-proclaimed atemporality. Similarly, the subjectivity represented in the poem is neither that of a secure landholder in an agrarian oligarchy nor that of a confident bourgeois. In fact, the consolidation of bourgeois ideology will be marked by the concealment of that which Marvell's poem reveals: the social construction of the historical actor in relation to time and the modes of production. What will soon be absorbed within an ideology of nature is shown, like Appleton House itself, under (re)construction. But poems do not simply reflect ideological changes; they also participate in them, and it is this mutual reflection, this reading of the self as it is represented in its literary products, that I have been most concerned to show. The Marvellian subject wears his temporal and epistemological predicament as the tortoise wears his shell. Like a fisherman whose head is shod in his canoe, he exists along a horizon between day and night, past and future, light and darkness. Irremediably outside the sign of himself in history and Providence, he can only terminate his contemplation and act by identifying himself with that sign, as equivocally determined in two distinct narratives, one of earth and one of heaven, one ironic, the other allegorical. The actor who emerges from this identification crosses the boundary of the poem and enters the material text of history.

Chapter 7

Experience, Negation, and the Genders of Time:

Milton and the Question of Woman

Wo Es war, soll Ich werden.[1]

> The object of the drive is to be situated at the level of what I have meta-
> phorically called a headless subjectification, a subjectification without a
> subject, a bone, a structure, an outline, which represents one side of the
> topology. The other side is that which is responsible for the fact that a sub-
> ject, through his relations with the signifier, is a subject with-holes (*sujet
> troué*). These holes came from somewhere. — Jacques Lacan[2]

1

It has been my contention that ideological tensions arising from the reorganization and modernization of social life in seventeenth-century England were
experienced as an inward division of the self, and that the poets of the time
represented this division with writings that are suspended between iconic
and verbal representation and lyric and narrative genres. In *Paradise Lost* we
encounter a poem in which the literary accommodation of the particular historical moment confronts at once an explicitly universalizing theme. To the
extent that Milton seeks to narrate the origin and destiny of history in the
punctual and decisive act of "Man's first disobedience," he also seeks to narrate a human condition that is the ground of all subsequent human conditions.
With *Paradise Lost,* we thus circle back to a commentary on the opening chapters of Genesis, the biblical place with which our literary historical excursus
began (in the thirteenth book of Augustine's *Confessions*). Milton's effort to
derive the conditions of man from the conditions of the creation of the universe would appear to necessitate a radically universalized understanding of
the historical subject. Yet it shall be my principal challenge in this chapter to
articulate the mythic thematics of *Paradise Lost* and the most historically immediate of Milton's political writings within a single rhetorical economy and
the construction of a determined historical experience.

The universal sweep of Milton's narration of the human self as an actor in the time and space of history necessitates that he begin with beginnings: the exaltation of the Son of God, the creation of the universe, and the creation of humankind. Given this early point of attack, it is at once unsurprising and brilliant that Milton poses the question of man's historical being in terms of the origin and performance of sexual difference. The injunction to increase and multiply immediately articulates difference both synchronically and dia-chronically: distinguishing Adam *from* Eve according to the division of labor in procreation and distinguishing Adam and Eve as progenitors *from* the un-folding futurity of their progeny.

In approaching Milton's genesis of gender, I note by way of literary his-torical context that we have examined in some detail the representative ways in which Augustine's mother is displaced by the unnamed woman who is the mother of his child—the son whose very name, Adeodatus (given by God), anticipates Augustine's coming renunciation of his mistress and of the sexual relation in favor of a paternal divinity. Preparing to read Milton's version of Genesis, we recall once more that Augustine's turn from the flesh is redupli-cated—as an explicitly linguistic turn—in his reading of "*crescite et multi-plicamini*" as an allegory of the faculty of using one word to signify many things or many words to signify one thing. Since, for Augustine, language arises from the child's exigent wish to ask for things, to name what he or she desires, the injunction to increase and multiply—language—represents two possible movements of desire. Desire may move along the chain of signifiers wanting one thing and then another (metonymy), or it may return toward the origin of the self by seeking to speak the Word that makes and includes all words (metaphor).[3]

In subsequent episodes we saw how Dante's Beatrice, Petrarch's Laura, Spenser's three Elizabeths, and Marvell's virgin Mary are—more or less—absorbed into their names, and, as counterpoint, how the unnamed girl of Donne's "Aire and Angels" and the Elizabeth Drury of his *Anniversaries* re-main symbolically functional only so long as they remain—in their differ-ent moral registers—interchangeably nondescript. Tracking these epideictic nominations of the female we also have been able to trace the various con-figurations of metaphor, metonymy, synecdoche, and irony underlying and supporting the symbolic cosmos in which they and the male subjects who speak them live.

With *Paradise Lost,* I reach the narrative turn of my literary history. If Augustine elides sexual difference in a refusal of the flesh, Dante and Petrarch in their different ways use the figure of an unattainable woman to mediate somatic and spiritual desires, and Spenser, Donne, and Marvell explore, each in his own way, the unstable relationship between the image of a woman, the naming of desire, and the symbolic organization of the cosmos, Milton marks the moment at which woman is restored to the status of a fully embodied subject, in whom and for whom the (re)convergence of spiritual and sexual desire is not only attainable but necessary. Paradoxically, however, she—Eve—attains this substantial being only insofar as she does not show her desire; only because she remains, for man, "a bone, a structure, an outline . . ." does she also and always substantially exceed the names by which *he* calls her.

In *Paradise Lost,* it is Adam who poses the question of woman, and poses it decisively; for it is his question that brings her into being. The newly created Adam is able to name all that he sees with the exception of God, whom he calls synecdochically by an attribute, "Author of this Universe" (8.360). The question of woman begins as a question asked of the Author that requires the able namer to call into being precisely what he does not see and for which he can find no unique symbolic designation. For this task he employs a reflexive periphrasis: "but with mee / I see not who partakes" (8.363–64).[4] Thus, woman enters Milton's creation as a lack, as the part-taker that Adam does not see. Without Eve, whom, throughout this account of her creation, he will give only the generic name "Woman," Adam has everything, "all," and can enjoy nothing: "In solitude / What happiness, who can enjoy alone, / Or all enjoying, what contentment find?" (8.364–66). Woman, then, is *not all;* she stands over against the rest of creation as what must be added to it before it may be enjoyed. On one side of creation, there is everything; on the other, woman, herself a creature, but also the creature that stands apart from creation.[5]

After successfully negotiating God's "trial" of his ability to express the divine Image (8.440–41), Adam receives divine assent, "I, ere thou spak'st, / Knew it not good for Man to be alone" (8.444–45), and assurance, "What next I bring shall please thee, be assur'd, / Thy likeness, thy fit help, thy other self, / Thy wish, exactly to thy heart's desire" (8.449–51). What follows is a dream in which the part is taken from his left side, and the partaker "form'd and fashion'd." There is an expedited "natural history" of sex in these verses (8.467–68): Adam is first made woman—"wide was the wound"—then impregnated

through a kind of self-coition — "But suddenly with flesh fill'd up and heal'd."
The rib, then, is the gamete that passes from the man to the woman, whose
womb (in-formed by God) fashions *for* the man an image or copy of himself:[6]

> Under his forming hands a Creature grew,
> Manlike, but different sex, so lovely fair,
> That what seem'd fair in all the World, seem'd now
> Mean, or in her summ'd up, in her contain'd
> And in her looks, which from that time infus'd
> Sweetness into my heart, unfelt before,
> And into all things from her Air inspir'd
> The spirit of love and amorous delight. (8.470–77)

The interplay of "all" or "nothing" invoked to assert the need of a partaker is
reinscribed within the fancied creature. "All" is contained and summed up in
her; through her mediation the *all* that she is *not* may be enjoyed.

When Adam wakes to find his dream come true, he speaks at once to creator
and creature, naming she-who-partakes with him, with man: "Woman is her
Name, of Man / Extracted," and she differs from the rib that she was and is in
one salient way: she may be seen. Standing before the fleshed vision of his flesh,
the visible incarnation of his bone, Man shall leave Father and Mother to find
himself, "one Flesh, one Heart, one Soul," a wish, exactly to his heart's desire
(8.494–99). Adam's desire to view his own rib becomes comprehensible when
we consider that the lack he sees in creation, "the one who partakes with me," is
literally himself. Before the creation of Eve, he is the one thing in Eden that he
cannot behold. Recognizing that he has no proper analog among the beasts, he
turns to God, whose image he is, but also, recognizing his unbridgeable difference from God, he insists on another of his kind so as to make himself visible to
himself, so as to realize and remedy his always already defective human nature:

> Thou in thyself art perfet, and in thee
> Is no deficience found; not so is Man,
> But in degree, the cause of his desire
> By conversation with his like to help,
> Or solace his defects. No need that thou
> Shouldst propagate, already infinite;
> And through all numbers absolute, though One;

> But Man by number is to manifest
> His single imperfection, and beget
> Like of his like, his Image multipli'd,
> In unity defective, which requires
> Collateral love, and dearest amity. (8.415–26)

These lines replay in reverse the allegory in which Augustine surgically excises flesh from the word so as to clear his way to the Word made flesh. Recall that the instrument which the church father used for this textual circumcision was a word, the participle *volatilia,* which, in his reading, articulated the flying birds of the fifth day's "increase and multiply" and the flying words implied by the repetition of the injunction on the sixth day (see fig. 1). In the above passage Milton uses a word "conversation" to suture Adam's wound and make him whole. In the seventeenth century "conversation" may have the sense of intercourse as well as discourse.[7] Adam's reference to propagation makes clear that he intends both denotations. Adam makes his desire the fleshly image of his word. He speaks to it (her) so as to possess that interior and excessive rib, which lies concealed in his side until it appears before him as Eve. What had been the dark perception of the empty place occupied by Adam's body moves into the sunlight carrying "Heav'n in her Eye" (l. 488), and Adam exclaims this is I, "My self / Before me" (ll. 495–96).

But this restoration is not without consequences. The visible projection of his heart, soul, rib (חוה, life), when she speaks, becomes her own "I" to his eye, not Adam's "I" but another, "Manlike, but different sex." When Adam confronts this other who is not himself, his previous vocabulary of containment, his plan to partake of all with his partaker, is disrupted. Gazing on this other, who is and is not himself, has the effect of purloining the very self from which its part was taken. He had hoped to hold Eve in his eye but instead feels himself drawn through that beholding eye into this something that exceeds an object.[8]

Thus, before he completes the conversation with Raphael, of which this creation narrative is a part, Adam will rewrite his imagined autocosm of man and woman, containing "all" within their partaking, as an anxiety concerning the autonomy of woman, in whom man is contained; that is, an anxiety over an inside that has somehow gotten outside, a part that has become independent, amputated:[9]

> transported I behold,
> Transported touch; here passion first I felt,
> Commotion strange, in all enjoyments else
> Superior and unmov'd, here only weak
> Against the charm of Beauty's powerful glance.
> Or Nature fail'd in mee, and left some part
> Not proof enough such Object to sustain,
> Or from my side subducting, took perhaps
> More than enough. (8.529–37)

And so Adam reposes the question of woman, obtaining woman as an eye in which to behold himself, only to fear that he will be held fast in "Beauty's powerful *glance*." The name of the partaker adds "wo" to "man"; the part taken is "perhaps more than enough."[10] The introduction of difference (sex) within the same (my self) changes things. The excess that is Eve, "more than enough" because she discloses the self by being another like the self, requires a reorganization of the economy of man, and the need of a peer, a partaker in "Collateral love," ironically, installs a hierarchy. The price of the subjectification of Adam is to be the subjection of Eve. In the economy of Milton's Eden, Eve is to be for Adam; she becomes excessive when she is for herself.[11] But, within the chronology of Milton's telling, she is for herself and speaks for herself before Adam speaks for her.[12]

Eve's version of the story, given, in Book 4, not to Raphael but to Adam, who was there to witness the events himself (or was he dreaming?), supplies a crucial episode that Adam pointedly omits: the story of an initial, "narcissistic" engagement with her own image. In Milton's myth of the origin of difference, the episode of the image in the pool, suppressed in Adam's account, disposes what it means to be "Manlike but different sex." Because he is created first, Adam requires an image. Eve is created to be an image for him, but, unlike him, she first encounters her own image. And, to her delight, this image, which she is, partakes with her:

> A Shape within the wat'ry gleam appear'd
> Bending to look on me, I started back,
> It started back, but pleas'd I soon return'd,
> Pleas'd it return'd as soon with answering looks
> Of sympathy and love. (4.461–65)[13]

Eve's version of her creation thematizes the scandal of Adam's desire for himself by discovering Narcissus at the "origin" of "collateral love" and the necessary interplay of subjectification and subjection that attends it. Milton's universe requires Eve's complicity in her own decapitation. To fulfill Adam's need for conversation, she must remain an empty place in which he finds himself:

> O thou for whom
> And from whom I was form'd flesh of thy flesh,
> And without whom am to no end, my Guide
> And Head. (4.440–43)

This submission is neither simple nor simpleminded.

What promise induces Eve to embrace this subjection? A new name. Eve admits that she would have remained enraptured of her image in the pool and "pin'd with vain desire" had not a voice warned her that the image lacked the requisite difference, was the shadow of herself and not its other. The voice draws her from her image with a compensatory offer:

> but follow me,
> And I will bring thee where no shadow stays
> Thy coming, and thy soft imbraces, hee
> Whose image thou art, him thou shalt enjoy
> Inseparably thine to him shalt bear
> Multitudes like thyself, and thence be call'd
> Mother of the human Race. (4.469–75)[14]

The name is "Mother," and it is delivered as a style, a title.[15] Having been generic woman, "Manlike, but different sex," Eve is now to be something generically unique, styled "Mother of the human Race." In return for this style, she must defer the pleasure of her self-possession in the pool and invest her desire in Adam, whose image she is. The promised return on this investment is to be "Multitudes like thyself."[16] It is in view of Adam's role in the future productivity of her "different sex" that Eve confers upon Adam the title that Adam had conferred upon God, and which, interestingly enough, the young Milton had, in view of his future productivity, appropriated to himself, "Author" (4.634).

2

To understand what is at stake in this displacement in the appellation of Eve from Woman to Mother it will be necessary to think a little more about the nature of Eve's encounter with the watery image and the compensation that she receives by turning from it. In the course of making distinct arguments, James Holstun and Mary Nyquist both recognize that Eve's momentary engagement with her reflection evokes a crucial moment of pre-Adamic female subjectivity.

For Holstun, the encounter "creates a normative model of feminine identity, not identity in general" ("Will You Rent Our Ancient Love," p. 854), but that model is quickly contained and neutralized by a periodizing nostalgia that locks it into a superseded past:

> The mere fact that [Eve] narrates [the reflection] scene indicates that she cannot return to it. She has gained the power of language only by renouncing her mute sapphic communion with her image. A narcissistic or lesbian moment that can be spoken of only indirectly and in the past tense by a speaker who has left it behind cannot threaten a cosmos ruled by paternal authority. (p. 858)[17]

In this reading, in an abrupt transition from the literary to the historical that is characteristic of the New Historicism which Holstun has criticized elsewhere, the very inclusion of the moment of Eve's pre-Adamic subjectivity somehow contains whatever contemporary performativity it may encode.[18] Thus, citing Adam's omission of the episode in his own account of the creation of Eve in Book 8, Holstun asserts that "we are quite free to follow Adam in this act of forgetting, to see Eve's sapphic autocosm as a safely periodized phase, and to see the formation of the Edenic couple as a natural and rational act of psychological maturation" (p. 862). The inclusion of the scene periodizes it in a way that places it safely as a stage of human development that has already been passed through: "Milton allows us to hear from within the Puritan nuclear family a critical recollection of the traumas accompanying its birth. Here, sandwiched between Eve's pious and submissive orations to God the Father and his image Adam, we find her quietly memorializing a lost sapphic moment" (p. 862). Later, I shall want to explore a possibility which Holstun neglects: that Adam's "forgetting" of the reflection scene suggests not that the scene has been rendered innocuous, but rather that it remains for him an unspeakable scandal.

But first I think we can come closer to the scene's content. Although Nyquist ultimately joins Holstun in the insufficiently mediated turn from Milton's text to the historical development of the bourgeois family, her contextualization of the episode is more carefully specified, and she is more attentive to the formal motivation of the scene within the narrative diegesis of *Paradise Lost*. Thus, she correctly identifies Milton's Divorce Tracts and the Puritan desire for companionate marriage as the immediate textual and historical contexts of the scene, and she understands the formal implication of Adam's desire and Eve's subjectivity:

> If Eve is created to satisfy the psychological needs of a lonely Adam, then it is necessary that *Paradise Lost*'s readers experience her from the first as expressing an intimately subjective sense of self. From the start she must be associated in a distinctive manner with the very interiority that Adam's need for another self articulates. Or to put this another way, Eve's subjectivity must be made available to the reader so that it can ground, as it were, the lonely Adam's articulated desire for another self. (p. 119)

Nyquist is precise in explicating the nature of this represented subjectivity. Recalling that before the intervention of the divine voice, "the 'Smooth Lake' into which Eve peers seems to her 'another Sky,' as if the waters on the face of the earth and the heavens were for her indistinguishable or continuous," Nyquist hears in the divine voice an echo of the paternal Word's division of the waters in Genesis 1:6–7. This insight leads Nyquist to an identification of the nature of Eve's engagement with the watery image more perspicuous than Holstun's "lesbian autocosm":

> Before describing her watery mirror and her other self, Eve mentions "a murmuring sound / Of waters issu'd from a Cave" — murmurs, waters and cave all being associated symbolically with maternality, as critics have pointed out. When the paternal Word intervenes, Eve's specular auto-eroticism seems to become, paradoxically, even more her own, in part because it no longer simply reflects that of Ovid's Narcissus. And when Eve responds to the verbal intervention by rejecting not only his advice but also Adam, "hee / Whose image" she is, preferring the "smooth wat'ry image," an analogical relationship gets established be-

tween female auto-eroticism and the mother-daughter dyad. But — and
the difference is of crucial importance — this implicit and mere analogy
is based on specular reflection and error alone. (pp. 121–22)

Nyquist's argument moves quickly here; the relationship between "the interiority that Adam's need for another self articulates" and the analogy of female
autoeroticism to the mother-daughter dyad in the reflection scene can be further spelled out.

When Adam awakes to his creation, he turns his "wond'ring Eyes" toward
heaven, springs upward "by quick instinctive motion," and surveys his sur-
roundings. He then turns his attention to himself:

> Myself I then perus'd, and Limb by Limb
> Survey'd, and sometimes went, and sometimes ran
> With supple joints, as lively vigor led:
> But who I was, or where, or from what cause,
> Knew not. (8.267–71)

When Adam recounts that he did not know who or where or why he was,
he fails to mention that he also did not know what he was. His visual self-
interrogation would have picked up a collection of parts — "Limb by Limb" —
but, without a specular encounter such as the one had by Eve, he could not
have seen himself as an organized whole, and, most importantly, he has not
seen the human face, the place from which he sees. Having exhausted his
visual capabilities without an adequate self-discovery, Adam turns to verbal
inquiry, asking the Sun, the Earth, and the Creatures for the story of his origin
and his Maker (8.273–82). When these inquiries receive no answer, Adam sits
down to think and is overtaken by sleep.

During this sleep he first encounters, in a dream, the creator in whose image
he has been formed:

> One came, methought, of shape Divine,
> And said, thy Mansion wants thee, *Adam,* rise,
> First Man, of Men innumerable ordain'd
> First Father, call'd by thee I come thy Guide
> To the Garden of bliss, thy seat prepar'd. (8.295–99)

Thus, Adam is named and called into being first as Man and then as Father,
inwardly, in a dream, and the image of himself he organizes through this call-

ing must correspond to something that he can describe only as "One . . . methought, of shape Divine." It is against this scene of paternal calling and self-recognition that Eve's autoerotic investment of the mother-daughter dyad must be read. It is only after this inward calling that Adam awakes to find another before him, in whose "Presence Divine" he recognizes the shape he had dreamed (8.314). His sense of self as Man and Father is mediated *inwardly* through God and through his speculative intellect, which conceives of the Maker and calls on him to reveal himself, while Eve's first sense of self is reflected to her by the watery *surface,* returning to her an image of herself. Of course, the discursive economy of institutional patriarchy within which Milton writes privileges the conceptual mediation yielding the divine appellation of Father over the visual mediation of Eve's virtual image, but the resistance that the maternal fact offers the paternal concept remains to be read.

Nyquist goes beyond Holstun's "lesbian autocosm" in seeing the etiology of Eve's affection for her image in an analogical relationship between the image and Eve on the one hand and the mother-daughter dyad on the other. What is curious, however, is the speed with which Nyquist dismisses this analogy as speculation and error. She understands the scene as one that establishes Eve's subjectivity specifically within the frame of a female genealogy, but rather than explore the ground of the analogy in a speculation of the self as other, she seeks the meaning of the scene in what she takes to be its ideological performance:

> Grounded in illusion, Eve's desire for an other self is therefore throughout appropriated by a patriarchal order, with the result that in *Paradise Lost*'s recasting of Ovid's tale of Narcissus, Eve's illusion is not only permitted but destined to pass away. In its very choice of subject, Milton's epic seems to testify to the progressive privatization and sentimentalization of the domestic sphere. That this privatization and sentimentalization make possible the construction of a novel female subjectivity is nowhere clearer than in Eve's first speech, in which the divine voice echoes the words originally dividing the waters from the waters, words which in their derived context separate Eve from the self which is only falsely, illusorily either mother or other. (pp. 121–22)

For both Holstun and Nyquist, then, in their different ways, Eve's pre-Adamic subjectivity, what Freud would call her primary narcissism, is fully recuperated by and within the patriarchal text of a historically developing set of social practices. Adam, however, is a key dissenter from this recuperative view:

> For well I understand in the prime end
> Of Nature her th'inferior, in the mind
> And inward Faculties, which most excel,
> In outward also her resembling less
> His image who made both, and less expressing
> The character of that Dominion giv'n
> O'er other Creatures; yet when I approach
> Her loveliness, so absolute she seems
> And in herself complete, so well to know
> Her own, that what she wills to do or say,
> Seems wisest, virtuousest, discreetest, best;
> All higher knowledge in her presence falls
> Degraded, Wisdom in discourse with her
> Loses discount'nanc't, and like folly shows;
> Authority and Reason on her wait,
> As one intended first, not after made
> Occasionally; and to consummate all,
> Greatness of mind and noblesness thir seat
> Build in her loveliest, and create an awe
> About her, as a guard Angelic plac't. (8.540–59)

The question is: if Adam, whose ego is formed first in a dream (8.292–310) and then in colloquy with the paternal maker (8.311–451), so fully subsumes Eve's *merely* specular identification with the maternal image — why, even after Raphael's corrective indoctrination, does she *seem* so absolute to him? The fact of the Fall is enough to establish the inadequacy of Raphael's remonstrance. When we recall that Adam will fall "Against his better knowledge, not deceiv'd / But fondly overcome with Female charm" (9.998–99), we must acknowledge that far from being fully contained and recuperated by patriarchal appropriation, the privacy of Eve, the inassimilable (by Adam) remainder of her feminine subjectivity, is in Milton's telling the universal ground of the human condition. An attempt to answer the question of Eve's seeming absoluteness would reengage the tense relations of history and form that inhere in the very notion of literary history, allowing us to rewrite Nyquist's too quick historicization in terms of the material history of form.

To begin, let us reconsider the "mere analogy" of Eve's autoeroticism and the mother-daughter dyad by confronting it with the following aphorism, empirically obvious but also implicit in the distinction between Adam's conceptual and Eve's visual self-discoveries: *Paternity is a concept; maternity is a fact.* This statement cross-couples with the thematics of vision and voice that have worked their way through the foregoing literary history to form a design that can be conveniently mapped in terms of the metaphorization of "speculation"; that is, the compression into the word "speculate" of a literal or concrete albeit reflective sense—to see, as in a mirror—and a figurative sense—to engage in intellectual surmise. In the story told by Nyquist, Adam's speculation of Eve, that is, his calling her into being according to his concept of her, overpowers and appropriates for patriarchy the moment of visual speculation in which Eve encounters her image reflected in the water; the concrete visual moment in which Eve comes to know herself as an integral whole *like* the image in the lake becomes merely "speculative," and the conceptual moment becomes concretely visual, as Adam awakes and sees Eve "such as I saw her in my dream" (8.482). The resistance that I want to locate emerges in the fact that, for Adam, this cross-coupling of thought and being does not actually occur. He knows it intellectually, but he also recognizes in the strange commotion of his passion that something is left over, an absoluteness about Eve that cannot be sublated into thought. What is the nature of this remainder that resists Adam's speculation?

Paternity is a concept; maternity is a fact. The complexly layered relations implicit in what we might call the scandal of patriarchy may be visualized on a square of oppositions (fig. 5). Begin with Adam, generic man, in the upper righthand corner of the square (A). In Milton's telling, Adam, like the narrator of "Aire and Angels," is marked for desire; he perceives Eve first as lack, as what is missing from his world, loves her before he sees her, and asks that she be made in accord with his desire for another *like* himself. Remembering the positions in the dialectic of rhetorical tropes outlined in chapter 2, we may call this the pole of identity, or metaphor. From Adam's point of view, Eve will be a metaphoric representation of himself; as his love, she will return to him in visible form the desire that seems to issue from within him and of which he is the subject. By knowing her, he will know what is intangible in himself.

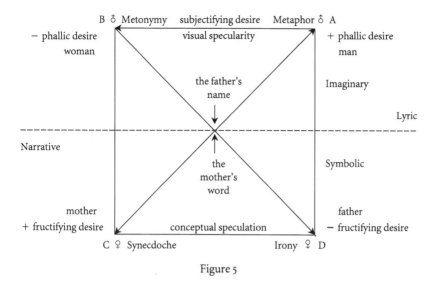

Figure 5

Eve appears at the upper left of the square (B). She does not apprehend her-self as "manlike but different sex." On the contrary, her first identification is with the image in the lake, whose appearance she prefers to Adam's. When she accepts the style of Mother, she understands herself to be deferring that one image on the promise of "multitudes like thyself." She is unmarked for desire, which is to say that while she makes concretely visible Adam's desire, her sub-jectivity, formed first on a fair surface and then ceded to Adam, cannot certify her own desire. Adam discovers himself in her as different, as future boys will discover themselves as boys only insofar as they realize that they differ from those who nurse them. Eve, however, matched with the maternal image in the lake, remains self-same. In terms of our rhetorical dialectic, we can think of her position as that of metonymy. Her first apprehension of Adam is not of identity but of difference, and she is formed as subject in the temporal slide be-tween two contiguous images: the one in the pool and that of God as reflected in Adam. If we were to stop here, with the top half of the square, we would have the Petrarchan dyad, whose impasse is exemplified in "Aire and Angels."[19]

When Eve accepts the style of Mother, however, time intervenes, and the bottom half of the square comes into play. Unlike generic woman, the Mother (C) is marked for desire, both by her visible affection for children and by the earlier sexual encounter that they imply. Insofar as the children make concretely visible the desire of father and mother, I propose to associate this position with synecdoche. Not incidentally, this is also the position of "the privatized and sentimentalized domestic sphere" in which desire is captured and contained within a "family" wholly represented by and wholly representing each of its members, the historical moment that Holstun and Nyquist identify in relation to Milton's inclusion of the reflection scene. Thus, I am not arguing against their social contextualization, but rather I am attempting to supply the formal mediation of literary history and history, which Holstun and Nyquist omit.

Before proceeding to the remaining and difficult position marked as the position of the Father (D), I need to say something about why I have labeled the rectangle above the bisecting dotted line, lyric, and the one below, narrative. I use these terms here to suggest, very generally, the literary historical event that occurs when the halves of the square are joined—as they are, in exemplary fashion, by the articulated displacement from Man to Father and from Woman to Mother in Milton's creation stories. This event may be thought of as no less than a door opening in the universalizing Petrarchan impasse into a particularized narrative time: a door resembling the one that Hamlet walks through when he negates Gertrude's assertion of the *common* fate of man, with a historicizing assertion of the sordid particulars of her *common* sexuality.[20] As Eve is to reappropriate the maternal image that she must leave for Adam by becoming pregnant, narrative attempts to reappropriate the lyric moment when desire and its object coincide by becoming *pregnant* with meaning, which it will *deliver* only retrospectively (as the child retrospectively confers the style of Father on the man so certified by the mother's word) when it has come to term. The patrilinearity, which underpins patriarchy, gathers up children under a name, the father's name, and thus extends its moments into a speculatively unified historical time. Narrative, in which a sequence of events is gathered into a plot that renders it consequential, is thus the formal rhetorical structure of unified historical time. In Milton's story, in particular, a promise is extended beyond the boundaries of the text that, in the end of time, all the disparate episodes within its "Race," those represented in the poem and those omitted, will be gathered up without remainder in the name of the signifying Father: "God shall be All in All" (3.341).

But something remains, unwritten, inassimilable, incapable of certification, the Mother's Word, for only she can speak the Father's name.

MIRANDA   Sir, are not you my father?
PROSPERO   Thy mother was a piece of virtue, and
                       She said thou wast my daughter; and thy father
                       Was Duke of Milan, and his only heir
                       And princess no worse issued. (*The Tempest* 1.2.55–58)

The diagonal lines BD and AC indicate implication. AC represents the positive, mutual implication of phallic desire and maternal desire. The fact of motherhood implies a completed sexual encounter. BD, however, indicates a negative or unmarked implication. The complication introduced by the resistance of the maternal word to the patriarchal appropriation of female subjectivity appears as irony at position D on the square in figure 1: the position of the Father, wherein the unrepresentability of female desire indicated at B is supplemented by the unrepresentability of paternity. The unmarked nature of female desire, the utmost privacy with which it may be invested, implies the radical uncertainty of paternal attribution.[21]

At the crotch of the square, where the lines of implication cross, the Father's name is revealed at last to be the inverted mirror of the maternal word on which the patriarchal Symbolic is propped. The coming of the child to the Father's name, the attribution of this child to this Father, which institutes the patrilinearity necessary to patriarchal appropriation, rests uneasily upon the mother's word. Thus, the position of the Father is also the position of irony because the feminine interiority that it suppressed, contained, and appropriated is also the ground on which it stands. Patriarchal appropriation, understood here in its most elemental institutional mediation as appropriation of the children, succeeds only insofar as it fails.

Be it conscious or otherwise, Milton's preoccupation with this insight is evident again, for example, in *Paradise Regained*, where the Son, who is the Father's Word, reaches the Father through the medium of the Mother's Word:

These growing thoughts my Mother soon perceiving
By words at times cast forth, inly rejoic'd,
And said to me apart: High are thy thoughts
O Son, but nourish them and let them soar

To what height sacred virture and true worth
Can raise them, though above example high;
By matchless Deeds express thy matchless Sire.
For know, thou art no Son of mortal man. (1.227–34)

The unusual prominence of Mary in *Paradise Regained* has been clarified in an important essay by Dayton Haskin in ways that particularly point toward the formal alliance of narrative and the mother's word. Haskin notes that when in the first book of the brief epic Jesus is called and retreats into the desert to "cast in his mind" the meaning of his baptism:

> He is doing what his mother had done when she received her calling, and he soon brings to mind that his mother had told him the *story* of his divine conception when she noticed that his noble aspirations required to be "nourish[ed]" and also to be properly challenged. Then, in relation to the Father's *sudden declaration* of his favor, the Son reviews the rest of what his mother had taught him: about the virgin birth, the arrival of the shepherds and wise men at the manger, etc. In this way, as he gives us access to the Son's memory of his mother's actual words, Milton has Mary *weave together* various details that came down to him and his readers piecemeal, from Matthew and Luke. He makes this dramatically functional in the story by showing that Mary had told Jesus all this at the right time and that Jesus now remembers it when he needs it. Mary has been a bearer of the Word, mediating to her son information that proved timely for his mission long before the penmen wrote it down for aftertimes.[22]

The alliance between narrative and Mary's "weaving" of "various details" is clear. In her maternal role, Mary, Mother of God, bears the Word into the world and its historical time, and she narrates the words to the Word that allow him to execute, in himself, his Father's will, which now may be extended, patrilinearly, as legacy. Clearly posed against the extension into history facilitated by the mother's narration is the "sudden declaration" of paternity at his baptism, which Jesus finds perplexing until he can clarify it with Mary's mediation.

   Returning now to the square in figure 5, we can see, as we saw in Augustine's displacement of sexual to allegorical reproduction that the name of the father — circulating on the top of the square — supports a return to the origin through the immediate collapse of time, like the sudden announcement at the baptism of Jesus, which, as Milton's retelling emphasizes, immediately calls Jesus from temporal engagement into the wilderness. The extension into history through propagation is obviated by the return to the creative uttering of the deity. The mother's word — on the bottom of the square — supports a return to the origin by way of a detour through the future, which sacrifices the fact, the thing, the visible to the speculative, the conceptual, the symbolic — but only on the condition that it will be returned, retrospectively, in the form of meaning.

Thus, the square of rhetorical desire is also the square of representation per se as understood in this literary historical moment. If we imagine Adam in the position of generic man, at the upper right, and Eve as generic woman, called into being by his desire, at the upper left, representation at its deadliest appears with Cain at the lower left. Precisely when his sacrifice fails to return to its divine origin, remaining as an empty sign, Cain, whose destiny is to be reduced to the sheer mark, the negating signifier, reenacts in inverted form the primal scene of Eve's birth from Adam's side:

> [Abel's] Off'ring soon propitious Fire from Heav'n
> Consumed with nimble glance, and greatful steam;
> The other's not, for his was not sincere;
> Whereat hee inly rag'd, and as they talk'd,
> Smote him into the Midriff with a stone
> That beat out life; he fell, and deadly pale
> Groan'd out his Soul with gushing blood effus'd. (11.441–47)

As Augustine had (re)gathered all words into the Word, Cain perversely kills the second son, as the pure signifying mark begins to negate all relations other than those that can be symbolically mediated. The mother's word, which preserves the immediate relationship of maternity and the subjectivity formed on a primal specular identification with the mother, as seen by Eve in the lake, resists this premature (insufficiently worked, like the "First Fruits, the green Ear, and the Yellow Sheaf, / Uncull'd" [*Paradise Lost* 11.435–36] of Cain's sacrifice) absorption. The various historical performances of this resistance are complex and variable.

3

So, the need for another like the self provokes difference; subjectification requires subjection; "collateral love" installs hierarchy, and the recompense for hierarchy is a multitudinous repetition of an originary image. Where else in the system of differences that is *Paradise Lost* may we follow this curious path? If Eve's sexual difference generates the human race in time, what generates Milton's text?[23] What is its originary event?

In Book 5, Raphael recounts the earliest event in the chronology of *Paradise Lost*. The chain of events that is Milton's plot begins when the Father, having called the angels into plenary session, announces the regency of the Son:

> This day I have begot whom I declare
> My only Son, and on this holy Hill
> Him have anointed, whom ye now behold
> At my right hand; your Head I him appoint:
> And by my Self have sworn to him shall bow
> All knees in Heav'n, and shall confess him Lord:
> Under his great Vice-gerent Reign abide
> United as one individual Soul
> For ever happy. (5.603–11)

The similarities between the exaltation of the Son for the angels and the creation of Eve for Adam are striking. The Son whom the angels "now behold" makes the divine glory visible not only to them but to the Father himself: "Son, thou in whom my glory I behold / In full resplendence" (5.719–20). This visible glory is offered to the eyes of the spiritual angels to perfect their collateral love by partaking with them "United as one individual Soul," much as corporal Adam perfects his collateral love by partaking with Eve as "one flesh, one Soul." To confirm and implement this union, the angels are to submit to the Son and accept him as their "head."[24] Abdiel's explanation of the submission by which the angels are to rise to closer union makes explicit the paradox of difference:

> And of our good, and of our dignity
> How provident he is, how far from thought
> To make us less, bent rather to exalt
> Our happy state under one Head more near

> United. But to grant it thee unjust,
> That equal over equals Monarch Reign:
> Thyself though great and glorious dost thou count,
> Or all Angelic Nature join'd in one
> Equal to him begotten Son, by whom
> As by his Word the mighty Father made
> All things, ev'n thee. (5.827–37)

To increase the opportunities of conversation in heaven, the Father offers a part of himself to the eye, but the equality of all "United in one Soul" can only be preserved through the recognition of a natural or prior difference, a transcendent and originary merit that, as it were, chooses the Son as the head of the angels and makes of them a *body* politic.

But if the Son is positioned toward the angels as Adam is toward Eve, he is also positioned toward the Father as Eve is toward Adam. He is the image in which the Father beholds his glory in "full resplendence." There is, however, a difference. Where the "I" of Eve becomes autonomous once outside the eye of Adam (in the separation scene, for example), the Son always perfectly expresses the "I" of the Father, whose eye cannot be evaded. The incarnation may thus be looked to as the literal inscription of the Son's *embodiment* of the Father's "head." Complementing this all-important difference between Eve and the Son is a striking similarity between the creation of the Son and that of generic Man, whom he is to save through a painful renunciation of the mortality/immortality difference: paternal birth. The Son, like Adam and Eve, lacks a mother.

At first. Eve, though second in order of creation, taken from Adam as a part, is repaid for her submission to the paternal claim of "authority" with the belated priority of "Mother of Mankind." Through a similar reversal, her descendant, Christ, is to be twice begotten: once, through the masculine authority of the Father and *later,* as the second Adam, in the womb of Mary, who may be styled henceforth "Mary, mother of God."[25] At this point, we may return to Eve's encounter with her image in the pool. The narrative presents this image as one that must be rejected because its love is self-love and consequently sterile. To achieve her destiny as progenitor, Eve must submit to Adam. Adam, we remember, is the primal namer, and Eve is called into being to help him name himself. She transfers her desire from her image in the pool to Adam, in return for the deferred multiplication of that image, "Multitudes like thyself." In the economy of this exchange she surrenders her image to the intervention of he-who-names on the advice of a voice that promises, a voice that names, not what is present before her, but what is to come. Eve is thus bound on both sides by the language of denomination, bound to embrace he-who-names so that she may, after a time, bear a daughter whose womb will bring forth the Father's Word.[26] When Eve trades the image in the pool for the head of Adam, she leaves the image of herself to accept the male word and become the transmitter of his difference; which is to say, she becomes *literature.*

The difference between Eve and the Son is precisely the allegorical difference, the difference between Speech, the living Word whose presence guarantees the Father's being, and Writing, the (more or less) autonomous reproduction of a *historical* utterance. The swerve from Speech to Writing, which had marked the ironic collapse of the lyric subject, is thus recorded in Milton's narrative as a swerve into history. Milton celebrates in a powerful way the trace of difference belatedly constituting itself as an originary moment. The Mother becomes the deferred text in which a male image is reproduced, just as Writing becomes the deferred transcription of a living speech that can only be found within it. Thus, Milton's narrative situates difference as a formal category whose historical origin is sexual difference. Adam asks for a partaker whom he understands to be she without whom he cannot enjoy *all* else. When Adam sees Eve for the first time, Milton compresses the entire dialectic of sameness and difference into what must be one of the most traumatic understatements in literary history: "Under his forming hands a creature grew, / Manlike, but different sex" (*Paradise Lost,* 8.470–71). Out of Adam's rib grows a creature manlike but for the absence of the visible signpost of desire, who may or may not want what he wants, a creature who, generically speaking, is another man, yet not a man at all, on and through whom man will reproduce images that are *not all* his.

To recapitulate: Adam asks for Eve so that he may see himself in her, and she must be guided away from her virtual (reflected) image by the promise that through her sexual congress with him she will multiply her image in her children. He recognizes her as "manlike but different sex," as showing him himself as self-difference, and she, recognizing him as different from her, agrees to resolve the difference by deferring it to future generations, which will reflect them both. Thus, *différance,* the differing and deferring of text (in the broadest sense) from itself over time, is situated within sexual difference as an irre-ducible aporia, at the empty center of which hovers the tantalizing possibility — implied when we mapped the dialectic of desire and of representation on the same rhetorical square — that sexual difference functions historically as the paradigm of difference as such. The dialectic of desire, which we saw played out in the two senses of "my love" in "Aire and Angels," is here deferred to a nar-rative temporality in which the metonymic dispersal of the signifier is under-stood to be recuperated from the point of view of the future, when it will have been subsumed into a metaphoric return to the origin. In Milton's dramati-cally naked re-rendering of Donne's "So thy love may be my loves spheare," the visible difference between Adam and Eve, which is the phallus as signifier of desire as such, is precisely the pen with which Adam will write the future unity of desiring and desired in and as the future of the world. Augustine's allegori-cal displacement of sexuality in reading the injunction to increase and multi-ply as the providential gift of using one word to mean many things, and many words to mean one thing, is written back into and as the history of the world.

The insight into the mystery of Narcissus accorded Eve by her encounter with her image marks, however, another difference between her and Adam, a difference that is historical rather than anatomic. She has a vision of herself before she sees another, a vision of her image, and this vision is her mother, the model on which an utterly self-contained conception of her subjectivity is formed. Thus, Adam and the Father find their image in an other whom they recognize as different from themselves. But Christ and Eve are always endowed with a dual nature; they always know themselves as a one that unifies two, be-cause they each have a mother. The questions of governance, of equality and hierarchy, of subject and subjection that resonate through Milton's work are all thus included in the question of woman. Woman styled as mother, the ori-gin who is herself both primary and secondary, is the object of Adam's scopic drive, "a headless subjectification, a subjectification without a subject, a bone, a structure, an outline."

The antithesis of the Son and of Eve is Sin, mother not of multitudes but of parasitic and incestuous images. Sin is not a partaker with Satan but the image of his rebellious thought. She is formed not by a divine author but by Satan's autonomous fancy. When Satan engenders with her, he donates only thoughts, and so materializes only the phantasy products of primary process. Satan is unable to establish himself as subject because he is subjected to his own internal economy and is unable to give of himself to mother or Son.[27] The cannibalistic relation of the hellhounds to their mother thus figures their inability to differ or defer the original, which they repeat but do not represent. Collapsing immediately back into a metaphoric identification with Sin and Death, they mark the difference between the textual *différance* of narrative "history" and the obsessive repetition of a hellish lyric.

Thus, to say that the subject, in the modern philosophical sense, is represented in *Paradise Lost* as originating in a desire for the mother is not only to recapitulate Freud, but also to install this formation of the subject or ego within a specific temporality.[28] For the mother is here implicitly understood as the deferred origin of a subject that presupposes her and confers upon her, by the testimony of its being, the title Mother. The mother is the place the subject creates in order that he may issue from the interior space which is the outline of his own being and of which he is the visible testimony. One becomes an author ("Author of the Universe," "My author, my disposer") by appropriating the difference of the other as a representative of the self. Within the Miltonic dialectic of sexual difference, woman, as mother, is the means of the (re)production of the paternal image, the place on which and in which the father writes his name and reproduces his style. But she is refractory, possessed of her own style, the mother's style, which must be subordinated under one (paternal) head, which she must herself identify and name. The subject as ego installs itself on the objectified other under the promise and offer of a head, a reunification, which is always deferred, always to come, when the "single defect" is made up and difference has run its course: "Then thou thy regal Sceptre shalt lay by, / For regal Sceptre then no more shall need, / God shall be All in All" (3.339–41). The temporality of deferral that underlies the providential and apocalyptic view of history is the historical projection of the temporality of the mother and the ego's deferred appropriation of her origin.

4

Paradise Lost, by virtue of its exhaustive intention, discloses the suppressed and deferred authority of the Mother underlying the superimposition of subjectification and subjection in the Miltonic text. It is the epic of the origin of generic Man and could hardly not include within it the origin of sexual difference. In fact, one could say with justice that it is the necessary relation of subjectivity to subjection that is obscured in the "great argument." At this point I should like to turn to an earlier, much less ambitious, but biographically decisive text, *Eikonoklastes,* in which this foreground and background are reversed.[29] Milton's attack upon the King's Book, or more precisely, the image of the king in the image of his book, his purloined style, deals explicitly with the dialectic of head and body, leader and citizen, service and freedom in the functioning of a body politic, the commonwealth. We find, however, that the author disposes his arguments against the *Eikon Basilike* in images that inscribe the problematic interdetermination of subjectification and subjection within what I have called the temporality of the Mother. The question of woman is thus raised along with the question of the persistence of the image of a king, who, like her, has surrendered his head. The juxtaposition of the two texts will therefore further illuminate the relationship of sexual and social difference in Milton's discourse, exemplifying in a particular instance the historical performance of the maternal word.

Two of the principal issues of the *Eikonoklastes* are the king's authority over the book, which represents his image, and the negative voice he claimed to exercise over parliamentary legislation. The king's image in the King's Book is a purloined image, cobbled together by a ghostwriter and, in the notorious case of "Pamela's prayer," plagiarized from another author, an inappropriate genre, and a female speaker.[30] Milton's tract consistently distinguishes the image and the reality of the king by presenting Charles with a choice of mothers: the Parliament (which Milton portrays as preceding the commonwealth and thus providing the entity over which the king rules) and three papistical women: his grandmother, Mary Stuart; his (in the Roundhead view) overweening wife, Henrietta Maria; and her mother, Marie de Médicis. Within this economy of mothers, the true king is not Charles, but a role or style created by Parliament. Thus, Milton divides the king's rule from his physical body and reassociates it with an originary Parliament, asserting that those "who fought for the King divided from his Parliament, fought for the shadow of a King" (3.530).

Examination of the passages in which Charles is shown to embrace one of his female mothers and thus to sacrifice his head to an inappropriate authority shows the temporality of the Mother underlying Milton's attempt to create the commonwealth as historical subject through the subjection of an emasculated king. In Milton's version of events, the king's uxorious submission of his head to a woman leads inexorably to the Parliament's literal reappropriation of the royal capital.

In the *Eikon Basilike,* the king (with the help of John Gauden, his clerical and posthumous ghostwriter) appropriates the style of royal martyr, portraying himself at his devotions before his execution.[31] Against this portraiture, Milton warns that "the deepest policy of a Tyrant hath bin ever to counterfet Religious":

> *Andronicus Comnenus* the *Byzantine* Emperor, though a most cruel Tyrant, is reported by *Nicetas* to have bin a constant reader of Saint *Pauls* Epistles; and by continual study had so incorporated the phrase & stile of that transcendent Apostle into all his familiar Letters, that the imitation seem'd to vie with the Original. Yet this availd not to deceave the people of that Empire; who notwithstanding his Saints vizard, tore him to peeces for his Tyranny." (3.361)

Following the analogy to Andronicus, the dismemberment of the king is justified by his acts, which must be divided from the false divinity of his misappropriated style. Milton's method in *Eikonoklastes* is, in fact, to dismember the king's text by inserting hostile commentary into a string of always fragmentary quotations from the *Eikon Basilike;* he disrupts the king's style by dispersing the king's text and reinscribing it as a series of falsehoods, distortions, and thefts.

Once the king's royal style has been divided from his acts, those acts are attributed to the queen, whose shrewish machinations miscarry the king's policies into a hysterical pregnancy that delivers only sterile imaginings. Thus, Charles enters Parliament with an armed force attempting to arrest five members suspected of, among other crimes, plotting against the queen, because he had not "*resolv'd to bear that repulse with patience,* which his Queen by her words to him at his return little thought he would have done" (3.378), and the indictment of the five members for treason is called for on the basis of "pregnancies" and "just motives" that come to nothing:

> *He mist but little to have produc'd Writings under some mens own hands.* But yet he mist, though thir Chambers, Trunks, and Studies were seal'd up and search'd; yet not found guilty. *Providence would not have it so.* Good Providence, that curbs the raging of proud Monarchs, as well as of

madd multitudes. *Yet he wanted not such probabilities* (for his pregnant is now come to probable) *as were sufficient to raise jealousies in any Kings heart.* And thus his pregnant *motives* are at last prov'd nothing but a Tympany, or a Queen *Maries* Cushion. (3.379)[32]

This unsavory intrusion into other men's "Chambers, Trunks, and Studies" is later recompensed when the "King's Cabinet" is captured, and writings produced under *his own hand* reveal that "to sum up all, they shewd him govern'd by a Woman" (3.538), while the text he now presents as his own is shown to contain a word, "*Demagogues*," "above his known stile and Orthographie" that "accuses the whole composure to be conscious of som other Author" (3.393).

    The king, whose words are not his own and whose text is conscious of some other author, fails to maintain authority over the commonwealth or over what purports to be his own text, in part because he fails to subject his wife: "how good shee was a Wife, was to himself, and be it left to his own fancy; how bad a Subject, is not much disputed" (3.419). Failing to install a paternal authority that defers the woman's style to the male testimony of motherhood (that is, to the accession of *her* son), Charles allows Henrietta Maria to continue the arc of an unsubjected matriarchy: "it need be made no wonder, though shee left a Protestant Kingdom with as little honour as her Mother left a Popish" (3.419).[33] Milton places Charles in a line of woman-governed governors that extends ultimately to Adam and makes it clear that Charles's devotion to his queen was at the expense of Parliament:

> He ascribes *Rudeness and barbarity worse then Indian* to the English Parlament, and *all vertue* to his Wife, in straines that come almost to Sonnetting: How fitt to govern men, undervaluing and aspersing the great Counsel of his Kingdom, in comparison of one Woman. Examples are not farr to seek, how great mischeif and dishonour hath befall'n to Nations under the Goverment of effeminate and Uxorious Magistrates. Who being themselves govern'd and overswaid at home under a Feminine usurpation, cannot but be farr short of spirit and autority without dores, to govern a whole Nation. (3.420–21)

The corrective to such a succession of "Vice-gerent" mothers is included as a repressed episode in Charles's family history: his father's quiet betrayal of Mary Stuart's head to the literal subjection of the sexually ambiguous Elizabeth.[34] But, unfortunately, Charles chooses to imitate not his father's but his grandmother's model, chooses, that is, a maternal over a patrilinear genealogy:

> The rest of his discours quite forgets the Title; and turns his Meditations upon death into obloquie and bitter vehemence against his *Judges and accusers;* imitating therin, not our Saviour, but his Grand-mother *Mary Queen of Scots;* as also in the most of his other scruples, exceptions and evasions: and from whom he seems to have learnt, as it were by heart, or els by kind, that which is thought by his admirers to be the most ver-tuous, most manly, most Christian, and most Martyr-like both of his words and speeches heer, and of his answers and behaviour at his Tryall. (3.597)

This exchange, in which Charles eschews the model of the paternal Word and instead confronts his execution in the style of his papist grandmother, is more thorough than may appear at first glance. On the one hand, Mary Stuart had stood precisely on the claim of indivisible majesty that Milton set out to undermine: "she made no exception against their [the judges' and commis-sioners'] persons, only stood upon her Majesty as a Queen and chose a thou-sand deaths rather than descend to the capacity of a subject."[35] On the other, Jesus descended to the capacity of a subject for the express purpose of at once affirming and transcending the paternal Law. While Mary Stewart took the occasion of her execution as an opportunity to excoriate her persecutors one last time, Jesus refused to extend the word of judgment, offering his accusers the cryptic response, "Thou sayst." Christ's voluntary humiliation, his sub-mission of his body to the paternal death sentence, ensures his deferred ascent to the Father and, along with him, the ascent of generic Man: "thy Humilia-tion shall exalt / With thee thy Manhood also to this Throne" (*Paradise Lost* 3.313–14). It also fulfills as it repeats the promise made to Eve in return for her submission to Adam, a promise that bridges the covenants when it is rewrit-ten, after the Fall, as the protevangelium: the mysterious promise in Genesis 3:15 that the seed of the woman shall bruise the head of the serpent (*Paradise Lost* 10.179–81). In *Paradise Lost* the procreation of a "race of worshippers" is first secured when the divine Word offers Eve the style "Mother of the human

Race," and it is secured again when Adam and Eve are rescued from the despair of sin by memory of the promise of renewal that the Son had delivered to Eve:

> calling to mind with heed
> Part of our Sentence, that thy Seed shall bruise
> The Serpent's head; piteous amends, unless
> Be meant, whom I conjecture, our grand Foe
> *Satan,* who in the Serpent hath contriv'd
> Against us this deceit. (10.1030–35)

After the Fall, the promise of/to the mother is clearly the promise of the text, the opportunity of allegorical interpretation. Milton recapitulates as historical narrative Augustine's conversion of procreation into allegorization in what I have suggested is a founding trope of the Christian ego in the *Confessions.* The hermeneutic shift from Augustine's allegory to Milton's typology also effects a shift from a lyric transaction between text and subject in a single moment to a narrative transaction between text and temporally deferred text. In the typological narration of *Paradise Lost,* first Eve is "Mother of the human Race," but second Eve transmits the style of Providence, retrospectively signifying the meaning of history and its transcendence.

In the political context of *Eikonoklastes,* Milton juxtaposes the unpleasant historical model of James's acquiescence in the judicial murder of his mother with the providential model of the Passion as the alternative that Charles rejects. Milton's allegorical reading of Charles and Henrietta as generic Man and Woman allows him to rewrite the story of Charles's refusal to emulate his father, James, by palliating Parliament with the offer of his queen as a refusal to emulate the heavenly Father's perfect Son, and, at the same time, to foreclose any scenario in which Charles and Parliament are reconciled. By the time of *Eikonoklastes,* the only issue in the king's life is his manner of leaving it. More important, the relations of king and Parliament are rhetorically inscribed within the relations of man and creator, which, in turn, inscribe them within Milton's economy of sexual difference. We may note, in particular, that the analogy of Henrietta Maria's subversive position in a Protestant commonwealth to that of Marie de Médicis's position in a Catholic one makes clear that the issue of male subjection to the mother's rule precedes the issue of religious reformation. The fall of Charles I comes before the definition or institution of any earthly church because it is a ritual reenactment of the Fall of man, when Adam was "fondly overcome with Female charm" (*Paradise Lost* 9.999). Within Milton's rhetorical economy the monarchist's identification of the king's two bodies reiterates Eve's identification with her image in the pool. The disruption of that identification transforms woman from image to signifier and opens the text of history to providential meaning. It also divides the king's body from his style as it divides him from female control over the continuity of the male line and delivers him to what Milton identifies as the law of nature that installs that which is learned from the mother "as it were by heart, or els by kind." Milton's rhetorical surgery reverses the traditional claim of the king to speak the law (Rex Lex Loquens), replacing it with the claim that the law (the writ of Parliament) speaks the king.[36]

The clearest view of this strange pre-Oedipal struggle of the mothers appears in what is certainly the most astonishing passage in *Eikonoklastes*. Milton rebuts the king's contention that the Parliament had placed itself in the livery of public tumults with the assertion that the more urgent threat to Parliament was the king's "encroaching Prerogative." The king's mistrust of Parliament results from his "overdated minority" and "Pupillage under Bishops," who have failed to explain to Charles that the "Parlament had *that part to act* which he had fail'd in" (3.466):

> Yet so farr doth self opinion or fals principles delude and transport him, as to think *the concurrence of his reason* to the Votes of Parlament, not onely Political, but Natural, *and as necessary to the begetting,* or bringing forth of any one *compleat act of public wisdom as the Suns influence is necessary to all natures productions.* So that the Parliament, it seems, is but a Female, and without his procreative reason, the Laws which they can produce are but windeggs. Wisdom, it seems, to a King is natural, to a Parlament not natural, but by conjunction with the King: Yet he professes to hold his Kingly right by Law; and if no Law could be made but by the great Counsel of a Nation, which we now term a Parlament, then certainly it was a Parlament that first created Kings, and not onely made Laws before a King was in being, but those Laws especially, wherby he holds his Crown. (3.467)

Thus, and too late, Milton takes over and corrects the tutorship of the bishops, explaining the facts of life to the eternally pubescent king. The king is born of the commonwealth and the commonwealth is born of the law and the law is born of a parliament. Here, then, is the masculine line of descent obscured by Charles's refusal to subjectify the king by subjecting the queen. The king does not rule according to an image, neither the precedent image of his father's rule (which he has refused), nor the eternal image of his heavenly Father's rule (to which he is inadequate). The king rules, if he rules at all, according to the laws produced by the natural wisdom of Parliament.

The king thus stands to Parliament as Eve stands to Adam. He may subjectify himself by being subject to its always precedent laws. As the son of the law, he may be liberated from the scandal of female originality and execute the royal authority that has, because of his failure, been reassumed by Parliament. To stand on the prerogative of the king's "negative" is to mistake the nature of law and Parliament in a way that reinscribes, in deadly form, the king's adolescent malady: to account the Parliament "but a Female":

> He ought then to have so thought of a Parlament, if he count it not Male, as of his Mother, which, to civil being created both him, and the Royalty he wore. And if it hath bin anciently interpreted the presaging signe of a future Tyrant, but to dream of copulation with his Mother, what can it be less then actual Tyranny to affirme waking, that the Parlament, which is his Mother, can neither conceive or bring forth *any autoritative Act* without his Masculine coition: Nay that his reason is as Celestial and lifegiving to the Parlament, as the Suns influence is to the Earth: What other notions but these, or such like, could swell up *Caligula* to think himself a God. (3.467)

If the Parliament be female and require his "Masculine coition" to "bring forth," then it is the king himself who is a "windegg." The *OED* defines "windegg" as "an imperfect or unproductive egg, esp. one with a soft shell, such as may be laid by hens and other domestic birds" and cites Milton's only other use of the word, in *Colasterion:* "From such a windegg of definition as this, they who expect any of his other arguments to be well-hatched [etc.]." The king, in his "outdated Minority," is softshelled and ill-defined; his boundaries fail to differentiate him from his mothers, in whom he attempts to engender paternal laws through an incestuous copulation. I risk this admittedly strong reading of Milton's allusion to Caligula because, in the context that I have been developing, the transgression and maintenance of boundaries, the separation of the subject from its origin and its peers, is so much the point. Caligula failed the test that God administers to Adam before the creation of Eve in Book 8; he failed to distinguish the mortal from the divine and fell into incest (with his sister). Is not copulation with the mother the too literal execution of a desire to be one's own original, "self-begot, self-rais'd / By our own quick'ning power" (*Paradise Lost* 5.860–61)? A desire as literal as this, returning to the image of its origin without the displacement of figuration, looking for itself in the past rather than the future of "Multitudes like thyself," must, within the economy of Milton's text, be answered with the counterliteralization of decapitation. The dismembered king figures itself, too late, as the object of its own drive: "a headless subjectification, a subjectification without a subject, a bone, a structure, an outline," a "windegg," a woman. On and in the text of the king's body, reposed, as it were, in the King's Book, Milton writes a new masculine birth; the law, freed from the image of the king, brings forth the commonwealth. Failing to grasp that the Parliament created "both him, and the Royalty he wore," the king failed to recognize that he embodied the superimposition of the two senses of "subject." He refused Eve's bargain and, because he would not subjectify the commonwealth by subjecting himself to the universal reason manifest in parliamentary law, he lost his head in deed.

Milton figures the movement from fantasy to execution of the king's incestuous attempt to make Parliament accept his head, the movement from "presaging signe" to "actual Tyranny," as a verbal act. Charles's waking affirmation that the Parliament "can neither conceive or bring forth" laws "without his Masculine coition" is the affirmation of a falsity and thus the true image of the king's negative. The rhetorical movement from a dream of copulation to the sin of waking affirmation anticipates three crucial moments in *Paradise Lost*: Eve's refusal in Book 5 to affirm waking the dream of flight induced by Satan; Adam's waking from his dream of Eve to find it true; and, most clearly, Satan's parthenogenesis of, and incest with, Sin, after his denial of the Father's Word. In the first instance, Eve refuses to execute the fantasy of autonomy that Satan's dream has offered. With the help of Adam and God, she chooses not to make the journey from "signe" to "sin." In the second instance, Adam accepts the loss of a part for the boon of a partaker and affirms waking the masculine genesis of the mother. In Satan's embrace of Sin, we see the self-engenderment that *Eikonoklastes* imputes to Charles, and we see, in the hell of *Paradise Lost*, Book 2, the body politic that rises from it. Over against these three moments of textual repetition, we may place the originary and putatively successful parthenogenesis that begins the plot of Milton's epic and has all human history as its consequence: "This day I have begot whom I declare / My only Son." The Father begets and declares, engenders and names. His Word restores the womb and gives God a mother. His style is "Author." The Word of the Father validates his style by accepting subjection to crucifixion and death. The Son is "by merit rais'd" because he perceives and acts out the superimposition of subject and subjectification to which Charles and his grandmother were blind.

5

What then is an author? The handmaiden and the sister of Truth:

> Truth indeed came once into the world with her divine Master, and
> was a perfect shape most glorious to look on: but when he ascended,
> and his Apostles after him were laid asleep, then strait arose a wicked
> race of deceivers, who as that story goes of the *Ægyptian Typhon* with
> his conspirators, how they dealt with the good *Osiris,* took the virgin
> Truth, hewd her lovely form into a thousand peeces, and scatter'd them
> to the four winds. From that time ever since, the sad friends of Truth,
> such as durst appear, imitating the carefull search that *Isis* made for the
> mangl'd body of *Osiris,* went up and down gathering up limb by limb
> still as they could find them. We have not yet found them all, Lords and
> Commons, nor ever shall doe, till her Masters second comming; he shall
> bring together every joynt and member, and shall mould them into an
> immortall feature of lovelines and perfection. Suffer not these licencing
> prohibitions to stand at every place of opportunity forbidding and dis-
> turbing them that continue seeking, that continue to do our obsequies
> to the torn body of our martyr'd Saint. We boast our light; but if we look
> not wisely on the Sun it self, it smites us into darknes. (*Areopagitica,*
> *CPW* 2.549–50)

Five years before the publication of *Eikonoklastes,* Milton addressed this plea to mother Parliament that she not interpose her prevenient law between authority and the limbs of Truth. I quote the passage in full to linger over its peculiar vocabulary, its images of dismembering and remembering, the subtle interplay of genders — of masculine master and feminine Truth, of sis-terly Isis and the company of (male) writers who reassemble the "torn body of our martyr'd Saint" — and because I want to read this passage as an allegorical preinscription of Eve's encounter with her image in the lake and the exchange which she subsequently accepts for relinquishing that image. Truth came into this world once, with Christ, *embodied* in "a perfect shape most glorious to look on," the shape of the Son. But that shape was dismembered on a cross, broken, and finally removed from the eye of man and returned to heaven, leaving only its "written Records pure" (*Paradise Lost* 12.513). The mangled body of Truth, indeterminate of sex (virgin), is fragmented and then reproduced infinitely, yet "with difference of sex" until the master's return, when we, Isis-like collectors of its dismembered limbs, will remember its torn face. But this memory of the future, this (re)membering of the truth of and in the body is deferred beyond the grasp of writers who must accept the fragmentary nature of their achievement until the master returns. We remember his torn visage that we might behold it, returned before our eyes. But we — whose authority is that of writers — play the female part, the part of Isis, lest "we look not wisely on the Sun it self" and "it smites us into darknes."

Like Oedipus, the writer brings what is dark to light, but unlike that unfortunate king of the city founded by that same Cadmus who brought the alphabet to Greece, he must not prematurely bring to light the Truth that smites and blinds, the truth of his own incestuous conjunction with the mother, his masculine appropriation of the mother's style:

> For Books are not absolutely dead things, but doe contain a potencie of life in them to be as active as that soule was whose progeny they are; nay they do preserve as in violl the purest efficacie and extractions of that living intellect that bred them. I know they are as lively, and as vigorously productive, as those fabulous Dragons teeth; and being sown up and down, may chance to spring up armed men. (*CPW* 2.492)

Oedipus, too, is reason's child, whom reason sends back into the dark place whence he came, and in the wake of his failure and his discovery "spring up armed men."

The writer, at least the prophetic writer whom Milton seeks to be, performs, with and through his text, the function performed for the angels by the begotten Son, for Adam by Eve, and for Christendom by Christ; he puts before our eyes that which we cannot otherwise see or name — that Truth which is shrouded at once in the interior darkness of the heart and the excessive brightness of the Sun: "as good almost kill a Man as kill a good Book; who kills a Man kills a reasonable creature, God's image; but hee who destroyes a good Booke, kills reason it selfe, kills the Image of God, as it were in the eye" (*CPW* 2.492). How is it that a text (be)holds the image of God in the eye, while its author avoids the fate of Oedipus?

In the self-exculpating preface to the second book of *The Reason of Church Government,* Milton records his anxieties over his use of his own talents and the purchase of "ease and leasure" for his "retired thoughts" "out of the sweat of other men," particularly the "ceaselesse diligence and care" of his father (*CPW* 1.804, 808). In response to his perceived obligation to repay this paternal investment, he converts ease and leisure to "labour and intent study," which "joyn'd with strong propensity of nature" will enable him to "leave something so written to aftertimes, as they should not willingly let it die" (1.810).[37] What will keep this something alive, what "potencie of life" will it offer to aftertimes? Milton bases his expectations in part on the opinion of his "sundry masters and teachers": "It was found that whether ought was impos'd me by them that had the overlooking, or betak'n to of mine own choise in English, or other tongue, prosing or versing, but chiefly this latter, the stile by certain signes it had, was likely to live" (1.809).

Milton goes on to recount his efforts to perfect this "stile," to make of it a "violl" that will carry into the "progeny" of his soul, "the purest efficacie and extractions of that intellect that bred them": "I apply'd my self . . . to fix all the industry and art I could unite to the adorning of my native tongue; not to make verbal curiosities the end, that were a toylsom vanity, but to be an interpreter & relater of the best and sagest things among mine own Citizens throughout this Iland in the mother dialect" (1.811–12).

This perfect conversation in the mother dialect, the presentation of a poem "doctrinal and exemplary to a Nation" (1.815), is to remain latent some twenty-four years, during which time Milton will give himself to the "carelesse and interrupted listening of these tumultuous times," choosing a "manner of writing wherein knowing my self inferior to my self, led by the genial power of nature to another task, I have the use, as I may account it, but of my left hand" (3.807–8).

During this extended gestation, however, Milton's muse is not inactive. She goes up and down like the good Isis picking up, here and there, the limbs of Truth. She will not find them all, but those she finds will contribute, according to the time of the Mother, to the re-membering of the "torn body" of a "martyr'd Saint." When this re-membered body is complete, it will form a text in that life-preserving style that at once expresses the propensities of nature and the diligence of the father. This text will reveal not an imitation of the sensible past, but the sensible signifier of the intelligible future. It will be not the "toylsom vanity" of "verbal curiosities" but the reasoned image of Truth's master brought out of the darkness of interior and personal revelation into the womb of a text where it can educate a "race of worshippers" for the blinding light of that day when the Father returns as the exalted presence of his Son.[38] In the matured style of that text, Milton gives birth to himself as "Author" and sees before him — as Dante had once beheld his heart and Adam his bleeding rib — the hidden part he had perceived in 1642 as an "inward prompting which now grew daily upon me" (1.810).

The interplay of subjection and subjectification that marks the marriage of Adam and Eve, the Son's vicegerent reign over the angels, and the Parliament's violent appropriation of the king's head is (re)played in Milton's account of his own temporal deferral in favor of the commonwealth's appropriation of his righthanded style, his long gestation, and his submission to the muse's delivery of "unpremeditated verse," until he can behold in the text those "inward promptings" that mark the presence of his style, tracing along the intersection of history and desire, subjection and subjectification, the fragmented, yet remembering, image of a woman, a mother, always about to answer the question in/of the text. The answer, however, remains and will remain deferred, the purloined image of an appropriated origin, until the return of the Master, the visibly present and perfectly voiced Word of the Father, who, with his Virgin Mother, Truth, withdrew — for a time — to his heavenly throne, leaving behind only a "written record pure."

Epilogue

The Hyphen in the Mouth of Modernity

> Shee, shee is gone; shee is gone; when thou knowest this,
> What fragmentary rubbidge this world is
> Thou knowest, and that it is not worth a thought.
> —John Donne, *The Second Anniversary*

> Things must expect to come in front of us
> At many times — I don't say just how many —
> That varies with the things — before we see them.
> One of the lies would make it out that nothing
> Ever presents itself before us twice.
> Where would we be at last if that were so?
> Our very life depends on everything's
> Recurring til we answer from within.
> —Robert Frost, "Snow"

> Life goes on long after the thrill of living is gone.
> —John Mellencamp, "Jack and Diane"

Some prologue is necessary. In 1988 I was asked to speak about Milton at a conference on "Postmodernism Across the Ages."[1] The title suggested both persistence in and movement through time, and the inclusion of Milton on a program about postmodernism indicated the intention of the organizers to disrupt, or at least to question, the linear narrative of contemporary periodization. This talk and parts of one given at a second conference, "Rethinking Culture," at which I contributed a talk on John Donne and literary history to a panel on "The Remains of Culture," have been absorbed into this epilogue, in which I attempt to extend the foregoing episodic history of the literary subject of modernity to a brief consideration of periodization and the postmodern.[2]

1

One wants to take the "postmodernism" of "Postmodernism Across the Ages" in a singular and unitary way as some substantive formation enduring endlessly in an ocean of history, washing up, wearied but intact, on the pebbled shores of diverse ages, shaking off the brine and supplementing, with its tearful eyewitness, the account of itself that it finds to be already oft-told in this strange place. However, in this age, if it is, when it is done, to have been an age, though one may think postmodernism, one sees postmodernisms, diversely rooted in their particular discursive histories.

At the time of writing the essay to be presented at "Postmodernism Across the Ages," and now to be incorporated in this epilogue to *The Story of All Things,* I lived, as I had for most of my life, in Brooklyn, where from the window of my apartment I had found recently imposed on my vision a sixteen-story, polygonal building of red brick. The oddly angled facets of this building, which is, naturally, still there, rise in slabs until they are topped by what I take to be a fake copper mansard roof, to which is added, on one side, a small, fake copper pyramid. On each side of this roof is a stone facing, containing — like a clock lacking a dial — a red neon circle.[3]

I take the copper to be fake because the day it was put up, its color approximated — in a way — the green copper-oxide color that *real* copper acquires as it weathers. I say approximated in a way, because the material in question — whatever it is — does not imitate a weathered appearance but rather seems to take a stab at what the familiar color of weathered copper would look like if clean and new, excepting the fact that clean and new copper is an entirely different color.

The building, which obscures and dwarfs the two-story public library that had previously organized the site, was put there — in the face of community objections — by the Morgan Stanley Guaranty Trust Company, which I know to be, in another register — that of the multinational financial operator and master of the transcendental tender offer — a postmodern entity, or, to impart to my meditation the rigor of Jürgen Habermas's translated discourse, an operator of "postmodernity."[4] Insofar as this building serves to signify the agency of postmodernity and its relation to the subject or agent of modernity, the advent of which has been the theme of the present study, it strikes me that the use of a building material that constructs the nonexistent newness of an aged coinage metal together with the absence of the clock hours within the neon circles of finance give this building a sort of absolute monumentality.

A monument marks the place, localized in time and space, at which something has been transferred from space and time to memory — has become, in effect, a tradition. This building, which by its bulk asserts hegemony over its neighbors and the nearby Williamsburg Savings Bank clock tower (to which its empty clock faces allude), razes the buildings whose style it expropriates from their contexts in the history of Brooklyn (a venerable history by American standards) and absorbs the motifs of the past and the archaeological strata in which they reside into its own decontextualized allusiveness. As an *absolute* monument, it encumbers the future by turning back to a past that it preserves only as what is lost — just as the green roof points at once to its always already aged quality with respect to its models and the loss of the historical process of weathering by which aging occurs.

I know this building to be an example of what architects call postmodernism, and I wonder if the temporal disruptions of its clockless clocks and not exactly pre-aged, not quite copper, roof might be clues to the temporality of postmodernism or, at least, to the defining attributes of postmodernism as a specifically temporal predicament. I will return later, and in a very different context, to the definition of a specifically postmodern monumentality and temporality.

But, first, tempted as I am to read what my window framed, more or less synchronically, and to derive from it a postmodernity that would bind to a finite and specifiable set of attributes the postmodernities I saw there, I am stopped by my casual knowledge that the postmodernity of the building ought to be situated diachronically with respect to the great age of the Bauhaus and architectural modernism against which it reacts, or to which it alludes, while the postmodernism of Morgan Stanley must be understood in relation to the age of industrial capitalization through which it has passed, the time when its function was to underwrite the productivity, as opposed to the performativity, of American capital. As for the burial of the 1950s social-realist branch library beneath this conglomerate pile, I must meditate on the fact that the library had, prophetically, in the time before Morgan Stanley, converted half of its space to "the Brooklyn Business Library."

While it certainly appears that these transitions of style and changing modes of production are connected, I would hesitate too quickly to assimilate, one to the other, their histories and modes of change, because I fear that to do so would lead to a totalizing idealization in which a virtual master code, operating at or near the modes of production, would appear to govern and rationalize the internal developments of the historically distinct (though

intertwined) disciplines involved. And I suspect that my hesitation in this respect is itself an instance of the postmodern moment in criticism.

Thus, each of the postmodernisms that appeared in my window back in
1988 seems more integral with its own immediate modernism than with something dragging its cunning self, intact, across the ages, and so too would it
seem that postmodern literature, painting, and music stand in a more determinate (if not necessarily more determinable) relationship to each of their
disciplinary pasts than to each other.

How, then, to talk about postmodernism across the ages? Since my interest in postmodernism is theoretical, which is to say that it is an interest not
in the *beings* of postmodernism but in its possibilities of *Being,* I propose to
leave aside — but only for the moment — the empirical patterns that insisted
through my window in Brooklyn, and, beginning with the term *postmodernism,* to sketch something of a conceptual morphology. My question, then,
will be not what is postmodernism through the ages but what might a postmodernism, properly so called, be?

As the foregoing study makes obvious, I come to this question, by virtue of
my own preparation and interest, from a *particular* age, the Renaissance, and
a particular perspective, literary history. I will begin, therefore, in the manner
of a Renaissance rhetorician by making a threefold division of the subject, addressing in turn: the semiotic function of the "post-," a contextual definition
of "modernity," and Milton's canonicity as a poet on the late Renaissance cusp
of modernity, in relation to modernism and postmodernism.

2

What precisely is transacted across the conjunction of *post-* and *modern?*
While the *post-* carries us past what follows it, it retains, by virtue of its
lexical attachment, precisely that which has been passed in time. The use of
compounds like postwar or poststructuralist depends on the persistent significance of the war or structuralism in the contexts that they are used to
address. Thus, the *post-* form is transitional; it distinguishes the moment at
which something that had been experienced as currently unfolding is felt, not
as ended, but as a more or less institutionalized presence. When a succeeding
configuration gets its own name, that which it supersedes may be regarded as
other in a way that is directly impeded by the *post-* formation. There is thus a
double dependence of the postmodern on the modern. Early modern people,

as those who lived in the Renaissance are now properly called, were evidently and indisputably aware of their modernity, but they do not seem to have conceived of themselves and their works as *post-medieval* or even *post-dark ages.* On the contrary they often worked hard to obscure their ruptures with the immediate past and to represent them as pervasive continuities. Looking ahead to our discussion of Milton, we might take as an example the way in which the Reformation, in order to claim its continuity with the "primitive" Catholic church, situated the Roman church and its history as a corrupt parenthesis opened at the Constantinian Donation and now to be closed. Modernism eventually constituted the Middle Ages as an otherness that lay behind it, and it seems now to have constituted postmodernism not as an otherness that lies before it but as the ever recursive image of its own exhaustion.

The *post-* form, then, indicates not the othering of the modern, in the way that the Renaissance achieved the othering of the Middle Ages, but rather it establishes a moment after the modern during which we seem to be bound in a present that is present only as the presence of a present that is lost, that is belated, and that remains. Insofar as modernity is the way of the "now," postmodernism installs that "now" as a remainder, or more properly a memory. In the postmodern, then, what is *present* is present as past, as a reminder of its own monumentality. Thus, the empty circles of neon *decorating* the odd faces of the Morgan Stanley building refer at once to the nearby clock tower of the Williamsburg Savings Bank (by which generations of Brooklynites told time) and to the belatedness of clock time itself in the digital realm of *Morgan Stanley.* Similarly, the weatherproof, "weathered copper" of its roof *remembers,* without *being in* the time in which a copper roof's durability inheres, the time in and through which it acquires the protective cover of copper oxide that *eventually* stabilizes it in and over time. Through such elements, the postmodern incorporates the past without *recycling* it, retaining it rather as an out-of-phase aspect of the present, as memory—or what amounts to the same thing, an allusion. Thus, the hyphen, invisible or printed out, that joins *post* to *modern* functions—to reengage the analogy of the microcosm and the macrocosm—as a mouth; for the transaction that takes place at this hyphen is the sucking inside of the world, so that experience may be retained, in its loss, as a property of consciousness, that is, as memory. Memory installed in this way is best called nostalgia. In it the markers of different times—public clocks, copper roofs, asymmetrical edifices—are held out of time in an expansive, yet dimensionless present — a present that remains absent to itself by virtue of its having been given over to recollection. Augustine catches this absence of memory to itself in the famous discourse on time in Book 11 of the *Confessions*:

> For if there be times past, and times to come; fain would I know where they be: which yet if I be not able to conceive, yet thus much I know, that wheresoever they now be, they are not there yet: if there also they be past, then are they not there still. Wheresoever therefore and what-soever they be, they are not *but as present* [*non sunt nisi praesentia*]. Although as for things past, whenever true stories are related, out of the memory are drawn *not the things themselves which are past* [*non res ipsae, quae praeteriereunt*], but such words as being conceived by the images of those things [*sed verba concepta ex imaginibus earum*], they, in their passing through our senses, have, as their footsteps, left imprinted in our minds.[5]

If the world that is swallowed and internalized by the *post-* of postmodernism is the modern world, then it remains to define the period of that modernity by defining a contextually relevant modernism. Having referred to the Renaissance as the early modern period, I have already tipped my hand about the broad historical parameters that my definition will entail. In proposing this broad definition of *modernism,* I forgo any attempt to characterize the variety of *modernisms* that articulate the various local regions of its career. My intent, rather, is to describe a signal rhetorical move, a trope, if you will, that formalizes the variety of modernist moments and, at the same time, limns, by its coming into and receding from view, the dimensions of a modernist epoch: what characteristic, that is, might encompass and unify, in some restricted, yet contextually relevant way, the expanse of Western cultural development from, say, Shakespeare to Joyce? I will take my examples from the restricted field of English literature, but similar examples could be found in other arts and other endeavors.

> Seems, madam? nay, it is, I know not "seems."
> 'Tis not alone my inky cloak, good mother,
> Nor customary suits of solemn black,
> Nor windy suspiration of forc'd breath,
> No, nor the fruitful river in the eye,

Nor the dejected havior of the visage,
Together with all forms, moods, shapes of grief,
That can denote me truly. These indeed seem,
For they are actions that a man might play,
But I have that within which passes show;
These but the trappings and the suits of woe.[6]

Thus, near the beginning of the modern, Hamlet tells Gertrude to disregard the legible signs of his state of mind and to equate Being precisely with that which once having been taken in can never be securely brought out. My second example, closer to the end of the modern, is spoken by Stephen Dedalus in a diary or record not of the world but of the world lost and epiphanically transferred into a personal and invisible cognitive possession: "O life! I go to encounter for the millionth time the reality of experience and to forge in the smithy of my soul the uncreated conscience of my race."[7]

With these two literary historical moments as a temporal frame, I would propose that modernism records the adventures of an *ethical* subject, determined and self-identified, according to its cognitive possessions. By ethical I mean one whose story or mythos is represented (to itself) as having been shaped by its own choices and decisions, and whose character is to be deduced from the genre of story so shaped. In short, the subject of modernism is the subject whose being resides in his or her generally proprietary knowledge and whose knowledge is the summation of his or her experience.[8]

Remaining within the confines of a formal analysis, I would suggest that the swallowing of the world signified by the *post-* of postmodernism is a second ingestion of what modernism itself had already swallowed when, sometime in and around the time of Shakespeare — for whatever reasons — the relation of Being to its symbolic representations became competitive; that is to say, the being of representation itself began to intrude upon its referential function.[9] For the modern subject, any immediate relation with the world (that is, its *Umwelt*) is subject to an epistemological reservation. What one sees are "actions which a man might play," but what one knows is "that within which passes show."

Where the Being of things is hopelessly doubtful, the relation to one's own knowledge is secured as the familiar hegemony of the individual consciousness. Thus, the trajectory of modernism can be seen as a progressive interiorization of the world of experience, ranging from the language games of Shakespearean "postepideictics" to the internalization of oceanic nature in Molly Bloom's interior monologue, or, in a theoretical register, T. S. Eliot's bizarre comparison of the mind of the poet to a platinum filament, catalytically converting individual "emotions" and "feelings" into *objectively* correlative art objects, in which the continual sacrifice of the self to the objective world insures, ironically, the publication of one's own experienced emotions in the form of an objectively evoked and effectively universalized "feeling":

> What is to be insisted upon is that the poet must develop or procure the consciousness of the past and that he should continue to develop this consciousness throughout his career.
>
> What happens is a continual surrender of himself *as he is at the moment* to something which is more valuable. The *progress* of an artist is a continual self-sacrifice, a continual extinction of personality.
>
> There remains to define this process of depersonalization and its relation to the sense of tradition. It is in this depersonalization that art may be said to approach the condition of science. I, therefore, invite you to consider, as a suggestive analogy, the action which takes place when a bit of finely filiated platinum is introduced into a chamber containing oxygen and sulphur dioxide.[10]

In an image that recalls Donne's alchemical limbeck, Eliot compares the poet's mind to "a receptacle for seizing and storing up numberless feelings, phrases, images, which remain there until all the particles which can unite to form a new compound are present together" (p. 8).

The "continual self-sacrifice" of Eliot's artist is, actually, a continual self-extrication from time and place and the restrictions of material life, in lieu of which he reconstitutes himself as a timeless eye, recording, yet untouched by, *all but* the present moment. Moreover, by appropriating the objects of his intersubjective world as the correlatives of his interior feelings, Eliot's artist reduces that world to the making present of *his* own interiorization of the past: his memory. Thus, it is not the artist but the world that is sacrificed.

It is, in fact, the play's failure to adequately reduce circumstance (the out-of-joint social and political times of Denmark) to the consciousness of its hero that causes Eliot to judge *Hamlet* an "artistic failure."[11] Eliot rejects *Hamlet* because the emotion it evokes is greater than that which can be attributed to the actions portrayed. Thus, the play leads us back to an excess that remains personal, remains Shakespeare's. Rather than converting its mythos to a purely objective showing, it insists on a prince and a world inhabited uneasily by an author who converts neither wholly to the symbolization of himself, but exists in tension with each. It is precisely in this way that *Hamlet* gives evidence of "that within which passes show."

We have now the outline of a persistence and a career for the modernist subject as I have described it. Just as much as our Freudian analysis of *The Faerie Queene* repeated and recapitulated Spenser's deferrals and retrospections, Eliot's complaint against *Hamlet* coincides with and repeats Hamlet's complaint. There is no objective correlative—no mere sign that will certify adequately a *particular* emotion and make it public. Hamlet, in thematizing this problem, submits his subjectivity to time and the iteration of a story ("Absent thee from felicity a while, / And in this harsh world draw thy breath in pain, / To tell my story" [5.2.347–49]). Eliot, standing, perhaps, near the end of Hamlet's career as an intelligible subject, has lost this faith in time as a medium in which things are revealed. He is, as it were, Hamlet inside out:

> The levity of Hamlet, his repetition of phrase, his puns, are not part of a deliberate plan of dissimulation, but a form of emotional relief. In the character Hamlet it is the buffoonery of an emotion which can find no outlet in action; in the dramatist it is the buffoonery of an emotion which he cannot express [*ex-press,* as to press out "that within which passes show"] in art. The intense feeling, ecstatic or terrible, without an object or exceeding its object, is doubtless a subject of study for pathologists. ("Hamlet and His Problems," pp. 125–26) [12]

What is pathological for Eliot is not the feeling but its tenacious resistance to artistic catharsis, its refusal to suture completely the shadow cast by the ineffable reality of the material world.

When the processes of postmodernity, however, put in question the security even of the epistemological subject of modernity—making present to it its various disseminations and the paucity of its future—the functional substitution of knowledge for Being becomes, itself, a memory. This memory reproduces, or remembers, the two forms of an older epideixis—the encomium and the execration—as nostalgic reverence and nostalgic travesty, respectively. In practice, these two logical possibilities for postmodern representation are often combined — as in, for example, the closing scene of Stanley Kubrick's film *Full Metal Jacket* (1987), in which U.S. Marines, stunned and battered by the Tet offensive, sing the Mickey Mouse Club song as they fan out over a Vietnamese landscape (constructed, one might add, on an English location).

What distinguishes this mixed nostalgia from the phenomenological presence of modernism is a disruption in narration. Hamlet cannot reliably make visible "that within which passes show" because the black clothes, teary eyes, and dejected facial expression that might signify his inner reality are "actions that a man might play." But the inner truth can be written out in a person's life and perceived retrospectively in the narrative that life generates. When the action is completed and all its embedded plays have been played out, each episode receives its meaning and the "rest is silence." Narrative, when it closes, converts all of its included actions into elements in an atemporal design, each element deriving its meaning in relation to the whole structure. Thus, it represents the plenitude of knowledge as a terminal retrospection, the journey of its subject, through time, to the proprietary truth that rewards its efforts. Hamlet knows that "murther, though it have no tongue, will speak / With most miraculous organ" (2.2.593–94), and that to make it speak, he must present it to itself as already known: first in dumb show, and then displaced into the appropriated banalities of an old script. "The story is extant, and written in very choice Italian" (3.2.262–63). The appropriation of *The Murder of Gonzago* as the miraculous organ that makes Claudius speak what is in Hamlet's mind reduplicates the situation of *Hamlet,* an old story, known in the choice French of Belleforest, and appropriated to Shakespeare's uses from an earlier version, played on the London stage in the 1580s and now lost. The price of this recursive speech is the end of Hamlet, his conversion from a life raveling out into time, to a story bounded on each side by silence, a bare stage, hard covers.

3

By the time of Milton the crisis of being that opens before Hamlet's inability to identify himself with his observable actions was being recuperated by the conversion of *questions of being* into *narratives of knowing*. Milton is a canonical author precisely with respect to the literary historical endurance of his consolidation, particularly in *Paradise Lost,* of the modernist subject as the subject of ethos, the subject of the story of the choices it has made and will make on the basis of what it knows.[13]

Milton engaged this modernist subject directly in a permutation of the *grand récit* of the Christian West — the story of creation, fall, apocalypse, and resurrection. For reasons both formal — his exhaustive working out of the rhetorically possible situations from which this subject could issue — and pragmatic — the production of his major works in the immediate aftermath of the failure of the English revolution — he also located, with considerable precision, the postmodern moment embedded within the formal possibilities of the ethical subject.

Take, for example, the 1671 volume in which *Paradise Regained* and *Samson Agonistes* first appeared. The Jesus of *Paradise Regained* is the highest of modernists. He acts in utter privacy "to forge in the smithy of his soul the uncreated conscience of his race," and his acts are undertaken in a state of totally illuminated anticipation, a completely epiphanic unity of "light" and action. Moreover, the change he effects — though it will transform the world — is presented as wholly interior and private — a transformation of the self that will empower and enable others to be similarly transformed. Having "said, and stood" (4.561), Milton's Jesus is proclaimed by angels to have reached the fullness of time: " 'on thy glorious work, / Now enter, and begin to save mankind' " (4.634–35), but in the poem's final lines, "hee unobserv'd / Home to his Mother's house private return[s]" (4.638–39).[14]

"To which is added," as it says on the title page, not the triumphant spectacle of the Passion, as we might well expect, but rather *Samson Agonistes: A Tragedy.* In contrast to the celibate Jesus, we meet, posteriorly in the volume, his profligate and uxorious prefiguration. Positioned in this way, presented as the failed *imitatio* of an as yet unborn Christ, Samson's story is, we might say, "post-Hebraic," and, Samson's nazerite vow (the word "nazerite" *now* unable to shed its anticipatory whisper of Nazareth) suspends him, as a post-Jew, between the exhaustion of the Law and the belatedness of Spirit.[15] More Hamlet than Jesus, Samson suffers from the hopeless in-mixing of his motives — indistinguishably divine and libidinous — and he is driven to express the putative divinity of his inner knowledge by all too literally pressing out what remains inside.

Dr. Johnson's famous censure of the structure of Milton's "dramatic poem" is very much to the point: "It is only by a blind confidence in the reputation of Milton that a drama can be praised in which the intermediate parts have neither cause nor consequence, neither hasten nor retard the catastrophe."[16] The subject of an ethos depends on the proleptic narrativization of its experi-

ence; its self-identity through time is constituted retrospectively and continu-
ously in a mimesis of its actions, and this is precisely what is missing from
Samson Agonistes. However, this structural absence, analogous to the absence
of the trace of the weathering process in the Morgan Stanley building's ersatz
roof, attains a thematic insistence within the poem, for only *blind* confidence
in Samson could allow Manoa, or the chorus, or the reader, to be more than
agnostic with regard to Samson's ability to distinguish his own suicidal desire
from the inward-speaking voice of God. Unlike Milton's reputation as a poet,
Samson's reputation as a judge instills no such confidence.[17] Dr. Johnson's use
of the adjective *blind* is particularly pointed, not just for its sly reference to
Milton's affliction, but because it would be precisely the faculty of sight that,
taking in its scene all at once, would perceive the lack of a unified design and
challenge the continuity of a story presented to the ear. Recalling the Greek
derivation of *theory* from *theorein,* we could say that, lacking a *visible* set of
causal relations to link episode to episode, Milton's tragedy remains insufficiently theorized.

The events of Samson's life, especially the judgments and choices of his married life, vary too drastically and too inexplicably from the story announced
by divine intervention at his birth. Unable to author a story to fit the autho-
rized story, Samson loses the light of a cognitively secure and private interior
knowledge — which is to say, he loses himself. Unable to act because the story
of his acts has become destructured in this way, Samson prematurely becomes
his own monument: "Myself my Sepulchre, a moving Grave" (l. 102).

Stanley Fish points out that it is only by dying and thus removing his excessive self from the stage that Samson can become the monumental narrative he
seeks to generate.[18] But even then, the Israelite uprising Samson sought to in-
spire never occurs; God fails to validate Samson's invisible ethos by writing it
out as the mythos of history. No Fortinbras comes on stage to clear away the
bodies and call flights of angels to carry him to rest. On the contrary, Samson remains, strangely installed in his posterior position in Milton's volume,
as that which is added to the story of the perfected warrior who will in time
succeed him. The orthodox Christian reading of the Samson story points out
that Samson's failure conduces to and explicates the glory of Jesus' success.
Milton's volume complicates this facile typology, reversing the expected order
and situating Samson, as it were, in the shadow of that unknown thing, which

he cannot remember — because it has not yet occurred — and for which, in the exigence of his circumstances, he cannot wait.

As a drama, *Samson Agonistes* bears a certain resemblance to the Morgan Stanley building. It tells and retells a tale of timely action from which time — understood as the medium in which human ethos is written on the world — has been expunged. It refers to a future that can only arrive as its own revision, its post-. Moreover, Samson, who was his own sepulcher, brings down on himself and his audience the temple in which the tragedy of classical heroism plays its scene. Henceforth, he is to be contained within and supplemented by the tomb that his father proposes as a *memorial* to inspire the Hebrew youth. This memorial also marks the scene of a catastrophic conversion from drama to narrative, from presence to story. Milton's play is thus a monument to Samson's monumentality. It marks at once the becoming of memory of a certain scene of heroic human action in the world *and* of the Greek drama in which its ethos was preserved as the working out of a series of causally related events.

As the roof falls in on the theatrical stage of the Temple of Dagon in the climax of *Samson Agonistes,* so too collapses the duration of ethos, the dialectic of ethos and mythos for which Greek drama stood and which Christ is made to reject in *Paradise Regained* (4.285–364). The story that Milton needs to tell is one not of the strength that follows enlightenment but of historically urgent action in the dark, the problematic discovery that "strength is not lost, though light denied." To tell his story, Milton chose a classic form, Euripidean tragedy, but the material which he put into that form cannot but travesty what the form reveres.

To return one last time to Brooklyn: We might distinguish the pathos of blind strength in *Samson Agonistes,* which, as Herman Rapaport has pointed out, mourns and celebrates the passing of classical tragedy along with the darkness of its hero, and the Morgan Stanley building's *bathetic* assertiveness as two distinct modes of the postmodern, corresponding respectively to the reverent encomium and travesty execration modes of postepideictic nostalgia.[19] Undermining the twin pillars of Aristotelian poetics and Christian historiography that were to hold it up, it brings the temple down, installing the memory of its ruins to mark the place where what will be was. It may be in this place — rather than at any specifiable time — that we might best situate the postmodern moment.

4

The three epigraphs to this epilogue are thus intended to suggest, roughly, a transit across three connected moments in a highly compressed history of the broadly epistemological literary tradition that reacts to the failure of metaphysics recorded in English Renaissance narrative poetry. This tradition posits experience as a determined relationship between a subject and his or her knowledge.

If the epigraph from *The Second Anniversary* records (as I hope I have shown it does) the shock and desolation initially brought about by the failure of mimesis and the fall from metaphysical ontology into critical epistemology, the epigraph from Frost normalizes it, takes it for granted, while that from Mellencamp ironically returns to it as a scene of a failed resignation. I allude — epigraphically, superficially — to the two succeeding moments because it is in their nuanced repetitions that the Renaissance is constituted as a seminal moment for the subject of modernity.

Just as Donne's anatomized world retained the wan ghost of a lost object that remained, modernism, in some obscurely crippled way, which marked the tomb from which that ghost escapes, now remains, soliciting from us that most Romantic of monuments: a ruined tomb — the remains of *Samson Agonistes,* marking the remains of storied Samson. What remains at the site of this ruin? Is it still haunted? Will it remain so?

I have argued that in 1611 Donne's world had become post-epideictic, but it did not remain so. Similarly, the postmodernity of *Samson Agonistes* remains embedded in Milton's highly personal experience of the failure of the English revolution. Neither the *Anniversaries* nor *Samson Agonistes* institutes the conventions of a new period. Moments such as these of Donne and Milton are transitory and transitional in the early modern period. We see in the Enlightenment, the career of a new fetish: reason and the individual consciousness, which emerges to replace the de-sublimed fetish of a macrocosmic perfection *embodied* in microcosmic form. The differences between these two signifying systems are great; the worlds they support dissimilar.

Semantically housed, as it is, in a neologism bordering on oxymoron, "postmodernism," as we have seen, does not indicate the othering of the modern. Rather, we find ourselves *after* the modern only in the sense that the modern lives on into its own impossibility, simultaneously asserting and denying what is qualitative in the passage of time. Like Donne's "wan ghost" or ruined

Samson's ruined tomb, modernity continues to inhabit a corpse tradition; the privilege it had accorded to the individual consciousness as the experiencing pole of a dialectical ex-sistence becomes visible, theorized, but no new sublimation, no new enlightenment, yet replaces it. As we shall see, there are reasons, moreover, to admit the possibility that none will.

In our own de-sublimated moment, then, what remains for us, for whom tradition is the object of a profession? Perhaps we can defy the erasure of experience to the degree that we are careful to articulate the experience of its erasure? Perhaps we can articulate the dim outlines of a self apart from fetishistic mediation? In seeking to look beyond this present, we meet ourselves, and the image becomes speculative.

For the sake of discussion, however, I will indulge two brief speculations. The first is that in our "administered society" (to use Adorno's term), past, present, and future are reified in the "now" of a reified memory in which tradition becomes, sardonically, immemorial.[20] In chapter 5, I noted some of the obvious ways in which Kepler's elliptical orbits did not support Petrarchan epideixis so well as Ptolemy's circular orbits did. Similarly, electronic communication does not support historical causality nearly so well as steam power did. One cannot see the moving parts in the contemporary locomotive. One cannot see movement at the speed of light, and yet the static traces of such movement render the interval between thought and expression perceptible, not just metaphorically, but physically. What is present is present as always already past, reminding us of its own reflexive monumentality.[21] If the fetish of presence remained for Donne (and after) a monument — literally, a memorial — what remains for us is absolutely monumental; remembering only itself, the absolute monument incorporates the past without *recycling* it, retaining it as an out-of-phase aspect of the present, as a memory — or, what amounts to the same thing, an allusion.

Thus, the hyphen, invisible or printed out, that joins post- to modern would seem to mark a second introjection of the world, so that experience may be retained in its loss as a property of consciousness. Marking not the persistence of continuity but the insistence of discontinuity, this memory of memory marks the "wan ghost's" failure to appear, and this failure — since it is a failure of memory — also erases her earlier appearances. Insofar as a monument marks the place, localized in time and space, at which something has been transferred from space and time to memory, the *absolute* monument memorializes the monumental itself. It is a monument without contents, an empty tomb; the mode of its remembering is oblivion and the extent of its reach limitless. This peculiar temporality can be seen, for example, when Elizabeth Drew, writing in *The New Yorker* in 1989, gives us this postmodern moment in politics: "Republican strategists believe," she writes, "that Reagan's popularity stemmed in part from the fact that by last fall he had become a nostalgic figure; by the time he left, he had in effect been gone for some time." [22] This is the popularity of the absolutely monumental, standing in to mark its own effaced memory.

Approaching modernity, Hegel saw work—in the dialectic of lordship and bondage—as an *activity* mediating between the negativity of Desire on the one side and the recalcitrance of Nature on the other:

> Desire has reserved to itself the pure negating of the object and thereby its unalloyed feeling of self. But that is the reason why this satisfaction is itself only a fleeting one, for it lacks the side of objectivity and permanence. Work, on the other hand, is desire held in check, fleetingness staved off; in other words, work forms and shapes the thing. The negative relation to the object becomes its *form* and something *permanent,* because it is precisely for the worker that the object has independence. This *negative* middle term or the formative *activity* is at the same time the individuality or pure being-for-self of consciousness which now, in the work outside of it, acquires an element of permanence. It is in this way, therefore, that consciousness, *qua* worker, comes to see in the independent being [of the object] its *own* independence.[23]

In the disjunct saturation of postmodernity, desire, work, and permanence elude dialectical mediation because of a perpetual temporal displacement that enfolds the *activity* of work in an anticipation of its memory. Never quite "com[ing] to see" its own independence "in the independent being" of the object, consciousness and its objects are encountered as anachronistic, as sharing the evanescence of the sort of conceptual art that exists only as the documentation of its having (once) been performed. History is thus transposed from a story whose proper ending is at all times anticipated to the compulsive recapitulation of a terminal event.

What then remains for us—that is, for literary historians—to do? It may be that a closer attention to the history of technology and particularly to the development of instrumental mathesis and its impact on natural language may offer more help in holding onto and historicizing the phenomenal nature of the experiences that I have been describing than a continued reliance on the totalizing categories of modes of production and class struggle into which technological developments have tended to be subsumed.

Thus, my second speculation specifies a particular direction for the study of the assimilation of technology in language. I suggested earlier that the Renaissance marked a de-sublimated moment that passed into the Enlightenment. One of the things that occurred during this period to enable the Age of Reason was the bringing of the post-Copernican universe into natural language. New pictures in the sky were met by new metaphors; poetic trajectories could modulate from the circular to the parabolic. Our present situation is more resistant to natural language because, in significant ways, mathesis has become paralinguistic. How does one put unified field theory or quantum mechanics into words? What is the status of history in a world that cannot be verbally modeled? Perhaps this difficulty accounts in part for the time lag, the resistance, that we have named postmodernity? And perhaps it signals a new and less central role for language in the mediation of desire? Having historicized history, can we follow the (algebraic) letter in its step outside the impasse of our ex-centricity—and be otherwise?

Notes

Preface

1 Ferdinand de Saussure, *Course in General Linguistics,* ed. Charles Bally and Albert Sechehaye, in collaboration with Albert Reidlinger, trans., with an introduction and notes by Wade Baskin (New York: McGraw-Hill, 1966), p. 66: "The linguistic sign unites, not a thing and a name, but a concept and a sound-image. The latter is not the material sound, a purely physical thing, but the psychological imprint of the sound, the impression that it makes on our senses."

1. Literary Forms and Historical Consciousness in Renaissance Poetry

1 The locus classicus would be "The Mirror Stage and the Formation of the I," *Écrits: A Selection,* trans. Alan Sheridan (New York: Norton, 1977), pp. 1–7. The point is re-inforced by the appearance of the accusative in the predicate nominative position where the grammatically more "correct" nominative gives the distinctly uncollo-quial "That's I." As a pictorial representation, the baby picture offers what Lacan would term an Imaginary encounter with the self; it is through identification with a verbal signifier that the subject discovers itself. The self-identity of the adult and the infant in the picture is mediated as well as asserted by the word; both are "me."

2 The Augustinian affiliations of the notion of memory implied in this statement are discussed in chap. 3 below.

3 For the classic investigation of the implications of this assimilation of the mascu-line and the generically human, see Simone de Beauvoir, *The Second Sex,* trans. H. M. Parshley (New York: Knopf, 1953). For a more recent discussion, more lit-erary in method, see Mieke Bal, *Lethal Love: Feminist Literary Readings of Biblical Love Stories* (Bloomington: Indiana University Press, 1987), pp. 104–30.

4 All citations of Shakespeare are to *The Riverside Shakespeare,* ed. G. Blakemore Evans et al. (Boston: Houghton Mifflin), 1974.

5 See, for example, Freud's remark, in the first of the Clark Lectures, that *"our hys-terical patients suffer from reminiscences"* (Freud's italics), *Five Lectures on Psycho-analysis* (1910), *Standard Edition of the Psychological Works of Sigmund Freud,* ed. and trans. James Strachey and Anna Freud, 24 vols. (London: Hogarth, 1953-74), 11: 16. (Subsequent references to this edition will be given with the abbreviation SE.) The singular aspect of these afflicting reminiscences is that being under a re-pression they are represented rather than remembered — in the case of the hysteric, by a symptom.

6 *The Seminar of Jacques Lacan,* ed. Jacques-Alain Miller, Book 7, "The Ethics of Psychoanalysis, 1959-1960," trans. Dennis Porter (New York: Norton, 1992), p. 12.

7 "Renaissance Literary Studies and the Subject of History," *ELR* 16 (1986): 5-12. The quoted passage appears on p. 6. See also Jean E. Howard's survey, "The New His-toricism in Renaissance Studies," in the same issue of *ELR* (pp. 13-43), and Stephen Greenblatt's introduction to *The Power of Forms in the English Renaissance* (Nor-man, Okla.: Pilgrim Books, 1982), pp. 3-6. An enormous number of (often generic) critical appraisals of the New Historicism have now appeared. Notable among the more valuable are Alan Liu, "The Power of Formalism: The New Historicism," *ELH* 56 (1989): 721-71, James Holstun, "Ranting at the New Historicism," *ELR* 19 (1989): 189-225, and the essays collected in H. Aram Veeser, ed., *The New Historicism* (New York: Routledge, Chapman and Hall, 1989). I feel a particular affinity with Charles Altieri's careful exposition of the inability of the New Historicists to take proper account of time from within the spatial metaphors on which they depend; see "Temporality and the Necessity for Dialectic: The Missing Dimension of Con-temporary Theory," *NLH* 23 (1992): 133-58. For the argument against the New His-toricism, see esp. pp. 135-38. For another argument for the irreducibility of *literary* history contra the New Historicists, see Sanford Budick, "The Experience of Liter-ary History: Vulgar Versus Not-Vulgar," *New Literary History* 25 (1994): 749-77.

8 I take the phrase "poetics of culture" from Stephen Greenblatt, *Renaissance Self-Fashioning from More to Shakespeare* (Chicago: University of Chicago Press, 1980), p. 5.

9 See, in particular, Michel Foucault, *The Order of Things: An Archaeology of the Human Sciences* (New York: Pantheon, 1971), and *The Archaeology of Knowledge,* trans. A. M. Sheridan (New York: Pantheon, 1972). It is curious, but explicable, that these (early) works, which posit synchronies that are radically disjoined diachroni-cally (see n. 14 below), should be appropriated for the recuperation of an *essentially* narrative history. The explanation lies, I believe, in Foucault's strategic need to sup-press the *explicitly* totalizing tendency of contemporary structuralism, on the one hand, and classical Marxism, on the other, by positing radical discontinuities at precisely the points at which either of these precursor discourses applies its "mas-

ter narrative" — the signifying system or class struggle — to articulate the historical transformation of one *épistème* to another (see chap. 2, pp. 52–53). The relation of American style "New Historicism," which appends itself to a structuralist-inspired anthropology of signs, and British "Cultural Materialism," which is explicitly neo-Marxist in its present readings of the past, neatly reproduces this fissure, already present within Foucault's seminal work.

10 Joel Fineman, "The History of the Anecdote: Fiction as Fiction," in Veeser, *The New Historicism*, pp. 49–76; rpt. Joel Fineman, *The Subjectivity Effect in Western Literature: Essays Toward the Release of Shakespeare's Will* (Cambridge, Mass.: MIT Press, 1992; hereafter cited as TSE). The quoted passage appears in TSE, p. 72. The title of Fineman's essay alludes to Greenblatt's "Fiction and Friction" in *Shakespearean Negotiations: The Circulation of Social Energy in Renaissance England* (Berkeley: University of California Press, 1988), pp. 66–93.

11 On narrative as a way of comprehending events from within a closed rhetorical structure, see Louis O. Mink, "History and Fiction as Modes of Comprehension," *New Literary History* 1 (1970): 541–58.

12 On the relation of sequence to consequence in narrative, see Roland Barthes, "Introduction to the Structural Analysis of Narratives," in *Image Music Text,* trans. Stephen Heath (New York: Hill and Wang, 1977), pp. 97–104.

13 For the classic example of the use of literary theory to sophisticate historiography, see Hayden White, *Metahistory: The Historical Imagination in Nineteenth-Century Europe* (Baltimore: Johns Hopkins University Press, 1973). On the nonexistence of a "specifically historical approach to the study of history," see White's irenic contribution to Veeser, *The New Historicism*, "New Historicism: A Comment," pp. 293–302; the quoted phrase appears on p. 302. For specific examples of the New Historical tendency to create or assume textual hierarchies, see chap. 4, pp. 109–12, 151–53.

14 My notion of the relationship of literature to "reality" draws on Lacan's definition of "the Real" as what is lacking in the Symbolic order, what can be represented neither as image nor symbol. See, for example, *The Four Fundamental Concepts of Psycho-Analysis,* ed. Jacques-Alain Miller, trans. Alan Sheridan (New York: Norton, 1978), pp. 53–56. Access to this "Real," which manifests itself as an irruption or discontinuity within symbolic representation, is necessarily belated and retrospective, following, as it must, the ripples that are left in the surface of representation by its disappearance.

15 Foucault, *The Order of Things*: "Now, this archaeological inquiry has revealed two great discontinuities in the *épistème* of Western culture: the first inaugurates the Classical age (roughly half-way through the seventeenth century) and the second, at the beginning of the nineteenth century, marks the beginning of the modern age" (p. xxii).

16 Greenblatt later moderates the claim of ideological containment, at least with respect to the theater, in the direction of a notion of "negotiations" that are accomplished through the "circulation of social energy," but without specifying any operations of subjective will. See "The Circulation of Social Energy," in *Shakespearean Negotiations*, pp. 1–20.

17 This rhetorical unconscious precedes and includes Jameson's "political unconscious." Like the political unconscious it identifies elements of a *combinatoire* that determines history but also opens a space within which the subjects of history make choices in consultation with an ability to imagine their situation otherwise — what Jameson calls "utopia." *The Political Unconscious: Narrative as a Socially Symbolic Act* (Ithaca, N.Y.: Cornell University Press, 1981), pp. 281–99. The rhetorical unconscious differs from the political unconscious, however, in that it pertains only to cognitive configurations and to ways in which material circumstances may be represented — that is, to ideology — while making no claim to describe social and economic developments except as they are mediated by the tropic dialectic. Joan Copjec cogently articulates the limitations of the Foucauldian subject with respect to a theory of ethical agency in "The Orthopsychic Subject: Film Theory and the Reception of Lacan," *October* 49 (1989): 52–71, rpt. in *Read My Desire: Lacan Against the Historicists,* An October Book (Cambridge, Mass.: MIT Press, 1994).

18 "The Decay of Lying" in *The Works of Oscar Wilde,* ed. G. F. Maine (London, 1948), rpt. in *The Modern Tradition: Backgrounds of Modern Literature,* ed. Richard Ellmann and Charles Feidelson, Jr. (New York: Oxford University Press, 1965), pp. 21–22.

19 For an explanation of an instance of the priority of signification over experience, see Fineman's argument (contra Greenblatt) for the necessary priority of language over experience in the derivation of desire in *Twelfth Night* ("History of the Anecdote," TSE, pp. 83–87, n. 34).

20 The foregoing argument has much in common with Altieri's argument for a "humble dialectic" in "Temporality and the Necessity of Dialectic," particularly its interest in a nontotalizing dialectic that would submit spatial (or what I call structural) metaphors to temporal mediation. I differ from Altieri in preserving dialectic, which does not seem to me recuperable without at least a provisional totalization, specifically *as a feature of representation.* Thus, my reservations about deconstruction are far more modest and specified than his; which is to say that although I am less optimistic than he about preserving an integral subject — one moving through time and capable of taking responsibility for its actions — from deconstructive dissemination, I am less concerned about the practical force of such dissemination because in social practice it leaves intact the subject, who is constituted as a historical agent always and necessarily on the level of the signifier, when we take

responsibility for what we will have done. In other words, responsible agency is not a question of matching unified and prior wills to actions, but of acknowledging and accepting an open-ended temporal process in which the relevant act of will *is* our identification with or acceptance of our own signifiers, our *will*ingness to name ourselves "I."

21 Jacques Derrida, *Positions,* trans. and annotated by Alan Bass (Chicago: University of Chicago Press, 1981), pp. 40–41. Interpolations from the original French are supplied from *Positions: Entretiens avec Henri Ronse, Julia Kristeva, Jean-Louis Houdebine, Guy Scarpetta* (Paris: Les Éditions de Minuit, 1972), p. 55.

22 On deconstruction's tendency to privilege metonymy, see Slavoj Žižek, *The Sublime Object of Ideology* (London: Verso, 1989), pp. 154–56. The need for the reservation here noted, which becomes important in the context of Derrida's critique of psychoanalysis, is elaborated in chap. 4 below.

23 See Paul Ricoeur, *Time and Narrative,* trans. Kathleen McLaughlin and David Pellauer (Chicago: University of Chicago Press, 1984), esp. pp. 52–87.

24 Aquinas comments on Aristotle, *Peri Hermeneias,* 16 ab8, n. 7, in *Aristotle: On Interpretation, Commentary by St. Thomas and Cajetan [Peri Hermeneias],* trans. from Latin with intro. by Jean T. Oesterle (Milwaukee: Marquette University Press, 1962).

25 *The Works of Francis Bacon,* collected and ed. by James Spedding, Robert Leslie Ellis, and Douglas Denon Heath, 13 vols. (Boston: Taggard and Thompson, 1863), 8:350. *John Milton: Complete Poetry and Major Prose,* ed. Merritt Y. Hughes (Indianapolis: Odyssey, 1957), *Paradise Lost* 5.498.

26 On conceptions of time, see Achsah Guibbory, *The Map of Time: Seventeenth-Century English Literature and Ideas of Pattern in History* (Urbana: University of Illinois Press, 1986). Guibbory notes three distinct conceptions of time in the seventeenth century; it is (1) the medium of decay, (2) cyclic, and (3) the medium of progress. Under the pressure of exigent events, the cyclic, I would argue, gives way to polarized conceptions of decay or progress. J. G. A. Pocock discusses three ways of conceiving time in relation to human agency in *The Machiavellian Moment: Florentine Political Thought and the Atlantic Republican Tradition* (Princeton, N.J.: Princeton University Press, 1975), "Part One: Particularity and Time: The Conceptual Background." For more general studies of the experience and conceptualization of time in the Renaissance, see Ricardo Quinones, *The Renaissance Discovery of Time* (Cambridge, Mass.: Harvard University Press, 1972), and Hershel Baker, *The Race of Time* (Toronto: University of Toronto Press, 1947). With the horizon of nuclear apocalypse now deferred, will a more open-ended experience of time recur? Time, I suppose, will tell.

27 On technological and agricultural development, see Christopher Hill, *The World Turned Upside Down: Radical Ideas in the English Revolution* (New York: Penguin,

1972, esp. pp. 40–45; and "The Agrarian Legislation of the Revolution," in *Puritanism and Revolution: Studies in the Interpretation of the English Revolution of the Seventeenth-Century* (New York: Schocken, 1964), pp. 153–96; Eric Kerridge, *The Agricultural Revolution* (New York: Augustus M. Kelley, 1968); and Lawrence Stone, *The Causes of the English Revolution, 1529–1642* (New York: Harper and Row, 1972), pp. 66–67. On the emergence of the concept of the market regulation of trade, see Joyce Oldham Appleby, *Economic Thought and Ideology in Seventeenth-Century England* (Princeton, N.J.: Princeton University Press, 1978), and Keith Tribe, *Land, Labour and Economic Discourse* (London: Routlege and Kegan Paul, 1978). The historiography of the English civil war has been much contested since the work of Hill and Stone. The controversy is characterized by a revisionist movement that sought to minimize or entirely deny the revolutionary character of the "English Revolution." While Hill and Stone tend to see the civil war as the result of large-scale social and economic forces, the revisionists argue for the continuity of English social life before and after the civil disturbances of the mid-century. For them, the civil war is not the inevitable result of broad conflicts of interest that build up over a period of time, but an entirely avoidable accident arising suddenly from a series of contingent misfortunes. See, for example, *The Origins of the English Civil War,* ed. Conrad Russell (New York: Barnes and Noble, 1973), and Conrad Russell, *Unrevolutionary England: 1603–1642* (London: Hambledon Press, 1990). More recently, a reaction against the revisionists has begun to critically assess their work and to restore the social and radical dimensions to the history of the period while benefiting from more recent work in local history and avoiding the "Whig" assumptions of some earlier social history. This work is well represented in Ann Hughes, *The Causes of the English Civil War* (New York: St. Martin's Press, 1991), and *Conflict in Early Stuart England,* ed. Richard Cust and Ann Hughes (New York: Longman, 1989). I shall not be interested in relating literary events to local political and social changes, but rather to the sort of slow and large-scale effects of technology, population growth, and economic reorganization indicated in my discussion of the experience of time. To the extent that I am able to find the traces of these changes in the literary history of the period, my argument lends support — in its broadest outlines — to the "Whig" over the "Tory" versions of English history.

28 *"Authors to Themselves": Milton and the Revelation of History* (Cambridge: Cambridge University Press, 1987), esp. pp. 12–25.

29 To carry these comparisons a little further, Renaissance humor psychology sees in any particular behavior the contextualized manifestation of an essential character, a specific and controlling combination of choler, bile, blood, and phlegm. Psychoanalysis is also interested in originary moments — primal scenes, seductions, traumas — but it is governed by the logic of narrative deferral, according to which the

meaning of an event is always reflected backward from its future. Where the theory of humors accounts for character as the manifestation of an ontic logos, psychoanalysis reconstructs a narrative contingency. Similarly, tropological hermeneutics understands a biblical text (or anecdote) as a moral allegory, allowing the reader to move directly from the scriptural exemplar to his or her own behavior; typological hermeneutics first refers the reader to a later text and a later event, so as to displace the meaning of the history of Israel to its future fulfillment in Christ. This meaning remains ontic, but it must be discovered through a temporal process of experience and reconstruction.

30 All citations of Marvell refer to *The Poems and Letters of Andrew Marvell,* ed. H. M. Margoliouth, 3rd rev. ed., by Pierre Legouis, with the collaboration of E. E. Duncan-Jones, 2 vols. (Oxford: Clarendon Press, 1971), vol. 1.

31 On the play of the supplement at the origin, see Jacques Derrida, *Dissemination,* trans. Barbara Johnson (Chicago: University of Chicago Press, 1981), pp. 156–71, and *Of Grammatology,* trans. Gayatri Spivak (Baltimore: Johns Hopkins University Press, 1976), pp. 269–316.

32 It is perhaps worth the brief detour into Freudian terminology to note that with these lines Marvell depicts the displacement of object libido onto the ego-ideal, as in Freud's description of secondary narcissism, *and* he associates this withdrawal with the retreat from language into a single (but still wounding) identification of self and name. See "On Narcissism: An Introduction," SE, p. 14. See also the speaker's identification with the plants in "Upon Appleton House," stanza 71.

33 William Empson, *Some Versions of the Pastoral* (London: Chatto and Windus, 1935), pp. 131–32. Empson also points out that "melon" is the Greek for apple.

34 In the King James Version: "And the glory of the Lord shall be revealed, and all flesh shall see it together: for the mouth of the Lord hath spoken *it.* The voice said, Cry. And he said, What shall I cry? All flesh *is* grass, and all the goodliness thereof *is* as the flower of the field: The grass withereth, the flower fadeth; because the spirit of the Lord bloweth upon it: surely the people *is* grass. The grass withereth, the flower fadeth: but the word of our God shall stand for ever. O Zion, that bringest good tidings, get thee up into the high mountain; O Jerusalem, that bringest good tidings, lift up thy voice with strength; lift *it* up, be not afraid; say unto the cities of Judah, Behold your God!" (Isaiah 40:5–9). Rosalie Colie finds the "stern Biblical meanings of the 'fall' " (163), but she still remarks the thematically reflexive splitting of Marvell's poem: "Among the substantive meanings of 'garden,' so generously alluded to in the poem . . . , lies the cliché literary meaning as well, the garden of eloquence, the paradise of pleasure or of dainty devices, the garden of the muses, its particular beauties, the particular flowers of rhetoric, all gathered into a mixed posie. At the same time, under all these positive meanings, so rich in their evocations, run

the qualifications of *vanitas,* the vanity of human wishes and human expectations. Human effort, human fame, human love, all human experience and all things are subject to time and in fact must pass away." *"My Ecchoing Song": Andrew Marvell's Poetry of Criticism* (Princeton, N.J.: Princeton University Press, 1970), p. 156.

35 Colie remarks: "When our poet carves trees, he will carve only the names of his beloved—namely, of the trees themselves. Misled by the normal connotations of 'wound' and the general *pathétique* of pastoral, we cannot expect this particular turn: the poet has carried us by this trick into the empty ground between words and things, has collapsed 'trees' into their names . . . , the parts of the metaphor into each other" (p. 159). See the arrested and arresting discourse of the birds in "Upon Appleton House": "And where I Language want, my Signs / The Bird upon the Bough divines; / And more attentive there doth sit / Then if She were with Lime-twigs knit" (ll. 571–73).

36 *Shakespeare's Perjured Eye: The Invention of Poetic Subjectivity in the Sonnets* (Berkeley: University of California Press, 1986) pp. 3–14.

37 See the poet's crucifixion by the briars in "Upon Appleton House": "Bind me ye *Woodbines* in your 'twines, / Curle me about ye gadding *Vines,* / And Oh so close your Circles lace, / That I may never leave this Place: But, lest your Fetters prove too weak, / Ere I your Silken Bondage break, / Do you, *O Brambles,* chain me too, / And courteous *Briars* nail me through" (ll. 609–16).

38 *Being and Time,* trans. John Macquarrie and Edward Robinson (New York: Harper and Row, 1962), pp. 276–311, esp. pp. 276–77.

39 In view of the fact that the promise of a life after death still represents an exit from time, the presumptive Christianity of the Marvellian subject complicates but does not obviate the existential relation to temporality grounded in a reflection on death. Thus, I am tempted to include Marvell's man in the garden among those sharing the "larger continuity of concern" indicated in the following remark of Fineman's: "In all these cases—Husserl, Heidegger, Derrida, and, let me say, what goes without saying, that I mention these three names only as a way of pointing to a larger continuity of concern—the self-completing self-reflecting of Hegelian historicity is turned over on itself, turned over and turned inside out, so as to open up in space a space for space to take its place, and to open up the temporality of time so that time can have its moment" (TSE, p. 71).

40 See also TSE, p. 78, n. 24: "Lacan's formulation of an unimaginable and unspeakable 'real' accounts for my use of the word 'anecdote,' which, at least etymologically, means that which is 'unpublished.'"

41 "Temporality and the Necessity for Dialectic," p. 149.

42 The exclusion of prose narrative from this study reflects my belief that Renaissance prose does not significantly participate in the evolution of the subject. The fact

that English prose in the Renaissance continues to be written as though English were an inflected language suggests that prose begins to be thought of as a vehicle for the mimesis of subjectivity only *after* the development of the narrative subject in poetry. Thus, as I hope to show in a subsequent study, it is in Dryden's essays, dialogues, and prefaces that the development of a prose style based on subject-verb-object word order prepares the way for the passage of the subject of history from Milton's epic into the novel. (The inclusion of Augustine's *Confessions* in chap. 3, of course, reflects the fact that for Augustine, Latin was the mother tongue and the *Confessions* is presented precisely as a mimesis of thought.)

2. The Subject of Narrative and the Rhetoric of the Self

1 Such was the apparent conclusion of a memorable conference of literary theorists, historians, anthropologists, psychologists, psychoanalysts, writers, and philosophers devoted to the consideration of narrative, held at the University of Chicago in 1979. The papers presented, originally published as the December 1980 issue of *Critical Inquiry* were reissued as a book, *On Narrative,* ed. W. J. T. Mitchell (Chicago: University of Chicago Press, 1981). For a systematic argument, largely within the conventions of Anglo-American philosophy (although with some phenomenological detours), see Charles Taylor, *Sources of the Self: The Making of Modern Identity* (Cambridge, Mass.: Harvard University Press, 1989), esp. pp. 47–52, 288–89.

2 The essays are collected in *Problems in General Linguistics,* trans. Mary Elizabeth Meek (Coral Gables, Fla.: University of Miami Press, 1971). The quotation is from "Categories of Thought and Language," p. 56. See also "Remarks on the Function of Language in Freudian Theory": "What is intentional in motivation obscurely controls the manner in which the inventor of a style fashions common material and, in his own way, releases himself therein. For what is called unconscious is responsible for the way in which the individual constructs his persona, and for what he accepts and what he rejects or fails to recognize, the former being motivated by the latter" (p. 75). For a sense of Benveniste's importance and the filiations of his work, see the festschrift honoring his retirement from the Collège de France, *Langue, discours, société: pour Émile Benveniste,* ed. Julia Kristeva, Jean-Claude Milner, Nicolas Ruwet (Paris: Éditions du Seuil, 1975). See also Lacan's discussion, in the seventh seminar, of unconscious thought processes in relation to the reality principle: "Freud tells us that the thought processes are only known to us through words, what we know of the unconscious reaches us as a function of words." *The Seminar of Jacques Lacan, Book 7, The Ethics of Psychoanalysis, 1959–1960,* ed. Jacques-Alain Miller, trans. Dennis Porter (New York: Norton, 1992), p. 32.

3 Benveniste, "Subjectivity in Language," in *Problems in General Linguistics,* p. 224.

4 Ibid., p. 225.

5 Taylor, *Sources of the Self,* p. 34-35. Subsequent citations are given parenthetically in the text.

6 By attributing this polarity to narrative, I shall be, to some extent, subverting a distinction that Benveniste draws between *histoire* and *discours,* that is, between represented and active discourse. The justification for this subversion should be apparent in the argument that follows. See "The Correlations of Tense in the French Verb," in *Problems in General Linguistics,* pp. 205-15. For a more detailed discussion of the relation of narrative to discourse, see Gérard Genette, "Boundaries of Narrative," *New Literary History* 8 (1976): 1-13, esp. 8-13.

7 *The Seminar of Jacques Lacan, Book 2, The Ego in Freud's Theory and in the Techniques of Psychoanalysis, 1954-1955,* ed. Jacques-Alain Miller, trans. Sylvana Tomaselli, with notes by John Forrester (New York: Norton, 1988), p. 169.

8 "The Cognitive Dimension of Narrative Discourse," *New Literary History* 7 (1976): 447, n. 5. Similarly, Gerald Prince, "Aspects of a Grammar of Narrative," *Poetics Today* 1 (1980): 50: "Narrative is the representation of *at least two* real or fictive events in a time sequence."

9 *The Poetics of Prose,* trans. Richard Howard (Ithaca, N.Y.: Cornell University Press, 1977), p. 233.

10 *Poetics,* 1448b, 1450a, 1450b.

11 *Anatomy of Criticism* (Princeton, N.J.: Princeton University Press, 1957), pp. 133-35.

12 See, for example, the discussion of the "barred subject" in *The Four Fundamental Concepts of Psychoanalysis,* ed. Jacques-Alain Miller, trans. Alan Sheridan (New York: Norton, 1978), pp. 138-42. For Derrida the differing and deferring [*différance*] of the speaking subject with respect to the subject inscribed in its speech is but one trace of a structural relation that underlies any and all signification. See, for example, "Différance," in *Margins of Philosophy,* trans. with additional notes by Alan Bass (Chicago: University of Chicago Press, 1982), pp. 3-27: "It is because of *différance* that the movement of signification is possible only if each so-called 'present' element, each element appearing on the scene of presence, is related to something other than itself, thereby keeping within itself the mark of the past element, and always letting itself be vitiated by the mark of its relation to the future element, this trace being related no less to what is called the future than to what is called the past, and constituting what is called the present by means of this very relation to what it is not: what it absolutely is not, not even a past or a future as modified present" (p. 13). In the context of the present argument it will suffice to note that the relationship of difference and deferral that exists between the uttering subject and the subject of the utterance installs and operates the temporal forward motion of narrative and its attendant proclivity for totalization. Only an apocalyp-

tically exhaustive narration could capture and hold the mobile speaking subject within the web of its representations.

13 There is a certain affinity here with Claude Lévi-Strauss's understanding of myths as a means of resolving existential contradictions. See *Structural Anthropology,* trans. Claire Jacobson and Brooke Grundfest Schoeph (New York: Basic Books, 1963), pp. 206-31. However, I shall be concerned to discover what can be learned from precisely those specific aspects of narrative form that Lévi-Strauss's method seeks to filter out as irrelevant to the interpretation of myth. I am interested in the process of relationship through which narrative "resolves" existential anomalies.

14 *Illuminations,* ed. with an intro. by Hannah Arendt, trans. Harry Zohn (New York: Schocken, 1977), p. 94.

15 See Lacan's famous claim that life is lived in the *future anterior* tense: "I identify myself in language, but only by losing myself in it like an object. What is realized in my history is not the past definite of what was, since it is no more, or even the present perfect of what has been in what I am, but the future anterior of what I shall have been for what I am in the process of becoming." "The Function and Field of Speech and Language in Psychoanalysis," *Écrits: A Selection,* trans. Alan Sheridan (New York: Norton, 1977), p. 86. See also Peter Brooks, "Freud's Master Plot: Questions of Narrative," *Yale French Studies* 55/56 (1977): 280-300.

16 Brooks, "Freud's Master Plot," p. 294.

17 *The Faerie Queene* 1.10.61. Unless otherwise noted Spenser is cited from: *The Works of Edmund Spenser,* a variorum ed., ed. Edwin Greenlaw, Charles Grosvenor Osgood, and Frederick Morgan Padelford (Baltimore: Johns Hopkins University Press, 1932).

18 On the dialectic of static and dynamic semantic elements in discourse, see Jan Mukařovský, "On Poetic Language," in *The Word and Verbal Art: Selected Essays by Jan Mukařovský,* trans. and ed. John Burbank and Peter Steiner (New Haven, Conn.: Yale University Press, 1977), pp. 46-47. See also Lacan, "The Agency of the Letter in the Unconscious or Reason Since Freud," *Écrits: A Selection,* p. 154: "There is in effect no signifying chain that does not have, as if attached to the punctuation of each of its units, a whole articulation of relevant contexts suspended 'vertically,' as it were, from that point."

19 Jonathan Culler, "Fabula and Sjuzhet in the Analysis of Narrative: Some American Discussions," *Poetics Today* 1 (1980): 32. Taylor makes a similar observation with specific reference to the temporal realization of the disengaged subject in the seventeenth century. See *Sources of the Self,* pp. 288-89.

20 Thus, as frequently happens in any discussion of narrative, we come back to the

Russian formalists' division of the literary work into material and device — a debt that Culler acknowledges in the title of his essay.

21 Culler, "Fabula and Sjuzhet in the Analysis of Narrative," p. 32.

22 Compare the discussion of the time and place of the preface in the *"Hors Livre"* to Jacques Derrida, *Dissemination,* trans. Barbara Johnson (Chicago: University of Chicago Press, 1981), pp. 3–59, esp. pp. 9–36. I derive my use of the term "master narrative" primarily from Jean-François Lyotard's discussion of the *"grand récit."* See, for example, *The Postmodern Condition: A Report on Knowledge,* trans. Geoff Bennington and Brian Masumi, foreword by Fredric Jameson (Minneapolis: University of Minnesota Press, 1984). See also Charles Altieri, "Temporality and the Necessity for Dialectic: The Missing Dimension of Contemporary Theory," *New Literary History* 23 (1992): 133–58, esp. 150–55.

23 See Jan Mukařovský, *Aesthetic Function, Norm and Value as Social Facts,* trans. Mark E. Suino, Michigan Slavic Contributions 3 (Ann Arbor: Department of Slavic Languages and Literature, University of Michigan, 1970), p. 20: "Collective awareness is a social fact. It can be defined as the locus of existence of individual systems of cultural phenomena such as language, religion, science, politics, etc. These systems are realities even though they cannot be perceived by the senses. They reveal their existence by exerting a normative influence on empirical reality."

24 I am indebted on this point to Hayden White, "The Problem of Change in Literary History," *New Literary History* 7 (1975): 97–111, esp. 107–8.

25 "The Archaeology of Knowledge," in *The Archaeology of Knowledge and the Discourse on Language,* trans. A. M. Sheridan Smith (New York: Harper and Row, 1976), p. 55.

26 On the use of rhetoric to innovate new predicative categories, see Paul de Man, "Semiology and Rhetoric," in *Textual Strategies: Perspectives in Post-Structuralist Criticism,* ed. Josué V. Harari (Ithaca, N.Y.: Cornell University Press, 1979), pp. 121–40. For an exhaustive discussion of the relationship of rhetorical tropes to predication, see Paul Ricoeur, *The Rule of Metaphor,* trans. Robert Czerny, with Kathleen McLaughlin and John Costello, S.J. (Toronto: University of Toronto Press, 1977), esp. pp. 65–100. The necessity of predication to the formation of an adequate grammar for historical description is one of the points on which my reservations about deconstruction parallel Altieri's. See his critique of Lyotard's "phrase grammar," in "Temporality and the Necessity of Dialectic," pp. 150–54. Lacan, who sees metaphor as the rhetorical vehicle of what psychoanalysis calls identification, also argues the crucial role of "predicative articulation" in the formation of the subject. See the two chapters on metaphor and metonymy in *The Seminar of Jacques Lacan, Book 3, The Psychoses, 1955–1956,* ed. Jacques-Alain Miller, trans. with notes by Russell Grigg (New York: Norton, 1993), pp. 214–30, esp. pp. 218–19.

27 Kenneth Burke, *A Grammar of Motives* (Berkeley: University of California Press, 1969), pp. 503–17. White's tropology is now developed in a sizable body of work (all published by Johns Hopkins University Press). See esp. *Metahistory: The Historical Imagination in Nineteenth-Century Europe* (1973), *Tropics of Discourse: Essays in Cultural Criticism* (1977), and *The Content of the Form* (1987). For an extended discussion of the literary historical implications of White's work, see also my review essay, "Hayden White and Literary Criticism: The Tropology of Discourse," *Papers on Literature and Language* 17 (1981): 424–45.

28 White credits Vico with the reduction of the tropes to four integral classes, but the reorganization of rhetoric "according to method" undertaken by Ramus and his disciple Taleus (Omar Talon) in the fifteenth century had already effected this logical arrangement. See, for example, Abraham Fraunce's *The Arcadian Rhetorike* (1588), an English adaptation of Taleus: "There be two kinds of tropes. The first conteineth *Metonymia,* the change of name: and *Ironia,* scoffing or iesting speach: the second comprehendeth a *Metaphore* and *Synecdoche*" (ed. Ethel Seaton, published for the Luttrell Society [Oxford, 1950], p. 4, abbreviations expanded). The naming of rhetorical tropes was in the Renaissance already a vexed and confusing issue, as George Puttenham emphasized in *The Arte of English Poesie* (1589), Book 3, chap. 9. I want to stress that my denomination of metaphor, metonymy, synecdoche, and irony refers to the categorical manipulations that I ascribe to each rather than to any comprehensive historical claim about the usage of the terms. Although the fourfold distinction I am making is at least implicit in some Renaissance rhetorics, my interest at this point is the logical possibilities implied, not the provenance of the names assigned to them. To forestall confusion and avoid fruitless argument, I will define in context the rhetorical tropes and figures to which I refer. I make no particular historical claims for my nomenclature.

29 See Jacques Derrida's classic essay on the effacement of metaphor in philosophical discourse, "White Mythology," in *Margins of Philosophy,* pp. 207–71.

30 Puttenham emphasizes the intellectual reach of *synecdoche* in joining things rather than simply manipulating names: "The Greeks . . . call it *Synecdoche,* the Latines *sub intellectio* or understanding, for by the part we are enforced to understand the whole, by the whole part, by many things one thing, by one, many, by a thing precedent, a thing consequent, and generally one thing out of another by maner of contraiety to the word which is spoken, *aliud ex alio,* which because it seemth to aske a good, quick, and pregnant capacitie, and is not for an ordinarie or dull wit so to do, I chose to call him the figure not onely of conceit after the Greeke originall, but also of quick conceit." *The Arte of English Poesie* (1589), ed. Edward Arber (London, 1869; rpt. New York: AMS Press, 1966), p. 196.

31 *Paradise Lost* is cited from *John Milton: Complete Poetry and Major Prose,* ed. Mer-

ritt Y. Hughes (Indianapolis: Odyssey, 1957). I offer a more elaborate and somewhat different analysis of these lines in *"Authors to Themselves": Milton and the Revelation of History* (Cambridge: Cambridge University Press, 1987) pp. 26–28.

32 See also *Paradise Lost* 3.285–89: "Be thou in *Adam's* room / The Head of all mankind, though *Adam's* Son. / As in him perish all men, so in thee / As from a second root shall be restor'd, / As many as are restor'd, without thee, none."

33 The case for this mediation in *Paradise Lost* is argued at length in *"Authors to Themselves."* The classic study of the reader's active induction into *Paradise Lost* remains Stanley Fish's *Surprised by Sin: The Reader in "Paradise Lost"* (New York: St. Martin's Press, 1967).

34 It becomes necessary at this point to refer to the familiar metaphor-metonymy polarity advanced by Roman Jakobson in "Two Aspects of Language and Two Types of Aphasic Disturbances," in Jakobson and Morris Halle, *Fundamentals of Language,* 2nd rev. ed. (The Hague: Mouton, 1975), pp. 67–96, and to explain my use of two additional terms. Metaphor and metonymy represent, for Jakobson, paradigmatic and syntactic operations, respectively. They are linguistically derived without reference to their impact on the conceptualization of a given syntagm. I am interested precisely in the conceptual or logical distinctions that are elided by the high level of generality at which Jakobson distinguishes the tropes. I distinguish synecdoche from metaphor and metonymy because the conceptual distinctions of inclusion, resemblance, and exclusion that hold among the three tropes are manifested in the kinds of narratives that may be generated to articulate the relationships presumed to hold among objects and between subject and object. Further, I am interested in the transformations that relate one narrative configuration to another, and, I believe, the tropes may be dialectically linked to account for these transformations. In this dialectic, metaphor (resemblance) mediates between metonymy (difference) and synecdoche (identity). Moreover, this figural dialectic accounts for the *temporal* transitions from one configuration to another that characterize narrative. Irony is included as a fourth trope because it functions to clear the way for new articulations by undermining the apparent referentiality of the articulation to be superseded. It is thus the negative moment of the dialectic. See also Ricoeur's discussion of the metaphor/metonymy polarity in *The Rule of Metaphor,* pp. 173–87.

35 Hayden White argues in *Metahistory* that "dialectic is nothing but a formalization of an insight into the tropological nature of all the forms of discourse which are not formally committed to the articulation of a world view within the confines of a single modality of linguistic usage" (p. 428). See Hegel's discussion of the unhappy consciousness, in which consciousness passes through three different relations to the Unchangeable (*Phenomenology of Spirit,* B, IB). For a highly suggestive analysis

of the dialectical contradiction of identity and difference immanent in predication per se, see Julia Kristeva, "*La fonction prédicative et le sujet parlant,*" in *Langue, discours, société,* pp. 229–59.

36 I would give priority neither to dialectic as a logic nor to rhetoric as a determinant of dialectic. It seems as useless to separate these poles into substantive entities as it is to envisage a monological discourse.

37 *Group Psychology and the Analysis of the Ego,* SE 18, pp. 135–36.

38 See Lacan, "Agency of the Letter in the Unconscious or Reason Since Freud," *Écrits: A Selection,* pp. 166–67: "And the enigmas that desire seems to pose for a 'natural philosophy' — its frenzy mocking the abyss of the infinite, the secret collusion with which it envelops the pleasure of knowing and of dominating with *jouissance,* these amount to no other derangement of instinct than that of being caught in the rails — eternally stretching forth toward the *desire for something else* — of metonymy." The "true referent of desire," the Oedipal wish to supplant the father, is sent by repression below the bar of signification. As a substitute for the father, the *ego* ideal moves, through its metonymic substitutions, between the rails formed by the chains of signification, organized not simply by the metaphors of symptom formation and the metonymies of desire, but by the formal-logical apparatus of narrativization.

39 *The Order of Things* (New York: Pantheon, 1971).

40 I discuss the complicated relationship of the "postmodern" present to the *épistème* of modernism in the Epilogue.

41 "Foucault Decoded: Notes from Underground," in *Tropics of Discourse,* pp. 230–60. Quotations used in the following discussion appear on pp. 252–54 of White's text. See also "Foucault's Discourse: The Historiography of Anti-Humanism," in *The Content of the Form: Narrative Discourse and Historical Representation* (Baltimore: Johns Hopkins University Press, 1987), pp. 104–41, esp. pp. 115–25.

42 Lacan remarks: "Events are engendered in a primary historicization. In other words, history is already producing itself on the stage where it will be played out, once it has been written down, both within the subject and outside him." "The Function and Field of Speech and Language in Psychoanalysis," *Écrits: A Selection,* p. 52.

43 *Beyond the Pleasure Principle,* SE 18, pp. 14–17. My use of the pronoun "he" in this paragraph and the following one corresponds to the fact that the child in question is Freud's grandson. Apart from this historical fact, one could read "he or she" in these sentences. The story I recount is extrapolated from Freud's observation of this particular child, and it is to him that I refer, while obviously taking him to be exemplary. No gender exclusion is intended, nor is the masculine pronoun being used as gender neutral in my text.

3. Augustine and the Rhetoric of the Christian Ego

1 *Soliloquiorum,* 2: 17. Augustine's Latin is quoted from J.-P. Migne, ed., *Patrologiae,* Series Latina Prior (Paris, 1861), vol. 32, p. 892; the English translation by Rev. Charles C. Starbuck is from the *Select Library of the Nicene and Post-Nicene Fathers,* ed. Philip Schaff, 1st ser. (Grand Rapids, Mich.: Wm. B. Eerdmans, 1956), 7:552. Lacan is quoted from "The Function and Field of Speech and Language in Psychoanalysis," in *Écrits: A Selection,* trans. Alan Sheridan (New York: Norton, 1977), p. 86.

2 Margaret W. Ferguson relates the way in which narratives of exile and attempted return are exuded at the site of this linguistic-temporal impasse. See "Saint Augustine's Region of Unlikeness: The Crossing of Exile and Language," *Georgia Review* 29 (1975): 842–64, esp. 843: "The metaphysical exile is defined as flawed because he is absent from an original unity of being. This absence may be conceived either in temporal or spatial terms. The exile is defined negatively with reference to what he is not; his essence is determined by a *difference* portrayed as a lack."

3 In contrast to narrative, "theory," as such, reduces temporal sequence to synchronic structures—more or less by definition: OED: "Theory": "from the Greek, Θεωρία: "a looking at, viewing, contemplation, speculation, theory, also a sight, a spectacle." Thus, if lyric suppresses time by absorbing it into a pictorial present, and narrative represents time as a motivated sequence of verbal predications, theory, which shares with lyric a certain aspiration toward the universal, sublates time in the form of spatial structure or design. Lyric "sees" an exemplary moment (metaphor); narrative "recounts" a sequence of moments (metonymy); theory "sees" that sequence as an always already determined structure. For a more fully illustrated discussion of the relation of narrative to theoretical discourse with reference to literary historiography, see my "The Fruits of One's Labor in Miltonic Practice and Marxian Theory," *ELH* 59 (1992): 77–105.

4 "Shakespeare's Ear," *The Subjectivity Effect in Western Literature: Essays Toward the Release of Shakespeare's Will* (Cambridge, Mass.: MIT Press, 1992, pp. 222–31; the quoted passage appears on p. 224. The challenge of sight and to sight is neatly (if rather generally) summed up by Macbeth's response to the spectral dagger in 2.1.44–45: "Mine eyes are made the fools o' th' other senses, / Or else worth all the rest." It is worth noting with respect to the role played by ambient sound in my discussion of Augustine's conversion narrative that Macbeth's hallucinatory equivocation in this crucial moment is resolved by the commonplace *sound* of a bell ringing the hours: "I go, and it is done; the bell invites me. / Hear it not, Duncan, for it is a knell, / That summons thee to heaven or to hell" (62–64).

5 *Shakespeare's Perjured Eye: The Invention of Poetic Subjectivity in the Sonnets* (Berkeley: University of California Press, 1986), pp. 24, 165–67, and 283–85.

6 The generic shape of such a narrative is aptly summarized in the *Consolation of Philosophy*, Book 3, 2:34–38: "*Repetunt proprios quaeque recursus / Redituque suo singula gaudent / Nec manet ulli traditus ordo / Nisi quod fini iunxerit ortum / Stabilemque sui fecerit orbem.*" ["Each thing seeks its own way back / And coming back is glad; / None is consigned to any ordered course / Save that which links the end to the beginning / And makes its cycle firm."] Cited from Boethius, *Tractates, De Consolatione Philosophiae*, trans. H. F. Stewart, E. K. Rand, S. J. Tester, Loeb Classical Library (Cambridge, Mass.: Harvard University Press, 1973), pp. 238, 239; Tester's translation. As Patricia A. Parker has argued, with particular reference to Spenser, the unassigned and unordered course that links the end to the beginning becomes the particular matter of Renaissance narrative *dilatio*. *Inescapable Romance: Studies in the Poetics of a Mode* (Princeton, N.J.: Princeton University Press, 1979), pp. 54–65. (The passage quoted from Boethius is discussed on pp. 57–58.) It is the special province of narrative to articulate the temporal unfolding of a meaning realized through a spatial design. On the expectations of progress in the British Renaissance, see chap. 1, pp. 21–25. On the ideological implications of this expectation, see the discussions of "emergent capitalism" in Christopher Kendrick, *Milton: A Study in Ideology and Form* (New York: Methuen, 1986), and Andrew Milner, *John Milton and the English Revolution: A Study in the Sociology of Literature* (Totowa, N.J.: Barnes and Noble, 1981).

7 Peter Brown, *Augustine of Hippo: A Biography* (Berkeley: University of California Press, 1967), p. 212. For a psychoanalytic reading of Augustine's identification of mother and church, see Charles Klegerman, M.D., "A Psychoanalytic Study of the 'Confessions of St. Augustine,'" *Journal of the American Psychoanalytic Association* 5 (1957): 469–84. On the Neoplatonic element in the *Confessions*, see Pierre Courcelle, *Les Confessions de Saint Augustin dans la Tradition Littéraire: Antécédents et Postérité* (Paris: Études Augustiniennes, 1963), pp. 17–88.

8 Andrew Fichter, *Poets Historical: Dynastic Epic in the Renaissance* (New Haven, Conn.: Yale University Press, 1982), p. 50.

9 On the conjunction of Augustinian theology and the church's transition from persecuted sect to state religion, see Elaine Pagels, *Adam, Eve, and the Serpent* (New York: Random House, 1988), pp. 98–126.

10 See Arnaldo Momiligliano's characterization of Eusebius's history as a development of Jewish-Hellenistic historiography in "Pagan and Christian Historiography in the Fourth Century A.D.," in Momiligliano, ed., *The Conflict Between Paganism and Christianity in the Fourth Century* (Oxford: Clarendon Press, 1963), pp. 90–91. More generally, Fineman sees "the motive to allegoricize emerg[ing] out of recuperative originology": "The Old Testament is revived when interpreted as typologically predictive of the New Testament, and the Gospels themselves receive

the benefit of spiritualizing exegesis when the apocalypse they prophesy is indefinitely deferred. Here, allegory acquires what will be in our tradition its primarily intermediate position between interpretive extremes. . . . Between a literalism pure and simple and what today might be called an exegesis of the free-floating signifier, allegory becomes, for literature as for theology, a vivifying archaeology of occulted origins and a promissory eschatology of postponed ends — all this in the service of an essentially pietistic cosmology devoted to the corroboration of divinely ordered space and time." "The Structure of Allegorical Desire" (TSE, p. 6). My understanding of Augustine is greatly indebted to Fineman's essay (TSE, pp. 3–31), which views the desire of and for allegory in terms of the problem of getting time into structure. Fineman argues that a thwarted desire for the lost origin arises within structure in consequence of an initial repression necessary to institute signification through a system of diacritical binaries (the primal /pa/ of /ma/ and /pa/ in his pointedly Oedipal example!): "In short, the structure of significant sounds must erase the original marking of diacriticality upon which it depends, and from which it emerges, in order to signify anything at all" (p. 17). The sense of a lost origin is thus constitutive of the subject as such. See n. 17 below.

11 See, for example, Quintilian, *Institutio Oratoria* 8.6.14–15. Fineman points out that "allegory will be defined up through the Renaissance as the temporal extension of trope" (p. 6).

12 See Ferguson, "Saint Augustine's Region of Unlikeness," n. 1 above.

13 *St. Augustine's "Confessions" with an English Translation by William Watts* (1631), Loeb Classical Library, 2 vols. (Cambridge, Mass.: Harvard University Press, 1961), Book 13, chap. 24, 2:438–42. Subsequent citations will be given parenthetically in the text. Page numbers refer to the Latin text; English translations appear on facing pages.

14 In the quoted passage the Platonic preoccupation with the distinction between perception and conception, sense and intelligence, is restated in semiotic terms. On Augustine's division of the word (*verbum*) into acoustic signifier and associated concept, see the discussion of *De Magistro* in Jacques Lacan, *The Seminar of Jacques Lacan: Book I: Freud's Papers on Technique, 1953–1954*, ed. Jacques-Alain Miller, trans. by John Forrester (New York: Norton, 1988), pp. 247–65. Lacan adverts to Augustine's dialogue with Adeodatus on the efficacy of teaching to support, illustrate, and, finally, to distinguish the linguistic turn of Lacanian analysis: "What is at the heart of things for Saint Augustine is not the restoration of the hegemony of things over signs, but the casting of doubt on the hegemony of signs in the essentially spoken activity of teaching. This is where the break occurs between *signum* and *verbum, nomen,* the instrument of knowing in as much as it is the instrument

of speech." In Lacan's reading, "because Saint Augustine wants to involve us in truth's very own dimension, he abandons the linguist's domain. . . . As soon as it is established, speech moves in the dimension of truth. Except, speech does not know that it is what makes truth. And Saint Augustine does not know it either, and that is why he tries to meet up with truth as such, through illumination" (p. 259). As we shall see, Augustine (re)turns to the original identity of an inner voice and the divine Logos in order to enter a domain of Truth beyond (prior to) signification. Lacan admits no such transcendence: "In fact, in grasping the function of the sign, one is always referred from one sign to another. Why? Because the system of signs, as they are concretely instituted, *hic et nunc,* by itself forms a whole. That means that it institutes an order from which there is no exit" (p. 262). Thus, in the end, Augustine's ascription of truth to the atemporal Word of an originary Logos represents to Lacan "a total inversion of perspective" (p. 259).

15 For Augustine's views on prelapsarian sexuality, see James Turner, *One Flesh: Paradisal Sexuality in the Age of Milton* (Oxford: Clarendon Press, 1987), pp. 41–55.

16 This extension from and return to an originary word is a defining characteristic of allegory. See, for example, Abraham Fraunce, "The excellencie of tropes is then most apparent, when either manie be fitlie included in one word, or one so continued in manie, as that with what thing it begin, with the same it also end: and then it is called an Allegorie or Inversion," *The Arcadian Rhetorike* (1588), ed. Ethel Seaton (Oxford: Basil Blackwell, 1950), pp. 3–4; quoted in Fineman, "The Structure of Allegorical Desire," TSE, p. 7. It will be the burden of the following discussion to elaborate in some detail the structure of associations that both generates and contains Augustine's allegory of allegory, constraining it to begin and end in the Divine Word.

17 See Jacques Derrida, *Of Grammatology,* trans. Gayatri Chakravorty Spivak (Baltimore: Johns Hopkins University Press, 1976), pp. 269–316. But see also Fineman's argument that Lacan's notion of the lack, installed by the entry into language, thematizes and ultimately controls *différance* and its traces ("The Structure of Allegorical Desire," TSE, pp. 47–51). The supplement appears as a kind of suture, covering over the place where the origin (of absolute diacriticality, of difference) has been repressed and (placed "under erasure") by structure. Augustine's allegory sacrifices the system of differences deriving from sexual difference, the difference, that is, between *men and women*—procreation and kinship—to a system of differences deriving from *man's* relationship to God, a relationship in which all *men* are *brothers* and *sons,* and each man addresses himself to *the Father.* On the general implications of this move, see the "Postscript" to Freud's *Group Psychology and the Analysis of the Ego,* SE 18, pp. 134–43.

18 *The City of God Against the Pagans,* trans. Eva Matthews and William McAllen Green, Loeb Classical Library, 7 vols. (Cambridge, Mass.: Harvard University Press, 1965), Book 18, chap. 13, 5:446 (my translation).

19 On the aporias of time in the *Confessions,* see Paul Ricoeur, *Time and Narrative,* trans. Kathleen McLaughlin and David Pellauer (Chicago: University of Chicago Press, 1984), pp. 1, 5–30. The passage about the ability of words to arrest the passage of time, quoted from Augustine, is discussed below in relation to the epideictic tradition. See pp. 82–83.

20 I refer here to the highly stylized and abstract figure of the fish seen in ancient iconography as a (perhaps covert) sign of Christ and his earthly brotherhood.

21 On metaphor as the appropriation of a sign to be the signifier of another sign, see the discussion of connotation in Roland Barthes, "Elements of Semiology," in *Writing Degree Zero and Elements of Semiology* (Boston: Beacon Press, 1970), pp. 89–92.

22 In Jewish tradition the Decalogue's prohibition against graven images precludes iconic representation of the deity. The force of this prohibition is intimately related to the narrated context of Abraham's dissent from the idolmakers and the subsequent struggles of his nation with its neighbors. Within the terms of Genesis, the proscription of the icon founds the nation. It is the fundamental *social* element of the covenant, effectively separating Abraham and his seed from the communal practices of the (now established as such) gentiles. This gesture of separation (rewritten on the flesh through ritual circumcision) is precisely that which Augustine must supplement to achieve the evangelical (universalizing) revision of Christianity prefigured in the Pauline argument against the need to circumcise gentile converts to Christianity. Thus, one might say that Augustine's separation of flesh and spirit in the Word is offered as a supplemental alternative to the Jewish *script* of circumcision and the prohibition of the image.

23 See Freud's discussion of "switch words" in the *Fragment of an Analysis of a Case of Hysteria:* "Now, in a line of association ambiguous words (or, as we may call them, 'switch words') act like points at a junction. If the points are switched across from the position in which they appear to lie in the dream, then we find ourselves on another set of rails; and along this second track run the thoughts which we are in search of but which still lie concealed behind the dream." SE 7, p. 65.

24 In this story of the formation of the Christian ego through the metaphoric inflection of a chain of metonymies, readers familiar with Lacanian psychoanalysis will recognize Lacan's relation of the symptom, understood as a metaphoric foreclosure, to the metonymic movement of the subject along the defiles of desire. See, for example, "Agency of the Letter in the Unconscious Or Reason Since Freud," *Écrits: A Selection,* pp. 163–66. I would emphasize that the relation between the

theological and the psychoanalytic explanations is neither trivial nor determinative. Rather the shared structure of these discourses marks their engagement with
a similar conception of the self as a temporal movement along the border between
doing and suffering.

25 See, for example, the experience shared by Augustine and Monica just before her
death (Book 11, chap. 10).

26 "The Fig Tree and the Laurel: Petrarch's Poetics," in *Literary Theory / Renaissance
Texts,* ed. Patricia Parker and David Quint (Baltimore: Johns Hopkins University
Press, 1986), p. 23. This essay was originally published in *Diacritics* 5 [1975]: 35–40.
See also David Norbrook's illuminating discussion of the scriptural word in *Poetry
and Politics in the English Renaissance* (London: Routledge and Kegan Paul, 1984),
pp. 36–40.

27 Alain de Lille, *Theologicae Regulae,* Regula 7: "*Deus est sp[h]aera intelligibilis, cu-
jus centrum ubique, circumferentia nusquam*" (Migne, *Patrologiae,* vol. 210, p. 627).
I am indebted to Tom Moser, Jr., for this reference.

28 As in, for example, Herbert's poem, "H. Scripture's II":
>Oh that I knew how all thy lights combine,
>>And the configurations of thy glorie!
>>Seeing not onely how each verse doth shine,
>>But all the constellations of the storie,
>>This verse markes that, and both do make a motion
>>>Unto a third, that ten leaves off doth lie:
>>>Then as dispersed herbs do watch a potion,
>>These three make up some Christian's destinie:
>>Such are thy secrets, which my life makes good,
>>>And comments on thee: for in ev'ry thing
>>>*Thy words do finde me out, & parallels bring,*
>>*And in another make me understood.*
>>>Starres are poor books, & oftentimes do misse
>>>This book of starres lights to eternal blisse.

The Works of George Herbert, ed. with a commentary by F. E. Hutchinson (Oxford:
Clarendon Press, 1941), p. 58 (emphasis mine).

29 "The Fig Tree and the Laurel," p. 25.

30 Reading *silently* indicates a special spirituality for Augustine, a spirituality marked
by indifference to the presence or absence of human discussants. See, for example,
Confessions, Book 6, chap. 2, where Augustine remarks approvingly on Ambrose's
habit of reading silently and of ignoring the petitioners who stand by waiting to be
recognized: "*sed cum legebat, oculi ducebantur per paginas et cor intellectum rima-*

batur, vox autem et lingua quiescebant" (1.272). ("But when he was reading he drew his eyes along over the leaves, and his heart searched into the sense, but his voice and tongue were silent").

31 On the distinction between following and having followed a story, see Louis O. Mink, "History and Fiction as Modes of Comprehension," *NLH* 1 (1970): 542–58. See also Marshall Grossman, *"Authors to Themselves": Milton and the Revelation of History* (Cambridge: Cambridge University Press, 1987), pp. 5–12.

32 Is the slide in the first sentence from *codex* to *liber* significant? Bible bindings from Augustine's period do not survive, though presumably they were flat paper books in coptic bindings (as opposed to scrolls of rolled skin, for which one would expect neither *codex* nor *liber* but *volumina*). Both *codex* and *liber* refer to the wood used for writing. See the entries for *caudex* and *liber* (4) in Charlton T. Lewis and Charles Short, *A New Latin Dictionary* (New York: American Book, 1879). In view of Augustine's metaphoric use of *skin* and *fold* here, it would be interesting to know whether *codex* and *liber* in this passage are simply synonyms or are intended to discriminate two different physical forms of the book. I am indebted to Frank Mowery of the Folger Shakespeare Library for his help in considering the physical forms of Augustine's books.

33 I have modified Watts's translation in the direction of greater literalness. The full Latin text of the passage is quoted on p. 69.

34 For an excellent discussion of Augustine's use of the incarnate Word to mediate "the paradox which allows language to be seen as both the region of unlikeness and the way of escaping that region," see Ferguson, "Saint Augustine's Region of Unlikeness." The quoted words are from p. 848.

35 Citations of *La Vita Nuova* are from Dante Alighieri, *Vita nuova e Rime*, ed. Guido Davico Bonino (Milan: Arnoldo Mondadori Editore, 1985). Translations are my own. The quoted passage appears on p. 74. With reference to Part 2 of this book, it should be noted that the circulation of *La Vita Nuova* in Renaissance England was limited. It did not serve, in the way that Petrarch's *Rime* certainly did, as a model for imitation by Renaissance poets. I mention it here because of its importance for Petrarch, whose influence on English poetry is profound, and because it provides an early example of the embedding of lyric poems within a post facto narrative frame.

36 See Robert Pogue Harrison's discussion of the ending of *La Vita Nuova*, in *The Body of Beatrice* (Baltimore: Johns Hopkins University Press, 1988), pp. 144–57, which includes a review of the relevant scholarship. My discussion of Dante is greatly indebted to Harrison's extraordinary book.

37 See Charles S. Singleton's influential characterization of the temporal division of

the authorial voice in *La Vita Nuova*: "The poet who is her [Beatrice's] lover, and whose Book of Memory this is, becomes as it were two persons, distinguishable according to the principle of time so established. He is the protagonist of the action, moving forward along the line of events in their first occurrence. And then he is that same person who, having lived through all these happenings, looks back upon them and sees their meaning now as it was not possible for him to do at the time. As the first of these persons he knows nothing before it happens. But as one reading in the book of memory he knows the end, the middle and the beginning of all that happened" (*An Essay on the "Vita Nuova"* [Cambridge, Mass.: Harvard University Press, 1949], p. 8). But, contra Singleton, see Harrison, *The Body of Beatrice*, pp. 5–13. Harrison accepts that *La Vita Nuova* posits a narrating "I" who interprets the experiences of his former self, but he objects to Singleton's assumption that "the *libello* contains a temporal, teleological endpoint that guarantees the closure of the hermeneutic circle" (p. 11). Against this assumption, Harrison argues persuasively that "the most distinctive feature of the *Vita Nuova*, after all, is that its author does not end his narrative but effectively interrupts it with a promise that he will accomplish at a later date what he has not managed to accomplish in the *libello*" (ibid.). I will argue that the provisional retrospective narration recognized by Harrison enables the narrative construction of the self.

38 The distinction between the *Idealich* and the *Ichideal*, left ambiguous by Freud, has been developed by Lacan in a direction pertinent to literary historical analysis. Lacan understands the ideal ego to refer to "the formation of an ideal," the image according to which the ego is initially constructed, and the ego ideal to refer to the "mirage of the ego," which the ego retains in itself as that of which it would be worthy. In Lacan's graph of desire ("The Subversion of the Subject and the Dialectic of Desire in the Freudian Unconscious," *Écrits: A Selection*, p. 315), "the big I designates the identification of omnipotence with the signifier, with the ego ideal. On the other hand, as image of the other, it is the *Urbild* of the ego, the original form on the basis of which the ego models itself, sets itself up, and operates under the auspices of pseudomastery." *The Seminar of Jacques Lacan, Book 7, The Ethics of Psychoanalysis, 1959–1960*, ed. Jacques-Alain Miller, trans. Dennis Porter (New York: Norton, 1992), pp. 98, 234. Lacan continues: "We will now define the ego ideal of the subject as representing the power to do good, which then opens up within itself the beyond that concerns us today. . . . As for the ideal ego, who is the imaginary other which faces us at the same level, it represents by itself the one who deprives us" (*The Seminar of Jacques Lacan, Book 1*, pp. 129–42).

39 See Fineman, *Shakespeare's Perjured Eye*, p. 6: "Praise is an objective showing [*deixis*] that is essentially subjective 'showing off' on the part of the poet."

40 The obsessive nature of the poet's repetition of Laura's praise is thematic in, for example, *Rime* 23 ("*Ne dolce tempo de la prima etade*"), in which the poet sings incessantly so as to make his pain less bitter.

41 Nancy J. Vickers reports that in the *Rime sparse*, "*Spargere* appears in some form ... forty-three times, and the pattern of its application is telling: nineteen (almost half) apply specifically to Laura's body and its emanations (the light from her eyes, the generative capacity of her footsteps); and thirteen (almost a third) to the speaker's mental state and its expression (tears, voice, rhymes, sighs, thoughts, praises, prayers, and hopes). The uses of *spargere* thus markedly gravitate toward not one but two poles; not just to Laura, but also to 'I.' " "The Body Re-membered Petrarchan Lyric and the Strategies of Description," in *Mimesis: From Mirror to Method, Augustine to Descartes,* ed. John D. Lyons and Stephen G. Nichols, Jr. (Hanover, N.H.: University Press of New England, 1982), p. 103.

42 Petrarch's poems are cited from: *Petrarch's Lyric Poems: The Rime sparse and Other Lyrics,* ed. and trans. Robert M. Durling (Cambridge, Mass.: Harvard University Press, 1976). Translations are Durling's. See Harrison's reading of *Rime* 1 in *The Body of Beatrice,* pp. 105–9.

43 See Freud's "Remembering, Repeating, Working-Through," SE 12, pp. 145–56.

44 Following the same historical path we have traveled—from Augustine's Logos, symbolized by the Fig Tree under which he is converted, past Dante's transcription of Love's dictation, to Petrarch's Laura, Freccero concludes: "for the laurel to be truly unique, it cannot *mean* anything: its referentiality must be neutralized if it is to remain the property of its creator. Petrarch makes of it the emblem of the mirror relationship *Laura-Lauro,* which is to say, the poetic lady created by the poet, who in turn creates him as poet laureate" ("The Fig Tree and the Laurel," pp. 26–27).

45 See Salvatore Battaglia, *Grande Dizionaraio Della Lingua Italiana* (Turin: Unione Tipographico-Editrice Torines, 1972): *Impresa*[2]: (1) *segno ... che gli antichi cavalieri ricevevano dalla propria dama impegnandosi a difenderne l'onore e a comportarsi valorosamente nella guerra, nel duello o nel torneo; figura simbolica che il cavaliere portava ricamata sulla veste oppure dipinta o scolpita sullo scudo o sull'elmo— Amche: insegna, emblema. ...* (2) *Arald. Figura* (corpo dell'impressa) *che, accompagnata per lo più da una frase allegorica* (anima dell'impressa), *serve come divisa o stemma gentilizio di personaggi, famiglie, Stati, città, communità, ecc. (e richiama, più or meno chiaramente, le origini, il nome, li attività, le gesta delle persone o degli enti a cui si riferisce).*

46 See Vickers's illuminating discussions of Petrarch's use of Ovid in *Rime* 23, in "The Body Re-membered," pp. 105–9, and "Diana Described: Scattered Woman and Scattered Rhyme," *Critical Inquiry* 8 (1981): 265–79; esp. 266–70.

47 See chap. 4, pp. 117–18; 300–301 nn. 18, 19.

48 *The Body of Beatrice,* pp. 93–109.

49 On the immanence of nostalgia to the pastoral tradition, see Judith Haber, *Pastoral and the Poetics of Self-Contradiction: Theocritus to Marvell* (Cambridge: Cambridge University Press, 1994). I thank Professor Haber for allowing me to read a prepublication copy of her book, the fourth chapter of which greatly informs my discussion of Marvell's mower poems. See also Rosalie Colie's discussion of pastoral in the mower poems in *"My Ecchoing Song": Andrew Marvell's Poetry of Criticism* (Princeton, N.J.: Princeton University Press, 1970), pp. 30–42. Annabel Patterson has noted the intrusion of georgic into pastoral signaled in the different occupations of Damon the Mower and Corydon, his pastoral counterpart in Vergil's *Eclogue* 2: "The match between their personalities should only emphasize the difference in their occupations, Marvell's Damon being unmistakably a worker, a georgic figure, whose 'Sweat' the sun 'licks off' and who deliberately contrasts himself to the 'piping Shepherd' (l. 49). He is therefore socially a correction of his Vergilian prototype, whose *otium* was signified by his own mention of 'reapers weary in the consuming heat.'" *Pastoral and Ideology: Virgil to Valéry* (Berkeley: University of California Press, 1987), pp. 154–55. Also standing behind and broadening the ideological implications of the intrusion of the georgic sweat of the mower into the pastoral otium of Marvell's mower poems is the displacement from the land of the shepherd Meliboeus by Roman expropriations of land for returning soldiers in Vergil's *Eclogue* 1. (See Haber, *Pastoral and the Poetics of Self-Contradiction,* pp. 104–5.) In *The Matter of Revolution: Science, Poetry, and Politics in the Age of Milton* (Ithaca, N.Y.: Cornell University Press, 1996), John Rogers finds a more local political context for Marvell's mower poems as "a distanced ironic reflection" on "the green idealism of a passive revolutionary" of the sort represented by Winstanley and the Diggers on St. George's Hill: "The tension inherent in Winstanley's prose between human and organic agents of revolution resurfaces, in a modified, highly literary key, in the Marvellian pastoral" (pp. 61–62).

50 All citations of Marvell refer to *The Poems and Letters of Andrew Marvell,* ed. H. M. Margoliouth; 3rd rev. ed., by Pierre Legouis, with the collaboration of E. E. Duncan-Jones, 2 vols. (Oxford: Clarendon Press, 1971), vol. 1. For Colie (*"My Ecchoing Song"*), the mower's complaint is too excessive and dogmatic to be taken seriously: "Really, all that is going on is that, through this mad argument, the poet is again questioning pastoral values and conventions. By making the Mower take elements of the pastoral program absolutely, the poet manages to make us think afresh about a convention in praise of naturalness which is distinguished for its fixedness, its cliché qualities, its artificiality. As we sort out the levels of artificiality involved in this poem, we are drawn to consider conventional thought and behavior in contexts beyond the pastoral" (p. 38). That the poem asks its readers to reflect on the

limitations of its genre is clear, but it seems wrong—and uncharacteristically defensive—to assert that this questioning of generic assumptions is "all that is going on." Rather, the pointedness of the poem derives from the way in which—precisely by detailing the agricultural and commercial innovations of the garden—the poem historicizes the generic failure that is surreptitiously its theme. It is not simply pastoral that is at stake, but the viability of "the pastoral *paragone* of art and nature" (p. 36) represented in a modernity that undermines its categorical distinctions.

51 See, for example, *Richard II* 3.4.29–66. For a discussion of the treatment of the enclosure movement in seventeenth-century "country" poems, see James Turner, *The Politics of Landscape: Rural Scenery and Society in English Poetry, 1630–1660* (Cambridge, Mass.: Harvard University Press, 1979), pp. 141–47.

52 See Marx's discussion of use and exchange value in *Das Kapital,* vol. 1, chap. 1. Lacan links the commodification of desire implicit in the abstract desire for goods (that is, the desire unashamedly articulated in the yuppie aphorism, "whoever dies with the most toys wins") to the emergence of the ethical imperative: "The long historical development of the problem of the good is in the end centered on the notion of how goods are created, insofar as they are organized not on the basis of so-called natural and predetermined needs, but insofar as they furnish the material of a distribution; and it is in relation to this that the dialectic of the good is articulated to the degree that it takes on effective meaning for man" (*The Seminar of Jacques Lacan, Book 7,* pp. 228–29).

53 The quotation is from Margoliouth's note, Marvell, *Poems and Letters,* 1:262.

54 See Haber, *Pastoral and the Poetics of Self-Contradiction,* p. 107, on the absence of the first-person singular from this poem.

55 Compare the senses of *use* in the concluding couplet of Shakespeare's sonnet 20: "But since she [Nature] prick'd thee out for women's pleasure, / Mine be thy love, and thy love's use their treasure." Not at all coincidentally, this sonnet, which presents the inverse of Damon's complaint against man's supplementing of nature —Nature's doting "addition" to the young man results in the perversion of Will— culminates the sequence's opening group in which the young man is first advised to *use* a woman to reproduce his image and then assured that his image will endure in the art of the sonnets.

56 See Turner, *The Politics of Landscape,* pp. 117–18: "Marvell is not belittling the mower by giving him absurd or heterodox ideas. Nor does he make him rustic or incompetent. The argument and structure of the poem are well-matched. Luxury, stagnation, doubleness, pretence, forbidden dealings, tyranny, and vexation—all these are forms of violence against nature, and violence forms the crux of the argument and pivot of the poem: ' 'Tis all enforc'd. . . .' "

57 The concept of *interpellation,* drawn from Louis Althusser, "Ideology and the Ideo-

logical State Apparatuses," in *Lenin and Philosophy and Other Essays,* trans. Ben Brewster (New York: Monthly Review Press, 1971), pp. 127–86, describes the appearance of the subject as the answer to an ideologically posed question. The subject recognizes itself as subject by answering to a socially established role — father, daughter, citizen, worker, critic. For an especially useful discussion of interpellation, see Slavoj Žižek, *The Sublime Object of Ideology* (New York: Verso, 1989), pp. 120–21.

58 Colie, "*My Ecchoing Song,*" describes the tension between the pastoral symbolic and the lover's Imaginary in terms of a passion that results in loss of self because it exceeds the generic decorum: "Passion in its gripping reality tends to rob the pastoralist of 'himself,' to distract him from going through the rites required in his free but carefully programmed landscape and society. The overriding domination of love destroys the delicacy and detachment of the pastoral artifice" (p. 31).

59 See the use of the sun in Augustine's adaptation of Plato's allegory of the cave in the *Soliloquiorum* I, 23.

60 See Haber, *Pastoral and the Poetics of Self-Contradiction,* p. 120: "Damon is wounded when the scythe in which he had seen his reflection 'glances' back at him. He is defeated, in effect, by his own diminished image. The triumph of fiction seems now to be complete."

61 On "The Garden," see chap. 1, pp. 26–32. On "Appleton House," see, chap. 6.

62 *Beyond the Pleasure Principle,* SE 18, pp. 14–17.

4. Spenser and the Metonymies of Virtue

1 *Othello* 1.1.42–44, 56–60. Shakespeare is cited from *The Riverside Shakespeare,* ed. G. Blakemore Evans et al. (Boston: Houghton Mifflin, 1974).

2 The locus classicus for this argument is, of course, Stephen Greenblatt, *Renaissance Self-Fashioning from More to Shakespeare* (Chicago: University of Chicago Press, 1980). In Greenblatt's view, the attempts of the subject to manipulate the social order from which his subjectivity emerges are generally recuperated by that order: "one of the highest achievements of power is to impose its fictions upon the world and one of its supreme pleasures is to enforce the acceptance of fictions that are known to be fictions" (p. 141). Louis Adrian Montrose articulates a more reflexive and therefore more liberal version of self-fashioning in "The Elizabethan Subject and the Spenserian Text," in *Literary Theory / Renaissance Texts,* ed. Patricia Parker and David Quint (Baltimore: Johns Hopkins University Press, 1986), p. 331: "Perhaps we could say, then, in response to Greenblatt's brilliant provocation, that one of the supreme pleasures available to the subject of power is to impose upon the fictions whose enforced acceptance signifies his subjection, the marks of his own subjectivity."

3 "Psychoanalysis and Renaissance Culture," in *Literary Theory / Renaissance Texts*, pp. 210–24; the quoted passage appears on p. 210. My remarks on this essay will pertain specifically to the issue of belatedness. For a fully elaborated psychoanalytic response to Greenblatt, see Elizabeth J. Bellamy, *Translations of Power: Narcissism and the Unconscious in Epic History* (Ithaca, N.Y.: Cornell University Press, 1992), pp. 1–22.

4 For an account of this sixteenth-century tale of imposture, which functions for Greenblatt as the exemplary anecdote of the New Historicism (its foundational Oedipus, so to speak), see Natalie Zemon Davis, *The Return of Martin Guerre* (Cambridge, Mass.: Harvard University Press, 1983).

5 In Natalie Zemon Davis's assessment, the evidence tends to support Arnaud's assertion that he had never met Martin Guerre, but, after having been mistaken for Martin, had prepared his imposture with material learned from others who had. See Davis, *The Return of Martin Guerre*, pp. 38–41. Bellamy displaces Greenblatt's dichotomy of legal and psychoanalytic subjects with a much more nuanced analysis of their emergence within the dialectic of self and other: "The sociocultural and contractual field that Jean de Coras's court draws from to make a legal determination concerning who is allowed to *be* Martin Guerre (that is, husband, son, nephew, heir to property) is precisely the psychic field of the other that Arnaud appropriates for the successful representation of himself as Martin. When the Law becomes implicated in the 'arresting' of the psychic other as the place of the signifier, it begins to lose its metaphysical grounding as the final arbiter of the identity. One could say that Arnaud 'knows' that his claim to be Martin resides in the 'unarrested' and sliding chain of signifiers that constitutes his 'dialectic of desire' to *be* Martin. In short, he seeks no higher authority beyond the other to ground his act of imposture. But the court at Artigat falls into the paradoxical trap of claiming that it *is* the 'other' for the other, that it *is* the metaphysical grounding for the signifier" (p. 9). The point is that both the legal and the psychoanalytic subjects are defined by sliding discursive interactions in which Arnaud is addressed as Martin and in which he answers to that address. Greenblatt's assertion of the primacy of the Law as the ground of these interpellations simply repeats the assertion of the court itself, while Bellamy's contention that Arnaud assumes Martin's identity by occupying the place Martin had left unoccupied in the web of signifying practices and interpersonal relations in Artigat conforms closely to Arnaud's own account before the court.

6 When Bellamy responds to Greenblatt so as to defend the historicism of her own psychoanalytic history of dynastic epic, she reaches a conclusion that is in many ways close to my own, though tied more restrictively to the specific requirements of dynastic epic (p. 253). Both of us are concerned to demonstrate a structure of

deferral shared by Spenser's narrative and thematized by Freud, but my literary historical aims are at once more general and more specific than hers.

7 In another response to Greenblatt, G. W. Pigman III argues: (1) Greenblatt's historicist claims rely on a distancing of the historical other that unduly suppresses an empathetic engagement with what remains the same in human experience across the ages; (2) the assumption of the "body's uniqueness and irreducibility," which Greenblatt ascribes to Freud, is shared by Renaissance commentators on the case; and (3) the empathetic "self psychology" of Hans Kohut and his followers (as opposed to the "Hegelian psychoanalysis" of Lacan) more accurately represents psychoanalytic practice than does Greenblatt's representation of psychoanalysis. "Limping Examples: Exemplarity, the New Historicism, and Psychoanalysis," in *Creative Imitation: New Essays on Renaissance Literature in Honor of Thomas M. Greene*, ed. David Quint, Margaret W. Ferguson, G. W. Pigman III, and Wayne A. Rebhorn (Binghamton, N.Y.: Medieval and Renaissance Texts and Studies, 1992), pp. 281–95. In respect of the dialectical genesis of the "belatedness effect" and of Pigman's "empathy" as well, I would agree with Greenblatt that the "Hegelianized psychoanalysis" of Lacan is more pertinent than the clinical pragmatics of Kohut. The clinical claims of psychoanalysis to one side, neither history nor literary history need aspire to be therapeutic.

8 See esp. *Shakespeare's Perjured Eye: The Invention of Poetic Subjectivity in the Sonnets* (Berkeley: University of California Press, 1986), and the essays now collected in *The Subjectivity Effect in Western Literary Tradition: Essays Toward the Release of Shakespeare's Will* (Cambridge, Mass.: MIT Press, 1991). For Fineman's compressed but pointed analysis of Greenblatt's premature privileging of a supracategorical but largely unarticulated history, see "The History of the Anecdote: Fiction as Fiction," TSE, pp. 59–90. See chap. 1, n. 8, above.

9 TSE, pp. 143–64. Fineman's discussion of Iago's "I follow him to serve my turn upon him" speech appears on p. 148.

10 Greenblatt, by producing Hobbes as a mediating term between literary and material social practice, comes, in the end, to a similar conclusion. In arguing that with his "conception of a person as a theatrical mask secured by authority, Hobbes seems far closer than Freud to the world of Shakespeare and, of course, Arnaud du Tilh" (p. 223), Greenblatt misses the point that Hobbes's absolutist resort to an "artificial person" who secures identity in the absence of a "layer deeper, more authentic, than theatrical self-representation" (p. 222) is a response to the same linguistically structured instability that Freud will later theorize. Thus, rather than establishing a self-evident hierarchy of historical authenticity, Greenblatt's recourse to Hobbes reiterates the Renaissance's experience of the self as something in excess of mean-

ing and thus in need of theoretical elucidation. (I am indebted to David Lee Miller for directing my attention to Greenblatt's use of Hobbes.)

11 See chap. 1, pp. 30–31.

12 For the critical history of Iago's narration of "Cassio's dream," see Bruce R. Smith, *Homosexual Desire in Shakespeare's England: A Cultural Poetics* (Chicago: University of Chicago Press, 1991), pp. 61–63.

13 The exchange thus illustrates an instance of Lacan's assertion that "the sender . . . receives from the receiver his own message in reverse form." "Seminar on 'The Purloined Letter,'" trans. Jeffrey Mehlman, *Yale French Studies* 48 (1973); rpt. in *The Purloined Poe: Lacan, Derrida and Psychoanalytic Reading,* ed. John P. Muller and William J. Richardson (Baltimore: Johns Hopkins University Press, 1988), pp. 52–53. A further instance of the inversion and transference of the primal fantasy in *Othello* would be Iago's otherwise notoriously unmotivated assertion that "it is thought abroad that 'twixt my sheets / [the Moor] H'as done my office" (1.3.387–88). See also 2.1.296–99.

14 I follow here Fineman's discussion of the evolution of the case history in relation to the New Historicist use of the anecdote in "The History of the Anecdote." On the logic of event and context in the medical case history, see TSE, pp. 65–67.

15 Jacques Lacan, *The Seminar of Jacques Lacan,* ed. Jacques-Alain Miller, Book 1, "Freud's Papers on Technique, 1953-1954," trans. with notes by John Forrester (New York: Norton, 1988), p. 36 (my emphasis). The original French appears in *Le Seminaire de Jacques Lacan,* vol. 1, ed. Jacques-Alain Miller (Paris: Éditions du Seuil, 1975), p. 46.

16 "Remembering, Repeating and Working Through," in the *Standard Edition of the Psychological Works of Sigmund Freud,* trans. James Strachey 24 vols. (London: Hogarth, 1953-74), 12:145–56. See also *Beyond the Pleasure Principle,* SE 18, pp. 18–19.

17 The persistent questioning of Iago's motivations in the history of the reception of *Othello* marks the play's complex thematization of this literary historical moment: to the extent that Iago is merely evil, Othello is also merely a Moor. The devil targets the convert, who is vulnerable because his ungodly origin retains the determining force of an essence. The literary historical pathos of the play derives from the way that both Iago and Othello struggle to represent themselves (to themselves) as self-made men.

18 "Seminar on the 'Purloined Letter,'" p. 53. For an early and important deconstructive response to Lacan's location of "truth" within an indivisible narrative closure, see Jean-Luc Nancy and Phillippe Lacoue-Labarthe, *The Title of the Letter: A Reading of Lacan,* trans. François Raffoul and David Pettigrew (Albany: State University

of New York Press, 1992), esp. pp. 86–104. Contra Nancy and Lacoue-Labarthe, see Slavoj Žižek, *The Sublime Object of Ideology* (London: Verso), p. 158.

19 Jacques Derrida, "Le Facteur de la Vérité," in *The Post Card: From Socrates to Freud and Beyond*, trans. Alan Bass (Chicago: University of Chicago Press, 1987), p. 414. Derrida's concern with the investment of psychoanalysis in recovering the scene of a narration is given more general scope in the earlier "Freud and the Scene of Writing," in *Writing and Difference*, trans. Alan Bass (Chicago: University of Chicago Press, 1978), pp. 196–231.

20 Freud's manifesto, taken from the *New Introductory Lectures*, 31, SE 22, p. 80: "[The] intention [of psychoanalysis] is, indeed, to strengthen the ego, to make it more independent of the super-ego, to widen its field of perception and enlarge its organization, so that it can appropriate fresh portions of the id. *Where id was, there ego shall be. It is a work of culture—not unlike the draining of the Zuider Zee*" (my italics). I prefer to Strachey's translation a more literal rendering—"Where it was, shall I become," because it retains the scheme of chiasmus from the original and makes clearer the elements of estrangement and appropriation incurred in Freud's effort to bring the dark parts of the psyche to light. See Lacan's discussion of the phrase in "La chose freudienne: ou sens du retour à Freud en psychanalyse," in *Écrits* (Paris: Seuil, 1966), p. 417. (I cite the French edition here because, although this essay is included in *Écrits: A Selection*, a comparison of alternative French translations of a German text, carried out in English, is of limited help.)

21 "Fragment of an Analysis of a Case of Hysteria," SE 7, p. 10.

22 Freud situates the secondary revision as external to the dream, a process that occurs principally at the moments of waking and recounting, when the return of conscious life supplies an exigent end to the primary dream work. Thus, the secondary revision represents the narrativizing aspect of the dream work, the *dilatio* through which the dream's figurations will ultimately return to their proper form. See *The Interpretation of Dreams* in SE 5, p. 499.

23 See Žižek's remarks on the psychoanalytic import of the proper noun in *The Sublime Object of Ideology*, p. 92. See also Fineman, TSE, pp. 154–56.

24 "From the History of an Infantile Neurosis," SE 17, see esp. pp. 37–38, n. 6. Although the comments in the analysis of the "Wolfman" are the locus classicus for a theoretical elaboration of *Nachträglichkeit*, the term appears in writings as early as the 1895, *Project for a Scientific Psychology*. See the entry "Deferred Action, Deferred," in J. Laplanche and J.-B. Pontalis, *The Language of Psycho-Analysis*, trans. Donald Nicholson-Smith (New York: Norton, 1973).

25 It is at this point that Freud, determining that there is no functional difference between a real and a phantasied traumatic origin, begins to abandon the seduction

theory according to which the etiology of every neurosis includes an early sexual trauma. Freud's acceptance of the constitutive ambiguity of the analytic presentation of sexual trauma as either the precipitating cause *or a pro dromo* symptom of obsessional neurosis thenceforth fully incorporates metalepsis in the rhetoric of the case history.

26 *Écrits: A Selection,* trans. Alan Sheridan (New York: Norton, 1977), p. 86.

27 *The Works of Edmund Spenser: A Variorum Edition,* ed. Edwin Greenlaw, Charles Grosvenor Osgood, and Frederick Morgan Padelford, 10 vols. (Baltimore: Johns Hopkins University Press, 1932–57), 1:168–69. All citations of Spenser refer to this edition.

28 See Jonathan Goldberg's deconstructive etiology of the interminable nature of *The Faerie Queene,* esp. as figured in the marriage of the Medway and Thames, pp. 134–44 and passim. *Endlesse Worke: Spenser and the Structures of Discourse* (Baltimore: Johns Hopkins University Press, 1981). John Guillory explores the coincidence in *The Faerie Queene* of the "quest for origins" and the "quest for the gratification of desire." See *Poetic Authority: Spenser, Milton and Literary History* (New York: Columbia University Press, 1983), pp. 23–45. See also Elizabeth J. Bellamy, "The Vocative and the Vocational: The Unreadability of Elizabeth in *The Faerie Queene,*" ELH 54 (1987): 1–30. For Bellamy the lack of a metaphoric closure to *The Faerie Queene* marks Spenser's inability to "name his queen, to call forth her image from behind her 'couert vele' (2 proem 5.2) as the ultimate sanctioner of his epic task" (1): "Because the metonymies which seek to name Elizabeth proliferate rather than coalesce toward Pure Name, the poet must construct a 'figural superposition,' the realm of faerie and of Gloriana, that narrates the unreadability of Elizabeth's name — and for that matter of a Briton *telos.* Even as the poet seeks to name Elizabeth, the superposition of the faerie Gloriana narrates his failure to do so" (pp. 5–7). The literary historical question raised by Spenser's proliferating metonymies is: why do they proliferate rather than coalesce? Is it because of Spenser's inadequacy as a dynastic poet or the inadequacy of dynastic romance to Spenser's material circumstances? Once this question is opened, it is possible for psychoanalysis to find what is beyond itself: the possibility that the "figural superposition" is not simply a formal requirement of dynastic romance (we know empirically — from the *Gerusalemme Liberata,* for example — that it is not), but rather a historical choice — indeterminately made by Spenser as poetic subject or by his text as material process or by the collaboration of the two — that formally opens the anecdote of the text and keeps the text open to exigent events by refusing the allegorical closure of History as destined and determined cause.

29 The ambiguous temporality of Spenser's "I" is already inscribed in his archaicizing

choice of "wote," a present tense verb formed on the present preterit stem of OE "wit," as its first predicate. See *OED* wot 1 and wit, vol. 1.

30 The *Discorsi* was not published until 1594, but Tasso mentions what appears to be a first draft (probably of the 1587 *Discorsi del'arte poetica*) in a letter to Bartolomeo di Porzia, 13 November 1574. Irene Samuel suggests 1561–62 as the likely time for the first composition of the *Discorsi*. See Torquato Tasso, *Discourses on the Heroic Poem*, trans. with notes by Mariella Cavalchini and Irene Samuel (Oxford: Clarendon Press, 1973), pp. xi–xii. (Subsequent citations of the *Discourses* refer to this edition and are given parenthetically.) Mazzoni invokes the distinction between the icastic and phantastic imaginations in his 1587 *Difesa della comedia di Dante*, which Tasso cites and criticizes (*Discourses*, pp. 28–29). Some of the discussion of Ariosto appears in Tasso's, *Discorsi dell' arte poetica; et in particolare del poema eroico*, 1587. Given his obvious knowledge of Tasso and Ariosto and the Italian controversies over the romance elements in the *Orlando Furioso*, we are on safe ground in assuming Spenser's familiarity with the substance of Tasso's argument whether or not he had actually read any portion of the *Discorsi* before the 1590 publication of *The Faerie Queene*. For an excellent (and concise) discussion of Spenser's involvement with Tasso's response to the attack on Ariosto during the composition of the 1590 *Faerie Queene*, see Richard Helgerson, *Forms of Nationhood: The Elizabethan Writing of England* (Chicago: University of Chicago Press, 1992), pp. 40–62. Helgerson sees the Counter Reformation controversy about the romance elements in the *Orlando Furioso* mapped out on the historically specific landscape of England as a tension between epic containment and chivalric individualism in *The Faerie Queene*, with Spenser finally, if covertly, favoring chivalric and implicitly Protestant initiative against the enclosing state power of epic containment. For a useful discussion of Spenser's handling of the question of whether "imagination represents an object or begets it," see Guillory, *Poetic Authority*, pp. 35–38.

31 See *Summa Theologica*, 1.48.1. Tasso (or Spenser) could have found an even more pointed formulation in the *Soliloquia* (2.18), where Augustine's "R[eason]" argues that art is always true by being false, because it is truly itself only insofar as it is not that which it imitates: "What think you, unless that all these things [poems, jests, and other imitative trifles] are in certain aspects true, by this very thing that they are in certain aspects false, and that for their quality of truth this alone avails them, that they are false in another regard? Whence to that which they either will or ought to be, they in no wise attain, if they avoid being false. For how could he whom I have mentioned have been a true tragedian, had he been unwilling to be a false Hector, a false Andromache, a false Hercules, and innumerable other things? or how would a picture, for instance, be a true picture, unless it were a false horse? or how could

there be in a mirror a true image of a man, if it were not a false man?" (trans. Charles C. Starbuck in *A Select Library of the Nicene and Post-Nicene Fathers*, 7: 553).

32 For a similar argument relating principally to *De Magistro*, see Linda Gregerson, *The Reformation of the Subject: Spenser, Milton, and the English Protestant Epic* (Cambridge: Cambridge University Press, 1995) pp. 62–69. Guillory's observation that "A certain parallel is established very early in Spenser's career between restraint as a poetic necessity and restraint as a principle of sexual morality" and that the "two themes are usually equated allegorically only where they both fail: in the disastrous collapsing together of desire and fantasy" (*Poetic Authority*, p. 41) also points to the homologous structure of the allegory of the birds and fishes in Augustine's *Confessions*.

33 See Lacan's "algorithmic" representation of the interplay of metonymy ("the connection between signifier and signifier") and metaphor ("the substitution of signifier for signifier") in the production of the subject, whose desire is "split between a refusal of the signifier and a lack of being." "Agency of the Letter in the Unconscious," *Écrits: A Selection*, pp. 163–66.

34 Torquato Tasso, "The Allegorie of the Poem," cited from *Godfrey of Bulloinge or the Recoverie of Ierusalem Done into English Heroicall Verse*, by Edward Fairfax, Gent. (London, 1600). No pagination. *The Faerie Queene*, like the *Gerusalemme Liberata*, is a dynastic romance, and Tasso's "Allegorie of the Poem" is almost certainly the model for Spenser's "Letter to Ralegh." The "Allegory" is included in the 1581 Ferrara and subsequent editions of the *Gerusalemme Liberata*. On Spenser's access to, and use of it, see Helgerson, *Forms of Nationhood*, pp. 47–50, 310, n. 42. Paul J. Alpers, in *The Poetry of "The Faerie Queene"* (Princeton, N.J.: Princeton University Press, 1967), pp. 19–22, argues, without reference to "The Allegorie," that Spenser's narrative mode rejects Tasso and follows Sidney in making *The Faerie Queene* "a continual address to the reader rather than . . . a fictional world" (p. 21). The polemic of Alpers's larger argument seems to me to lead to an overestimation of the difference between Tasso and Spenser. My argument that *The Faerie Queene* registers a tension between "imitation" and "allegory" does not imply that the poem's mimesis offers a coherent fictional world.

35 See David Lee Miller's excellent discussion of "The Aesthetic Theology of *The Faerie Queene*," in *The Poem's Two Bodies: The Poetics of the 1590 "Faerie Queene"* (Princeton, N.J.: Princeton University Press, 1988), pp. 71–82, esp. p. 76.

36 See Bellamy's remark: "As the muse of history, Clio serves to undermine Calliope as the unceasing flux of historical fact threatens to expose the potential hypocrisy of dynastic epic. In the final analysis, the reader cannot know who presides over the 'euerlasting scryne' " which holds the story of *The Faerie Queene*—the historical

fiction of Calliope or the fictive history of Clio." "The Vocative and the Vocational," p. 26, n. 10.

37 Maureen Quilligan notes that the fashioning of a "gentleman or noble person" in the "Letter to Ralegh" applies at once to the fashioning of the character of Prince Arthur in the text and to the poem's constructive effect on its readers, making the important observation that the phrase "gentleman or noble person" admits the fashioning of a female as well as a male audience. *Milton's Spenser: The Politics of Reading* (Ithaca, N.Y.: Cornell University Press, 1983), p. 38.

38 See Bellamy in *Translations of Power*, pp. 236–38: "Spenser's epic is highly self-conscious of its unfinished status. . . . In his prefatory 'Letter to Ralegh,' Spenser has to admit to a potential temporal confusion posited by his epic's putative twelve-book structure. . . . Because, as Spenser also admits in his 'Letter,' the beginning of his epic 'depends vpon other antecedents' that are almost impossible to consolidate, *The Faerie Queene* traces a complex network of retrogressions, interruptions, and reiterations. Repeatedly it finds itself stalling in the temporal lassitude of being positioned 'in the middest' or, even more ambiguously, on the deferred threshold of 'a-while' " (p. 237).

39 David Lee Miller remarks, in "Spenser's Vocation, Spenser's Career," *ELH* 50 (1983): 215: "Spenser's work seems marked by the combination of urgency and subtlety with which he engages contemporary history; if his sense of poetic vocation is one measure of his confidence . . . [in transcendence], the dynamics of self-presentation in his work are a measure — one among many — of his engagement with history, specifically of his engagement *as a poet* with the cultural and political institutions of late sixteenth-century England."

40 See *Discourses*, pp. 40–41, for Tasso's reasons for choosing a subject "neither very recent nor very ancient."

41 Elizabeth Boyle's covert entry into *The Faerie Queene* is further abetted by allusions to the *Epithalamion* in FQ 6.10.10, 14, 15, and 16. See also Kenneth Gross's excellent discussion of the evocation of the fourth grace on Mount Acidale. *Spenserian Poetics: Idolatry, Iconoclasm, and Magic* (Ithaca, N.Y.: Cornell University Press, 1985), pp. 218–19. The identification of the fourth grace as Elizabeth Boyle is considered but rejected in favor of "ideal feminine courtesy," in R. F. Hill, "Colin Clout's Courtesy," *Modern Language Review* 57 (1962): 492–503; see esp. 500–503.

42 See Charles Grosvenor Osgood, ed., *A Concordance to the Poems of Edmund Spenser* (Washington, D.C.: Carnegie Institution, 1915), under "midst." Osgood records six occurrences of "midst" or "middest" in 6.10.10–23, by far the highest concentration in the poem. For purposes of comparison, the next highest concentration occurs in 4.10, where three occurrences are spread over stanzas 8, 39, and 52. See

also Michael Bayback, Paul Delany, and A. Kent Hieatt, "Placement 'In the Mid-dest' in *The Faerie Queene*," *Papers on Language and Literature* 5 (1969): 227–34.

43 In this paragraph and the following one I am much indebted to Guillory, *Poetic Authority*. See esp. pp. 28–33. For an acute discussion of the etiology and implications of the appearance of Colin Clout on Mount Acidale, see Miller, "Spenser's Vocation, Spenser's Career," p. 218. Miller remarks, in *The Poem's Two Bodies*, p. 142: "From a point of view that remains firmly in 'the middest,' the difference between randomness and design will always be undecidable, and this is as true for the reader as it is for the protagonist: the final form, or 'centered structure,' of the poem itself is never more than an attempted sublimation of copious textuality into meaning, a conjectural grid by which we seek to invest interpretive errancy with the illusion of inevitability."

44 On the general case of the Lady or "She" subject to incomparable comparison in Renaissance epideictics, see Fineman, *Shakespeare's Perjured Eye*, pp. 21–24. See also Gross's comparison of "the crisis of allegory" on Mount Acidale to that in Petrarch's "Ascent of Mount Ventoux" (*Spenserian Poetics*, pp. 221–24).

45 The ironic (re)turn to sender of *The Faerie Queene* is chiastically concealed in Cali-dore's name, which can be derived from (among other etymologies), *kallidoron* "beauty-gift" or "gift of grace." Thus, the "not happy" Colin is deprived of the gifts of the graces by his encounter with the "unhappy" gift of grace (6.10.20.1–2); or, one might say, Calidore delivers the coup de grace to *The Faerie Queene*. On the complex play of names in *The Faerie Queene*, see Alastair Fowler, "Spenser's Names," in *Unfolded Tales: Essays on Renaissance Romance*, ed. George M. Logan and Gordon Teskey (Ithaca, N.Y.: Cornell University Press, 1989), pp. 32–48. The derivation of Calidore from *kallidoron* appears on p. 36. Patricia Parker observes of the generally recursive tendency of Book 6: "The poem itself seems to be re-turning to its beginnings, as Serena recalls Una, Acidale the House of Holiness, the Hermit Contemplation, and the 'harrowing' of the brigands' cave the recovery of Eden. The legend is even generically in touch with origins, in its return to pastoral, a traditional and, for Spenser, actual early mode. But the Book which asks to be shown the source of its own virtue also calls into question the return to origins or the possibility of their recovery, emphasizing the gap as often as the link between origin and issue, including the 'origin' which is etymology ('Of Court it *seemes*, men Courtesie doe call . . .,' i. 1. 1)" (*Inescapable Romance: Studies in the Poetics of a Mode* [Princeton, N.J.: Princeton University Press, 1979], p. 107; Parker's italics). See also James Nohrnberg, *The Analogy of "The Faerie Queene"* (Princeton, N.J.: Princeton University Press, 1976), pp. 663–64. In discussing "the motif of secret or concealed *origins*" in Book 6, Nohrnberg precedes me in referring to the vision on Acidale as a discovery of the primal scene (p. 664).

46 Many critics have noted that Calidore's interruption of Colin and the Graces in canto 10 repeats his earlier interruption of Calipine and Serena in canto 3, and that it is this earlier interruption that elicits the first appearance of the Blatant Beast. See, for example, A. Bartlett Giamatti, *Play of Double Senses: Spenser's "Faerie Queene"* (Englewood Cliffs, N.J.: Prentice-Hall, 1975), pp. 69; Humphrey Tonkin, *Spenser's Courteous Pastoral: Book Six of "The Faerie Queene"* (Oxford: Clarendon Press, 1972), pp. 48–53, 122; and Harry Berger, Jr., *Revisionary Play: Studies in the Spenserian Dynamics* (Berkeley: University of California Press, 1988), p. 31.

47 For further discussion of Spenser's ironic presentation of Calidore's courtesy, see Richard Neuse, "Book VI as Conclusion to *The Faerie Queene,*" *ELH* 35 (1968): 329–53; esp. 342–44. Neuse sees in Book VI an ironic presentation of the failure of courtesy. In my view, Spenser's text goes beyond Neuse's assumption that there is a *right* courtesy which Spenser's England gets wrong to a questioning of the civil / savage binary that provides the architecture of its narrative. Calidore's courteous deception of Priscilla's father is just the most *blatant* instance in a series of episodes designed to disclose the presence of the savage in the civil and the civil in the savage. The lethal mix of reverence and brutality with which the cannibals approach Serena (discussed by Neuse, "Book VI as Conclusion," pp. 347–48) would be another.

48 See Annabel Patterson, *Pastoral and Ideology: Virgil to Valéry* (Berkeley: University of California Press, 1987), pp. 131–32, for a persuasive account of Spenser's ironic allegorization of pastoral as a child of the court.

49 *Revisionary Play,* pp. 215–42; see esp. pp. 216–17. Berger makes a similar point in "Narrative as Rhetoric in *The Faerie Queene,*" *ELR* 21 (1991): 3–48. "The question is, does it make a difference if, instead of merely reading the poem as a piece of storytelling, we approach it as a poem that *represents* storytelling, and does so in a manner that isn't innocent, a manner that interrogates the values and motives, the politics and ideology, embedded in the structure of storytelling?" (p. 3). On the "metadiscursivity" of *The Faerie Queene,* see the "Afterword" to Berger, *Revisionary Play,* pp. 462–73.

50 See, for example, the confrontation of courtly pastoral and the sensuous materiality of sheepherding staged by the country boy, Shakespeare, in the dialogue of Corin and Touchstone in *As You Like It* 3.2.11–85.

51 On the sexual content of Britomart's dream, see Gross, *Spenserian Poetics,* pp. 174–80, and Julia M. Walker, "Spenser's Elizabeth Portrait and the Fiction of Dynastic Epic," *Modern Philology* 90 (1992): 172–199, esp. 192–94, 197.

52 "Salmacis and Hermaphroditus," *Metamorphoses,* Book 4. On Spenser's use of Ovid's story of the Hermaphrodite, see Donald Cheney, "Spenser's Hermaphrodite and the 1590 *Faerie Queene,*" *PMLA* 87 (1972): 192–200, and Lauren Silberman, "The Hermaphrodite and the Metamorphosis of Spenserian Allegory," *ELR*

17 (1987): 207–23. Dorothy Stephens notes the "proprietary voyeurism of the 'rich Romane' who once erected a marble hermaphrodite, which he himself had carved." "Into Other Arms: Amoret's Evasion," *ELH* 58 (1991): 374.

53 See S. K. Heninger, Jr., "The Orgoglio Episode in *The Faerie Queene*," *ELH* 26 (1959): 171–87.

54 The story of the incest of Myrrha and her father, of which Adonis is issue, appears in Book 10 of *The Metamorphoses*. For an excellent elaboration of the originary role of incest throughout Spenser's Legend of Chastity, see Nohrnberg, *The Analogy of "The Faerie Queene,"* pp. 436–52, esp. his discussion of Spenser's use of the story of Myrrha in connection with the depictions of Malecasta and Britomart, pp. 442–48.

55 Montrose aptly remarks: "This female other is represented as threatening the male subject with more than sexual enthrallment: the climactic image of the bare bosomed witch cradling the slumbering youth in her lap makes it evident that she is also threatening him with maternal engulfment" ("The Elizabethan Subject and the Spenserian Text," p. 329). In "Narrative as Rhetoric in *The Faerie Queene*," Berger explores "the fantasy of male disempowerment by virulent or erotic female forces" in several parallel episodes in Book 2, most notably the "Acrasian variant" in Phedon's tale, 4:17–18 ("Narrative as Rhetoric," p. 19).

56 On the *anaclisis*, or propping, of desire on the infantile relation to the breast, see Freud, *Three Essays on the Theory of Sexuality*, SE 7, pp. 222–30, and Jean Laplanche, *Life and Death in Psychoanalysis*, trans. Jeffrey Mehlman (Baltimore: Johns Hopkins University Press, 1976), pp. 14–18. In the psychoanalytic notion of anaclisis, the desire for an object ultimately derives from the infantile desire to incorporate the mother as the source of food and security. By a metonymy of the container for the contained, the desire to incorporate the mother becomes the desire to be (re)incorporated in her—as Adonis is reincorporated within the Mount of Venus in 3.6.48. In both Freud and Spenser the maternal object thus figures as a metaphoric origin from which desire proceeds metonymically along its errant ways. For a useful discussion of the mother's breast as "the origin of representation," see Elizabeth J. Bellamy, "Reading Desire Backwards: Belatedness and Spenser's Arthur," *SAQ* 88 (1989): 789–809, esp. 798–809. The persistent reemergence of the maternal figure in *The Faerie Queene* may also be compared with the mediating role played by the death of Monica (who, we recall, had earlier been abandoned at Ostia in a reenactment of Aeneas's desertion of Dido) in Augustine's more successful return to an originary Father in the *Confessions*. See chap. 3 above. Spenser's punning superimposition of French *blesser* and English *bliss* to denote the wound of love is noted by Quilligan, *Milton's Spenser*, p. 199.

57 See Jacques Lacan, "Television," trans. Denis Holier, Rosalind Krauss, and Annette Michelson in *October* 40 (1987): 34: "The sexual impasse exudes the fictions that

rationalize the impossible within which it originates. I don't say they are imagined; like Freud, I read in them the invitation to the real that underwrites them." See also Fineman's discussion (TSE, pp. 143–64) of the impasse in "The Sound of O in Othello," where Lacan's statement appears as an epigraph.

58 *"Il n'y a pas La femme, article défini pour désigner l'universal. Il n'y a pas La femme puisque . . . de son essence, elle n'est pas toute."* Le séminaire de Jacques Lacan, ed. Jacques-Alain Miller, vol. 20, Encore (Paris: Éditions du Seuil, 1975), p. 68. See also Marshall Grossman, "Servile / Sterile / Style: Milton and the Question of Woman," in *Milton and the Idea of Woman,* ed. Julia Walker (Urbana: University of Illinois Press, 1988), pp. 148–68.

59 *Civilization and Its Discontents,* SE, vol. 21, p. 106, n. 3 (chap. 4). For yet another striking (and unusually aggressive) example, see the stripping of Serena by the savage *cannibals* culminating in the exposure of "Her goodly thighes, whose glorie did appeare / Like a triumphall Arch, and thereupon / The spoiles of Princes hang'd, which were in battel won" (6.8.427–29).

60 For an apt discussion of the limitations of the diagnostic approach of applied psychoanalysis, see Shoshana Felman, *Jacques Lacan and the Adventure of Insight: Psychoanalysis in Contemporary Culture* (Cambridge, Mass.: Harvard University Press, 1987), pp. 32–46.

61 Max Horkheimer and Theodor W. Adorno, *Dialectic of Enlightenment,* trans. John Cumming (New York: Continuum, 1990). On Spenser's contribution to the revaluation of work, see Anthony Low, *The Georgic Revolution* (Princeton, N.J.: Princeton University Press, 1985), pp. 35–70. What I here refer to as the radical contingency of the event corresponds to what Lacan calls, after Aristotle, the touché, the "encounter with the real." *The Four Fundamental Concepts of Psycho-Analysis,* ed. Jacques-Alain Miller, trans. Alan Sheridan (New York: Norton, 1978), pp. 53–64.

62 *PMLA* 101 (1986): 9–23.

63 See Marshall Grossman, *"Authors to Themselves": Milton and the Revelation of History* (New York: Cambridge University Press, 1987).

64 On Spenser's (Aristotelian) treatment of virtue as habit, see Ernest Sirluck, "Milton Revises *The Faerie Queene,*" *Modern Philology* 48 (1950): 90–96, and Teskey, "Imagining Error in Spenser and Milton," p. 10.

65 See also Isabel G. MacCaffrey, *Spenser's Allegory: The Anatomy of Imagination* (Princeton, N.J.: Princeton University Press, 1976), pp. 178–87. Opposing psychologizing readings of Spenser's characters, MacCaffrey cautions: "To insist that all the poems's actions must occur in some character's psyche is to muddle the considerable complications of Spenser's ontology in *The Faerie Queene.* It will not do to rationalize the poem too far, or to say that the poet is invariably consistent in suggesting the kind of reality possessed by the various inhabitants of Fairy Land"

(pp. 180–81). MacCaffrey comes especially close to Teskey when she observes that "Spenser does not ordinarily embody in other human knights aspects of his heroes' psychic life; such minor characters are related to the hero rather as alternative versions of his virtue, or instances of it in other contexts" (p. 181).

66 The general case of what happens to dialectical negation in Spenser's text may be elaborated in terms of Žižek's psychoanalytic transcription of the Hegelian subject: "The Hegelian subject . . . is nothing but the very gap which separates phenomena from the Thing, the abyss beyond phenomena conceived in its negative mode, i.e., the purely negative gesture of limiting phenomena without providing any positive content which would fill out the space beyond the limit. . . . The standard notion of the gradual becoming-subject of the substance (of the 'active' subject leaving its 'imprint' on the substance, molding it, mediating it, expressing it in his subjective content) is here doubly misleading. First, we must bear in mind that with Hegel this subjectivization of the object never 'turns out': there is always a remainder of the substance which eludes the grasp of 'subjective mediation'; and far from being a simple impediment preventing the subject's full actualization, this remainder is *stricto sensu* correlative to the very being of the subject. We reach thereby one of the possible definitions of [the Lacanian] *objet a:* that surplus of the Substance, that 'bone,' which *resists subjectivization; objet a* is correlative to the subject in its very radical incommensurability with it. Secondly, we have the opposite notion according to which the subject is that very 'nothing,' the purely formal void which is left over after the substantial content has wholly 'passed over' into its predicates-determinations: in the 'subjectivization' of Substance, its compact In-itself is dissolved into the multitude of its particular predicates-determinations, of its 'beings-for other,' and 'subject' is that very X, the empty form of a 'container,' which remains after all its content was 'subjectivized.' These two conceptions are strictly correlative, i.e., 'subject' and 'object' are the two left-overs of this same process, or, rather, the two sides of the same left-over, conceived either in the modality of form (subject) or in the modality of content, of 'stuff' (object): *a* is the 'stuff' of the subject qua empty form." (*Tarrying with the Negative: Kant, Hegel, and the Critique of Ideology* [Durham, N.C.: Duke University Press, 1993], pp. 21–22). The dialectical and the diegetical alternatives, represented by Spenserian and Miltonic narration, respectively, are realized according to whether, at the site of the negation of the negation, the remainder or "stuff" of the object is deferred to the fulfillment of the Spirit, i.e., placed at the limit of the narrative frame—as in Milton's evocation of a time beyond time when "God shall be All in All" *Paradise Lost* 3, 341)—or cycled back into history as a subjective agency to be realized in yet another narrative segment—as in the doubling of Arthur and Gloriana, not only

by Artegall and Britomart, but also, respectively, by the individual (Aristotelian) knight-virtues and Amoret, Belphoebe, Florimell, Medina, et al.

67 On the dialogic nature of psychoanalytic transference, see Felman, *Jacques Lacan and the Adventure of Insight,* pp. 56–58.

68 George T. Wright, *Shakespeare's Metrical Art* (Berkeley: University of California Press, 1988), p. 152.

69 Ibid., p. 158.

70 On "Amoret's fear of sexual love in marriage," see Thomas P. Roche, Jr., *The Kindly Flame: A Study of the Third and Fourth Books of Spenser's "Faerie Queene"* (Princeton, N.J.: Princeton University Press, 1964), pp. 72–88.

5. Refiguring the Remains of the World in Donne's *Anniversaries*

1 What is at stake for Renaissance thought in relating the particular to the universal in ways that make intelligible the "particular event in time" is brilliantly rendered in J. G. A. Pocock's *The Machiavellian Moment: Florentine Political Thought and the Atlantic Republican Tradition* (Princeton, N.J.: Princeton University Press, 1975), pp. 3–80.

2 The same failed exchange is dramatized in the third act "closet scene," when Gertrude's "Hamlet, thou hast thy father much offended," elicits the reply, "Mother, you have my father much offended" (3.4.9–10). Similarly, Hamlet's repression of Gertrude's name under the generic "woman," in "Frailty, thy name is woman!" in his first soliloquy, delivered near the close of Act 1, Scene 2, prepares the way for the transfer of his hostility toward his mother to Woman in general and then to Ophelia, emptied of her particular accidents and rendered as generic Woman: "I have heard of your paintings, well enough. God hath given you one face, and you make yourselves another. You jig and amble, and you lisp, you nick-name God's creatures and make your wantonness your ignorance" (3.1.142–46). Hamlet's complaint is that women differ from themselves and thus exceed the categories that ought to contain them.

3 Joel Fineman, *Shakespeare's Perjured Eye: The Invention of Poetic Subjectivity in the Sonnets* (Berkeley: University of California Press, 1986), p. 12. Aristotle is quoted from *Poetics,* 1459a, pp. 16–18, in the Loeb Classical Library, ed. E. Capps (New York: G. Putnam and Sons, 1927). See also Tasso's "signs having the power to perfect," discussed in chap. 4, p. 124.

4 *Confessions,* Book 13, chap. 24, discussed in chap. 3 above. See esp. chap. 3, n. 10.

5 One might note that what unfolds in this analysis is the rhetorical operation underlying the Heideggerean ontology of the logos as the distancing of the thing. See

"The Thing," in *Poetry, Language, Thought,* trans. Albert Hofstadter (New York: Harper Colophon Books, 1975), pp. 163–86, esp. 176–77.

6 See chap. 4 above.

7 Martin Heidegger, *An Introduction to Metaphysics,* trans. Ralph Manheim (New Haven, Conn.: Yale University Press, 1959), pp. 128–34.

8 Martin Heidegger, "The Thing," p. 177: "The presence of something present . . . comes into its own, appropriately manifests and determines itself, only from the thinging of the thing." See also the discussion of Heidegger's notions of alethia, logos, and the thing in Mikkel Borch-Jacobsen, *Lacan: The Absolute Master,* trans. Douglas Brick (Stanford: Stanford University Press, 1991), esp. pp. 104–13.

9 See Jacques Lacan, "The Agency of the Letter in the Unconscious or Reason since Freud," in *Écrits: A Selection,* trans. Alan Sheridan (New York: Norton, 1977), pp. 153–59, on the relation of metaphor to metonymy in the constituting of the self as the subject of desire.

10 For example, see Arthur Marotti, *John Donne: Coterie Poet* (Madison: University of Wisconsin Press, 1986); David Aers, Bob Hodge, and Gunther Kress, *Language, Literature, and Society in England, 1580–1680* (Totowa, N.J.: Barnes and Noble, 1981); John Carey, *John Donne: Mind and Art* (New York: Oxford University Press, 1981). See also the political contextualizations of Donne by David Norbrook, in "The Monarchy of Wit and the Republic of Letters: Donne's Politics," and Annabel Patterson, in "All Donne," both in *Soliciting Interpretation: Literary Theory and Seventeenth-Century English Poetry,* ed. Elizabeth D. Harvey and Katharine Eisaman Maus (Chicago: University of Chicago Press, 1990). Stanley Fish's, "Masculine Persuasive Force: Donne and Verbal Power," also in the Harvey and Mauss volume, comes closer to the concerns of this chapter.

11 Samuel Johnson, *Lives of the English Poets,* ed. George Birbeck Hill, 3 vols. (Oxford: Clarendon Press, 1905), 1: 18–35. Johnson identifies the metaphysical element as specifically non-mimetic or antimimetic: "These writers will without great wrong lose their right to the name of poets, for they cannot be said to have imitated any thing: they neither copied nature nor life; neither painted the forms of matter nor represented the operations of the intellect" (p. 19). T. S. Eliot, "The Metaphysical Poets," in *Selected Essays: 1917–1932* (London: Faber and Faber, 1932), pp. 267–77. I am anticipated on this point by Barbara Lewalski, who remarks: "Analysis of Donne's occasional poetry of compliment in relation to contemporary exercises in the kind has revealed that his characteristic approach to the poetry of praise is in a strict sense metaphysical—that his praises are directed not to the particular qualities of individuals, but to the image of God which they severally may bear." *Donne's* Anniversaries *and the Poetry of Praise: The Creation of a Symbolic Mode* (Princeton, N.J.: Princeton University Press, 1973), p. 111.

12 Donne initiates the division of Jack Donne from Dr. Donne in a 1619 letter, which he sent to Sir Robert Ker, along with a manuscript of *Biathanatos:* "Let any that your discretion admits to the sight of it, know the date of it; and that it is a Book written by *Jack Donne,* and not by *D. Donne.*" *Letters to Severall Persons of Honour* (London, 1651), p. 22. It is worth noting that in the context of this *original* letter, the two Donnes are already at once sequential and contemporaneous; the present Doctor mediates the superseded Jack to Ker and the readers with whom Ker chooses to share the enclosed text.

13 For a fully elaborated discussion of *The Anniversaries* as a variety of epideictic verse, see Lewalski, *Donne's* Anniversaries *and the Poetry of Praise,* pp. 11–70.

14 All citations of the *Anniversaries* refer to *John Donne: "The Anniversaries,"* ed. Frank Manley (Baltimore: Johns Hopkins University Press, 1963).

15 "Donne's Anatomy Lesson: Vesalian or Paracelsian?" *John Donne Journal* 3 (1984): 35. Although I develop different implications of the distinction than does Willard, I am indebted to him for emphasizing its importance.

16 On Donne's personal and social situation as the impoverished son of a distinguished recussant family, see Carey, *John Donne: Mind and Art.* On his place as a gentlemen amateur within the system in which courtly literature was produced and distributed, see Richard Helgerson, *Self-Crowned Laureates: Spenser, Jonson, Milton and the Literary System* (Berkeley: University of California Press, 1983), and Marotti, *John Donne: Coterie Poet.*

17 For details of the commission and Donne's subsequent relations with the girl's father, see R. C. Bald, *Donne and the Drurys* (Cambridge: Cambridge University Press, 1959).

18 *Ben Jonson,* ed. Ian Donaldson (Oxford: Oxford University Press, 1985), p. 596.

19 For a remarkably detailed and informative history of Donne's "idea," see Edward W. Tayler, *Donne's Idea of a Woman: Structure and Meaning in the Anniversaries* (New York: Columbia University Press, 1991). Although I am substantially in agreement with Tayler about the scholastic etiology of Donne's "idea," my analytic methods and vocabulary should make clear my dissent from Tayler's polemic. Briefly, I justify the division of Tayler's historical analyses from his polemic on the basis of a disagreement about philology. Tayler seems to believe that once a word or phrase has been established as a philosophical term of art it can be walled off from other meanings and usages, contemporary and subsequent. Most notably, he attempts to isolate the Aristotelian notion of "idea," as it is principally established in *De Anima* and commentaries on *De Anima,* from the Platonic or Platonically inflected "idea" also active in the Renaissance. My own sense of how language works and my reading of Renaissance discussions of the two "ideas" convince me that, in general, linguistic usages inevitably bleed into each other and, in particular, the distinction

between Aristotelian and Platonic "ideas" was not well understood in the Renaissance. (See, for example, the constant and seamless slippage between Plato and Aristotle in Sidney's "An Apology for Poetry.")

20 Edmund Gosse, ed. *The Life and Letters of John Donne,* 2 vols. (London: William Heinemann, 1899), 1: 305–6. My emphases.

21 Elaine Scarry, in "Donne: 'But Yet the Body is his Booke,'" in *Literature and the Body: Essays on Populations and Persons,* Selected Papers from the English Institute, 1986, n.s., no. 12, ed. Scarry (Baltimore: Johns Hopkins University Press, 1988), pp. 70–105, cites and discusses numerous examples of Donne's penchant for figuring the passage from material to immaterial worlds in terms of the material properties of language and writing: "The passage from body to voice, or body to language is itself one instance of the spectrum that leads from the material to the immaterial, and that passage in turn can be charted by including a thing, a picture of the thing, and a name for the thing within the space of a poem or passage" (p. 78). Janet E. Halley discusses the textualization of Anne Donne in "Textual Intercourse: Anne Donne, John Donne, and the Sexual Politics of Textual Exchange," in Sheila Fisher and Halley, eds., *Seeking the Woman in Late Medieval and Renaissance Writings: Essays in Feminist Contextual Criticism* (Knoxville: University of Tennessee Press, 1989), pp. 187–206. "Rather than demand that an overwhelmingly masculine historical record make Anne Donne *present* to us, we might ask whether, in the man's writing, we can read the woman's *absence.* Can we respect the subjective, historical existence of Anne Donne not only by recognizing her presence in history, but also by acknowledging her absence to us? Is it possible to hear her silence?" (pp. 190–91). It is interesting to note that in the letter to "Sir G. F.," Donne seems to hear Anne's silence and to imply by juxtaposition (metonymic contiguity) that his writing of Elizabeth Drury as "the best he could conceive" preemptively supplies and subsequently costs Anne Donne's presence, though, as we shall see, her trace remains precisely as syllable — in The *Ann*-iversaries, or worse, the trace and the process by which it is inscribed, *Ann-I-vers[e]-aries.* See also, the discussion of "inanimate," n. 35 below.

22 John Donne, *The Elegies and the Songs and Sonnets,* ed. with an intro. and commentary by Helen Gardner (Oxford: Clarendon Press, 1965).

23 Witness *John Donne Journal* 9 (1990), no. 1, a special issue devoted to "Interpreting 'Aire and Angels,'" ed. Achsah Guibbory. For a comprehensive review of the criticism on "Aire and Angels," see in the same issue, John R. Roberts, "'Just such disparitie': The Critical Debate About 'Aire and Angels,'" (pp. 43–64).

24 A similar point is made by Peter De Sa Wiggins, "'Aire and Angels': Incarnations of Love," *English Literary Renaissance* 12 (1982): 87–101: "The first sestet poses the difficulty love must contend with as a passion in search of an object, and the first

octave solves the difficulty by having love discover its object in the person of the woman to whom the whole poem is addressed" (p. 88).

25 On Donne's use of double entendre, see Albert C. Labriola, " 'This Dialogue of One': Rational Argument and Affective Discourse in Donne's 'Aire and Angels,' " *John Donne Journal* 9 (1990): 77–83.

26 See Jacques Lacan, *The Four Fundamental Concepts of Psycho-Analysis*, ed. Jacques-Alain Miller, trans. Alan Sheridan (New York: Norton, 1978). *Objet petit a* is Lacan's term for "the object as cause of desire" (p. ix). This object is not the woman to whom the poem is addressed, but rather "a small part of the subject that detaches itself from him while still remaining his" (p. 62) and which is encountered as gaze or voice. "This *a* is presented precisely, in the field of the mirage of the narcissistic function of desire, as the object that cannot be swallowed, as it were, which remains stuck in the gullet of the signifier. It is at this point of lack that the subject has to recognize himself" (p. 270). More generally, the *objets a* are object-representatives or figures of "libido, qua pure life instinct, that is to say, immortal life, or irrepressible life, life that has need of no organ, simplified, indestructible life. It is precisely what is subtracted from the living being by virtue of the fact that it is subject to the cycle of sexed reproduction" (p. 198). As a representative of the nonspecular real, as that which resists signification, the *objet a* appears as a disturbance in the signifying chain: some sound (e.g., an incomprehensible voice) or motion (e.g., the flickering of a flame). The temporality of this object is always *nachträglich*. The "trauma of the real" preexists the *objet a*, but not as trauma. Like the primal scene in Freud's case history of the wolfman, it is felt only as trauma when it later emerges as a disturbance in the symbolic (see chap. 4 above).

27 On the poem's restaging of the Petrarchan encounter, see Janel Mueller, "The Play of Difference in Donne's "Aire and Angels," *John Donne Journal* 9 [1990]: 85–94. Following Arnold Stein, *John Donne's Lyrics: The Eloquence of Action* (Minneapolis: University of Minnesota Press, 1962), p. 141, Mueller notes that each stanza of the poem "takes shape as an upside-down Italian sonnet, with sestet preceding octave" (85), and she sees the blazon at the end of stanza 1 as an inversion of the speaker-lover's "enactment of his desire . . . imaged as an outward disclosure" in Wyatt and Surrey's versions of *Rime sparse* 145 (Mueller, "The Play of Difference," p. 88). I would add that the speaker's instructions to Love: "And therefore what thou wert, and who, / I bid Love aske" (ll. 11–12) recall, in inverted fashion, Love's instruction of Dante in *La Vita Nuova*. See also Barbara Estrin, "Donne's Injured 'I': Defections from Petrarchan and Spenserian Poetics," *PQ* 66 (1987): 175–93.

28 See chap. 3, pp. 64–73. See also Ronald J. Corthell, "Donne's 'Disparitie': Inversion, Gender, and the Subject of Love in Some Songs and Sonnets," *Exemplaria* 1 (1989): 17–42. While I am generally sympathetic to Corthell's attempt to track the

ideological work performed by the love lyric, I have in mind something more nar-
rowly defined than the analysis he offers.

29   For the argument from angelology, see A. J. Smith, "Theory and Practice in Renaissance Poetry: Two Kinds of Imitation," *BJRL* 47 (1964): 228, cited and summarized
in Roberts, " 'Just such a disparitie,' " pp. 48–49. See also Wiggins, " 'Aire and Angels': Incarnations of Love," pp. 94–95 and Raymond B. Waddington, " 'All in All':
Shakespeare, Milton, Donne and the Soul-in Body Topos," *ELR* 20 (1990): 40–68.

30   The "pinnance overfraught," connoting at once a prostitute and "penis" (see Waddington, " 'All in All,' " pp. 60–64) drolly concentrates the poem's play on "my
love" as at once male desire and its desired object — the becoming visible of masculine desire in the woman — as desire for the woman.

31   For a Lacanian reading of this dialectical moment, see Slavoj Žižek, *Tarrying with
the Negative: Kant, Hegel, and the Critique of Ideology* (Durham, N.C.: Duke University Press, 1993), p. 156: "Insofar as the relationship between contingency and
necessity is that of becoming and being, it is legitimate to conceive of *objet a,* this
pure semblance, as a kind of 'anticipation' of being from the perspective of becoming. That is to say, Hegel conceives of matter as correlative to incomplete form,
i.e., to form which still is 'mere form,' a mere anticipation of itself qua complete
form. In this precise sense, it can be said that *objet a* designates that remainder of
matter which bears witness to the fact that form did not yet fully realize itself, that it
did not become actual as the concrete determination of the object, that it remains
a mere anticipation of itself." The woman, contingently encountered, in "Aire and
Angels" becomes "my love" when she is informed by the speaker's desire, which
momentarily anticipates itself as concretely determined in her. The persistence of
desire, paradoxically multiplied by its division among her discrete attributes (eyes,
lips, brow) results in her dissolution as determined object, thus allowing an oblique
glimpse of "my love" as condition of the being of the subject, as precisely a lack in
being (*manque-à-être*).

32   See Tayler, *Donne's Idea of a Woman,* esp. pp. 21–33. See also Emily and Fred S.
Michael, "Corporeal Ideas in Seventeenth-Century Psychology," *JHI* 50 (1989): 31–
48.

33   This epistemological process is given climactic force in *The Second Anniversary,* ll.
435–42. See Tayler's discussion of this passage, *Donne's Idea of a Woman,* pp. 32, 64;
see also n. 44 below. Compare Marvell's "The Mind, that Ocean where each kind /
Does streight its own resemblance find" in "The Garden," ll. 43–44.

34   "The Harbinger to the Progress," p. 7, in Manley, ed., *John Donne: "The Anniversaries."* For attribution of "The Harbinger of the Progress" and "To the Praise of
the Dead" to Joseph Hall, see Manley, ibid., pp. 120–21, and *John Donne: The Epi-
thalamions Anniversaries and Epicedes,* ed. with intro. and commentary by Wesley

Milgate (Oxford: Clarendon Press, 1978), pp. xxx–xxxi. Rosalie L. Colie, characterizing the "Shee" of *The Anniversaries* as the epitome and purification of ladies loved
by poets," remarks that Hall "noted the right association . . . when he wrote 'Let thy
Makers praise / Honor thy Laura,' a beloved woman who, like our poet's lady was
particularly celebrated and particularly effective *in morte*." " 'All in Peeces': Problems of Interpretation in Donne's Anniversary Poems," in *Just So Much Honor:
Essays Commemorating the Four-Hundredth Anniversary of the Birth of John Donne,*
ed. Peter Amadeus Fiore (University Park: Pennsylvania State University Press,
1972), p. 210. The obscurity of the *Anniversaries* has been the occasion for a number of esoteric readings, glossing the figure of Elizabeth Drury as, for example, the
Logos embodied in the celestial Venus (Manley) or Queen Elizabeth (Nicolson).
For surveys of these identifications, see Lewalski, *Donne's* Anniversaries *and the
Poetry of Praise,* pp. 108–11, and Tayler, *Donne's Idea of a Woman,* pp. 9–13. Lewalski
usefully identifies four positions concerning the "shee" of *The Anniversaries:* (1) she
is "simply a point of departure for a poem about some other identifiable person
or persons"; (2) she is "an ambiguous symbol arbitrarily or paradoxically invested
with profound significances and transcendent values"; (3) she is a figure of the
Christian Neoplatonic notion of Wisdom; and (4) the poems are about the soul of
Elizabeth Drury (pp. 108–10). Lewalski herself argues that the "shee" of the poem
represents the restored image of God in man. In treating the figure of Drury as that
of a generic Petrarchan lady, I mean to imply that she is represented as having been
visibly beautiful and physically unattainable and as having disappeared. It is my intention to thicken the figure of the absent woman at the center of the poems so as to
appreciate (1) the resistance it offers before yielding to one or another identification
and (2) the ways in which that resistance leads Donne to explore the literary historical function of such a female figure. Lewalski argues against carrying the analogy
of Elizabeth Drury and Petrarch's Laura into an identification of Petrarchan elegy
as the genre of *The Anniversaries* (pp. 13–15). I would in fact recognize the impossibility of writing Petrarchan elegy in his present time as one of Donne's literary historical themes. For Lewalski's comments on Hall's Petrarchan reading of *The Anniversaries,* see *Donne's* Anniversaries *and the Poetry of Praise,* pp. 222–25 and 265.

35 This same estrangement survives to be reiterated in Lacan's notorious assertion in
Encore that "*il n'y a pas La femme,*" which, in context, asserts women (*species*) over
the Woman (*genus*). See chap. 4, n. 57, above.

36 See Fish, "Masculine Persuasive Force," pp. 223–52. In a wonderfully concise sketch
of the critical history of Donne's poetry, Fish attributes the persistent and persistently changing contemporaneity of Donne to the failure of criticism to learn that
Donne's "masculine persuasive force . . . can only be deployed at the cost of everything it purports to incarnate — domination, independence, assertion, masculinity

itself. In much of Donne criticism that lesson has been lost or at least obscured by a concerted effort to put Donne in possession of his poetry and therefore of himself" (*Soliciting Interpretation*, p. 250). For Fish, "these romances all make the mistake of placing Donne outside the (verbal) forces he sets in motion and thus making him a figure of control," while Fish offers a Donne who is "always folded back into the dilemmas he articulates" (p. 250–51). I note, along with Fish, that the critical history of Donne is marked by the sense that his poems are fundamentally about something current that the critics know. The question, then, becomes, as they say, "What did Donne (as opposed to the poems) know and when did he know it?" Fish's own "masculine persuasive force" attempts to separate from Donne long enough to posit the subject of Donne's poems as the victim of what he, Fish, knows to be the limit of a subjectivity that is an inherently linguistic construction. But, by variously representing Donne's attempt to contemplate the failure of representation, the irresistible irony of Donne's texts bleeds into the critical discourses that attempt to possess his poems.

37 On the forms of nostalgia in postmodernity, see the Epilogue below.

38 *OED*, sv. inanimate, a: 1. Not animated or alive; destitute of life, lifeless; and inanimate, v¹: 1. *trans.* to animate, infuse life into. Compare Donne's superimposition of verbal and adjectival usages of *snow* in "Song: Goe and catch a falling star": "Till age snow white hairs on thee." Also, at the risk of an acknowledged battiness and with due diffidence, I continue the insistence on Anne More's syllables begun in n. 20 above, by noting the possible autobiographical reference to the decisive and not at all ideal female presence *in* Donne's life: *in-An[n]-I-mate*, a reference which becomes more credible when we recall Donne's caution in lines 4–6 that he who does not "see, and Iudge and follow worthiness. . . . May lodge an *In-mate* soule, but tis not his" (my emphasis). The dropping out of the syllables *An[n]-I* verbally enacts the loss of the relation between soul and body that attends the loss of the mediating female. The physical presence of Anne More, whose relationship with Donne began when she was around the age at which Elizabeth Drury had died, negated the career in state service he had imagined, a decisive episode on the way to the negation of Jack Donne by Dr. Donne after Donne's ordination in 1615. See R. C. Bald, *John Donne: A Life* (Oxford: Oxford University Press, 1970), pp. 128–54.

39 "Donne's Anatomy Lesson," p. 50. Given Donne's broad interests, his knowledge of contemporary medicine is unsurprising, especially in view of the fact that Donne's stepfather, John Syminges, was a prominent physician and past president of the Royal College of Physicians, who in 1583 moved the family to a house near St. Bartholomew's Hospital. See Bald, *John Donne: A Life*, pp. 37–38.

40 Oswald Crollivs, *Philosophy Reformed and Improved in Four Profound Tractates,*

"Both made English by H. Pinnell, for the increase of Learning and true Knowledge" (London, 1657), pp. 23–24.

41 See, for example, Socrates' account of the teaching of Diotima in the *Symposium:* "And remember, [Diotima] said, that it is only when he discerns beauty itself through what makes it visible that a man will be quickened with the true, and not the seeming, virtue — for it is virtue's self that quickens him, not virtue's resemblance. And when he has brought forth and reared this perfect virtue, he shall be called the friend of god, and if ever it is given to man to put on immortality, it shall be given to him" (*Plato: The Collected Dialogues,* trans. Michael Joyce, ed. Edith Hamilton and Huntington Cairns [Princeton, N.J.: Princeton University Press, 1961], p. 563).

42 Slavoj Žižek, *The Sublime Object of Ideology* (London: Verso, 1989), pp. 45, 71.

43 By way of extending the narrative of a proposed trajectory from Pauline *Spiritus* to Hegelian *Geist* and beyond, we may consider Lacan's remarks on an analogous desublimation:

> Of course, as it is said, the letter killeth while the spirit giveth life . . . but we should also like to know how the spirit could live without the letter. Even so, the pretentions of the spirit would remain unassailable if the letter had not shown us that it produces all the effects of truth in man without involving the spirit at all.
>
> It is none other than Freud who had this revelation, and he called his discovery the unconscious.

"The Agency of the Letter in the Unconscious or Reason Since Freud," *Écrits: A Selection,* trans. Alan Sheridan (New York: Norton, 1977), pp. 158–59.

44 See Julie Soloman, " 'To Know, to Fly, to Conjure': Situating Baconian Science at the Juncture of Early Modern Modes of Reading," *Renaissance Quarterly* 44 (1991): 513–58.

45 Tayler's polemical interest is to dispute the usual Neoplatonic reading of Donne's "Idea of a Woman," and, insofar as I identify something called the "subject" with the knower's intellect, I am giving this passage a Neoplatonic inflection that he would resist. (See n. 19 above.) I use the term "Petrarchan" to refer to a concrete and composite literary historical practice that variously grounds itself on the available wisdom of the "ancients" with minimal investment in philosophical consistency.

46 *Essays in Divinity,* ed. Evelyn M. Simpson (Oxford: Clarendon Press, 1952), p. 92. The *Essays* were first published by Donne's son in 1651. On the scholarly consensus around 1614–15 for the date of composition, see Simpson's introduction, pp. ix–x. See also Gosse, *Life and Letters,* 2: 321. For an enumeration of the "verbal links" between the *Essays* and the *Anniversaries,* see Simpson, *Essays in Divinity,* pp. xiii–xvii.

47 Tayler remarks: "In *The Confessions* Augustine comes close to identifying memory with the self, and Donne follows him in this tendency in arguing that the most important of the three psychological powers or faculties is not the reason or the will but memory" (*Donne's Idea of a Woman*, p. 40).

48 Manley and others note the pun on "hymes": "the hymns are also males, which may impregnate others" (*John Donne:* The Anniversaries, p. 176). For discussion of the generic implications of the hymn form for *The Second Anniversary*, see Lewalski, *Donne's* Anniversaries *and the Poetry of Praise*, pp. 267–72.

49 "The Uncanny," SE 17, 219–56.

50 Augustine's Latin for this and the following quotation is quoted in chap. 3, pp. 80–81.

51 The date and circumstances of "A Nocturnall Upon S. Lucies Day, being the shortest day," cannot be established with certainty, but the force of the poem is such that most commentators have assumed that the poem refers to a lived experience. For a review of the possibilities advanced, see Helen Gardner, "A Nocturnal upon St. Lucy's Day, being the shortest day," in *Poetic Traditions of the English Renaissance*, ed., Maynard Mack and George deForest Lord (New Haven, Conn.: Yale University Press, 1982), pp. 181–201. Gardner makes a persuasive case, on grounds of manuscript history, for the death of Anne Donne as the occasion of the poem. Other critics have suggested a 1612 illness of Donne's patron Lucy, Countess of Bedford, and Donne's fears for Anne while he was abroad with Drury in 1611–12 (recorded in the letter to G. F.) as possible occasions.

52 If the "Nocturnall" is indeed about the death of Donne's wife, it literally fulfills the despairing epigram on his marriage, "John Donne, Anne Donne, Vndone," he is said to have written in a "sad letter" to Anne Donne, after failing to regain the employment with Egerton lost because of their marriage. Unfortunately, the attribution of this compressed narrative of puns is tenuous. See Bald, *John Donne: A Life*, p. 139.

6. Authoring the Boundary

1 See C. G. A. Clay, *Economic Expansion and Social Change: England, 1500–1700*, 2 vols. (Cambridge: Cambridge University Press, 1984), 1:102–41; Christopher Hill, "The Agrarian Legislation of the Revolution," in *Puritanism and Revolution: Studies in Interpretation of the English Revolution* (New York: Schocken, 1964), pp. 153–96; Eric Kerridge, *The Agricultural Revolution* (London: George Allen and Unwin, 1967); Lawrence Stone, *The Causes of the English Revolution, 1529–1642* (New York: Harper and Row, 1972), pp. 66–67, and Joan Thirsk, "Agricultural Innovations and Their Diffusion," in *The Agrarian History of England and Wales*, vol. 5, *1640–1750*,

pt. 2, "Agrarian Change," ed. Thirsk (Cambridge: Cambridge University Press, 1985), pp. 533–71.

2 On the development of the rhetoric of the market economy, see Joyce Oldham Appleby, *Economic Thought and Ideology in Seventeenth-Century England* (Princeton, N.J.: Princeton University Press, 1978), and Joan Thirsk, *Economic Policy and Projects: The Development of Consumer Society in Early Modern England* (Oxford: Clarendon Press, 1978).

3 See Raymond Williams, *The Country and the City* (New York: Oxford University Press, 1973), pp. 54–59. For a useful discussion of the Fairfaxes' social position and expectations, see also Lee Erickson, "Marvell's 'Upon Appleton House' and the Fairfax Family," *ELR* 9 (1979): 158–68. On "landed society" and the gentry, see Clay, *Economic Expansion,* 1:142–64. Observing that Fairfax held in trust the royalist estates awarded him in sequestration, ensuring, for example, that the rents of the seigniory of the Isle of Man continued to be paid to the Countess of Derby, Michael Wilding remarks: "The big landowners maintained solidarity across supposed political lines," *Dragons Teeth: Literature in the English Revolution* (Oxford: Clarendon Press, 1987), p. 154.

4 "To Penshurst" is cited from *Ben Jonson,* ed. Ian Donaldson (Oxford: Oxford University Press, 1985). On the historical and ideological contexts of the poem, see Don E. Wayne, *Penshurst: The Semiotics of Place and the Poetics of History* (Madison: University of Wisconsin Press, 1984). In *The Politics of Landscape: Rural Scenery and Society in English Poetry, 1630–1660* (Cambridge, Mass.: Harvard University Press, 1979), James Turner argues that "Upon Appleton House" is not a "country house" poem because it goes so far beyond the panegyric of previous examples; he prefers to treat it as a "prospect poem," comprising "a progressive structure determined by the eye" (pp. 61–63). Although the poem clearly exceeds in scope the earlier examples of country house poetry to which it may be compared, its opening alludes specifically to "To Penshurst" in ways that invite comparison and emphasize the ideological differences between the two poems. Thus, at the very least, "Upon Appleton House" may be usefully thought of as a counter country house poem. Moreover, as my argument develops, it will become clear that the "structure determined by the eye" given in the poem finds its meaning in a conceptual rather than a visual register. The shading of "prospect" from a spatial to a temporal reference becomes very much its point.

5 "Marvell's 'Upon Appleton House, to my Lord Fairfax' and the Regaining of Paradise," in *The Political Identity of Andrew Marvell,* ed. Conal Condren and A. D. Cousins (Aldershot: Scholar Press, 1990), pp. 53–84; the quoted passage appears on p. 54.

6 *Literature and Revolution in England: 1640–1660* (New Haven, Conn.: Yale University Press, 1994), p. 325.

7 For the characterization of Marvell as a "loyalist," see John M. Wallace, *Destiny His Choice: The Loyalism of Andrew Marvell* (Cambridge: Cambridge University Press, 1968), and R. I. V. Hodge, *Foreshortened Time: Andrew Marvell and Seventeenth-Century Revolutions* (Ipswich: D. S. Brewer, 1978), esp. pp. 117–31. For a contrasting view, see Warren L. Chernaik, *The Poet's Time: Politics and Religion in the Work of Andrew Marvell* (Cambridge: Cambridge University Press, 1983), pp. 6–7. Wilding provides an explication of Marvell's political environment, with particular attention to the possibility of a position at once conservative and Cromwellian (pp. 114–37).

8 John Rogers, *The Matter of Revolution: Science, Poetry and Politics in the Age of Milton* (Ithaca, N.Y.: Cornell University Press, 1996), pp. 51–61.

9 Erickson, "Marvell's 'Upon Appleton House,'" pp. 159–60.

10 All citations of Marvell's poetry refer to H. M. Margoliouth, ed., *The Poems and Letters of Andrew Marvell*, 3rd rev. ed., by Pierre Legouis and E. E. Duncan-Jones, 2 vols. (Oxford: Clarendon Press, 1971).

11 I have defined allegory here with respect to the peculiar temporality it develops in "Upon Appleton House." In *The Language of Allegory: Defining the Genre* (Ithaca, N.Y.: Cornell University Press, 1979), Maureen Quilligan argues against the assumption that allegory and *allegoresis* (the allegorical interpretation of nonallegorical texts) are identical procedures. Rejecting the traditional understanding of allegory as a "vertical" system that uses narrated actions to imply and conceal an allegorical truth, she argues that "all allegorical narrative unfolds as action designed to comment on the verbal implications of the words used to describe the imaginary action" (p. 53). This conversion of allegory from a "vertical" to a "horizontal" procedure has tricky implications for the kind of temporal classification I am here proposing, since it moves allegory away from any aspiration toward iconic representation and makes verbal representation its theme and essence. As my argument develops it will become clear that Marvell does indeed allegorize in Quilligan's sense at some points—developing narrative sections of the poem as commentaries on the puns and etymologies employed in his own text. It is also true, however, that Marvell is thematically, even parodically, engaged with *allegoresis* as a general method of articulating the eternal and the temporal and that any generic classification of the poem along the lines suggested by Quilligan's definition would have to contend with this sophisticated and ambivalent inmixing. John Rogers believes that allegory is precluded because "the recurrent images of innocence, fall, and redemption function in 'Upon Appleton House' as indispensable units of a broader cultural discourse of history and change. Taking advantage of

the urgent theological controversies surrounding certain key moments in Christian history, Marvell explores the problem of the Reformation and change of the existing social order." "The Great Work of Time: Marvell's Pastoral Historiography," in *On the Celebrated and Neglected Poems of Andrew Marvell*, ed. Claude J. Summers and Ted-Larry Pebworth (Columbia: University of Missouri Press, 1992), p. 211. But this opposition between the allegorical and the historical is unnecessary. Allegory treats of the sorts of historical issues that Rogers enumerates by transposing historical choices and actions to specifically moralized landscapes (spatially and temporally removed) where they and their presumed consequences can be evaluated. *Piers Plowman*, for example, encounters no problem in allegorically exploring contemporary problems of court extravagance and baronial power. In advancing the definition given in my text, I am concerned not with allegory as a genre but as a trope, a manipulation of the text that encodes a specifiable relation of verbal representation to historical time. (I am indebted to Heather Dubrow for drawing my attention to this issue.)

12 See Paul de Man's argument that the textual features of allegory and irony are antithetical codings of "a truly temporal predicament." "The Rhetoric of Temporality," in Charles S. Singleton, ed., *Interpretation: Theory and Practice* (Baltimore: Johns Hopkins University Press, 1969), pp. 173–209; the quoted phrase appears on p. 203. This essay is also available in the revised edition of *Blindness and Insight: Essays in the Rhetoric of Contemporary Criticism* (Minneapolis: University of Minnesota Press, 1983), pp. 187–228. My argument departs from de Man's by demonstrating a dialectical linkage of allegory and irony in Marvell's poem, while de Man believes these two tropes to be historically distinct and incapable of mediation. In response to de Man's claim that irony supersedes allegory at a given literary historical moment, I seek to demonstrate the mutual implication of these two rhetorical codings of time at the moment of the inception of a narrative subject whose temporal predicament each, in its way, represents.

13 See the *DNB*, "Villiers, George, second Duke of Buckingham." On Ann Vere's Presbyterianism and her very public opposition to the regicide, see Steven Zwicker and Derek Hirst, "High Summer at Nun Appleton: Andrew Marvell and Lord Fairfax's Occasions," *Historical Journal* 36 (1993): 247–69.

14 "Marvell, St. Paul and the Body of Hope," in *Beyond Formalism* (New Haven, Conn.: Yale University Press, 1970), p. 164.

15 Hartman's use of the term *rebus* for Marvell's figure is opposed by Ann Berthoff in *The Resolved Soul: A Study of Marvell's Major Poems* (Princeton, N.J.: Princeton University Press, 1970). "A rebus is a visual pun . . . , wordplay made visible. The semantics of the rebus is absolutely different from that of the emblem, which always has a temporal ambience" (p. 25, n. 16). Berthoff argues, "an emblem is a narrative

moment from which the particular occasion has, to various degrees, been refined" (p. 24). But the figure with which I am concerned is not an emblem in Berthoff's sense. It does not "refine away" the "particular occasion." It effects a transfer or exchange of contexts so that the occasion represented in the poem may be read in the context of another occasion that is allegorically related to it. Rather than a visual moralization abstracted from a narrative context, as is the emblem, Marvell's rebus is the metonymy of a metaphor, the transfer of an analogy from one narrative context to another.

16 See Harold Skulsky, " 'Upon Appleton House': Marvell's Comedy of Discourse," *ELH* 52 (1985): 591–620. Skulsky argues that the poet of "Appleton House" invites his auditor to "regard one notion as a representation or icon of another" (p. 603), but he fails to consider the specific hermeneutic conventions at play in the poem, and consequently he produces a curiously unhistorical reading that reduces what I see as a comic but serious exploration of the nature of the self in the mid-seventeenth century to a celebration of the games that language plays.

17 Paul Ricoeur has written extensively on the notion of a double hermeneutic comprising an initial demystifying of the text followed by its restoration through a mythic interpretation. See, for example, *Freud and Philosophy: An Essay on Interpretation,* trans. Denis Savage (New Haven, Conn.: Yale University Press, 1970), esp. pp. 20–36.

18 I am much indebted here to Rogers's persuasive questioning of Marvell's commitment to a Calvinist understanding of providence. *The Matter of Revolution,* pp. 86–87. However, I remain convinced that Marvell's rebus engages the notion of "providential destiny." Even given the range of thought that Rogers identifies in the immediate social and intellectual contexts of "Upon Appleton House," Marvell could not have used the vocabulary of typology, destiny, and providence without putting in play the notion of a divinely ordered history and an accompanying range of expectations about how such an order was mediated. I shall argue, particularly in reference to the episode of the slain rail, that Marvell invokes typology not to assume a voluntarist predisposition of human history, but rather to suggest that destiny is a necessary and necessarily retrospective construction: the type only becomes typical in the presence of its antitype. In relation to this poem, destiny is not what was ordained before time, but what will have been recuperated after time: the medium of anticipated results in which moral choice occurs.

19 See Vitruvius, *On Architecture,* ed. from the Harleian MS 2767 and trans. by Frank Granger, Loeb Classical Library, 2 vols. (Cambridge, Mass.: Harvard University Press, 1970), 1:7. "Both in general and especially in architecture are these two things found: that which signifies and that which is signified. That which is signified is the thing proposed about which we speak; that which signifies is the demonstration

unfolded in systems of precepts." Commenting that "the whole poem, in short, is a perfect Vitruvian building," Turner offers the *frons scenica* of the Roman theater as the model for its architecture (*The Politics of Landscape,* pp. 80, 82).

20 Ibid., 1:161. The figure of the man circumscribed in a circle and square is also important in the construction of perspective pictures, whose anamorphic "now you see it; now you don't" reproduces the relationship of space and time given in Marvell's poem. See Ernest Gilman, *The Curious Perspective: Literary and Pictorial Wit in the Seventeenth Century* (New Haven, Conn.: Yale University Press, 1978), p. 22.

21 The literature on the Renaissance interpretation of the circle and the square is extensive. See, for example, Rudolph Wittkower, *Architectural Principles in the Age of Humanism* (London: A. Tiranti, 1952), p. 15. Particularly useful on Marvell's use of the figure are Kitty W. Scoular, *Natural Magic: Strategies in the Presentation of Nature in English Poetry from Spenser to Marvell* (Oxford: Clarendon Press, 1965), p. 180, n. 2, and Maren-Sofie Røstvig, " 'Upon Appleton House' and the Universal History of Man," *English Studies* 42 (1961): 342.

22 George Puttenham, *The Arte of English Poesie: Continued into three Bookes: the first of Poets and Poesie, the second of Proportion, the third of Ornament* [1589], a facsimile reproduction, intro. by Baxter Hathaway (Kent, Ohio: Kent State University Press, 1970), p. 113. The figure of the square in "Upon Appleton House" has been discussed by Wallace, *Destiny His Choice,* pp. 237–38. Rosalie Colie cites Wither on the cube in this context in *"My Ecchoing Song": Andrew Marvell's Poetry of Criticism* (Princeton, N.J.: Princeton University Press, 1970), p. 228, n. 25. See also Turner, *The Politics of Landscape,* p. 207, n. 76. Note that the sixteen syllables in each Marvellian couplet correspond to Vitruvius's diplomatic choice of a perfect number, *On Architecture,* 1:165.

23 "*In ordine di ruoto:* Circular Structure in 'The Unfortunate Lover' and 'Upon Appleton House,' " in K. Friedenreich, ed., *Tercentenary Essays in Honor of Andrew Marvell* (Hamden, Conn.: Archon Books, 1977), pp. 245–65.

24 Against Skulsky's objection that "nothing in what precedes the phrase ['light Mosaick'] allows 'light' to be construed as a noun meaning illumination" (" 'Upon Appleton House': Marvell's Comedy of Discourse," p. 619, n. 38), I offer his own substantial list of critics who have so read it. Against a theoretical restriction of semantic meaning to what is syntactically permitted stands the ample evidence that for many readers the resonances of the phrase exceed grammatical containment. See Peter Schwenger, " 'To Make his Saying true': Deceit in *Appleton House,"* *Studies in Philology* 77 (1980): 98: "[The Sibyl's leaves] are scattered to be recombined according to the poet's will rather than God's." But the point of Marvell's lines is that the poet's fancy, if properly schooled, can go on assembling innumerable and unexpected "leaves" in accord with the will of God, that it can read a

divine meaning in *all things,* past, present and to come. Though whether or not it has read correctly cannot be definitively known within time.

25 Wallace believes Marvell's source for these lines is Davenant's *Gondibert,* 2.5.45: "Now they the *Hebrew, Greek, and Roman* spie; / Who for the Peoples ease, yoak'd them with Law; / Whom else, ungovern'd lusts would drive awrie; / And each his own way frowardly would draw" (cited from Wallace, *Destiny His Choice,* p. 250). The "Hebrew, Greek, and Roman" of Davenant refer to wise but pre-Christian writers. Adopting this reference for Marvell's poem makes the stanza invoke the superiority of the covenant of Love to that of Laws and the subsumption of the Old Testament in the New. Although *Gondibert* may indeed be Marvell's source, the fact that he reads in "the light Mosaick" argues that the Roman, Greek, and Hebrew texts in Marvell's poem are the principal linguistic representations of the Bible, all of which are enlightened by the Spirit of the Gospels, which fulfill and unify them. Taking these texts as translations rather than precedent essays in "natural theology" is not essential to my argument, but the advantage of doing so will be clarified by the discussion of typology below.

26 On eschatological thought in Marvell, see Margarita Stocker, *Apocalyptic Marvell: The Second Coming in Seventeenth-Century Poetry* (Athens: Ohio University Press, 1986), pp. 46–66; for an opposing view, see Rogers, *The Matter of Revolution,* n. 18 above.

27 An important tradition of scholarship views typology as a Protestant hermeneutic opposed to the Thomistic allegory of the Jesuits and the even less restrained allegorical procedures of the Neoplatonists. See, for example, William Madsen, *From Shadowy Types to Truth: Studies in Milton's Symbolism* (New Haven, Conn.: Yale University Press, 1968), esp. pp. 83–85. Significantly different from these allegorical traditions though it may be, typology should be understood not as antiallegorical but as a specific kind of allegorical procedure. The definition of allegory given at the beginning of this essay certainly includes it. For the relationship of typology to history, see Erich Auerbach, "Figura," in *Scenes from the Drama of European Literature* (New York: Meridian Books, 1959), pp. 11–76.

28 *Protestant Poetics and the Seventeenth-Century Religious Lyric* (Princeton, N.J.: Princeton University Press, 1979), pp. 132, 131.

29 See Milton's description of Adam and Eve as "Authors to themselves in all / Both what they judge and what they choose" in *Paradise Lost* 3.122–23.

30 I am indebted to Amy Stackhouse for the characterization of Providence as collaborative.

31 "Answer to Davenant's Preface to *Gondibert* 1650," in J. E. Spingarn, ed., *Critical Essays of the Seventeenth Century,* 2 vols. (1908; rpt. Bloomington: Indiana Uni-

versity Press, 1968), 2:59 (my emphasis). See also Wallace, *Destiny His Choice,* pp. 238–41.

32 Hobbes, "Answer to Davenant's Preface," 2:60.

33 Compare, for example, Leone Battista Alberti, *Ten Books on Architecture,* trans. into Italian by Cosimo Bartoli and into English by James Leoni, Venetian Architect, 1755, ed. Joseph Ryhwert (London: A. Tiranti, 1955), p. xi: "We consider that an Edifice is a Kind of Body consisting, like all other Bodies, of Design and of Matter; the first is produced by the Thought, the other by Nature; so that the one is to be provided by the Application and Contrivance of the Mind, and the other by due Preparation and Choice. And we further reflected, that neither the one nor the other of itself was sufficient, without the Hand of an Experienced Artificer, that knew how to form his Materials after a just Design."

34 The *OED* records no uses of "subject" in the modern philosophical sense, "for the mind or ego considered as the subject of all knowledge," before the eighteenth century. Transitional uses are cited from 1682 and 1697. However, the late change in the use of the word *subject* is doubtless part of a general shift toward an experience of the mind as the center of the "cogito" that had been taking place for some time.

35 See Don Cameron Allen, *Image and Meaning: Metaphoric Traditions in Renaissance Poetry* (Baltimore: Johns Hopkins University Press, 1960), p. 147: "[The Thwaites and Mary Fairfax episodes] are brought together as history and prophecy, as 'Scatter'd *Sibyls* Leaves' and the light 'Mosaick.' " Rosalie Colie sees Mary Fairfax as the typological fulfillment of the antitype, Isabel Thwaites ("*My Ecchoing Song,*" p. 252).

36 Don Cameron Allen sees the episode of Thestylis and the rail as an allegory of the civil war, the rail representing the slain king (*Image and Meaning,* pp. 135–37). The possibility of such a reading is another illustration of the typological pattern. The narrated events refer at once to a scriptural and a historical context. In this way the historical event is understood in light of its putative providential significance.

37 See also Quilligan's argument that "allegorical narrative unfolds as a series of punning commentaries, related to one another on the most literal of verbal levels — the sounds of words," *The Language of Allegory,* p. 22.

7. Experience, Negation, and the Genders of Time in Milton

1 Freud's *New Introductory Lectures,* 31, SE 22, p. 80. See chap. 4, n. 20.

2 Jacques Lacan, *The Four Fundamental Concepts of Psycho-Analysis,* ed. Jacques Alain Miller, trans. Alan Sheridan (New York: Norton, 1978), p. 184.

328   Notes to Chapter 7

3 See John Freccero, "The Fig Tree and the Laurel: Petrarch's Poetics," in *Literary Theory / Renaissance Texts,* ed. Patricia Parker and David Quint (Baltimore: Johns Hopkins University Press, 1986), pp. 20–32. See also chap. 3 above.

4 All citations of Milton's poetry come from *John Milton: Complete Poems and Major Prose,* ed. Merritt Y. Hughes (Indianapolis: Odyssey, 1957). On Adam's naming of Eve after her creation, see John Leonard, *Naming in Paradise: Milton and the Language of Adam and Eve* (Oxford: Clarendon Press, 1990), pp. 35–50.

5 See chap. 4, n. 58, above. Mary Nyquist frames the historical context of Milton's emphasis on Adam's desire in the colloquy preceding the creation of Eve in "The Genesis of Gendered Subjectivity in the Divorce Tracts and in *Paradise Lost,*" in *Re-Membering Milton: Essays on the Texts and Traditions,* ed. Nyquist and Margaret W. Ferguson (New York: Methuen, 1987), pp. 99–127, esp. pp. 116–18. See also Linda Gregerson, *The Reformation of the Subject: Spenser, Milton, and the English Protestant Epic* (Cambridge: Cambridge University Press, 1995): "Adam comes to know himself by knowing what he wants or lacks. Desire constitutes him, and while he arguably also 'discovers' desire in the sense of inventing it, this invention is rather a recursive process than a linear exercise of willful 'self-fashioning': subject formation is always in *Paradise Lost* the product — and the process — of discourse; desire is mediated" (p. 156). Gregerson's reading of Adam and Eve's creation scenes (pp. 148–68) anticipates many of the points I am about to make. The two accounts, Gregerson's and mine, differ significantly in the observation of details and in emphases — especially with reference to the authority I accord to Eve's feminine reserve and Adam's befuddlement before Freud's famous question, "*Was will das Weib?*" (What does woman want?), in relation to what I will call the resistance of the maternal fact. Thus, I offer the following discussion in the text as complementary and dialogic with respect to Gregerson's views rather than as redundant to them.

6 On the difficulty with which the male surrenders the piece of himself that contains the gamete, see Freud's "On Narcissism: An Introduction," SE 14, pp. 67–104; see also n. 8 below.

7 *OED,* s.v. *converse.* For a discussion of the relation of intercourse and discourse in the quoted passage, see my "Augustine, Spenser, Milton and the Christian Ego," *New Orleans Review* 11 (1984): 9–17.

8 Lacan's "mirror stage" and Hegel's dialectic of lordship and bondage converge in Milton's depiction of Adam's encounter with another who is a subject like himself, suggesting the common ground of both discourses in the historical foundation of the modern subject at the chiasmus of intending subjectivity and political subjection. See Lacan, "The Mirror State as Formative of the Function of the I," in *Écrits: A Selection,* trans. Alan Sheridan (New York: Norton, 1977), pp. 1–7; Hegel, *The Phenomenology of the Spirit,* B,IV,A.

9 See Freud, "On Narcissism: An Introduction," SE 14, p. 78: "The individual does actually carry on a twofold existence: one to serve his own purposes and the other as a link in a chain, which he serves against his will, or at least involuntarily. The individual himself regards sexuality as one of his own ends; whereas from another point of view he is an appendage to his germplasm, at whose disposal he puts his energies in return for a bonus of pleasure. *He is the mortal vehicle of a possibly immortal substance—like the inheritor of an entailed property, who is only the temporary holder of an estate which survives him.* The separation of the sexual instincts from the ego instincts would simply reflect this two-fold function of the individual" (my emphasis).

10 The *OED* records the pseudo-etymological association of wo-man and woe-man as frequent in the sixteenth and seventeenth centuries: Woman: I.l.k.

11 See Milton's discussion of Genesis 2:18 in the *Doctrine and Discipline of Divorce,* in *The Complete Prose Works of John Milton,* ed. Don M. Wolfe et al., 8 vols. (New Haven, Conn.: Yale University Press, 1953 and 1982), 2:245–46. (Subsequent citations of Milton's prose will refer to this edition, cited as *CPW,* by volume and page number.) Adam's expressed fear that Eve may be "more than enough" concerns precisely his anxiety that Eve may be for herself and that the loss of the rib will not be recompensed, that her fullness will manifest his interior emptiness.

12 On the placement of Eve's narrative before Adam's, see Nyquist, "The Genesis of Gendered Subjectivity," p. 119: "Set in juxtaposition to the rather barrenly disputational speech of Adam's which immediately precedes it in Book IV, Eve's narrative creates a space that is strongly if only implicitly gendered, a space that is dilatory, erotic, and significantly, almost quintessentially, 'private.' "

13 For an extended discussion of the allusion to Narcissus in this passage, with a full review of the literature, see Diane McColley, *Milton's Eve* (Urbana: University of Illinois Press, 1983) pp. 74–85. See also Richard J. DuRocher, "Guiding the Glance: Spenser, Milton, and 'Venus looking glas,' " *JEGP* 92 (1993): 325–41; Christine Froula, "When Eve Reads Milton: Undoing the Canonical Economy," *Critical Inquiry* 10 (1983): 321–47; James Holstun, " 'Will you rent our ancient love asunder?': Lesbian Elegy in Donne, Marvell and Milton," *ELH* 54 (1987): 835–67; Kathleen Kelley, "Narcissus in *Paradise Lost* and *Upon Appleton House:* Disenchanting the Renaissance Lyric," in *Traditions and Innovations: Essays on British Literature of the Middle Ages and the Renaissance,* ed. David G. Allen and Robert A. White (Newark: University of Delaware Press, 1990), pp. 200–213. See also Nyquist, "The Genesis of Gendered Subjectivity," pp. 119–24.

14 See William Kerrigan's explanation of the transfer of Eve's affection from her image in the pool to Adam, in *The Sacred Complex: On the Psychogenesis of "Paradise Lost"* (Cambridge, Mass.: Harvard University Press, 1983), p. 70.

15 *OED,* Style: II.b.18: "A legal, official, or honorific title, the proper name or recognized appellation of a person, family, trading firm, etc.; the ceremonial designation of a sovereign, including his various titles and the enumeration of his dominions." See, for example, *Paradise Lost* 2.312. A "style" is a proper name, but unlike the name "Eve," it is a hereditary surname, in English practice a patronymic. Eve receives her unique given name from Adam as a verbal gift. The title "Mother," which is her royal style, proclaiming the dominions and the legal status of her daughter successors, is also a gift of Adam's, but this time it is written on and in her body. As my argument develops, I hope the apparently disparate denotations of "style"—pen, phallus, title, literary mark of ownership and origin—will appear less distinct, the collection of signifieds under this signifier more motivated. For a related discussion of the semantic relations of the stylish and the feminine, see Jacques Derrida, *Spurs: Nietzsche's Styles / Eperons: Les Styles de Nietzsche,* trans. Barbara Harlow (Chicago: University of Chicago Press, 1979). On titles in *Paradise Lost,* see Leonard, *Naming in Paradise,* pp. 50–67.

16 In reading this scene, Gregerson follows an itinerary much like my own: "The onset of love's mirror stage in *The Faerie Queene* is described as narcissistic entrapment and despair . . . and in the *Confessions* of Augustine as abandonment to frank carnality. . . . The recognition scene that launches the reformation of the subject—conversion in Augustine's sense—is grounded in error. In *Paradise Lost,* this prototype is rendered in the gaze of a woman at the side of a lake, where the perfect circle of barren 'pining,' the narcissistic embrace that progressively diminishes the self, must be broken to allow for the self's progressive augmentation" (*The Reformation of the Subject,* pp. 156–57). On the deferral of Eve's image until she recognizes herself in her children, see James Earl, "Eve's Narcissism," *Milton Quarterly* 19 (1985): 13–16.

17 Holstun contextualizes Eve's reflection scene with representations of lesbian desire in Donne's "Sapho to Philaenis" and in the nunnery episode of "Upon Appleton House." Thus he assimilates Eve's "narcissism" to a lesbian erotics: "As 'Sapho to Philaenis' shows, early modern representations of narcissism in women are capable of modulating rather easily into representations of lesbianism, since both a woman's unmediated relation to herself and her unmediated relation to another woman are, in a male-dominated literary universe, fundamentally insignificant" (p. 854). This quick slide from desire of the same to desire of the same sex is questionable. However, Holstun's recognition of the scene as formative of a female subjectivity unmediated by male desire stands independently.

18 "Ranting at the New Historicism," *English Literary Renaissance* 19 (1989): 189–225.

19 See chap. 5, pp. 169–74.

20 See chap. 5, pp. 156–58.

21 In referring to the unmarked nature of female desire, I open a can of worms that

cannot be adequately collected and catalogued within the contexts of this book. Briefly: what must be confronted and circumscribed is the irreducibly anatomical ground of this determination, which, I quickly add, is asserted here specifically from the point of view of the Father as defined within the historically occurring rhetoric of patriarchy that I am trying to explicate. It must be acknowledged that from within this restricted discursive economy, the unrepresentability of female desire (Freud's "What does the woman want?") is to be understood in opposition to the visibility of phallic desire. Lacan's efforts to assert the independence of the phallus from the penis are, in my view, not entirely convincing. The primal signifying power of the phallus resides precisely in its being a *motivated* signifier, marked in a way that certifies (not merely signifies) the presence of desire. This is not to say that the divagations of desire described here are somehow biologically sanctioned or in any necessary sense universal. It is rather to say that from a particular historically occurring position, in which desire is subsumed as male desire, female desire is apprehended as the interiorizing invagination and consequent invisibility of the phallus; this economic transaction of exteriorization and disappearance is figured in the interiority Adam requires from Eve and the seeming absoluteness he perceives in her because her desire is precisely "that which passes show." For a more sustained discussion of Lacan's "deduction of the phallus," see Mikkel Borch-Jacobsen, *Lacan: The Absolute Master,* trans. Douglas Brick (Stanford, Calif.: Stanford University Press, 1991), pp. 205–27.

22 Dayton Haskin, "Milton's Portrait of Mary as Bearer of the Word," in *Milton and the Idea of Woman,* ed. J. Walker (Urbana: University of Illinois Press, 1988), pp. 169–84; the quoted passage appears on p. 176 (my emphasis).

23 The association of textual and sexual reproduction goes back at least as far as Augustine's curious reading of the biblical injunction to "increase and multiply" as pertaining to the generation of thoughts and words (*Confessions* 13.24). See chap. 3, pp. 64–74.

24 For a discussion of the begetting of the Son *for* the angels, see Albert C. Labriola, " 'Thy Humiliation Shall Exalt': The Christology of *Paradise Lost,*" *Milton Studies* 15, ed. James D. Simmonds (Pittsburgh: University of Pittsburgh Press, 1981), pp. 29–42.

25 See Maureen Quilligan's discussion of "cosmic femaleness" and the gender of Milton's muse. *Milton's Spenser: The Politics of Reading* (Ithaca, N.Y.: Cornell University Press, 1983), pp. 218–20.

26 We may recall again here that in the *Confessions,* 1.7., Augustine describes the acquisition of language in terms of learning the names of desired things so as to express the will to possess them.

27 For a phenomenology of the satanic subject, see my *"Authors to Themselves": Milton*

and the Revelation of History (Cambridge: Cambridge University Press, 1987), chap. 2.

28 The OED records no uses of "subject" in the modern philosophical sense "for the mind or ego considered as the subject of all knowledge" before the eighteenth century, but it does cite transitional uses from 1682 and 1697. The change in the use of "subject" is only one indication of a general shift toward understanding the self or mind as an interior space in which exterior objects are known, a conception already clear in the Cartesian "cogito." For a study of the development of an English vocabulary with which to express this interiority, see Anne Ferry, *The "Inward" Language: Sonnets of Wyatt, Sidney, Shakespeare, Donne* (Chicago: University of Chicago Press, 1983).

29 *Eikonoklastes,* which was a task assigned to Milton in his capacity as Secretary for Foreign Tongues, defined him in the public estimation as a regicide, a definition affirmed by the restoration government, which included his name on the list of those excepted from the general amnesty at the time of the Restoration. For a discussion of the ways in which the experience of *Eikonoklastes* molded Milton's poetic technique in *Paradise Lost,* see my "The Dissemination of the King," in *The Theatrical City: London's Culture, Theatre and Literature, 1576–1649,* ed. David Bevington, Richard Strier, and David Smith (Cambridge: Cambridge University Press, 1995), pp. 260–81. David Loewenstein, *Milton and the Drama of History: Historical Vision, Iconoclasm, and the Literary Imagination* (Cambridge: Cambridge University Press, 1990), pp. 51–73, discusses the ways in which Milton's polemical encounter with the *Eikon Basilike* contributes to "his perception of history as a process which may be altered and shaped by vehement polemic." Loewenstein argues that as "a specifically literary activity, Milton's iconoclasm represents a crucial dimension of his imaginative response to the historical process" (p. 52). Lana Cable also sees the composition of *Eikonoklastes* as a crucial event in Milton's intellectual development: "It is not until Milton makes his assault on the King's icon that the problems intrinsic to representation of truth become an explicit political, moral, philosophical, and rhetorical issue." "Milton's Iconoclastic Truth," in *Politics, Poetics, and Hermeneutics in Milton's Prose,* ed. David Loewenstein and James Grantham Turner (Cambridge: Cambridge University Press, 1990), pp. 135–51. The quoted passage appears on p. 138. See also, Sharon Achinstein, *Milton and the Revolutionary Reader* (Princeton, N.J.: Princeton University Press, 1994), pp. 162–68.

30 See Merritt Hughes's discussion of the Pamela's prayer controversies in *CPW* 3, 153–60. Noticing that the first of four prayers purporting to be the king's private devotions before his execution, all of which are included in Duggard's (1649) and subsequent editions of the *Eikon Basilike,* was a close paraphrase of Pamela's prayer in chap. 3 of the 1590 *Arcadia,* Milton declaims: "Who would have imagin'd so

little feare in him of the true all-seeing Deitie, so little reverence of the Holy Ghost, whose office is to dictat and present our Christian Prayers, so little care of truth in his last words, or honour to himself, or to his Friends, or sense of his afflictions, or of that sad howr which was upon him, as immediately before his death to poppe into the hand of that grave Bishop who attended him, for a special Relique of his saintly exercises, a Prayer stol'n word for word from the mouth of a Heathen fiction praying to a heathen God; & that in no serious Book, but the vain amatorious Poem of S' *Philip Sidneys Arcadia*" (*CPW* 3:362).

31 The debates about the authorship of the *Eikon Basilike* are summarized in Philip A. Knachel's introduction to his edition, *Eikon Basilike: The Portraiture of His Sacred Majesty in His Solitude and Suffering,* Folger Shakespeare Library (Ithaca, N.Y.: Cornell University Press, 1966). The scholarly consensus is that the book was produced by Dr. John Gauden, based on manuscript material composed by the king over a period of time and provided to Gauden in November or December 1647. For further discussion of its composition and its immediate polemical context, see Grossman, "The Dissemination of the King," n. 14. On the presentation of Charles as martyr, see Loewenstein, *Milton and the Drama of History,* pp. 55–62. For a useful account of contemporary reactions to the staging of the execution, see Nancy Klein Maguire, "The Theatrical Mask/Masque of Politics: The Case of Charles I," *Journal of British Studies* 28 (January 1989): 1–22. See also Robert Wilcher, "What was the King's Book For?: The Evolution of *Eikon Basilike,*" *Yearbook of English Studies* 21 (1991): 219–28.

32 *OED:* Cushion 2.b: "A swelling simulating pregnancy: sometimes called *Queen Mary's cushion,* after Mary Tudor." For further discussion of Milton's allusion to Mary Tudor's false pregnancy, see Cable, "Milton's Iconoclastic Truth," p. 138, Grossman, "The Dissemination of the King," p. 277–78.

33 Henrietta's mother, Marie de Médicis, notorious for the power she asserted as queen regent during the minority of her son, Louis XIII, was driven into exile by Richelieu. See *CPW* 3:419, n. 3.

34 On James's accession and his acquiescence in the execution of his mother, see Jonathan Goldberg, *James I and the Politics of Literature: Jonson, Shakespeare, Donne, and Their Contemporaries* (Baltimore: Johns Hopkins University Press, 1983), pp. 11–17. We should perhaps note that this appeal to family history represents a negative application of the same technique that Marvell used in the nunnery episode of "Upon Appleton House."

35 The quotation is from *Historicall Collections of Ecclesiastic Affairs in Scotland* (1615), as cited in *CPW* 3:597, n. 38.

36 See, for example, James I's "SPEECH TO BOTH HOUSES OF PARLIAMENT DE-LIVERED IN THE GREAT CHAMBER AT WHITE-HALL, The last Day of March

1607": "[F]or you all know that *Rex est lex loquens;* And you have oft heard mee say, that the Kings will and intention being the speaking Law ought to bee *Luce clarius . . . ,*" in *The Political Works of James I,* reprt. from 1616 ed., with intro. by Charles Howard McIlwain, Harvard Political Classics, 2 vols. (Cambridge, Mass.: Harvard University Press, 1918), 1:291. On James I's "projection of the self into language and of language into print" as speaking law, see Richard Helgerson, "Milton Reads the King's Book: Print, Performance, and the Making of a Bourgeois Idol," *Criticism* 29 (1987): 5–8; the quoted phrase appears on p. 5.

37 See William Kerrigan's view in *The Sacred Complex* of *Paradise Lost* as a sublimation of Milton's Oedipal ambivalence. For discussion of the specifically Oedipal thematics of *Eikonoklastes,* see Bruce Boehrer, "Elementary Structures of Kingship: Milton, Regicide, and the Family," *Milton Studies* 23 (1987): 97–117.

38 Milton follows Tasso's notion of "icastic imitation" in understanding prophetic poetry as a sensible signifier of intelligible Truth. See Torquato Tasso, *Discourses on the Heroic Poem,* trans. with notes by Mariella Cavalchini and Irene Samuel (Oxford: Oxford University Press, 1973), p. 31; see also discussion in chap. 4 above. See Paul Stevens, "Milton and the Icastic Imagination," *Milton Studies* 20, ed. James D. Simmonds (Pittsburgh: University of Pittsburgh Press, 1984), pp. 43–73.

Epilogue

1 "Postmodernism Across the Ages," an event organized by Bennet Schaber and Bill Readings, was held at Syracuse University in 1989 as the fall conference of the New York College English Association. An enlarged version of my conference presentation, "The Hyphen in the Mouth of Modernity," appears in *Postmodernism Across the Ages,* ed. Readings and Schaber (Syracuse, N.Y.: Syracuse University Press, 1993), pp. 75–87. I thank the University of Syracuse Press for permission to reprint and Schaber and Readings for providing an opportunity for me to work out and discuss the ideas herein. I am indebted to Schaber and Readings and to other conference participants, especially Bruce Robbins and Stephen Melville, for their comments. I am especially indebted to Bill Readings for suggesting a title more perspicuous and pithy than any I could have come up with.

2 "Rethinking Culture," a conference organized by Bill Readings and others at the University of Montreal in 1992. A slightly expanded version of my "Housing the Remains of Culture: Absolute Monuments to Absolute Knowledge" was published electronically, along with other papers from the conference, in *Surfaces* 2 (1993). The thoughts given preliminary expression in that essay have been reworked in this Epilogue and in chap. 5.

3 The Morgan Stanley Building, 1 Pierrepont Street, Brooklyn, designed by Haines, Lundberg, Waehler, Architects. The building, when it was put up, was owned by its

developer, Forest City Development of Cleveland. The Morgan Stanley bank is the principal tenant and the prime mover behind its construction. The neon circles are part of the building's lighting and were installed by the owner, not the architect. In response to my inquiry, the architect's spokesperson reports that the roof was designed to "reference the skyline," that the material used is "just metal," and that copper or slate would have been preferred but are now too costly to use. I would like to thank Ms. Jane Cohn of Haines, Lundberg, Waehler for her help and co-operation.

4 "Modernity Versus Postmodernity," *New German Critique* 22 (1981): 3–14.

5 *St. Augustine's Confessions,* with an English trans. by William Watts (1631), 2 vols. Loeb Classical Library (New York: G. P. Putnam's Sons, 1931), 2:247–49 (my emphasis).

6 *Hamlet* 1.2.76–86, quoted from *The Riverside Shakespeare,* ed. G. Blakemore Evans et al. (Boston: Houghton Mifflin, 1974). For further discussion of this passage, see chap. 5.

7 James Joyce, *A Portrait of the Artist as a Young Man* (London: Penguin, 1975), p. 253.

8 There is not enough space in these pages to elaborate—in a useful way—the relationship of this identification of the self and its accumulated knowledge to the emergence of protocapitalist and then capitalist modes of production, but one could usefully refer to the discussion of *Areopagitica* in Christopher Kendrick's *Milton: A Study in Ideology and Form* (London: Methuen, 1986) for the lineaments of such an argument.

9 For a discussion of the emergence and canonization of this specifically Shakespearean representation of the speaker as the subject of his or her own verbal duplicity, see Joel Fineman, *Shakespeare's Perjured Eye: The Invention of Poetic Subjectivity in the Sonnets* (Berkeley: University of California Press, 1985).

10 "Tradition and the Individual Talent," in *Selected Essays,* new ed. (New York: Harcourt, Brace and World, 1960), pp. 6–7 (my emphasis).

11 "Hamlet and His Problems," *Selected Essays,* pp. 124–25.

12 Compare (Eliot-) Prufrock's mocking self-identification as Hamlet's buffoonish other: "No! I am not Prince Hamlet, nor was meant to be; / Am an attendant lord, one that will do / To swell a progress, start a scene or two / . . . / At times, indeed, almost ridiculous— / Almost, at times, the Fool." "The Love Song of J. Alfred Prufrock," in *The Complete Poems and Plays, 1909–1950* (New York: Harcourt, Brace and World, 1952), p. 7.

13 I argue the case for this reading of Milton in *"Authors to Themselves": Milton and the Revelation of History* (Cambridge: Cambridge University Press, 1987).

14 All citations of Milton come from John Milton, *Complete Poetry and Major Prose,* ed. Merritt Y. Hughes (Indianapolis: Odyssey, 1957).

15 On the ideology of the Christian as "post-Jew," see my "The Violence of the Hyphen in Judeo-Christian," *Social Text* 22 (1989): 115–22.

16 *Lives of the English Poets*, ed. George Birbeck Hill, 3 vols. (Oxford: Clarendon Press, 1905), 1:189.

17 On Samson's complex and ambiguous reputation in the seventeenth century, see Joseph Wittreich, *Samson Agonistes: An Essay on Interpretation* (Princeton, N.J.: Princeton University Press, 1985).

18 "Spectacle and Evidence in Samson Agonistes," *Critical Inquiry* 15 (1989): 556–86.

19 *Milton and the Postmodern* (Lincoln: University of Nebraska Press, 1983).

20 See esp. *Minima Moralia: Reflections from a Damaged Life*, trans. E. F. N. Jephcott (London: NLB, 1974).

21 Fredric Jameson eloquently remarks the lack of a "capacity for representation" in "the technology of our moment" in *Postmodernism or, The Cultural Logic of Late Capitalism* (Durham, N.C.: Duke University Press, 1991), pp. 36–37, but Jameson, rather willfully (albeit hopefully), goes on to recuperate Marxist modernity by making that lack itself a representation: "Rather I want to suggest that our faulty representations of some immense communicational and computer network are themselves but a distorted figuration of something even deeper, namely, the whole world system of present-day multinational capitalism. The technology of contemporary society is therefore mesmerizing and fascinating not so much in its own right but because it seems to offer some privileged representational shorthand for grasping a network of power and control even more difficult for our minds and imaginations to grasp: the whole new decentered global network of the third stage of capital itself" (pp. 37–38).

22 "Letter from Washington," February 27, 1989, p. 77.

23 *The Phenomenology of the Spirit*, trans. A. V. Miller (Oxford: Oxford University Press, 1977), p. 118.

Index

Adam and Eve, 64–65, 329 n.12; Adam as father, 232; Adam as generic man, 230; Adam as prime namer, 237, 328 n.4, 329 n.15 (*see also* Proper names); and collateral love, 223–24, 236; conversation of, 222; and dreams, 227–28, 230, 248, 252; Eve and her image in the lake, 223–32, 238, 239, 246, 250, 330 nn.16 and 17; Eve as image of Adam, 224–25, 231; Eve as literature, 238; and the Fall, 28, 48, 95, 98, 102, 159, 220–22; and interiority, 227, 329 nn.11 and 12; marriage of, 226, 252; and procreation, 219; and the Son, 237, 239; and subjectivity, 224–26, 229, 236, 328 nn.5 and 8, 331 n.21

Adorno, Theodor, 141, 267, 309 n.61, 336 n.20

Agency, xiv, 5, 14, 16, 20–23, 25, 28, 44, 60, 63, 78, 84, 85, 94, 116, 123, 141, 145, 150, 211, 217, 254–56, 274 n.20, 310 n.66

Agriculture, 91, 198–99, 213, 320 n.1. *See also* Technology

Alberti, Leone Battista, 326 n.33

Allegory, xiv, 61–63, 65–66, 115–16, 123–27, 129–30, 132, 136, 140, 142, 147–48, 155, 164, 171, 203, 206, 208, 238, 245, 250, 287 n.10, 289 nn.16 and 17, 302

n.28, 306 n.44, 322 nn.11 and 12; and allegoresis, 76, 190–93, 197, 322 n.11, 326 n.27; temporality of, 203, 205, 211–12, 216–17, 327 n.37. *See also* Augustine, Saint; Tasso, Torquato

Allen, Don Cameron, 327 nn.35 and 36

Altieri, Charles, 30, 272 n.7, 274 n.20, 278 n.41, 282 n.22

Anaphora, 169

Aquinas, Saint Thomas, 21, 122–23, 257 n.24, 303 n.31, 326 n.27

Ariosto, Lodovico, 24, 303 n.30

Aristotle, 38, 145, 173, 206, 265, 280 n.10, 309 nn.61 and 64, 311 n.66; *De Anima*, 313 n.19; and epistemology of genus and species, 182–83, 189, 194; *Poetics*, 311 n.3

Augustine, Saint, xvii, 86, 92, 100, 134, 159, 163, 191, 193, 197, 286 n.2, 287 n.9, 288 n.14, 289 nn.16 and 17, 290 n.22, 292 nn.32 and 34, 294 n.44, 304 n.32, 308 n.56; allegorical interpretation of "increase and multiply," 63–79, 84, 116, 123–25, 147, 155, 159, 162, 171, 191, 219–20, 222, 234–35, 239, 279 n.42, 304 n.32, 331 n.23; *City of God*, 290 n.18; *Confessions*, xvi, 33, 59–86, 123–26, 159, 173, 189–90, 216, 218, 245, 258, 279 n.42,

Marshall Grossman is Professor of English at the

University of Maryland at College Park.

Library of Congress Cataloging-in-Publication Data

Grossman, Marshall.

The story of all things : writing the self in English Renaissance

narrative poetry / Marshall Grossman.

    p. cm. — (Post-contemporary interventions)

Includes bibliographical references (p.   ) and index.

ISBN 0-8223-2101-7 (cloth : alk. paper). — ISBN 0-8223-2117-3

(pbk. : alk. paper)

1. English poetry — Early modern, 1500–1700 — History and

criticism.   2. Self in literature.   3. Literature and history —

England — History — 17th century.   4. Literature and history —

England — History — 16th century.   5. Narrative poetry,

English — History and criticism.   6. Subjectivity in literature.

7. Narration (Rhetoric)   8. Renaissance — England.   I. Title.

II. Series.

PR545.S44G76   1998

821'.309384 — dc21   97-44322